MODERN
COLLEGE READING

MODERN COLLEGE READING

Techniques with Exercises

Deanne K. Milan

CITY COLLEGE OF SAN FRANCISCO

Charles Scribner's Sons   New York

11 13 15 17 19   H/P   20 18 16 14 12

PRINTED IN THE UNITED STATES OF AMERICA
SBN 684–41369–8
Library of Congress Catalog Card Number 72–145806

ACKNOWLEDGMENTS

On this and pages iv–ix, which constitute an extension of the copyright page,
acknowledgment is gratefully made to those publishers, agents, and individuals who
have permitted the use of the following materials in copyright:

From *Two Cheers for Democracy* by E. M. Forster. Reprinted by permission of
Harcourt Brace Jovanovich, Inc. and Edward Arnold Ltd.

For "Car Games" by Frank Conroy. Reprinted by permission of Robert Lantz-
Candida Donadio Literary Agency, Inc. Copyright © 1970 by Frank Conroy. Originally printed in *The New Yorker*.

For "The Greatest Man in the World" by James Thurber. Copyright © 1945 James
Thurber. From *The Thurber Carnival*, published by Harper & Row, Publishers, Inc.
Originally printed in *The New Yorker*.

For "The Wall" by Jean Paul Sartre. Copyright 1945 by Random House, Inc. Re-
printed from *Bedside Book of Famous French Stories* by Jean Paul Sartre, trans. by
Marie Jolas, by permission of New Directions Publishing Corp. and Random House,
Inc.

For "The Secret Heart" by Machado de Assis. Translated by Helen Caldwell, from
The Psychiatrist and Other Stories. University of California Press, 1966. Reprinted by
permission of the University of California Press.

For "Good Country People" by Flannery O'Connor. From *A Good Man Is Hard
to Find,* copyright 1953, 1954, 1955 by Flannery O'Connor. Reprinted by permission
of Harcourt Brace Jovanovich, Inc., and Harold Matson Company, Inc.

For "Eros Rampant" by John Updike. Copyright © 1968, by Harper's Magazine,
Inc. Reprinted from the June, 1968 issue of *Harper's Magazine* by permission of the
author.

For "Television's War," and "The Ten Most Shows" by Michael Arlen. From
Living-Room War by Michael J. Arlen. Copyright © 1967 by Michael J. Arlen. Orig-
inally appeared in *The New Yorker*. All rights reserved. Reprinted by permission of
The Viking Press, Inc.

For "When I Grow the Lord He'll Be a Real Big Man" by Robert Coles. Copyright
© 1964, 1965, 1966, 1967 by Robert Coles. From *Children of Crises: A Study of
Courage and Fear* by Robert Coles, by permission of Little, Brown and Company.

For "Uneasy Rider: The Unilateral Withdrawal of Private Weise" by Peter Collier. *Ramparts,* February, 1970. Reprinted by permission of the author.

For "A Generation in Search of a Future" by George Wald. Reprinted from the *Boston Globe,* March 8, 1969, by permission of the author.

For "The Cheerleaders" by John Steinbeck. From *Travels with Charley in Search of America* by John Steinbeck. Copyright © 1961, 1962 by The Curtis Publishing Company, Inc. Copyright © 1962 by John Steinbeck. Reprinted by permission of The Viking Press, Inc.

For "From Subway to Synagogue" by Alfred Kazin. From *A Walker in the City,* copyright 1951 by Alfred Kazin. Reprinted by permission of Harcourt Brace Jovanovich, Inc.

For "The Black Man's Stake in Vietnam," and "On Becoming" by Eldridge Cleaver. From *Soul On Ice* by Eldridge Cleaver. Copyright © 1968 by Eldridge Cleaver. Used with permission of McGraw-Hill Book Company.

For "Tummler" and "R.I.P." by A. J. Liebling. Copyright © 1938, 1963 by A. J. Liebling. Reprinted by permission of Simon and Schuster, Inc.

For "The Welfare Bureau" by Paul Jacobs. Copyright © 1967 by Paul Jacobs. Reprinted from *Prelude to Riot: A View of America from the Bottom,* by Paul Jacobs, by permission of Random House, Inc.

From *The American Way of Death* by Jessica Mitford. Copyright © 1963 by Jessica Mitford. Reprinted by permission of Simon and Schuster, Inc.

For "Apollo 11: The Time Machine" by Peter Collier. *Ramparts,* October, 1969. Reprinted by permission of the author.

For "Come on in, the Liability's Fine" by S. J. Perelman. From *The Road to Milltown.* Copyright © 1955 by S. J. Perelman. Reprinted by permission of Simon and Schuster, Inc.

From *Hell's Angels* by Hunter Thompson. Copyright © 1966, 1967 by Hunter Thompson. Published by Ballantine Books, Inc.

For "The Crime of Commitment" by Thomas Szasz. Reprinted from *Psychology Today* Magazine, March, 1969. Copyright © Communications/Research/Machines/Inc.

For "O Rotten Gotham—Sliding Down into the Behavorial Sink," and "The Automated Hotel" by Tom Wolfe. Reprinted with the permission of Farrar, Straus & Giroux, Inc. from *The Pump House Gang* by Tom Wolfe, copyright © 1968 by Tom Wolfe, copyright © 1966 by the World Journal Tribune Corporation, copyright © 1964, 1965, 1966 by the New York Herald Tribune, Inc.

For "Fish Are Jumping an' the Cotton Is High: Notes from the Mississippi Delta" by Mike Thelwell. Reprinted from *The Massachusetts Review,* © 1966 The Massachusetts Review, Inc.

For "Eco-Catastrophe!" by Paul Ehrlich. *Ramparts,* September, 1969. Reprinted by permission of *Ramparts.*

For "Baja's Bounty" by Lupi Saldana. Copyright 1969 by the *Los Angeles Times.* Reprinted by permission.

From *The Image* by Daniel J. Boorstin. Copyright © 1961 by Daniel J. Boorstin. Reprinted by permission of Atheneum Publishers.

For "The White Exodus to Suburbia Steps Up" by Herbert J. Gans. Copyright © 1968–1969 by The New York Times Company. Reprinted by permission.

For "The Rejects" by Michael Harrington. Reprinted with permission of The Macmillan Company from *The Other America* by Michael Harrington. Copyright © Michael Harrington, 1962.

For "Choose Your War: Or the Case of the Selective C.O." by Walter Goodman. Copyright © 1969 by The New York Times Company. Reprinted by permission.

From "Wallace" by Richard Rovere. Reprinted by permission of The New Yorker Magazine, Inc.

printed by permission of *Commentary* and the author. Copyright © 1967 by the American Jewish Committee.

From *Up Against the Ivy Wall* by Jerry L. Avorn, Robert Friedman, and Members of the Staff of the Columbia Daily Spectator. Copyright © 1968 by Member of the Board of Associates. Reprinted by permission of Atheneum Publishers.

From "Our Invisible Poor" by Dwight Macdonald. Reprinted by permission of *The New Yorker*.

From *Venomous Reptiles* by Sherman A. Minton, Jr. and Madge Rutherford Minton. Reprinted by permission of Charles Scribner's Sons.

From *Dark Ghetto* by Kenneth B. Clark. Copyright © 1965 by Kenneth B. Clark. Reprinted by permission of Harper & Row, Publishers, Inc.

From *Flowering Earth* by Donald Culross Peattie. Reprinted by permission of Noel R. Peattie and his agent, James Brown Associates, Inc. Copyright © 1939 by Donald Culross Peattie.

From *Technics and Civilization* by Lewis Mumford. Reprinted by permission of Harcourt Brace Jovanovich, Inc.

From *Brideshead Revisited* by Evelyn Waugh. Copyright 1944, 1945 by Evelyn Waugh. Reprinted by permission of Little, Brown and Company and A. D. Peters & Co.

From *The Sea Around Us* by Rachel Carson. Reprinted by permission of Oxford University Press.

From *A Story for Teddy and Others* by Harvey Swados. Copyright © 1961, 1962, 1963, 1964, 1965 by Harvey Swados. Reprinted by permission of Simon and Schuster, Inc.

From "Among the Aged" by Dorothy Rabinowitz. Reprinted from *Commentary*, by permission. Copyright © 1969 by the American Jewish Committee.

From *More in Anger* by Marya Mannes. Copyright © 1958 by Marya Mannes. Reprinted by permission of J. B. Lippincott Company.

From *Funk & Wagnalls Standard® College Dictionary*. Copyright 1969 by Funk & Wagnalls, a Division of Reader's Digest Books, Inc.

From *Webster's Seventh New Collegiate Dictionary* © 1970 by G. & C. Merriam Co., Publishers of the Merriam-Webster Dictionaries. By permission.

From *The Random House Dictionary of the English Language*. Copyright © 1966, 1970 by Random House, Inc. Reprinted by permission of the publisher.

From *Poverty in America*, Louis A. Ferman, Joyce L. Kornbluh and Alan Haber, eds. Copyright © by the University of Michigan, 1965.

From *Police Power* by Paul Chevigny. Copyright © 1969 by Paul Chevigny. Reprinted by permission of Pantheon Books, a Division of Random House, Inc.

From *So Human an Animal* by René Dubos. Reprinted by permission of Charles Scribner's Sons.

From *The Making of the Mind* by James Harvey Robinson (Harper & Row, 1921). Reprinted by permission of Harper & Row, Publishers, Inc.

From *The Nude: A Study in Ideal Form* by Kenneth Clark. Copyright © 1956 by the Trustees of the National Gallery of Art, Washington, D.C. Reprinted by permission of Princeton University Press.

From *The Edge of Day: A Boyhood in the West of England* by Laurie Lee. Reprinted by permission of William Morrow & Co., Inc. Copyright © 1959 by Laurie Lee.

From *The Adventures of Huckleberry Finn* by Mark Twain (Harper & Row, 1896).

From *Let Us Now Praise Famous Men* by James Agee and Walker Evans. Reprinted by permission of Houghton Mifflin Company.

From *Bullett Park* by John Cheever. Copyright © 1967, 1968, 1969 by John Cheever. Reprinted by permission of Alfred Knopf, Inc.

From *North America* by J. Russell Smith. Reprinted by permission of Harcourt Brace Jovanovich, Inc.

For "High Purpose?" Reprinted by permission of *The Arizona Republic.*

From "Reach, Touch and Teach" by Terry Borton. Copyright 1969 Saturday Review, Inc. Reprinted by permission of the author and Saturday Review, Inc.

For "Your Friend, the Fuzz," and "Is Sex Old-Fashioned?" by Arthur Hoppe. Reprinted from the *San Francisco Chronicle* by permission of the author.

From "The Parson" by Penelope Mortimer. Reprinted by permission of the author and *The New Yorker.*

From *Life on Man* by Theodor Rosebury. Copyright © 1969 by Theodor Rosebury. All rights reserved. Reprinted by permission of The Viking Press, Inc.

From "Sleep Well" by T.R.B. Reprinted by permission of *The New Republic,* © 1969, Harrison-Blaine of New Jersey, Inc.

From "The Face of a Starving Nation" by Edward M. Keating. Reprinted from The *San Francisco Chronicle* by permission of the author. Copyright 1969 by Edward M. Keating.

From "Mad Dogs in the Streets." Reprinted courtesy of the *Chicago Tribune.*

From "S.D.S. 'Tigers' a Sorry Sight" by Mike Royko. Reprinted with permission from the *Chicago Daily News.*

From "Message from the Moon." *The Wall Street Journal,* July 16, 1969. Reprinted with permission of *The Wall Street Journal.*

From "When If Ever, Do You Call in the Cops?" © 1968–69 by The New York Times Company. Reprinted by permission of *The New York Times,* Sanford D. Garelik, Andrew Schlesinger and Erich Wise.

From *Prejudices: Third Series,* H. L. Mencken. Copyright 1922 and renewed by H. L. Mencken. Reprinted by permission of Alfred A. Knopf, Inc.

From "The Fog," *Eleven Blue Men* by Berton Roueché. Copyright 1950 by Berton Roueché. Reprinted by permission of Little, Brown and Company. Originally appeared in *The New Yorker.*

From "The Emergence of Rock" by Albert Goldman. Copyright © 1968 by Albert Goldman. Preprinted by permission of The Sterling Lord Agency.

From *The Gathering Storm* by Winston Churchill. Reprinted by permission of Houghton Mifflin Company.

From "Sociological Habit Patterns in Linguistic Transmogrification" by Malcolm Cowley. From *The Reporter,* September 20, 1956. Copyright 1956 by Malcolm Cowley and reprinted by permission of the author.

For "In a Nutshell" and "On the Contrary" by Tom Turner. Reprinted by permission of Tom Turner (Pseudonym R. J. Bleauhard) from the *San Francisco Chronicle,* July 21 and 29, 1969.

From *The Best of Myles* by Myles na Gopaleen (Flann O'Brien). Copyright © 1968 by Evelyn O'Nolan. Used by permission of Walker & Co., New York.

From "The World Through Mark's Eyes" by Cynthia N. Shepard. Copyright 1969. Saturday Review, Inc. Reprinted by permission of the author and Saturday Review, Inc.

From *The Greeks* by H.D.F. Kitto. Reprinted by permission of Penguin Books, Ltd.

From *Environmental Conservation* by Raymond F. Dasmann. Reprinted by permission of John Wiley & Sons, Inc.

From *Psychology: An Introduction* by Jerome Kagan and Ernest Haveman, © 1968 by Harcourt Brace Jovanovich, Inc. and reprinted with their permission.

From *The National Experience,* 2nd. ed., by John Blum et. al., copyright © 1963, 1968, by Harcourt Brace Jovanovich, Inc. and reprinted with their permission.

From *The Secular City* by Harvey Cox. Reprinted with permission of The Macmillan Company. Copyright © Harvey Cox, 1965.

From *The Hidden Assassins* by Booth Mooney. Copyright © 1966 by Booth Mooney. Used by permission of Follett Publishing Company.

For "Annals of Agriculture: The Three-Hundred-and-Nineteenth Growing Season" (© 1969 The New Yorker, Inc.) and for "Love According to Madison Avenue" (© 1959, Morton Hunt) by Morton Hunt. Reprinted by permission of Robert Lescher Literary Agency.

From *The Haircurl Papers* by William K. Zinsser. Copyright © 1959, 1960, 1961, 1962, 1963, 1964 by William K. Zinsser. Reprinted by permission of The Sterling Lord Agency.

From "18-Year-Old-Vote—Nothing to It" by Nicholos von Hoffman. *The Washington Post,* February 25, 1970. Reprinted by permission of *The Washington Post.*

From "The Wind and the Sun" from *Aesop's Fables* edited by Boris Artzybaseff. Reprinted by permission of Viking Press, Inc.

From "A Morbid Spectacle" by Russell Baker. Copyright © 1968–69 by The New York Times Company. Reprinted by permission.

From *Across the Plains* by Robert Louis Stevenson (Charles Scribner's Sons, 1923).

From "Notes and Comment" in "The Talk of the Town." Copyright © 1970 by The New Yorker Magazine, Inc. Reprinted by permission.

From *The Urban Villagers* by Herbert J. Gans. Reprinted with permission of The Macmillan Company. Copyright © 1962 by The Free Press, a division of The Macmillan Company.

From *The World I Live In* by Helen Keller (Appleton-Century-Crofts, 1935).

From *Into Battle* by Winston Churchill (Cassell and Company, Ltd., 1941).

From *Sheppey* by W. Somerset Maugham, published by William Heinemann. By permission of The Literary Executor of W. Somerset Maugham, and William Heinemann Ltd.

From *The Portable Dorothy Parker* (The Viking Press, Inc., 1944).

PREFACE

MODERN COLLEGE READING is a textbook for reading improvement and developmental reading courses; it grows out of my experience in teaching students to improve their reading skills. The book is based on the obvious premise that comprehension is the single most important reading skill. Indeed, speed has been glamorized as an end in itself, but the truism remains that the 600 wpm reader who understands 10% of what he reads is performing at the same efficiency rate as the 60 wpm reader who understands everything. Neither is a good or efficient reader.

The book is divided in three parts. The twelve chapters of Part I cover techniques that any *good* reader employs, consciously or not. The first of these, finding the main idea, is central. Other skills are taken up in the order my students have found most useful: phrase reading; reading paragraphs—finding the main idea, coherent devices and methods of development; improving vocabulary—using context clues and the dictionary; denotation and connotation; making inferences and judgments; opinion and persuasion; tone and style; reading textbooks; and improving reading speed. It must be kept in mind, of course, that the good reader acquires many of these skills simultaneously and that separating them out, as I have done, is at best an artifice of organization.

Each chapter contains several illustrations, practice passages and exercises, and a final short reading selection. Comprehension and vocabulary tests accompany each selection, as well as scoring apparatus for measuring comprehension, vocabulary, reading rate, and reading efficiency rate. The last is a useful device for computing both comprehension and reading rate.

Part II is an anthology of twelve essays. The criteria I have used in choosing them are (1) their intrinsic literary and intellectual worth, (2) their relevance (a much-abused word these days) to the concern of all thinking and thoughtful persons, and (3) the affinity they have toward the sorts of writing college students must be able to read in their other courses. The selections progress in difficulty of subject, syntax, vocabulary, and style and they are measurably longer than the selections in Part I. Tests that measure comprehension and vocabulary follow each selection.

Part III is a collection of six short stories, where the student is invited to refine further his skills of connotation and inference by confronting the work of first-rate writers of imaginative literature. The questions after each story serve not only as a test of the student's understanding but as a guide to unraveling the complexities of theme, plot, meaning, and development.

Learning to read efficiently and well is not easy, and no one textbook ought to presume itself a cure-all. It has been my experience, though, that students who conscientiously apply the principles and techniques set forth here will not only get more from their other college courses, but will also enjoy them more.

CONTENTS

PART III SHORT STORIES FOR ENJOYMENT
          AND ANALYSIS

PART I

SKILLS FOR READING IMPROVEMENT

Chapter 1

GETTING THE MAIN IDEA

The first skill required for good reading is the ability to identify accurately the main idea of a selection. The main idea is the most important point or thought the writer wants to communicate; it is expressed as a *general statement,* while illustrations or examples that support the main idea are expressed as *specific statements.* The following simple exercise will help you to distinguish main ideas (general statements) from supporting illustrations or examples (specific statements). Read the selection that follows and then mark the statements as directed.

To the romanticists, it's the Sea of Cortes. To the realists, it's still the Gulf of California. But no matter what you call it, that blue ribbon of water between Mexico's mainland and Baja California is one of the best —if not *the* best—fishing ponds in the world.

This giant aquarium extends more than 600 miles from San Felipe, 125 miles below the California border, south to Cabo San Lucas at the tip of Baja California Sur.

According to biologists, the rocky shoreline and the deep blue water off shore is home for at least 857 species of fish ranging from tiny tropical specimens to huge blue and black marlin weighing more than 1,000 pounds.

The action in Baja waters is dealer's choice—and the fisherman is the dealer. He can choose one or more popular species from a list as long as a fishing rod—three varieties of marlin, broadbill swordfish, sailfish, yellowfin tuna, dolphin, yellowtail, wahoo, roosterfish, dorado, grouper, cabrilla, amberjack, white sea bass, totuava, sierra, triggerfish, snook, etc.

Mexican history books state that the honor of having discovered this fish-rich gulf and Baja belongs not to Cortes, but to one of his captains, Fortino Jimenez. In 1534, Jimenez sailed into the sleepy village of La Paz and was overwhelmed by what he found. He hurried back to regale Cortes with tales about a fabulous island whose waters were loaded with beautiful pearls and other treasures. Cortes was impressed, but he did not visit La Paz until May 3, 1535.

The famed Spanish conquistador and his faithful captain were dazzled by the pearls, but they overlooked Baja's richest prize—its seemingly unlimited supply of fish. This piscatorial treasure remained practically untouched until after World War II when adventurous anglers from Southern California discovered the underwater bonanza.

In the last decade, this bountiful marine resource has brought a wave of golden prosperity to Baja. The once barren shores of the gulf are now dotted with hotels—all monuments to the caliber of fishing which is bringing worldwide fame to Baja. The heart of this activity is from La Paz south to the tip (115 miles by air and 200 miles by boat), where the season for fishing is every day.

The key to the gulf's fisheries is the tremendous amount of feed available in the water. Due to the abundant feed and water warmed by the tropical sun, waters near the tip are the year-round playground for millions of game fish.

LUPI SALDANA, from "Baja's Bounty" *

The statements that follow summarize information found in the selection. For each, mark M in the space provided if the statement is a *main idea,* the principal point or idea the author tries to make, and S if the statement is a *specific* illustration or example to support the main idea.

1. ___S___ The Sea of Cortes, located 125 miles south of the U. S. border, is sometimes called the Gulf of California.
2. ___M___ The Baja waters, which offer some 857 varieties of fish, may be one of the best fishing areas in the world.
3. ___S___ One can find exotic varieties of fish there, such as the wahoo, dorado, amberjack, and triggerfish.
4. ___S___ Blue and black marlin caught there have weighed over 1,000 pounds.
5. ___S___ Mexican history books state that the Sea of Cortes was discovered not by Cortes, but by one of his captains, Fortino Jiminez.
6. ___S___ Jiminez found La Paz to be only a sleepy village in 1534.
7. ___S___ Strangely enough, Cortes was more interested in pearls and other treasures than in the abundant fish.
8. ___M___ Baja was left undisturbed for four centuries, when Southern California fishermen discovered the fishing bonanza.
9. ___S___ Many hotels have been built in Baja, proving that it is a popular resort.
10. ___M___ The important reasons for Baja's abundant fish are the warm tropical waters and the vast food supply.

From this exercise, you should have reached some new conclusions about reading. In the selection, the main ideas appeared at the beginning

* From *West,* July 13, 1969, p. 25.

and at the end. This is true often enough that it may help to read the first and last paragraphs before you read the whole selection. Think for a moment about what you have read, and then reread the entire selection. The middle portion of an article usually explains the main idea further, gives important facts or necessary background information, or gives illustrations and examples to support the main idea, as we have seen in this selection, "Baja's Bounty." The end of an article usually sums up or draws a conclusion.

A common reading error students make is attaching equal weight or significance to every sentence. You can't possibly remember everything you read; nor should you even make the attempt to. The sensible solution, then, is to ask yourself what must be retained. Bear in mind that the main idea is an unrestricted, unexamined and undeveloped idea that requires further explanation. In the selection "Baja's Bounty," for example, it is far more important to remember that the area has excellent fishing facilities than to remember that roosterfish are found there or that Baja is 200 miles by boat from La Paz.

The following paragraph illustrates a similar pattern: main idea, specific supporting statements, and conclusion.

MAIN IDEA

We have come a long way from the time when music was heard only on unique, formal occasions. When people heard music in concerts by live artists they expected the music itself to make the atmosphere. The event was the music. In a concert hall they listened to hear precisely what the composer or the performer had to offer at that particular moment. At home they listened while they themselves, a member of the family, or a friend sang or played an instrument. Nowadays, of course, we still have our occasional home concerts and special performances by particular artists in con-

SPECIFIC
DETAILS AND
ILLUSTRATIONS

cert halls and auditoriums. Many of us play instruments. But this is no longer the commonest way music reaches us. Far commoner is the sound from the car radio as we drive along; or from the AM-FM radio while we cook a meal, wash the dishes, or work in our basement; or from the automatic-record-playing hi-fi as we play cards, read a book, or make conversation. A normal feature of upper-middle-class domestic architecture today is the hi-fi radio-phonograph system with a speaker in every room. *We are music-soothed*

MAIN IDEA—
CONCLUSION

and music-encompassed as we go about our business. Now the appropriate music for any occasion is that which need not be followed but can simply be inhaled.
DANIEL BOORSTIN, from *The Image: Or What Happened to the American Dream**

* (New York: Atheneum Publishers, 1962), pp. 174–175.

Another way, then, to distinguish main ideas from less important ones is to ask yourself what would be important to remember if you were being tested on the material. Are dates, examples and statistics so important that they should be considered equal to main concepts? Probably not, unless the purpose of your reading is to collect statistical data. Once you learn to distinguish between general and specific statements, your reading will become more efficient, and that means less drudgery for you.

The exercise that follows is similar to the one just completed. After you read the passage, mark M in the space provided if the statement summarizes the *main idea,* and S for *specific supporting statements,* as you did before. To make the exercise more challenging, mark C for any *main idea* that draws a *conclusion* from the evidence.

In this unpredictable world, nothing can be predicted quite so easily as the continued proliferation of suburbia. Not only have American cities stopped growing for more than a generation, while the metropolitan areas of which they are a part were continuing to expand lustily, but there is incontrovertible evidence that another huge wave of suburban home building can be expected in the coming decade.

Between 1947 and about 1960, the country experienced the greatest baby boom ever, ending the slow-down in marriages and childbirths created first by the Depression and then by World War II. Today, the earliest arrivals of that baby boom are themselves old enough to marry, and many are now setting up housekeeping in urban or suburban apartments. In a few years, however, when their first child is 2 to 3 years old, and the second is about to appear, many young parents will decide to buy suburban homes. Only simple addition is necessary to see that by the mid-seventies, they will be fashioning another massive suburban building boom, provided of course that the country is affluent and not engaged in World War III.

The new suburbia may not look much different from the old; there will, however, be an increase in the class and racial polarization that has been developing between the suburbs and the cities for several generations now. The suburbs will be home for an ever larger proportion of working-class, middle-class and upper-class whites; the cities, for an ever larger proportion of poor and non-white people. The continuation of this trend means that, by the nineteen-seventies, a greater number of cities will be 40 to 50 per cent non-white in population, with more and larger ghettos and greater municipal poverty on the one hand, and stronger suburban opposition to open housing and related policies to solve the city's problems on the other hand. The urban crisis will worsen, and although there is no shortage of rational solutions, nothing much will be done about the crisis unless white America permits a radical change of public policy and undergoes a miraculous change of attitude toward its cities and their populations.

HERBERT J. GANS, from "The White Exodus to Suburbia Steps Up" *

* From *The New York Times Magazine,* January 7, 1968, p. 25.

1. ___M/C___ Not only have urban populations declined and suburbs grown rapidly, but there is evidence to suggest another wave of suburban home building in the next ten years.

2. ___S___ Before World War II, marriages and childbirths had declined to some extent.

3. ___S___ One reason for the growth of suburbs is the post-World War II baby boom.

4. ___S___ The greatest baby boom in America's history occurred between 1947 and 1960.

5. ___S___ The first post-war babies are now married and having children.

6. ___S___ Most newly married couples first rent an apartment in the city but move to the suburbs when they have one or two children.

7. ___M___ One result of the new suburbia will be an increase in class and racial polarization.

8. ___M___ By the mid-seventies some cities will have non-white populations of 40 or 50 per cent, which will cause greater poverty and stronger suburban opposition to solving the city's problems.

9. ___M/C___ Unless America changes its public policies and attitudes toward its cities, urban residents will witness a terrible crisis.

10. ___C___ Which of the following best describes the organization of the passage?

  A. Statement of the problem
     Mathematical figures for support
     Illustrations of specific cities
  B. Statement of the problem
     Illustrations of specific cities
     Conclusion based on examples
  C. Statement of the problem
     Historical reasons and probable outcome
     Conclusion and recommendation for the future

Good reading is following the direction of a writer's idea—from the initial statement, to the explanation, and through the conclusion. The reading selection for each chapter will provide further exercises in selecting main ideas.

The first chapter reading selection is similar to the exercises you have completed. As you read the article, concentrate on the direction of the writer's statement. In particular, look for the main ideas, the specific illustrations that support the main idea, and most important, the reasons that the writer gives to account for the rejects' plight.

After you read the selection, answer the ten comprehension questions and the ten vocabulary items. In addition, a formula is provided to convert your reading time into the number of words-per-minute, your reading rate.

READING SELECTION 1 Michael Harrington, "The Rejects" *

Michael Harrington has been actively involved in many social welfare agencies for several years. His famous book, The Other America: Poverty in the United States, *impressed President Kennedy and is often cited as the catalyst for the War on Poverty. In this excerpt, Mr. Harrington discusses the rejects, the helpless victims of urban unemployment and a fast-moving technological economy.*

In New York City, some of my friends call 80 Warren Street "the slave market."

It is a big building in downtown Manhattan. Its corridors have the littered, trampled air of a courthouse. They are lined with employment-agency offices. Some of these places list good-paying and highly skilled jobs. But many of them provide the work force for the economic underworld in the big city: the dishwashers and day workers, the fly-by-night jobs.

Early every morning, there is a great press of human beings in 80 Warren Street. It is made up of Puerto Ricans and Negroes, alcoholics, drifters, and disturbed people. Some of them will pay a flat fee (usually around 10 percent) for a day's work. They pay $0.50 for a $5.00 job and they are given the address of a luncheonette. If all goes well, they will make their wage. If not, they have a legal right to come back and get their half-dollar. But many of them don't know that, for they are people that are not familiar with laws and rights.

But perhaps the most depressing time at 80 Warren Street is in the afternoon. The jobs have all been handed out, yet the people still mill around. Some of them sit on benches in the larger offices. There is no real point to their waiting, yet they have nothing else to do. For some, it is probably a point of pride to be here, a feeling that they are somehow still looking for a job even if they know that there is no chance to get one until early in the morning.

Most of the people at 80 Warren Street were born poor. (The alcoholics are an exception.) They are incompetent as far as American society is concerned, lacking the education and the skills to get decent work. If they find steady employment, it will be in a sweatshop or a kitchen.

In a Chicago factory, another group of people are working. A year or so ago, they were in a union shop making good wages, with sick leave, pension rights, and vacations. Now they are making artificial Christmas

---

* From *The Other America: Poverty in the United States* (New York: The Macmillan Company, 1962), pp. 25–26.

trees at less than half the pay they had been receiving. They have no contract rights, and the foreman is absolute monarch. Permission is required if a worker wants to go to the bathroom. A few are fired every day for insubordination.

These are people who have become poor. They possess skills, and they once moved upward with the rest of the society. But now their jobs have been destroyed, and their skills have been rendered useless. In the process, they have been pushed down toward the poverty from whence they came. This particular group is Negro, and the chances of ever breaking through, of returning to the old conditions, are very slim. Yet their plight is not exclusively racial, for it is shared by all the semi-skilled and unskilled workers who are the victims of technological unemployment in the mass-production industries. They are involved in an interracial misery.

These people are the rejects of the affluent society. They never had the right skills in the first place, or they lost them when the rest of the economy advanced. They are the ones who make up a huge portion of the culture of poverty in the cities of America. They are to be counted in the millions.

Reading Selection 1

COMPREHENSION

Do not refer to the article to answer these questions. Choose one of the four items that best answers each question, and mark the letter in the space provided.

1. ___C___ 80 Warren Street is referred to as "the slave market" because (a) workers are actually bought and sold there (b) unemployed people can find high paying skilled jobs if they are lucky (c) the agencies provide the labor source for the economic underworld (d) the building contains only employment agencies.

2. ___A___ In order to get a job, the applicant must (a) pay a 10 percent fee from his prospective wages (b) have good references (c) compete fiercely with other applicants (d) bribe the employment counselor.

3. ___C___ Warren Street is a hang-out for the unemployed during the afternoon because (a) sometimes evening jobs are available (b) they can get free meals (c) to leave would be an admission of defeat (d) they have no home to return to.

4. ___B___ According to Harrington, one reason the rejects have trouble getting jobs is that (a) they are basically lazy, preferring handouts to honest wages (b) they lack the proper education and skills (c) there are not enough jobs to go around (d) they are unable to pay the required fee.

5. ___C___ Harrington states that in Chicago many Negro workers are unemployed because (a) Chicago employers refuse to hire them (b) Chicago has no employment agencies for day work as New York does (c) their skills are useless or their former jobs have been destroyed by technology (d) they have no contract rights guaranteed.

6. ___A___ The author says that the reason for interracial unemployment in Chicago is that (a) technological advances which mass-produce goods have made unskilled workers obsolete (b) the culture of poverty from which the workers come is too hard to break (c) unskilled workers refuse to accept salaries below minimum wage (d) the unions refuse to admit members from minority groups.

7. ___C___ Judging from the tone of the selection, whom does Harrington criticize most for the rejects' situation? (a) the employers who hire only skilled laborers (b) the rejects themselves who could go back to school and learn new skills (c) an affluent, technically advanced society that has passed the re-

jects by (d) the employment agencies whose only concern
is profit.

8. ___B___ Harrington never directly mentions welfare payments, but
what can you infer from his article about the rejects' *probable* attitude toward welfare? (a) welfare payments would
be the easy way out of their predicament, the solution most
of them probably take (b) welfare payments would be an
admission of defeat; they would rather earn their own way
even with poor salaries and uncertain jobs (c) welfare payments would mean a humiliating invasion of privacy from
social workers (d) welfare payments would be even less
than their low wages.

9. ___B___ The rejects' situation is particularly pathetic because (a)
they have always been poor and have never held decent
jobs (b) they were born poor, acquired skills, but lost their
jobs as the economy advanced (c) they are emotionally disturbed and unable to hold steady jobs (d) their economic
situation will never improve.

10. ___C___ The main idea of the selection is best expressed by the statement (a) the rejects are victims of racial and economic
prejudice (b) the rejects are poor only because they lack
education and skills (c) the rejects are the helpless victims
of a rich technological society that is indifferent toward
them (d) the rejects provide a cheap labor force for American cities.

VOCABULARY

From the lettered choices, find the best definition for each vocabulary
item, and mark the letter in the space provided.

1. ___F___ the trampled *air*
2. ___K___ they are *incompetent*
3. ___D___ to get *decent* work
4. ___H___ *artificial* trees
5. _____ foreman is absolute *monarch*
6. ___A___ fired for *insubordination*
7. ___E___ their *plight* is not racial
8. ___C___ not *exclusively* racial
9. ___B___ an interracial *misery*
10. ___I___ these people are the *rejects*

A. disobedience   E. difficult; dangerous
B. suffering; wretchedness   situation
C. only; solely   F. atmosphere
D. respectable; adequate   G. solemn; stately

H. not natural; made in imitation
I. worthless, useless people
J. limited; confined
K. unfit; lacking skills or ability

L. skilled; expert
M. honest
N. natural; genuine
O. ruler; autocrat

COMPREHENSION   No. right _____ × 10 = _____ %

VOCABULARY   No. right _____ × 10 = _____ %

No. of words 550 ÷ time in seconds _____ × 60 = _____ WPM
WPM × Comprehension % = Reading Efficiency Rate _____

Chapter 2

PHRASE READING

In the previous chapter you were introduced to some basic skills required for accurate comprehension of main ideas and supporting evidence. This chapter introduces a new skill, phrase reading, which will help develop both your comprehension and reading rate.

Speed reading techniques are helpful when applied to reading material you want to cover quickly, like news and magazine articles. Some of these techniques will be discussed in Chapter 12. However, speed techniques may not be useful for reading difficult college assignments. Textbook material, essays and fiction require careful attention and concentration. Further, if your comprehension and critical skills are weak, straining to read faster may cause you to misread or misinterpret. Phrase reading is a technique well-suited to difficult or complex reading material. Its purpose is to develop your comprehension skills and thereby improve your reading rate.

One of the most common reading errors students make is to read word-by-word or even syllable-by-syllable, which affects both comprehension and speed. Compare these two illustrations of reading styles. The diagonal slash marks (/) represent the points where the eye stops or jumps when reading.

> Of / all / the / issues / that / have / risen / out / of / the / conflict / in / Vietnam / to / trouble / America, / none / holds / a / more / secure / place / in / the / history / of / man's / moral / searchings / than / selective / conscientious / objection / to / war. / For / at / least / 2,000 / years / moralists / have / weighed / and / attempted / to / balance / the / duties / owed / to / Caesar / and / to / God, / and / for / nearly / as / long / they / have / sought / to / define / the / conditions / that / make / war / just / or / unjust. / Never / in / the / life / of / this / nation, / however, / have / these / enduring / questions / imposed / themselves / so / forcibly / on / so / many / thousands / of / young / men.

Of all the issues / that have risen / out of the conflict / in Vietnam /
to trouble America, / none holds / a more secure place / in the history /
of man's moral searchings / than selective / conscientious objection /
to war. / For at least / 2,000 years / moralists have weighed /
and attempted / to balance / the duties / owed to Caesar / and to God, /
and for nearly / as long / they have sought / to define / the conditions /
that make war / just or unjust. / Never in the life / of this nation, /
however, / have these / enduring questions / imposed themselves / so
forcibly / on so many thousands / of young men.

> WALTER GOODMAN, from "Choose
> Your War; Or the Case of the Selec-
> tive C. O." *

If the number of slash marks in the first illustration annoyed you or distracted you from understanding the selection, stop and think about it. If
you read word-by-word, this is in effect how you read, and both your
speed and comprehension may suffer from it. You may believe that a
difficult sentence or passage is easier to comprehend if you read even more
slowly than normal, pausing after each word to consider its meaning. But
nothing is more discouraging than plodding through a sentence, one word
at a time, only to forget at the end what was said at the beginning. And
the discouragement increases as your reading assignments become
heavier.

Word-by-word reading, as shown in the first illustration, is both unnatural and inefficient. When you speak, for example, you don't say each
word in the same tone of voice, nor do you pause equally between words.
Everyone who has had the misfortune of listening to a lecturer speak in
a monotone knows how annoying and boring it sounds. And reading is the
same, which explains why students frequently complain of falling asleep
when reading or of reading an entire chapter and not remembering a
thing. It is inefficient to emphasize the "and's," "the's," and "if's" as much
as the more obviously important words.

Turn back to the illustration and think about the words that are really
important in the first sentence. If the sentence were stripped of the filler
words which lend continuity, you would find something like "issues . . .
risen out of . . . Vietnam . . . trouble America . . . selective conscientious objection to war." It looks peculiar without the little words, but
it can be understood.

Phrase reading, shown in the second illustration, has two functions:

(1) it teaches you to recognize the phrase as a unit of meaning to im-
    prove your comprehension; and

* From *The New York Times Magazine*, March 23, 1969, p. 34.

(2) it teaches you to expand the number of words you take in at a
glance to improve your speed.

A phrase, as you may remember from grammar, is a group of words
that does not contain a subject and verb in combination and that, unlike a
sentence, does not express a complete thought. But phrases usually do express at least a portion of a thought or give a small picture. Phrases like
"I was sitting / on the floor / watching television / when the fire started /
next door" if written alone still make some kind of sense. And when
phrases are arranged grammatically, they form a complete thought, or a
sentence. Phrases, then, can be defined as *units of meaning*. One word of
caution: incorrect, unnatural or awkward phrasing may hurt your comprehension or even result in misreading. For example: "I / was sitting on
the / floor watching / television when the / fire started next / door" violates the rules of natural phrasing, and certainly would sound ridiculous
if spoken that way. An example of misreading can be seen by incorrectly
phrasing the old maxim "go west young man." Unless the writer were
clearly hip, it is unlikely he meant "go west young / man" which distorts
the original meaning of "go west / young man."

Another point must be emphasized. Phrase reading is first a comprehension tool and then a speed tool. Even the most efficient reader cannot
take in more than two words per eye stop. But once you begin to see that
sentences have a natural rhythm and that they are composed of small units
of meaning, you will feel more comfortable when reading and your rate
of comprehension will improve.

The following paragraph is printed without punctuation. Go through
it carefully and mark one diagonal slash (/) after each phrase. In addition, mark a double slash (//) at the end of every sentence. The first few
phrases are already marked. There is no one correct set of answers, but
be sure that your phrases make grammatical sense.

> the two / most expressive things / about him / were his mouth / and
> the pockets / of his jacket // by looking / at his mouth / one could tell /
> whether he / was plotting evil / or had recently / accomplished it / if he was /
> bent upon malevolence / his lips / were all puckered up / like those of a /
> billiard player / about to make / a difficult shot / after the deed / was done /
> the pucker / was replaced / by a delicate unearthly smile / how a teacher / who
> knew anything / about / boys / could miss the fact / that both expressions /
> were masks / of Satan / I'm sure / I don't know / Wallace's pockets were less
> interesting / than his / mouth perhaps but more spectacular in a way the
> side pockets of his jacket bulged out over his pudgy haunches like burro
> hampers they were filled with tools screwdrivers pliers files wrenches wire
> cutters nail sets and I don't know what else in addition to all this one
> pocket always contained a rolled-up copy of *Popular Mechanics* while
> from the top of the other protruded *Scientific American* or some such

other magazine his breast pocket contained besides a large collection of fountain pens and mechanical pencils a picket fence of drill bits gimlets kitchen knives and other pointed instruments when he walked he clinked and jangled and pealed

RICHARD ROVERE, from "Wallace" *

In the following exercise, phrases are supplied from the passage just presented. In the space provided, mark T—if the phrase is natural, grammatical, and makes some sense by itself; F—if the phrase is artificial, ungrammatical, or simply nonsense.

1. ___T___ the two most expressive things
2. ___T___ about him
3. ___F___ the pockets of his
4. ___T___ mouth one could tell
5. ___T___ he was plotting evil
6. ___T___ recently accomplished it
7. ___F___ malevolence his lips
8. ___F___ up like those of a
9. ___T___ delicate unearthly smile
10. ___T___ who knew anything
11. ___T___ both expressions were masks
12. ___F___ of his jacket bulged
13. ___T___ in addition to
14. ___F___ *Mechanics* while the
15. ___F___ of the other protruded a
16. ___T___ contained besides a large
17. ___F___ a picket fence of drill bits
18. ___F___ pens and mechanical
19. ___F___ knives and other
20. ___T___ he clinked

Increasing your reading speed is pointless if you don't understand what you read. A person who wants to learn to drive would be mistaken to begin at the Indianapolis Speedway in a racing car at 100 miles an hour. At this point in developing your reading ability, you should not strain for speed. If you practice phrase reading, your reading rate should improve naturally. Breaking habits like smoking or eating too much can be accomplished by effort only, the conscious effort of will power and concentration. Breaking the habit of word-by-word reading requires the same effort, but in this case, the side effects are much more pleasant. Once you begin to see words in groups rather than individually, your speed and comprehension should increase considerably. But like the smoker who kids

* From *The New Yorker*, February 4, 1950, p. 28.

himself through life by having endless "last cigarettes," you won't get very far by saying "the old way is more comfortable."

For more practice in phrase reading, you may find the technique of "reading between the lines" helpful. To do this, read the paragraph that follows by resting your eyes quickly on the black marks printed in the white space above each line. You may find the marks annoying at first, but you should also be aware of a new feeling as you are freed from seeing individual words while your eyes move smoothly across the line.

A short trip by helicopter from Saigon in almost any direction permits a ringside view of American bombing. Just beyond the truck gardens of the suburbs, you see what at first glance appears to be a series of bonfires evocative of Indian summers; thick plumes of smoke are rising from wooded clumps and fields. Toward the west, great blackish-brown tracts testify to the most recent results of the defoliation program; purplish-brown tracts are last year's work. As the helicopter skims the treetops, and its machine guns lower into position, you can study the fires more closely, and it is possible to distinguish a rice field burned over by peasants from neat bombing targets emitting spirals of smoke. But a new visitor cannot be sure and may tend to discredit his horrified impression not wishing to jump to conclusions. Flying over the delta one morning, I saw the accustomed lazy smoke puffs mounting from the landscape and was urging myself to be cautious ("How do you *know?*") when I noticed a small plane circling; then it plunged, dropped its bombs, and was away in a graceful movement, having hit the target again; there was a flash of flame, and fresh, blacker smoke poured out. In the distance, a pair of small planes was hovering in the sky, like mosquitoes buzzing near the ceiling, waiting to strike. We flew on.

MARY MCCARTHY, from *Vietnam**

As an exercise in identifying phrases, a more difficult passage by Mark Twain is reprinted without punctuation. Mark as you did before one slash to indicate each phrase and a double slash to indicate the end of each sentence. As you remember, a sentence is a complete and grammatical statement. However, in this passage, Twain uses semicolons to separate his thoughts. Strictly speaking, these thoughts are not sentences, but fragments or incomplete thoughts. In working through the passage, you should consider them as complete statements, as the first few slash marks indicate.

* (New York: Harcourt Brace Jovanovich, Inc., 1967), p. 31.

I can see the farm yet with perfect clearness I can see all its belongings all its details the family room of the house with a "trundle" bed in
one corner and a spinning-wheel in another a wheel whose rising and
falling wail heard from a distance was the mournfulest of all sounds to
me and made me homesick and low spirited and filled my atmosphere
with the wandering spirits of the dead the vast fireplace piled high on
winter nights with flaming hickory logs from whose ends a sugary sap
bubbled out but did not go to waste for we scraped it off and ate it the
lazy cat spread out on the rough hearthstones the drowsy dogs braced
against the jambs and blinking my aunt in one chimney corner knitting
my uncle in the other smoking his corn-cob pipe the slick and carpetless
oak floor faintly mirroring the dancing flame tongues and freckled with
black indentations where the fire coals had popped out and died a
leisurely death half a dozen children romping in the background twilight
"split"-bottomed chairs here and there some with rockers a cradle out of
service but waiting with confidence in the early cold mornings a snuggle
of children in shirts and chemises occupying the hearthstones and pro-
crastinating they could not bear to leave that comfortable place and go
out on the wind-swept floor space between the house and kitchen where
the general tin basin stood and wash.

Mark Twain, from Autobiog-
raphy*

Before you read the following selection, here are some suggestions to
consider. First, read to find the main idea and the evidence the author
musters to justify his point of view. Then, try to apply one of the phrase
reading techniques discussed in this chapter. You should attempt to read
each sentence in short phrases, by units of meaning. Or if you prefer the
technique of "reading between the lines," focus your eyes slightly above
the line of print as you practiced in the passage by Mary McCarthy. You
should not try, however, to combine the two methods at this point. Instead, you should feel free to use whichever method seems more comfortable.

Reading Selection 2 Wolf von Eckardt, from *A Place to Live: The
Crisis of the Cities*†

> *Cities have long been criticized for breeding anonymity and apathy, and
> the last two decades have witnessed an unprecedented number of middle
> class people fleeing to the suburbs to escape city life. In this excerpt,
> Wolf von Eckardt, the architecture critic for* The Washington Post, *takes
> a different approach. He examines the sterility of contemporary suburban
> life. As in Reading Selection 1, you will be reading for comprehension and
> vocabulary.*

* (New York: Harper & Row, Publishers, 1959), pp. 102–103.
† (New York: Delacorte Press, 1967), pp. 22–24.

"There is no there there," reported Gertrude Stein after she was shown
—I believe it was Oakland, California. It doesn't much matter where it
was. Oakland or Oklahoma City, urban America is much the same. If you
do much traveling in America, it is easy to forget just where you are when
you step out of your hotel in the morning. From coast to coast vast, gray
urbia and vast, green suburbia, rich man's luxury highrise or poor man's
public housing project are alike in their anonymous sameness. With rare
exceptions, there is no there there. There is no there there at all.

This is disturbing not only as a matter of appearance. In 1964, close to
an apartment house in Kew Gardens, a gray but by no means unpleasant
middle-class suburb of New York City, twenty-eight-year-old Catherine
Genovese was murdered on the street early one morning. She was stabbed
several times by a man who took half an hour to kill her. As you may
recall reading, thirty-eight people living on that street admitted having
heard her screams. Several watched the murder from their windows. Not
one bothered to call the police. No one, newspaper reporters were later
told, wanted to get involved. The anonymity of the place, I am sure, has
a good deal to do with this apathy. Who wants to be involved with row
upon row of gray apartment slabs? Yet without involvement with the
stage set you remain a mere spectator of the drama that takes place in it.

Vast, gray urbia came first. It was bad enough that in the industrial
revolution cities just grew and grew, row upon row of houses and tenements. They broke Aristotle's rule that a city, to be a good place to live,
ought to be large enough to encompass all its functions but not too large to
interfere with them.

Then, with affluence and the automobile came green suburbia. They
gave the white middle class the means to flee the city and move into
suburban miniature manors on diminutive country estates, sprawling
farther and farther out. The fact that people are spread so far apart also
dangerously dissipates the quality of urban life—the life seven out of ten
Americans lead today.

One penalty we pay is precious time. In the eighteenth century it took
man ten minutes to get from the outskirts to the center of his city. In the
nineteenth century it took twenty minutes. Today, despite the fact that
we own vehicles capable of transporting us at a hundred miles per hour, it
takes, on the average, forty minutes. The trouble in suburbia is not only
that it takes all that time to get downtown, but that people must mobilize
all of 250 horsepower whenever they want to buy a pack of cigarettes or
have a drink in the warm conviviality of a tavern. This makes the subur-
banite almost as deprived as the slum dweller. The irritated restlessness of
the itinerant suburban child, forever being dragged along on mother's far-
flung errands, can be as pathetic as the sad eyes of a slum child. Even the
affluent two-car family can no longer spontaneously do as it wants.
Johnny cannot attend his Boy Scout meeting or Jane her dancing lesson
while Dad is at work and Mother out shopping. How often do any of them

get to a theater? Or worse, how often do any of them meet people of different income, color, or persuasion? How many affluent Americans can experience the wealth of culture and civilization that cities are built to offer—not vicariously on television but in their heart and soul?

Gray urbia and green suburbia are now caught in the blender of unprecedented economic boom and out comes metropolis, a vast urbanized area that is, for the most part, neither city nor suburb. It has none of the advantages of either and all the disadvantages of both. The white affluent middle class, which used to give the city stability, moves out and, sped by federal superhighways and mortgage insurance, spreads the unsightly manifestations of its wealth all over the countryside. Poor immigrants from the country, sped by farm mechanization, which is aided by federal subsidies, move in and spread the diseases of their poverty all over the city.

While we're very democratic about spreading blight, we are very careful not to mix people. What not long ago we fancied was about to become a truly classless society has segregated rich and poor in its zoning system. Democracy in America, it seems, stops at the office or factory gate. On the job we frown at class distinctions. At home we insist on sticking strictly to our own class. Our residential areas are considered exclusive private clubs. The "wrong" kind of people are kept out because the "right" address, of course, is as much, or more, of a status symbol than club membership.

READING SELECTION 2

COMPREHENSION

Do not refer to the article to answer these questions. Choose one of the items that best answers each question, and mark the letter in the space provided.

1. ___C___ The main idea of the entire selection is (a) people don't want to get involved (b) cities offer a variety of experiences which suburbs don't (c) physical ugliness and loss of identity are the results of urbanization (d) suburbs are more attractive to live in than cities.

2. ___D___ Gertrude Stein's comment about Oakland "there is no there there" means that (a) the city didn't exist (b) she preferred Oklahoma City to Oakland (c) Oakland was physically unattractive (d) Oakland lacked distinction and identity.

3. ___B___ Thirty-eight people in New York watched a girl being murdered and failed to rescue her because (a) they feared for their own safety (b) they didn't want to get involved (c) the victim was a suspicious stranger (d) the police handled the matter quickly.

4. ___B___ The reader can infer that after the industrial revolution, cities expanded (a) according to a design or plan (b) randomly, haphazardly (c) quickly, because workers had to live near factories where they worked (d) slowly and efficiently.

5. ___C___ Aristotle's rule about cities was that they should be (a) carefully planned to be efficient (b) limited in size to discourage population expansion (c) only moderate in size, to include all functions without interfering with them (d) very small to give residents a sense of security.

6. ___B___ The author estimates that approximately (a) 50% (b) 70% (c) 20% (d) 85% of the American population lives in cities.

7. ___A___ One main disadvantage of living in the suburbs is that (a) one wastes valuable time getting to the center of the city (b) one must risk driving on dangerous freeways (c) cars must go at high speeds to be efficient (d) a family must have two cars.

8. ___C___ Von Eckardt lists several other disadvantages of living in the suburbs. Which was not mentioned? (a) few surburban residents can take advantage of what cities have to offer (b) spontaneous activities in the city are almost impossible (c) cheap public transportation is unavailable (d) suburban residents are cut off from members of different income or racial groups.

9. ___B___ The author emphasizes the idea that the new metropolis, formed by urban and suburban sprawl, (a) lacks the stability of rich inhabitants (b) has the advantages of neither suburb nor city and the disadvantages of both (c) has been possible because of technological advances (d) is responsible for urban blight and air pollution.

10. ___E___ From the conclusion, the author evidently thinks that (a) the middle class has fled to the suburbs to avoid close contact with the "wrong" people (b) suburbs are a clever and legal way of ensuring segregation in residential areas (c) middle-class people consider a suburban address as a kind of status symbol (d) suburban residents approve of racial and class integration at work, but not in their communities (e) all of the above

VOCABULARY

From the lettered choices, find the best definition for each vocabulary item, and mark the letter in the space provided.

1. ___G___ in their *anonymous* sameness
2. ___K___ with this *apathy*
3. ___I___ to *encompass* its functions
4. ___B___ with *affluence* and the automobile
5. ___N___ on *diminutive* country estates
6. ___E___ *dissipates* the quality
7. ___A___ the *itinerant* suburban child
8. ___D___ *spontaneously* do as it wants
9. ___M___ *vicariously* on television
10. ___F___ *unprecedented* economic boom

A. going from place to place; wandering
B. abundance of wealth
C. concern; involvement
D. impulsively; freely
E. drives away; disperses
F. never before experienced; without parallel
G. having no name, identity

H. poverty
I. contain; envelop
J. having distinct characteristics
K. indifference; lack of concern
L. very large; vast
M. enjoyed by imagination or substitution
N. small; tiny
O. chaotically; without plan

COMPREHENSION   No. right ____ × 10 = ____ %

VOCABULARY   No. right ____ × 10 = ____ %

No. of words 780 ÷ time in seconds ____ × 60 = ____ WPM
WPM × Comprehension % = Reading Efficiency Rate _____

Chapter 3

READING PARAGRAPHS:
Finding the Main Idea and Coherent Devices

In Chapter 1, you learned to identify the main idea and to see the relationship between the main idea and the supporting evidence. In Chapters 3 and 4, you will apply the same principles to reading paragraphs for more accurate comprehension. Because most of the required reading in college courses is informational or persuasive, the critical skills discussed in this chapter will improve your comprehension in these two difficult areas.

The paragraph, the main unit of composition, is a complete thought, expressed in a series of sentences. One sentence in each paragraph usually states the main idea, although occasionally a writer may communicate the main idea in two or even three sentences. Each of the other sentences acts as supporting evidence to explain, develop, and analyze the main idea. A paragraph may be any length, one sentence or several, as long as it holds to one idea.

An essay consists of several paragraphs, each of which must pertain to the general idea the writer wants to communicate. Paragraph divisions in an essay are a convenience for the reader; they help by separating one thought clearly from another. Paragraphs may have several functions in longer reading passages. They may serve to:

(1) introduce the main idea of the essay
(2) develop or analyze the secondary ideas
(3) link other paragraphs together logically; called *transitional* paragraphs
(4) sum up and draw conclusions.

Analyzing paragraph order and finding the main idea are not meaningless tasks. The purpose is to teach you to see quickly the organization and logical pattern of a paragraph, which leads to better comprehension of complex ideas, and, further, to train you to see how the paragraph func-

25

tions in the essay as a whole. In informational and persuasive writing, the position of the main idea determines the order of supporting evidence. Although the main idea can appear anywhere in the paragraph, writers generally follow these four basic methods of paragraph order:

most Common

(1) *Deductive Order*—Main idea at or near the beginning is followed by supporting evidence;

(2) *A Variation of Deductive Order*—Main idea at the beginning is followed by supporting evidence; main idea is restated at the end;

(3) *Inductive Order*—Supporting evidence at the beginning leads to the main idea at or near the end;

(4) *Implied Main Idea*—Main idea is unstated; evidence suggests the topic of the paragraph.

(1) Deductive Order

Deductive order is the most common method of paragraph organization. The writer states the main idea at the beginning, and then musters evidence to support it. This method is also the easiest to recognize, for you know immediately what the paragraph is about. Journalists call this pattern the "pyramid style," because a newspaper compositor often finds it necessary to cut some material from the bottom of the article to save space. For this reason, the news writer puts the most important information first and the remaining details in descending order of importance. Even if the printer deletes some details from the end, the reader will still have the essential information. The pyramid style is easy to visualize if you imagine an inverted triangle with the base at the top:

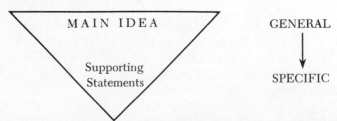

The following paragraph illustrates deductive order. After you read it carefully, answer the questions that follow. You may refer to the paragraph if necessary.

> Hostility to authority and disrespect for law are commonplace in Mississippi.[1] How could it be otherwise in a state that tolerates the cynical disregard of the Mississippi prohibition law and blithely collects a black market tax on liquor?[2] How can anything else be expected when the state itself brazenly tells the world it has achieved "separate but equal" school facilities, although in 1959–60 local school expenditures were

$81.86 per capita for the white child as against $21.77 for the colored.[3] Or when, as in 1951, the county superintendents of education, looking greedily toward the allocation of state equalization funds, reported 895,779 children of educable age (6–20) while the United States Census of 1950 listed the number of children from 5 to 19 as only 651,600? [4] What respect can there be for the legal process when one standard of justice prevails when a Negro commits a crime against a Negro, another when a Negro commits a crime against a white, still another when a white commits a crime against a white, and a fourth when a white commits a crime against a Negro? [5]

> JAMES W. SILVER, from *Mississippi: The Closed Society**

1. _____ Which sentence or sentences express the main idea?
2. _____ How does the supporting evidence relate to the situation described? Do the supporting statements appear to be (a) explanations (b) causes and effects (c) illustrations and examples (d) rationalizations and justifications?
3. _____ The author uses the question form for the supporting evidence probably because (a) he doesn't know the answers (b) it is a clever and effective persuasive device (c) he wants the reader to answer the questions (d) the statistics he presents may not be true.
4. _____ Does the author imply that (a) the Negroes (b) the white citizens (c) the state institutions (d) the Federal government—are responsible for the situation in Mississippi?
5. Look up the most accurate definition for each italicized word in an unabridged dictionary and write the answer in the space provided.

   (a) the *cynical* disregard _selfishness_
   (b) *blithely* collects a tax _cheerful, carefree_
   (c) *brazenly* tells the world _bold, bold_
   (d) *per capita* _per person_
   (e) the *allocation* of state funds _to allot, assign_

The term *main idea* is more sensible than the more common, "topic sentence." Although most writers state the main idea in one sentence, that is not a steadfast rule. It is a mistake to look for *the* topic sentence because some paragraphs may state the main idea in two or more sentences.

(2) A Variation of Deductive Order

Most college textbooks, newspapers, and magazines use deductive order extensively. Besides the first pattern, the writer may vary deductive order by restating the main idea in different words at the end. The paragraph,

* (New York: Harcourt Brace Jovanovich, Inc., 1966), p. 152.

then, begins and ends with a main idea. A diagram of this variation method looks like this:

MAIN IDEA
Supporting Statements
Restated Main Idea

In this example, Emerson reinterprets the main idea at the end and draws a conclusion. Read the paragraph, and then answer the questions.

A foolish consistency is the hobgoblin of little minds, adored by little statesmen and philosophers and divines.[1] *With consistency a great soul has simply nothing to do.* [2] He may as well concern himself with his shadow on the wall.[3] Speak what you think now in hard words and tomorrow speak what tomorrow thinks in hard words again, though it contradict everything you said today.[4]—"Ah, so you shall be sure to be misunderstood?" [5]—Is it so bad, then, to be misunderstood? [6] Pythagoras was misunderstood, and Socrates, and Jesus, and Luther, and Copernicus, and Galileo, and Newton, and every pure and wise spirit that ever took flesh.[7] *To be great is to be misunderstood.*[8]

RALPH WALDO EMERSON, from
"Self-Reliance" *

1. *1, 2, 8* What is the number of the sentences that express the main idea?
2. *D* In the phrase, "a foolish consistency," Emerson uses *consistency* to mean (a) firmness (b) nearness, density (c) logical connection between ideas (d) agreement between things.
3. *A* The main point of the paragraph is that (a) inconsistency is a virtue that great men share (b) great men should be consistent to avoid being misunderstood (c) philosophers deliberately contradict themselves (d) a man cannot be great unless he is inconsistent.
4. *B* To support his idea, Emerson (a) pokes fun at people who are always consistent (b) cites the examples of great religious figures and scientists (c) describes historical events (d) uses hard words.
5. *C* Emerson implies that consistency is the fault of (a) great inventors (b) great and wise men (c) small, petty minds (d) daydreamers.
6. For each italicized word, look up the best definition in an unabridged dictionary, and write your answer in the space provided.

* From *Essays, First and Second Series* (New York: Thomas Y. Crowell Company, 1926), p. 41.

(a) the *hobgoblin* of little minds ___evil goblin___
(b) adored by philosophers and *divines* ___clergymen___
(c) in *hard* words ___intense, real___
(d) that *ever took flesh* ___taking meat of Christ___

The variation method of deductive order may be used to disprove or re-define the main idea. The writer may begin with one idea and conclude with another that redefines or reinterprets the original. Hunter Thompson in the following paragraph describes the Hell's Angels' refusal to follow the "eye for an eye" custom. At the end, the conclusion redefines their concept of right and wrong. After you read the paragraph, answer the questions as directed.

> *Of all their habits and predilections that society finds alarming, the out-laws' disregard for the time-honored concept of an eye for an eye is the one that frightens people most.*[1] The Hell's Angels try not to do anything halfway, and outcasts who deal in extremes are bound to cause trouble, whether they mean to or not.[2] This, along with a belief in total retaliation for any offense or insult, is what makes the Angels such a problem for police and so morbidly fascinating to the general public.[3] Their claim that they don't start trouble is probably true more often than not, but their idea of provocation is dangerously broad, and one of their main difficulties is that almost nobody else seems to understand it.[4] *Yet they have a very simple rule of thumb; in any argument a fellow Angel is* always *right.*[5] *To disagree with a Hell's Angel is to be* wrong—*and to persist in being wrong is an open challenge.*[6]
>
> HUNTER S. THOMPSON, from
> *Hell's Angels**

1. __C__ The following statements are from the paragraph. Which accurately expresses the restated idea? (a) "they have a very simple rule of thumb" (b) "the outlaw's disregard for the time-honored concept of an eye for an eye" (c) "in any argu-ment a fellow Angel is *always right*. To disagree with a Hell's Angel is to be *wrong*" (d) "to persist in being wrong is an open challenge."

2. __B__ The author suggests that most people (a) believe in total re-taliation for an offense or insult (b) believe that an offender must be punished according to his crime (c) believe that right and wrong are clearly defined (d) believe that human error should be forgiven.

3. __D__ The author's statement that "their idea of provocation is dangerously broad" means that the Angels probably (a) never provoke trouble without good cause (b) are too sensi-tive to their public image (c) consider every act as a potential

threat (d) are quick to retaliate for any real or imagined wrong.

4. _____*B*_____ The Angels' notion of right and wrong is best described as (a) generous, tolerant (b) ruthless (c) extremist (d) shadowy; undefined.

5. _____*D*_____ According to the paragraph, it is evident that the public views the Angels with (a) fascination (b) respect (c) fear (d) disapproval (e) fear, fascination, and misunderstanding.

6.   For each of the italicized words, look up the best definition and write your answer in the space provided.

      (a) their habits and *predilections* _____

      (b) belief in total *retaliation* _____

      (c) so *morbidly* fascinating _____

      (d) *rule of thumb* _____

The remaining methods of paragraph order are not as common as the first two, but writers do employ them occasionally to break the monotony.

(3) *Inductive Order*

Modern writers use inductive order to provide relief from reading too many deductive paragraphs. Inductive order is just the reverse of deductive order. The writer first presents evidence and support, saving the main idea for the end. The reader must try to determine the conclusion in advance by doing a bit of detective work. For this reason, induction is more emphatic than other kinds of paragraph order. Inductive reasoning proceeds from the *specific* (supporting evidence) to the *general* (main idea), diagrammed as a triangle or pyramid with the base at the bottom:

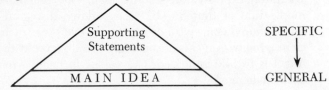

The following paragraph is a good illustration of how a paragraph builds suspense:

> His average annual income is one-half the amount which has been determined to be the general poverty level for the poor in the United States.[1] He can expect to live to age 42.[2] His segregation from the rest of society makes the Negro's degree of acceptance look good.[3] The level of unemployment among his people is seven or eight times that of his nation's average unemployment.[4] He suffers more from poor health, malnutrition and ignorance than does any other ethnic group in his country.[5] Who is he?[6] Any American school child should know that the American Indian and only the American Indian answers to that de-

scription.[7] Conquered, dispossessed, exploited, abandoned, the American Indian confronts the nation as its primary challenge.[8]

> "The American Indian, Dispossessed and Abandoned" *

Answer the questions as directed.

1. __2__ What is the number of the sentence that expresses the main idea?

2. __B__ The evidence to support the main idea is mainly concerned with (a) suggestions for programs to help the Indian (b) a comparison of the Indian's living standards with that of the national average or of other minority groups (c) exact statistics on income, unemployment, average years of education completed and health standards (d) reasons to account for the Indian's poverty.

3. __A__ The author builds up the reader's curiosity by (a) listing shocking facts and statistics (b) withholding the subject until the end (c) asking the reader to determine the subject at the beginning (d) using the question form for supporting evidence.

4. __A__ This paragraph is part of a longer editorial. Does it appear to belong to the (a) introduction (b) middle portion—development and analysis (c) conclusion?

5. Look up each of the italicized vocabulary words, and write the best definition in the space provided.

(a) suffers from *malnutrition* _insufficient diet_
(b) any other *ethnic* group _sociable group_
(c) conquered, *dispossessed* _deprive of possession_
(d) *exploited*, abandoned _make selfish or unethical use of —_

(4) Implied Main Idea

A writer may not always state the main idea in explicit terms. Instead, he gives illustrations, examples, or details that suggest the main thought, from which you, as reader, must infer his topic. After you have read the following paragraph, decide which statement best expresses the implied main idea:

> "THE No. 280 reflects character and station in life. It is superb in styling and provides a formal reflection of successful living." This is quoted from the catalogue of Practical Burial Footwear of Columbus, Ohio, and refers to the Fit-A-Fut Oxford, which comes in patent, calf, tan or oxblood with lace or goring back. The same firm carries the Ko-Zee, with its "soft, cush-

* From an editorial, "Help the Neediest First," *The Christian Century*, May 27, 1964, p. 693.

ioned soles and warm, luxurious slipper comfort, but true shoe smartness."
Just what practical use is made of the footwear is spelled out. Burial
footwear demonstrates "consideration and thoughtfulness for the departed." The closed portion of the casket is opened for the family, who
on looking see that "the ensemble is complete although not showing. You
will gain their complete confidence and good will." The women's lingerie
department of Practical Burial Footwear supplies a deluxe package, in
black patent box with gold-embossed inscription, of "pantee, vestee" and
nylon hose, "strikingly smart—ultimate in distinction." Also for the ladies
is the "new Bra-form, Post Mortem Form Restoration," offered by Courtesy Products at the demonstrably low price of $11 for a package of 50—
they "accomplish so much for so little."

JESSICA MITFORD, from The
American Way of Death*

American suppliers of burial attire:

(1) manufacture beautiful clothes and accessories so the survivors will
not be reminded of their grief.

(2) appeal to the survivors' wish to give the dead an image of distinction and luxury.

(3) promote fashion trends so that the dead can wear the same styles as
the living.

In addition, most descriptive paragraphs in novels and short stories do
not state the main idea in explicit terms. The writer implies the feeling
and the mood of the scene by using adjectives and adverbs or descriptive
words. In this way, he shows the reader without directly telling him.

Although the four patterns described in this chapter are most frequently
used, a writer may place the main idea wherever he thinks it will be most
emphatic.

Methods of Coherence

A skilled writer makes his ideas stick together and follow one another
logically. This is called paragraph *coherence.* Coherent devices link the
writer's ideas together and make the sentences read more smoothly, as the
italicized words illustrate in this paragraph:

> The catalog of L.A. gadgetry could go on forever, *but* I may as well
> close *it* with a note on what I found in one fairly modest "open house"
> last summer. *To begin with,* the house had a central vacuum-cleaning
> arrangement, with a socket in each room to which the cleaner could be
> attached. *It* had another central device, for the garden, that could spray
> water mixed with fertilizer on the plants. *It* had a soda-bar (for the
> young, one hopes) with standard soda-fountain equipment, including
> squirters for chocolate, coca-cola, and root-beer syrup; a soda spout;

* (New York: Simon & Schuster, Inc. 1963) p. 56.

and containers, with scoops attached to their covers, for pineapple and strawberry sundae sauce. *It also* had freezer space for ice-cream, and *all these things* were in impeccable stainless steel and labeled in conventional soda-fountain manner. *Of course* the house had a perfect technological kitchen, and outside *it* had a barbecue pit with a gas-jet for getting the charcoal started. This use of gas-jets, in barbecues and also fireplaces, is common in L.A., and *it* gives an idea of the difference between *that city* and *those* of the East Coast or Old World.

CHRISTOPHER RAND, from *Los Angeles: The Ultimate City**

If you read this paragraph aloud, omitting the italicized words, the difference will be obvious. It will sound choppy and uneven. Just as pancake flour will not adhere until you add milk and eggs, a paragraph will not *cohere* without these devices. There are four devices frequently used to produce coherent paragraphs; examples may be seen in the paragraph by Rand:

(1) repetition of a key word or phrase; in the paragraph, *house* is repeated twice.

(2) substitution of pronouns for key words; *it* refers several times to *house* to avoid monotony.

(3) transitional words or phrases; expressions like *to begin with, also, of course, for example, even though, furthermore,* and so forth.

(4) parallel phrase, clause, or sentence structure. In the preceding passage, Rand repeats the beginning words *it had* four times, keeping the sentences parallel in structure. Parallel structure is most effective in this famous speech by Winston Churchill:

> We shall go on to the end, we shall fight in France, we shall fight on the seas and oceans, we shall fight with growing confidence and growing strength in the air, we shall defend our Island, whatever the cost may be, we shall fight on the beaches, we shall fight on the landing grounds, we shall fight in the fields and in the streets, we shall fight in the hills; we shall never surrender, and even if, which I do not for a moment believe, this Island or a large part of it were subjugated and starving, then our Empire beyond the seas, armed and guarded by the British Fleet, would carry on the struggle, until, in God's good time, the New World, with all its power and might, steps forth to the rescue and the liberation of the old.

WINSTON CHURCHILL, from "Dunkirk: A Speech Delivered in the House of Commons, June 4, 1940" †

For practice in recognizing coherent devices, read the following paragraph by John F. Kennedy. The coherent devices are italicized and numbered.

---

* (New York: Oxford University Press, 1967), p. 147.
† From *Into Battle* (London: Cassell and Company, Ltd., 1941), p. 223.

A knowledge of history is more than a means of judgment; [1] *it is* [2] *also* a [3] *means of sympathy—a means of relating* our own experience with the [4] *experience* of other peoples and lands struggling for national fulfillment. We may sometimes forget, [5] *for example,* that the United States began as an underdeveloped nation which seized [6] *its* independence by carrying out a successful revolution against a colonial empire. [7] *We may forget that,* in the first few years of the new republic, George Washington laid down the principle of no "permanent alliances" and enjoined the United States to a course of neutralism in the face of the great-power conflicts then dividing the civilized world. [8] *We may forget that,* in the first stages of our economic development, our national growth was stimulated to a considerable degree [9] *by "foreign aid"*—[10] *that is,* investment from abroad—and [9] *by public investment and direction* on the part of our state and local [11] *as well as* our national government. [12] *We may forget that* our own process of economic change was often accompanied [13] *by the issue of wildcat paper money, by the repudiation of bonds, by disorder, fraud, and violence.* [14] *If we recall the facts of our own past,* we may better understand the problems and predicaments of contemporary "new nations" laboring for national development in circumstances far less favorable than our own—and we will, [15] *in consequence,* become less liable to the national self-righteousness which is both unworthy of our own traditions and a bane of international relations.

> JOHN F. KENNEDY, from "On History" *

From the key that follows, decide which method of coherence each word or phrase represents and mark the number in the space provided. In addition, for each pronoun, write the word from the paragraph by John Kennedy to which the pronoun refers. The first answer has been done for you. You may refer to the passage for help.

(1) repetition of key word or phrase
(2) substitution of pronoun for a key word
(3) transitional word or phrase
(4) parallel phrase, clause or sentence

1. it (2) pronoun substitute; refers to "knowledge of history"
2. also (3) Knowledge of history
3. a means of sympathy—a means of relating (4) Knowledge of history
4. experience (1) our own knowledge of history
5. for example (3) an instance of what we forget
6. its (2) United States
7. we may forget that (1) the American people
8. we may forget that (1)
9. by foreign aid, by public investment and direction (4) our national growth
10. that is (2) foreign aid

* From *American Heritage New Illustrated History of the United States,* Volume I (New York: American Heritage, 1963), pp. 4–6.

11. as well as (3) _national gov't._
12. we may forget that (1) _the American people of U.S._
13. by the issue of wildcat paper money, by the repudiation of bonds, by disorder, fraud, and violence (4) _economic change_
14. if we recall the facts of our own past (4) _Americas part_
15. in consequence (3) _less liable to self-righteousness_

EXERCISES

Here are several paragraphs for more practice. After you read each one carefully, answer the questions that follow. You may refer to the paragraph to answer each set of questions.

I.   *You must adjust . . .*[1] This is the legend imprinted in every school-book, the invisible message on every blackboard.[2] Our schools have become vast factories for the manufacture of robots.[3] We no longer send our young to them primarily to be taught and given the tools of thought, no longer primarily to be informed and acquire knowledge; but to be "socialized"—which in the current semantic means to be regimented and made to conform.[4] The modern report card reflects with horrible precision the preoccupations of our teachers and the philosophy of our educators.[5] Today, in the public schools, grades are given for the "ability" of a child to "adjust" to group activities, for whether he is "liked" by others, for whether he "enjoys" the subjects taught, for whether he "gets along" with his schoolmates.[6] In the private schools, especially in those which designate themselves "progressive," the situation is more frightening, in some cases known to me actually revealing a cynical kind of anti-intellectualism.[7] So the school takes up where the parent leaves off; and the children who emerge from it with a few shreds of individuality clinging to their blue jeans or bobby-socks are rare birds, indeed.[8] But even if they manage to retain some uniqueness after passing through the mill of primary and secondary education, the young who go on to institutions of higher learning are exposed to pressures to conformity that must surely deprive them of the pitiful remnants of singularity and independence they still have.[9]

ROBERT M. LINDNER, from *Must You Conform?* *

1. __A__ Which kind of paragraph order does the writer use? (a) deductive (b) variation of deductive (c) inductive (d) implied main idea.
2. __3, 9__ What is the number of the sentence (or sentences) that expresses the main idea?
3. __C__ In the phrase, *"you must adjust,"* the author means that children are forced to (a) learn (b) be independent (c) conform (d) think and acquire knowledge.

* (New York: Holt, Rinehart & Winston, Inc., 1956), pp. 168–169.

4. _C___ The author's supporting evidence is concerned with the idea that (a) parents expect the schools to train their children for them (b) schools are too bureaucratic to teach children to be individuals (c) schools grade children according to how well they adjust, not according to what they learn (d) grammar schools do not prepare children for the emphasis on individuality they will confront in college.

5. _D___ The reader can infer that the pressure to adjust exists (a) only in elementary schools (b) in elementary and high schools (c) only in private schools (d) from elementary school through college.

6.   Vocabulary: For each of the italicized words, look up the best definition and write your answer in the space provided.

     (a) in the current *semantic* _meaning in language_
     (b) which *designate* themselves _to indicate or specify_
     (c) a *cynical* kind of anti-intellectualism _motivated by_
     (d) the pitiful *remnants* _left over_   _selfishness_

II.   Psychologists studying race prejudice have many times made an interesting experiment.[1] They seat a few people in a row, show a picture to the first in line, and ask him to whisper a description of it in a few words to a second who will whisper the information to the third, and so on.[2] The picture is of a policeman and a badly dressed, uncouth Negro.[3] The policeman is holding a knife in his hand; the Negro is unarmed.[4] Almost never is the description transmitted to more than two or three individuals in succession, before the knife has passed from the hand of the policeman and is now being held in a threatening manner, by the Negro![5] *In other words,* the picture is transformed until it fits the preexisting concept in the mind, which is that an open knife is far more likely to be held by a Negro than a policeman.[6] *This sort of unconscious alteration* of what is perceived, to make it accord with what is already believed, is universal and is one of the most important of all the facts with which communication has to deal.[7]

> BRUCE BLIVEN, from *Preview
> for Tomorrow**

1. _D___ Which kind of paragraph order does the writer follow? (a) deductive (b) variation of deductive (c) inductive (d) implied main idea.

2. _4,7___ Mark the number of the sentence (or sentences) that expresses the main idea.

3. _C___ The point of the experiment was *specifically* to test (a) racial prejudice (b) public attitudes toward police (c) how people unconsciously substitute what they expect for what they

* (New York: Alfred A. Knopf, Inc., 1953), pp. 255–256.

actually see (d) how people transmit information from what they perceive.

4. ___C___ The experiment proved that the subjects (a) actually did perceive the picture accurately (b) could not accurately transmit their perceptions to others (c) carried with them unconscious concepts of racial stereotypes (d) reacted objectively to the picture.

5. _____ Find a coherent device that acts as a substitute for the key words in this statement: "the picture is transformed until it fits the preexisting concept in the mind."

6. Vocabulary: For each italicized word, look up the best definition and write your answer in the space provided.

(a) an *uncouth* Negro ___crude/unrefined / awkward___
(b) the description is *transmitted* ___to convey / to send___
(c) the *preexisting* concept ___one before___
(d) to make it *accord* ___agreement / settlement___

III.   The accommodations provisions of the new civil rights act were met with a sullen, partial compliance in the larger towns.[1] Even here, private eating clubs and exclusive recreational associations blossomed forth, and in the rural areas, where colored citizens were excluded from all but the segregated honky-tonks by economic necessity, the law had no meaning.[2] In a society where most Negroes were dependent on whites for their livelihood, there was no rush to take advantage of federal legislation.[3] Tallahatchie County Negroes were simply afraid to exercise their rights under a federal court order that they be registered without the application of Mississippi law.[4] There seems to be no way yet to induce a Mississippi white jury to look honestly at the facts in a case of assault on civil rights workers.[5] The degree of resentment built up among Mississippians against outside interference in what they considered their private affairs was vividly shown in the remarkable protest vote for Barry Goldwater in the November presidential election—87.1% of the voters, whose proud heritage had for a century known only the Democratic Party, cast their ballots for the Republican nominee.[6] In a Louis Harris poll published three weeks later, 19% of Mississippi's citizenry approved of Lyndon Johnson's over-all performance as against 58% approval for the South and 74% for the country.[7] When it came to the President's handling of racial outbreaks and civil rights problems, only 2% and 4% of the people of Mississippi responded favorably.[8] They had been forced to accept revolutionary change, but they most assuredly didn't like it.[9]

JAMES W. SILVER, from *Mississippi: The Closed Society**

1. ___D___ Which kind of paragraph order does the writer follow? (a) deductive (b) variation of deductive (c) inductive (d) implied main idea.

* (New York: Harcourt Brace Jovanovich, Inc., 1966), pp. 253–254.

2. ___/___ Mark the number of the sentence (or sentences) that expresses the main idea.

3. ___B___ To support the main idea, the writer gives (a) background information and reasons (b) statistics on voting behavior (c) the effects of the civil rights law (d) statistics from political preference surveys (e) all of the above.

4. ___D___ The reader can infer that Mississippi whites reacted to the civil rights law with hostility because (a) they resented the federal government's interference in their affairs (b) they were not consulted about the law's provisions (c) they planned to handle civil rights matters in their own way (d) they were bitter over Goldwater's defeat in the election.

5. Vocabulary: For each italicized word, look up the best definition and write your answer in the space provided.

(a) a *sullen*, partial compliance ___resentment / all one___
(b) for their *livelihood* ___support / subsistence___
(c) no way to *induce* a jury ___to persuade___
(d) was *vividly* shown ___distinct / intense / lifelike___

IV.   When I think of hills, I think of the upward strength I tread upon.[1] When water is the object of my thought, I feel the cool shock of the plunge and the quick yielding of the waves that crisp and curl and ripple about my body.[2] The pleasing changes of rough and smooth, pliant and rigid, curved and straight in the bark and branches of a tree give the truth to my hand.[3] The immovable rock, with its juts and warped surfaces, bends beneath my fingers into all manner of grooves and hollows.[4] The bulge of a watermelon and the puffed-up rotundities of squashes that sprout, bud, and ripen in that strange garden planted somewhere behind my finger tips are the ludicrous in my tactual memory and imagination.[5]

> HELEN KELLER, from *The World
> I Live In**

1. ___A___ Which method of paragraph order does the writer follow? (a) deductive (b) variation of deductive (c) inductive (d) implied main idea.

2. ___C___ This paragraph describes a blind person's memory of natural things according to her sense of (a) smell (b) taste (c) touch (d) hearing.

3. ___B___ One can infer from the paragraph that the writer (a) never went outdoors after she became blind (b) had to rely on her memory and imagination to enjoy nature (c) enjoyed gardening (d) never learned to enjoy life after becoming blind.

4. Vocabulary: For each italicized word, look up the best definition and write your answer in the space provided.

** (New York: D. Appleton-Century-Crofts, 1935), p. 11.

(a) the quick *yielding* _give in return_
(b) *pliant* and rigid _easily bent or flexed_
(c) *warped* surfaces _distortion, twist, out of shape_
(d) puffed-up *rotundities* _rounded, plump_
(e) are the *ludicrous* _absurdity or incongruity_
(f) in my *tactual* memory _appreciate situation_

V.   It was a very narrow street—a ravine of tall, leprous houses, lurching toward one another in queer attitudes, as though they had all been frozen in the act of collapse.[1] All the houses were hotels and packed to the tiles with lodgers, mostly Poles, Arabs, and Italians.[2] At the foot of the hotels were tiny *bistros*, where you could be drunk for the equivalent of a shilling.[3] On Saturday nights about a third of the male population of the quarter was drunk.[4] There was fighting over women, and the Arab navvies who lived in the cheapest hotels used to conduct mysterious feuds, and fight them out with chairs and occasionally revolvers.[5] At night the policemen would only come through the street two together.[6] It was a fairly rackety place.[7] And yet amid the noise and dirt lived the usual respectable French shopkeepers, bakers and laundresses and the like, keeping themselves to themselves and quietly piling up small fortunes.[8] It was quite a representative Paris slum.[9]

GEORGE ORWELL, from *Down and Out in Paris and London**

1. _c_ Which method of paragraph order does the writer follow? (a) deductive (b) variation of deductive (c) inductive (d) implied main idea.
2. _1_ What is the number of the sentence (or sentences) that express the main idea?
3. _leprous_ What word in the first sentence suggests metaphorically that the houses were decaying?
4. _c_ One can infer that a *bistro* is probably a (a) hotel (b) private lodging house (c) small bar and restaurant (d) French word for slum.
5. _b, d, c_ Mark any of the words that apply to the neighborhood according to Orwell's description. (a) unique (b) populated with all nationalities and classes (c) typical (d) dirty, dilapidated.
6.   Vocabulary: For each of the italicized words, look up the best definition and write your answer in the space provided.

(a) a *ravine* of tall houses _a deep narrow cleft_
(b) tall, *leprous* houses _a chronic infectious disease_
(c) in *queer attitudes* _strange beliefs_
(d) for the *equivalent* of _equal to, similar_

* (New York: Harcourt Brace Jovanovich, Inc., 1956), pp. 49–50.

READING SELECTION 3 James Reston, "The Pueblo Trial" *

Perhaps no international incident shocked and outraged the American public as much as the North Koreans' capture of the U.S.S. Pueblo. James Reston, the noted political analyst, examines the philosophic implications of Commander Bucher's ordeal.

Secretary of the Navy John H. Chafee says the Pueblo case is "closed," but an interesting philosophic question remains. Who is to judge the judges?

The men who make decisions about war and the men who carry them out live by different rules. The first volunteer for political office and most of the second are drafted to fight, and both, being human, make mistakes, but the fighters must answer for their missions and the men who ordered missions do not have to answer and even sit in judgment on their men.

It is easy to understand why the senior officers of the Navy recommended a court-martial for Commander Lloyd Bucher. He broke the Navy's tradition of going down with the ship, and tradition is important.

It is also easy to understand why Secretary Chafee rejected the court-martial, for the Pueblo was not only a naval and political disaster, but a rebuke to the United States as well as to Commander Bucher. And Secretary Chafee clearly wanted to bury it as soon as possible.

Any reasonable man would have done the same thing, but after the legal and political problems of the Pueblo are over, everybody is still vaguely uneasy. It is out of the headlines but not out of sensitive minds.

For Commander Bucher, while he may have been a weak and blundering captain, has become a symbol of the helpless individual directed and even humiliated by the judgments and power of the state—and this is almost the central conflict in our society today.

Consider, for example, the 303 Committee in Washington, which very few people, and probably not even Commander Bucher, have ever heard of, even now.

This is the committee charged with approving intelligence missions all over the world such as the Pueblo mission off the North Korean coast. It is composed of the Deputy Secretary of Defense, the Under Secretary of State, the Director of the Central Intelligence Agency, and the presidential assistant for National Security Affairs in the White House, among others.

These are human beings too, subject to human error. They have primary responsibility for recommending these spy missions. They are above even the Joint Chiefs of Staff, and the commanders in the Pacific, let alone Commander Bucher or his superior officers in Japan.

They approved the Pueblo mission. They made the judgment that

* From *The New York Times,* May 7, 1969.

even a spy ship outside territorial waters would not be attacked, or at least that the advantage of the spy mission was greater than the risk.

In the perspective of history, it was not an unreasonable recommendation to the President, but it proved to be wrong—and was even repeated by the 303 Committee and by the President after the Pueblo incident when they approved sending an unguarded spy-plane into the same area, only to have it shot down.

The blunders and tragedies in the Pueblo case are great enough to cover the field. A great deal was spent to gain very little, and it would be easy to bring a strong case against the President, the Joint Chiefs, the 303 Committee, the theater commander, and Commander Bucher and his crew.

All made mistakes of judgment, but only Commander Bucher was held accountable, and put through a medieval trial that exposed his agony and broke his spirit.

Maybe he was unfit for command. Maybe this orphan boy, pushed beyond his capacities, was too weak to be strong enough to risk the resentment of his crew. But other men chose him for command and pushed him into a situation beyond his capacities—and they are invisible, unidentified, and uncharged.

"Life is unfair," President Kennedy said, and this is the only point of the story. The misjudgments in the Pueblo incident were general. No one man was to blame, but everybody was to blame, and only Commander Bucher was blamed in the end.

"A time will come," H. G. Wells wrote many long years ago, "when a politician who has wilfully made war and promoted international dissension will be as sure of the dock and much surer of the noose than a private homicide. It is not reasonable that those who gamble with men's lives should not stake their own."

It is a hard philosophy and one wonders whether it will ever come true. But the Pueblo case dramatizes the inequality between the men who give the military orders and the men who have to carry them out.

There were politicians and naval officers who tried to prove that all would have been well if only Bucher had carried out the old tradition, and gone down with his men and his ship, but he defied the tradition and has now taken his rebuke.

It is the old Billy Budd dilemma of duty and conviction all over again. The individual has been punished and the institution has been spared.

Secretary Chafee tried to soften the tragedy by saying: "They have suffered enough and further punishment would not be justified," so the novelists and dramatists will have to take it from here.

READING SELECTION 3

COMPREHENSION

Do not refer to the article to answer these questions. Choose one of the items that best answers each question, and mark the letter in the space provided.

1. ___*d*___ Choose the statement that best expresses the main idea. The Pueblo incident showed that (a) military men are sometimes pushed beyond their capabilities (b) spy missions need more careful planning if they are to succeed (c) the institution which gave the orders was not held responsible for the mistakes of its men (d) men who undertake dangerous missions should be given psychological tests to see how they stand up under strain.

2. ___*B*___ The question Reston asks, "who is to judge the judges" means (a) Commander Bucher had an unfair trial (b) men who give orders must share the blame for disasters with those who carry them out (c) a judge must be subject to a higher law (d) the judges themselves must be free from any emotional bias toward the defendant.

3. ___*A*___ Reston says that the Navy recommended a court-martial for Bucher because (a) he broke naval tradition by abandoning ship (b) he refused to follow orders (c) the crew resented him (d) he was unable to endure imprisonment.

4. ___*C*___ Bucher was finally denied a court-martial because (a) the Secretary of Navy felt sorry for him (b) Bucher had no other choice but to be captured by the North Koreans (c) the incident was a naval and political disaster, best forgot (d) the institution that gave the order had to accept the blame.

5. ___*D*___ The group that approves spy missions like that of the Pueblo is (a) the Joint Chiefs of Staff (b) the Central Intelligence Agency (c) the National Security Affairs Board with the President's approval (d) the 303 Committee.

6. ___*A*___ The Pueblo mission was originally approved because the military (a) thought that North Korea would not attack a spy ship outside territorial waters (b) wanted to retaliate for North Korea's spy missions over American military bases in Japan (c) knew that North Korea's Navy was weak and that the Pueblo would be safe from attack (d) had no other way of gathering evidence of North Korea's military activities.

7. __B__ The Pueblo incident was repeated when the North Koreans (a) captured another spy ship in their waters (b) shot down a spy plane (c) seized a small fishing boat. (d) shot down a passenger aircraft.

8. __D__ According to the editorial, the blame for the mishap should have been shared by (a) the committee that authorized the mission (b) only Commander Bucher and his crew (c) the President, the Joint Chiefs of Staff, and the theater commander (d) everyone involved.

9. __A__ The Pueblo case shows that (a) the military institution was spared and the individual was unnecessarily humiliated (b) military spy missions should be abolished (c) the military code of ethics should be strengthened (d) military tradition should never be broken.

10. __C__ Reston says that Bucher was caught in a dilemma between (a) God and country (b) reason and emotion (c) duty and conviction (d) responsibility and personal ambition.

VOCABULARY

From the lettered choices, find the best definition for each vocabulary item, and mark the letter in the space provided.

1. __D__ political *disaster*
2. __A__ *rebuke* to the U.S.
3. __L__ not out of *sensitive* minds
4. __I__ *symbol* of the helpless individual
5. __N__ *humiliated* by the state
6. __K__ *blunders* in the Pueblo case
7. __C__ risk the *resentment* of the crew
8. __J__ promoted international *dissension*
9. __E__ he *defied* the tradition
10. __G__ old Billy Budd *dilemma*

A. expression of strong disapproval
B. embarrassed
C. anger; indignation
D. catastrophe
E. challenged boldly
F. threatened
G. perplexing predicament
H. symptom
I. representation of quality or trait
J. disagreement; discord
K. silly, careless mistakes
L. easily offended; touchy
M. injury; disability
N. shamed; suffered loss of integrity
O. friendship; accord

COMPREHENSION No. right _____ × 10 = _____ %

VOCABULARY No. right _____ × 10 = _____ %

No. of words 850 ÷ time in seconds _____ × 60 = _____ WPM

WPM × Comprehension % = Reading Efficiency Rate _____

Chapter 4

READING PARAGRAPHS
Methods of Development

In the previous chapter you learned that a paragraph is a complete thought, expressed in a series of sentences. You were introduced to some examples of paragraph organization, the pattern the writer imposes on those sentences. In addition to these matters, the writer must also determine the best way to muster evidence to support the main idea. There are seven basic methods of development. Learning each method will help improve your comprehension, for it is important to recognize the relationship between the main idea and the supporting evidence.

METHODS OF DEVELOPMENT

(1) Facts, illustrations and examples
(2) Description of a process
(3) Analysis
(4) Classification
(5) Comparison and contrast
(6) Analogy
(7) Cause-to-effect

Most writers use only one method for each paragraph; occasionally however, two or even three methods may be combined to support a complex subject.

(1) Development by Facts, Illustrations, and Examples

This is the simplest method to learn. In the last chapter, Kennedy supported the topic by citing several historical facts. Rand described the array of gadgets in Los Angeles homes by using several illustrations. Here is a third illustration, in which the writer lists several examples of "square" television commercials:

> For an English professor, the question of television advertising reduces itself to the most successfully misused preposition in the language.[1] *But why do the makers of Winstons persist in* deliberately *making the squarest ads on TV?* [2] It has to be intentional—all those Wildrooted men in checked sports coats and slacks riding cable cars, paddling canoes, or buying cuckoo clocks in the company of women cut whole from 1957 noontime Indianapolis.[3] And the whole genre of dumbhead ads:[4] Harry, the man whose dinner's getting cold because he's so in love with his hand-held fertilizer spreader that he's walking the center strip of Interstate 80;[5] Joe, who tests Sta-prest pants by having thousands of sexy broads sit in his lap and muss his hair and nothing else;[6] certain family situations where grandmothers leap into sinks while invisible plastic shields roll over kitchen floors: "It's beautiful, but will it last?" [7]
>
> JONATHAN MIDDLEBROOK, from
> *Smoke Good Like a Vile Worm**

In this paragraph, the main idea in the second sentence is expressed as a rhetorical question, which the writer does not intend to answer directly except through illustration and example of "square" and "dumbhead" ads. Complete the exercises that follow.

1. __D__ What method of paragraph order does the writer use? (a) deductive order (b) variation of deductive order (c) inductive order (d) implied main idea.

2. __D+C__ The "most successfully misused preposition" refers to the Winston slogan, "Winston tastes good *like* a cigarette should." By "successfully," the author means that (a) the grammatical error offends English teachers (b) the slogan is popular (c) the ad helps sell cigarettes, despite the error (d) the ad is famous because of the error.

3. __3__ What transitional sentence separates the illustrations of "square" and "dumbhead" ads?

4. __D__ The writer's intention is primarily to ridicule (a) advertisements that use ungrammatical slogans (b) advertisements that present unbelievable situations (c) advertisements that show out-of-date scenes (d) advertisements that are either stupid or unbelievable.

5. For each italicized word, look up the best definition and write it in the space provided.

   (a) the question *reduces* itself _lesson in extent_
   (b) the makers of Winstons *persist* _to hold firmly_
   (c) the whole *genre* _a distinctive class_

* From "Television as the Medium of Contempt," *Ramparts,* April 1969, p. 56.

(2) *Development by Describing a Process*

The process method is similarly obvious, for it simply describes step-by-step how something is done. Ordinarily the writer lists each step in order with the help of transitional words like *first, the second step,* and *then.* Cookbooks and how-to-do-it manuals use the process method extensively. Here is a different sort of example, that describes how Mississippi has devised methods to keep Negroes from voting. When you read the paragraph, you should notice that the writer begins by providing some background information to support the main idea expressed in the first sentence. Then you must look for the two transitional sentences that set up the process portion of the paragraph. They are italicized for you. The remaining italicized transitional devices act as signals to describe the two ways that Mississippi uses to deny Negroes their voting rights. When you have read the paragraph, complete the exercises that follow.

> *Negroes and whites agree in Mississippi that if Negroes were given full and free access to the ballot, the lot of the Negro would have to change for the better.*[1] Politics is perhaps the most popular of the southern arts.[2] It is an art, however, to which the Negro has not been allowed to contribute much in Mississippi.[3] If Negro suffrage were ever permitted to become widespread, there is little doubt that the white supremacists would be in serious trouble.[4] It is no surprise therefore that every effort is made by the minions of the closed society, whatever their level of office, to keep the Negro away from the polls.[5] *The essential technique of Negro exclusion from the polls is a matter of some interest.*[6] *There are two devices involved.*[7] The *first* is the poll tax—now forbidden by the Twenty-fourth Amendment to the Constitution as a qualification for voting in national elections, but still in force in local and state-wide contests.[8] The *second* is the requirement that a voter applicant appear before the county Registrar.[9] *In this proceeding* the citizen applies to vote by filling out a rather long application.[10] In *one section* of the application the applicant is asked to interpret in writing a section of the Mississippi constitution.[11] The Registrar, whose discretionary powers are virtually without limit, then decides whether the applicant is qualified to vote.[12] The Registrar is under no legal obligation to defend, explain, or state how he has reached his decision.[13] An appeal may be taken to the County Election Commission and *thence* to the appropriate Mississippi circuit court, but the more effective resort is in the federal courts, in a suit brought by the Department of Justice under the Civil Rights Act of 1960.[14]
>
> JAMES W. SILVER, from *Mississippi: The Closed Society**

1. _A_ Which method of paragraph order does the writer use? (a) deductive order (b) variation of deductive order (c) inductive order (d) implied main idea.

* (New York: Harcourt Brace Jovanovich, Inc., 1966), p. 105.

2. *A, C* Mark the two statements that would represent the effects if
voting rights were extended to Negroes in Mississippi (a) the
power of the white supremacists would be damaged (b) more
black officials would be elected (c) the Negro's situation
would improve (d) the devices used to prevent Negroes from
voting would be declared illegal.

3. *C + D* Who is responsible for the devices used to prevent Negroes
from voting in Mississippi? (a) the Negroes themselves who
are politically powerless (b) the federal government which
has not enforced the voting rights act (c) the white state and
local officials (d) the Registrar of voters.

4.   Mark the two inferences that can be accurately made.

A. _____ No other state outside of Mississippi has poll
taxes or literacy tests.

B. _____ Mississippi officials ignore the federal ban on poll
taxes in all elections.

C. _✓_ Most Negroes cannot qualify to vote because they
cannot afford the poll tax or because they fail the written section of the application.

D. _____ The application before the Registrar requires a
prospective Negro voter to read a passage from the State Constitution aloud.

E. _✓_ An applicant has a better chance of winning his
case against discriminatory voting practices by going to the
federal courts.

5.   Vocabulary: For each italicized word, look up the best definition, and write it in the space provided.

(a) the *lot* of the Negro _a large amount_
(b) Negro *suffrage* _the prowledge of voting_
(c) the *minions* of the closed society _followers (favorites)_
(d) whose *discretionary* powers _decision by own judgement_
(e) the more effective *resort* _thing turned to for aid or relief._

(3) Development by Analysis

Analysis is the most difficult method to recognize, because there are so
many variations. The word *analysis* means, in writing at least, to take
apart an idea and to examine each part in relation to the whole. For example, to analyze a wheel, one might first describe the form and function of each component part—the rim, spokes, hub, and axle. Then he
would "reassemble" the wheel, by describing how each part helps the
entire mechanism to function. Writers use the analysis method to examine,
to explore, to explain, to question, and to comment. The next paragraph,

written in 1968 just after Eldridge Cleaver's *Soul on Ice* was published, analyzes the development of the civil rights movement.

Before you read the entire paragraph, read the first sentence, the italicized coherent devices, and the last sentence. This information tells you that the evidence explains the development of the civil rights movement chronologically. Surveying a paragraph in this way before you read it through completely often proves helpful in comprehending and analyzing complex ideas. Then read the entire paragraph and complete the exercises that follow.

> *But let us look at what, in the meantime, had happened to the Afro-American struggle since it was propelled upon a new and promising course by the Supreme Court's desegregation decision of 1954.*[1] It had gone on to become one of the greatest mass protest movements in American history, had attracted such a powerful coalition of groups that the federal government was obliged to legislate more vigorously than ever before in behalf of desegregation and voting rights, which were particularly useful in the South.[2] *By 1966, however,* the movement had been overtaken by crisis, a crisis of success, so to speak.[3] *While* it had not done all that some people had mistakenly thought it would do, the civil-rights movement accomplished all that street marches and demonstrations reasonably could.[4] *That is to say,* it could fight for and achieve legislation in behalf of integration, but it could neither enforce such legislation nor make integration work.[5] *And while* it could raise questions concerning poverty and economic deprivation, it could not as a protest movement affect the country's economic institutions.[6] *Thus, although* middle-class blacks did benefit from desegregation and consequent opportunities in education and employment, the masses in the ghettos discovered that integration even when enforced was less relevant to their problems than they had believed, and that, in any case, they were still locked in poverty, joblessness, and slums.[7] *At this point,* aided by the indifference of the liberal coalition which was by now mainly preoccupied with the Vietnam war, the movement bogged down and splintered in different directions.[8] *Once monolithically dedicated to nonviolence and integration, the movement was now a chaos of ideologies: some turning to black nationalism and separatism, some calling for violence, some preaching the necessity for a black economy and black power, and some remaining faithful to the old strategy and objective of nonviolence and integration.*[9]
>
> JERVIS ANDERSON, from "Race, Rage and Eldridge Cleaver" *

1. __A & D__ Which two organizational devices does the author use in his analysis? (a) description of a process (b) cause-to-effect (c) analysis of historical trends from slavery to the present (d) chronological or time sequence.

2. __C__ In the beginning, the civil rights movement was organized to

* From *Commentary*, December 1968, p. 64.

promote (a) militancy and black economic power (b) a separate black state (c) non-violence and peaceful integration (d)
sit-ins and demonstrations.

3. _____ C _____ The primary reason that the civil rights movement failed was
that (a) the federal government paid little attention to its
demands (b) its tactics were not militant enough to effect
real changes (c) its members expected that civil rights legislation would effect real and lasting social and economic
changes (d) its demands were not geared to solve the overwhelming problems in the ghettos.

4. _____ B _____ The last sentence represents (a) a summary (b) the final result (c) a redefinition of the main idea (d) another reason
the movement failed.

5.   Vocabulary: For each italicized word, look up the best definition, and write it in the space provided.

(a) a powerful *coalition* of groups alliance or union
(b) economic *deprivation* drastic cline in economy
(c) integration was less *relevant* related to matter at hand
(d) once *monolithically* dedicated eg stone in architecture
(e) a chaos of *ideologies* ideas reflecting the social needs of a culture.

Here is another example in which the author analyzes the ways an individual changes his social role as he moves from youth to adulthood.
Notice that the author establishes coherence by repeating key words
from the main idea. After reading the paragraph, complete the exercises
that follow.

> *Youth ends when the individual moves into a more enduring social
> role,* whether because of a clear choice, or because of the passage of
> time that transforms the youthful amateur into an adult professional do-
> ing much the same thing but now "permanently" committed to it.[1] *As
> youth ends,* the individual accepts or is forced by age into a social role
> that hereafter is likely to define his relationship to society.[2] *This role, of
> course,* may be "deviant"—revolutionary, criminal, mental patient, crank,
> innovator, and so on.[3] *But when youth ends,* it is no longer necessary for
> the individual to proclaim repeatedly that he will not abandon his youth-
> ful commitments—that fact (or its falsity) is obvious in his social posi-
> tion.[4] *With the successful resolution of youth,* a man or woman is more
> able to compromise without feeling compromised and, conversely, to
> stand alone on principle without feeling isolated.[5] *With the end of youth,
> too,* the future becomes less open, and the individual establishes a more-
> or-less enduring mode of relationship to his society—be he critic or execu-
> tive, revolutionary or yeoman, radical or apologist, apathetic or indignant.[6]
>
> KENNETH KENISTON, from *Young
> Radicals**

* (New York: Harcourt Brace Jovanovich, Inc., 1968), pp. 270–271.

1. ___B___ Which method of paragraph order does the author use? (a) deductive order (b) variation of deductive order (c) inductive order (d) implied main idea.

2. ___b___ The primary event that occurs when youth ends is (a) the formation of fixed peer group values (b) the development of a permanent social role (c) the abandonment of one's youthful commitments (d) the availability of unlimited opportunities.

3. ___D___ In his analysis the author concedes that the end of youth (a) does not mean strict conformity to adult social values (b) may make compromise a little easier (c) may permit a deviant social role (d) may limit the individual's prospects for the future (e) all of the above (f) only b and c.

4. ___B___ The main point of the analysis is to describe (a) the emotional strain of reaching maturity (b) the development of a lasting social role and the young adult's relationship to society (c) the reason youthful commitments cannot last (d) the importance of establishing a permanent social position.

5. Vocabulary: For each italicized word, look up the best definition, and write it in the space provided.

(a) this role may be *deviant* ___bad / to turn aside___
(b) to *proclaim* repeatedly ___explain / announce officaly___
(c) more able to *compromise* ___settle / in one peace___
(d) revolutionary or *yeoman* ___petty officer___
(e) apathetic or *indignant* ___rude / unworthy___ anger –

subordinate
asst.

(4) Development by Classification

Classification is the method of dividing large groups into smaller categories according to their characteristics. For example, the general class, *mass media,* can be broken down into individual media like radio, television, film, and newspapers. The writer might describe how each medium fulfills its primary function—to communicate information to large numbers of people. In this example, E. B. White classifies New Yorkers into three groups. The first portion of the paragraph carries out the classification established in the first sentence. The remainder of the paragraph, signaled by the italicized transitional sentence, provides specific illustrations of the three types of New Yorkers. After reading the paragraph, complete the exercises that follow.

> There are roughly three New Yorks.[1] There is, *first,* the New York of the man or woman who was born here, who takes the city for granted and accepts its size and its turbulence as natural and inevitable.[2] *Second,* there is the New York of the commuter—the city that is devoured by locusts each day and spat out each night.[3] *Third,* there

is the New York of the person who was born somewhere else and
came to New York in quest of something.[4] *Of these three trembling
cities the greatest is the last—the city of final destination, the city
that is a goal.*[5] *It is this third city* that accounts for New York's high-
strung disposition, its poetical deportment, its dedication to the arts,
and its incomparable achievements.[6] Commuters give the city its tidal
restlessness; natives give it solidity and continuity; but the settlers give
it passion.[7] And whether it is a farmer arriving from Italy to set up a
small grocery store in a slum, or a young girl arriving from a small
town in Mississippi to escape the indignity of being observed by her
neighbors, or a boy arriving from the Corn Belt with a manuscript and
a pain in his heart, it makes no difference:[8] each embraces New York
with the intense excitement of first love, each absorbs New York with
the fresh eyes of an adventurer, each generates heat and light to dwarf
the Consolidated Edison Company.[9]

> E. B. WHITE, from *Here Is New
> York**

1. ___A___ Which method of paragraph order does the writer use? (a)
   deductive order (b) variation of deductive order (c) inductive order (d) implied main idea.
2. ___B___ Besides classification, which additional method of paragraph
   development does the author use? (a) analysis (b) illustration and example (c) description of a process (d) cause-to-
   effect.
3. ___C___ The writer says that the people who make New York hold
   together as a city are the (a) settlers (b) commuters (c) natives (d) tourists.
4. ___B___ New York attracts new people because it represents (a) a first
   love (b) a goal unobtainable anywhere else (c) a variety of
   things to do and see (d) a last resort.
5. ___a___ The author evidently feels that life in New York is (a) exciting, adventurous (b) impossible (c) harsh, cruel (d) restless,
   uncomfortable (e) exciting but disappointing.
6. Vocabulary: For each italicized word, look up the best definition, and write it in the space provided.

   (a) its size and its *turbulence* violently agitated
   (b) in *quest* of something seeking, to search
   (c) its poetical *deportment* correct conduct
   (d) to escape the *indignity* offense to one's dignity
   (e) each *generates* heat to bring in existence, produce

(5) Development by Comparison and Contrast

A writer uses the comparison and contrast method to describe the similarities and differences between two ideas. Usually we say that *compare*

* (New York: Harper & Row, Publishers, 1949), pp. 17–18.

means to describe the similarities and *contrast* means to describe the differences. A film reviewer might compare the similar themes of *Midnight Cowboy* and *Easy Rider*; a report on auto performance tests might contrast American cars with foreign imports. A paragraph may compare or contrast, or occasionally it may do both. In this paragraph, E. M. Forster compares America to life; after reading the paragraph, complete the exercises that follow.

> America is rather like life.[1] You can usually find in it what you look for.[2] If you look for skyscrapers or cowboys or cocktail parties or gangsters or business connections or political problems or women's clubs, they will certainly be there.[3] You can be very hot there or very cold.[4] You can explore the America of your choice by plane or train, by hitch-hike or on foot.[5] It will probably be interesting, and it is sure to be large.[6]
>
> E. M. FORSTER, from "The United States"*

1. In addition to comparing America metaphorically to life itself, the author also uses the method of (a) classification (b) illustration and example (c) analysis (d) description of a process.
2. The main point of the paragraph is that (a) a visitor can find anything he wants in America (b) a visitor can become easily confused by America's size and diversity (c) a visitor can never see everything in America (d) a visitor can travel by any means through America.
3. In relation to the first sentence, the last sentence serves as (a) a summary (b) a restatement (c) another analogy (d) another example.

The next paragraph contrasts postwar and contemporary attitudes toward American cities. Notice that most of the paragraph describes attitudes directly after the war, while the last two sentences briefly describe contemporary attitudes. After reading the paragraph, complete the exercises that follow.

> *To be clear about what is happening in the city today, present attitudes must be distinguished from those which were expressed in the early post-war migration to suburbia.*[1] This original exodus from the city started considerably before Negro urbanization was making itself felt on a large scale.[2] Most of the young people leaving the city then were seeking greater security, better living conditions (particularly for their children), and the higher status they felt came with home ownership and membership in a smaller community.[3] No doubt the suburbs served as a haven for the prejudiced, but in the main they represented a higher level of living— whatever their aesthetic limitations—than would have been within the means of most young couples of those days if they had remained within the city limits.[4] The motivation, in other words, was more positive toward the suburbs than it was negative with respect to the city.[5] *Today the feel-*

* From *Two Cheers for Democracy* (New York: Harcourt Brace Jovanovich, Inc., 1951), p. 332.

ing has been reversed.[6] Even those who have no intentions of leaving the city are inwardly abandoning it: few people expect it to solve its problems.[7]

DAVID DANZIG AND JOHN FIELD,
from "The Betrayal of the American City." *

1. ___C___ After the war, urban residents moved away from the city because the suburbs represented (a) a place to escape from the city's increasing minority population (b) a place where houses could easily be purchased (c) a better way of life (d) a more peaceful, relaxed way of life.

2. ___C___ The author says that people now move to the suburbs (a) for the same reason that people left the city after the war (b) to find a better way of life (c) because the city's problems seem hopelessly unsolvable (d) to escape urban poverty and decay.

3. ___C___ In sentence 4, the phrase "whatever their aesthetic limitations" directly refers to (a) cities (b) small communities (c) suburbs (d) suburban housing developments.

4. ___D___ One can infer most accurately that the migration to suburbia has caused the cities to witness (a) a decline in the population of old people (b) an increase in the population of young single people (c) an increase in hostility to minority groups (d) a decline in young middle-class families.

5. Vocabulary: For each italicized word, look up the best definition, and write it in the space provided.

   (a) early postwar *migration* _to move seasonally_
   (b) this original *exodus* _a lg. departure of people_
   (c) served as a *haven* _a place of sanctuary_
   (d) their *aesthetic* limitations _sensitive to the beauty_
   (e) *inwardly* abandoning it _within, privately_
   mentally, spiritually

(6) Development by Analogy

The analogy is often used in contemporary writing. An analogy is similar to a *metaphor,* a figure of speech which imaginatively compares an unfamiliar idea with something familiar. Metaphors are short: *her face was granite; death is an obscenity.* An analogy is simply an extended metaphor, comparing at length an unfamiliar idea in terms of something known. In this paragraph, Christopher Rand compares the unknown, Los Angeles, to a wheezing, smoking, complicated machine that is always about to break down; after reading the paragraph, complete the exercises that follow.

* From *Commentary,* June 1968, p. 53.

One way to view Los Angeles is as a machine.[1] *All modern cities are machines, but L.A. is more so than the others.*[2] It it a humming, smoking, ever-changing contraption, with mechanics incessantly working at it, trying to make improvements and to get the bugs out.[3] Being a populous near-desert, it depends crucially on imported water.[4] It is also under threat from floods, fires, and earthquakes, to which its technological daring makes it especially vulnerable.[5] Because of its scatteredness, furthermore, it is concerned, day in and day out, with keeping a transport system moving at high speed.[6] And finally it must deal with the waste products, the smog, and other obscenities, that its operations throw off.[7]

CHRISTOPHER RAND, from *Los Angeles: The Ultimate City**

1. _A_____ What method of paragraph order does the writer use? (a) deductive order (b) variation of deductive order (c) inductive order (d) implied main idea.

2. _B_____ The primary impression the author tries to give is that Los Angeles (a) is mechanically deficient (b) is extremely complicated and continually subject to breakdowns (c) offers its residents a variety of experiences (d) suffers from congestion and pollution.

3. _B,D,A_ The "mechanics" mentioned in the third sentence are probably (a) politicians (b) civil engineers and city planners (c) car mechanics (d) pollution controllers.

4. _D,D_ What kind of coherent device does the author use several times to make the paragraph stick together? (a) repetition of key words (b) substitution of a pronoun for key words (c) parallel sentence structure (d) transitional words and phrases.

5. Vocabulary: For each italicized word, look up the best definition, and write it in the space provided.

   (a) *incessantly* working at it _unceasing/w/out interruption_
   (b) it depends *crucially* on _decisive importance_
   (c) its technological *daring* _to challenge_
   (d) makes it *vulnerable* _susceptible to injury_
   (e) and other *obscenities* _offensive to accepted standards of decency._

(7) Development by Analyzing Cause and Effect

Writers use the cause-to-effect method to examine reasons and results. In this example, James Q. Wilson states the reasons that streetcorner gangs are rare in Southern California; then he examines the effects. In addition, the writer contrasts (in sentences 2, 3, and 4) California teenage hangouts with those of their eastern counterparts. After reading the paragraph, complete the exercises that follow.

* (New York: Oxford University Press, 1967), p. 33.

CAUSES

Low-density, single-family homes, a lack of public trans-portation, the absence of ethnic neighborhoods, and the use of cars combined to prevent the formation of streetcorner gangs, except in very central portions of Los Angeles and one or two older cities.[1] The principal after-school occupation of a teen-age eastern boy from a working class family is to "hang out" at the corner candystore, the icecream parlor, or in front of the drugstore with class and ethnic compatriots.[2] Having a "corner" of your own—or having "turf," in the case of the ambitious and imperialistic—would have made no sense to an equivalent group of young men in Southern California.[3] The eastern life-style produced a feeling of *territory*, the western life-style a feeling of *property*.[4] Teen-agers in Southern California hung out together, to be sure, but not in any fixed spot, and where they did hang out

EFFECTS

tended to be a place reached by a car, with lots of free parking for other cars.[5] The drive-in restaurant was the premier institution catering to this need.[6] But it was also a very democratic institution, since it was not (and because of its location some distance from one's home, could not become) the "turf" of any particular gang.[7] Rich and poor, Protestant and Catholic, anybody with a car could get there and, barring a losing fight over a girl, stay there.[8] There were rivalries, but like modern warfare they tended to be between large, heterogeneous, and impersonal rivals—one high school against another, not one ethnic group against another.[9]

JAMES Q. WILSON, from "The Political Culture of Southern California" *

1. __C__ The primary reason that teenagers in Los Angeles have never developed the eastern teenagers' sense of "turf" is (a) the absence of ethnic neighborhoods (b) the popularity of drive-in restaurants (c) the freedom generated by the use of cars (d) the prevalence of single-family homes.

2. __B__ The main point of the paragraph is to show (a) the difference between eastern and western teenage life styles (b) the peculiar characteristics of Los Angeles that helped promote a different kind of teenage hangout than exists in the east (c) the freedom and mobility western teenagers have developed compared to eastern teenagers (d) the reasons streetcorner gangs developed in the east.

3. __C__ The author says that teenage hangouts in Los Angeles (a) are limited to particular ethnic groups (b) create a feeling of "territory" (c) are not limited to any one neighborhood (d) are the scenes for local high school rivalry and gang fights.

* From *Commentary*, May 1967, p. 41.

4. _A/B_ The last sentence supports the idea that (a) streetcorner gangs are rare in Los Angeles (b) teenage hangouts in Los Angeles are relatively democratic (c) teenagers establish hangouts where parking is available (d) hangouts are confined to students from one high school.

5.   Vocabulary: For each italicized word, look up the best definition, and write it in the space provided.

powerful / dominate

(a) ethnic *compatriots* _fellow countrymen_
(b) the ambitious and *imperialistic* _national_ _____
(c) the *premier* institution _first (chief or principal)_
(d) large, *heterogeneous,* and impersonal _different (unlike)_ _unrelated elements_

The cause-to-effect method may be reversed so that the writer first states the effects, then examines the causes. _So that the writer first_

Occasionally you will find a paragraph that uses several methods at once. Here is a paragraph that combines the methods of analysis, cause-to-effect, and illustration to support a rather complex idea; after reading the paragraph, complete the exercises that follow.

> *In 1968 student unrest shifted noticeably from the national scene to the campus, for psychological and tactical reasons.*[1] Thrust into a frightening world, the individual tries to make sense of his existence and seeks gratification in having an effect as an individual on his social environment.[2] He is told that he is a citizen of a vast country and slowly learns that his relationship with the government of that country is one-sided.[3] Perhaps this is the failing of mass democracy.[4] Whatever the case, the individual's power extends as far as the ballot box which allows him to vote for officials whose actions and decisions in office can never be known beforehand.[5] His other "legitimate" source of power is dissent.[6] But dissent, students have learned from marching the streets of New York and the steps of the Pentagon, does not change men or their policies; it only incites them to enforce the law.[7] And so students turn back from the Pentagon, where the war machine muffled their protest in tear gas.[8] They are lost in the social context of the nation state.[9] They can protest the war only to find it being escalated before their placards.[10] They can work for McCarthy and pretend to forget that the New Hampshire euphoria will soon be smoke-screened behind the disenchantment of convention politics.[11] *And so they return to the framework of their universities, where they can be more effective as individual radicalizers or reformers, and where they hope to find an administration more receptive to their needs and demands.*[12]
>
> JERRY AVORN, et al. from *Up Against the Ivy Wall* *

1. _C_ The two legitimate sources of political power which failed to be effective were (a) protests and sit-ins (b) voting and

* (New York: Atheneum Publishers, 1969) p. 6.

campus violence (c) voting and dissent (d) protest and picketing at political conventions.

2. __B__ The primary reason that students turned to the campus to effect social changes is that their previous efforts (a) were looked on suspiciously by the public (b) had no effect on the country's political policies (c) caused the war to be escalated (d) caused repression rather than political change.

3. __C__ The author suggests that political activity on the campus may be (a) illegal (b) ineffective (c) more effective than national activity (d) a form of political compromise.

4. __B__ The author suggests that the students' inability to change national policy through legitimate means caused them to feel (a) bitter and revengeful (b) disillusioned and disenchanted (c) enthusiastic and dedicated (d) cynical.

5. Vocabulary: For each italicized word, look up the best definition, and write it in the space provided.

(a) *tactical* reasons __strategic / cleverly__
(b) seeks *gratification* __satisfaction__
(c) it only *incites* them __urges to action__
(d) *muffled* their protest __deaden sound by force__
(e) lost in the social *context* __setting / background__
(f) the New Hampshire *euphoria* __state of happiness__

EXERCISES

Here are nine more paragraphs for additional practice. After you finish reading each one carefully, answer the questions that follow. You may refer to the paragraph if necessary. In addition, the methods of paragraph development are repeated here for your reference.

(1) Facts, illustrations, and example
(2) Description of a process
(3) Analysis
(4) Classification
(5) Comparison and contrast
(6) Analogy
(7) Cause-to-effect (or effect-to-cause)
(8) Combination of methods

I. Statistics on poverty are even trickier than most.[1] For example, age and geography make a difference.[2] There is a distinction, which cannot be rendered arithmetically, between poverty and low income.[3] A childless young couple with $3,000 a year is not poor in the way an elderly couple might be with the same income.[4] The young couple's statistical poverty may be a temporary inconvenience; if the husband is a graduate student or a skilled worker, there are prospects of later affluence or at least comfort.[5] But the old couple can look forward only to diminishing earnings and increasing medical expenses.[6] So also geographically: A family of four in a small town with $4,000 a year may be better off than a like family in a city—lower rent, no bus fares to get to work, fewer occasions (or temptations) to spend money.[7] Even more so with a rural family.[8] Although allowance is made for the value of the vegetables they may raise to feed themselves, it is impossible to calculate how much money they *don't* spend on clothes, say, or furniture, because they don't have to keep up with the Joneses.[9] Lurking in the crevices of a city, like piranha fish in a Brazilian stream, are numerous tempting opportunities for expenditure, small but voracious, which can strip a budget to its bones in a surprisingly short time.[10]

DWIGHT MACDONALD, from "Our
Invisible Poor" *

1. _____ Which method of paragraph development does the author use?
2. _____ Write the number of the sentence (or sentences) that expresses the main idea.
3. _____ Does the author use (a) deductive order (b) variation of deductive order (c) inductive order (d) implied main idea?
4. _____ Write the number of the sentence which contains a metaphor.
5. _____ The author's point is that (a) old people are hurt by fixed incomes (b) statistics on poverty are deceptive because the variables of age and geography make "poverty" a relative term (c) although statistically poorer, rural families spend less money than people who live in cities (d) statisticians should pay attention to the distinction between poverty and low income.

6. Vocabulary: For each of the italicized words, look up the best definition and write it in the space provided.

(a) cannot be *rendered* arithmetically ____to give, to translate____
(b) prospects of later *affluence* ____wealth, abundance____
(c) small but *voracious* ____too eager, insatiable, greedy____

II. One of the most spectacular demonstrations of Oriental snake charming is seen in parts of Burma.[1] The snakes used are freshly captured king cobras, sometimes 10 feet long.[2] These snakes are sacred to two powerful mountain spirit gods and guard their shrines.[3] The snake charmers are frequently, but not invariably, young women.[4] The ceremony is held in a public place in the village and is a mixture of entertainment and religious ritual.[5] After preliminary prayers and music, the snake baskets are opened and the snakes are teased until they rear and strike repeatedly at the performers who deftly elude them.[6] At the climax of the display, the leading performer kisses one of the snakes on the top of its head as it rears poised to strike.[7] After this, the snakes are returned to their

* From *The New Yorker*, January 19, 1963, p. 8.

baskets and eventually released in accordance with the snake charmers' promise to the gods.[8]

SHERMAN A. MINTON, JR. and
MADGE RUTHERFORD MINTON, from
*Venomous Reptiles**

1. __/__ Write the number of the sentence (or sentences) that expresses the main idea.

2. Which method of paragraph development do the writers use?

3. Based on the evidence in the paragraph, mark T if the statement is an *accurate inference* and F if the statement is an *inaccurate inference.*

(a) __F__ the writers have traveled to Burma

(b) __F__ the snake ceremony is restricted to upper-class religious observers

(c) __T__ the snakes will strike the performers if they are not careful

(d) __T__ king cobra snakes are sacred in Burma

(e) __F__ the authors were evidently frightened by the ceremony

4. __C__ In the sentence, "the snake charmers are frequently, but not invariably, young women," the authors use "not invariably" to mean (a) always (b) often (c) not always (d) never (e) as an exception.

5. Vocabulary: For each of the italicized words, look up the best definition and write it in the space provided.

(a) religious *ritual* belief, ceremony, custom

(b) who *deftly elude* them skillfully, dodge

(c) *poised* to strike held in position, suspended

(d) *in accordance* with the promise agreement

III. The story of Harley-Davidson and the domestic motorcycle market is one of the gloomiest chapters in the history of American free enterprise.[1] At the end of World War II there were less than 200,000 motorcycles registered in the United States, very few of them imports.[2] During the 1950s, while H-D was consolidating its monopoly, bike sales doubled and then tripled.[3] Harley had a gold mine on its hands—until 1962–63, when the import blitz began.[4] By 1964 registrations had jumped to nearly 1,000,000 and lightweight Hondas were selling as fast as Japanese freighters could bring them over the ocean.[5] The H-D brain trust was still pondering this oriental duplicity when they were zapped on the opposite flank by Birmingham Small Arms, Ltd., of England.[6] BSA (which also makes Triumphs) decided to challenge Harley on its own turf and in its own class, despite the price-boosting handicap of a huge protective tariff.[7] By 1965, with registrations already up 50 percent over the pre-

* (New York: Charles Scribner's Sons, 1969), p. 140.

vious year, the H-D monopoly was sorely beset on two fronts.[8] The only buyers they could count on were cops and outlaws, while the Japanese were mopping up in the low-price field and BSA was giving them hell on the race track.[9] By 1966, with the bike boom still growing, Harley was down to less than 10 percent of the domestic market and fighting to hold even that.[10]

HUNTER S. THOMPSON, from
*Hell's Angels**

1. _____1_____ Write the number of the sentence (or sentences) that expresses the main idea.

2. _____A_____ Which of the following combinations of methods of paragraph development does the author use? (a) description of a process according to time sequence; cause-and-effect; facts and examples (b) description of a process; illustration and example (c) facts and illustration; classification (d) analysis; comparison and contrast.

3. _____B a)_____ The main reason cited for Harley-Davidson's failure in the domestic motorcycle market was (a) competition from other American manufacturers (b) competition from Japanese and British imported models (c) the lifting of the protective tariff (d) the increased popularity of inexpensive lightweight models.

4. _____B_____ Which of the following statements is an accurate inference? (a) Harley-Davidson did not try hard enough to retain its profitable lead in the motorcycle market (b) only outlaws and police buy heavy motorcycles (c) the reason for the increased popularity of owning motorcycles is the availability of inexpensive, lightweight import models (d) Harley-Davidson finally went out of business (e) the writer owns a Harley-Davidson motorcycle.

5. Vocabulary: Look up the best definition for each italicized word, and write it in the space provided.

(a) *consolidating* its monopoly __merging, uniting__
(b) the import *blitz* __campaign, attack__
(c) this oriental *duplicity* __deception__
(d) on its own *turf* __ground, land, own property__
(e) the monopoly was sorely *beset* __trouble, attack from all sides__

IV.   The privileged white community is at great pains to blind itself to conditions of the ghetto, but the residents of the ghetto are not themselves blind to life as it is outside of the ghetto.[1] They observe that others enjoy a better life, and this knowledge brings a conglomerate of hostility, despair, and hope.[2] If the ghetto could be contained totally, the chances of social revolt would be decreased, if not eliminated, but it cannot be

* (New York: Random House, Inc., 1966), p. 80.

contained and the outside world intrudes.[3] The Negro lives in part in
the world of television and motion pictures, bombarded by the myths
of the American middle class, often believing as literal truth their pictures of luxury and happiness, and yet at the same time confronted by
a harsh world of reality where the dreams do not come true or change
into nightmares.[4] The discrepancy between the reality and the dream
burns into their consciousness.[5] The oppressed can never be sure whether
their failures reflect personal inferiority or the fact of color.[6] This persistent and agonizing conflict dominates their lives.[7]

                                   KENNETH B. CLARK, from *Dark
                                   Ghetto**

1. __4, 7__ Write the number of the sentence (or sentences) that expresses the main idea.

2. __B__ Which method of paragraph order does the writer use? (a)
deductive order (b) variation of deductive order (c) inductive order (d) implied main idea.

3. __D__ Which combination of methods of paragraph development
does the writer use? (a) analysis; analogy (b) classification;
illustration and example (c) comparison and contrast; cause-
to-effect (d) analysis; cause-to-effect; illustration and example.

4. __D__ The following statements are taken from the paragraph.
__c__ Choose the one that explains why ghetto residents feel a kind
of helpless agony. (a) "the privileged white community is at
great pains to blind itself to conditions of the ghetto" (b)
"if the ghetto could be contained totally" (c) "the discrepancy between the reality and the dream burns into their consciousness" (d) "this knowledge brings a conglomerate of
hostility, despair, and hope."

5. __C__ According to the evidence, the primary reason that ghetto
residents feel confused and hostile is (a) television programs
and motion pictures (b) poverty, unemployment and a sense
of failure (c) the intrusion of the myths of middle class America from communications media (d) the constant threat of
social revolt.

6. Vocabulary: For each italicized word, look up the best definition and write it in the space provided.

(a) a *conglomerate* of hostility, despair __cluster, collection__
(b) *bombarded* by the myths __invaded, continuously__
(c) the *discrepancy* between __unsure reason, inconsistency__
(d) the *oppressed* can never be sure __kept down by__
__unjust power.__

V. It is a miracle that New York works at all.[1] The whole thing is implausible.[2] Every time the residents brush their teeth, millions of gal-

* (New York: Harper & Row, Publishers, 1965), p. 12.

lons of water must be drawn from the Catskill Mountains and the hills of Westchester.[3] When a young man in Manhattan writes a letter to his girl in Brooklyn, the love message gets blown to her through a pneumatic tube—*pfft*—just like that.[4] The subterranean system of telephone cables, power lines, steam pipes, gas mains and sewer pipes is reason enough to abandon the island to the gods and the weevils.[5] Every time an incision is made in the pavement, the noisy surgeons expose ganglia that are tangled beyond belief.[6] By rights New York should have destroyed itself long ago, from panic or fire or rioting or failure of some vital supply line in its circulatory system or from some deep labyrinthine short circuit.[7] Long ago the city should have experienced an insoluble traffic snarl at some impossible bottleneck.[8] It should have perished of hunger when food lines failed for a few days.[9] It should have been wiped out by a plague starting in its slums or carried in by ships' rats.[10] It should have been overwhelmed by the sea that licks at it on every side.[11] The workers in its myriad cells should have succumbed to nerves, from the fearful pall of smoke-fog that drifts over every few days from Jersey, blotting out all light at noon and leaving the high offices suspended, men groping and depressed, and the sense of world's end.[12] It should have been touched in the head by the August heat and gone off its rocker.[13]

E. B. WHITE, from *Here Is New York**

1. _l, 7_ Mark the number of the sentence (or sentences) that expresses the main idea.

2. _B_ Which combination of methods of paragraph development does the writer use? (a) analysis and classification (b) illustration and analogy (c) analysis and analogy (d) comparison and contrast; description of a process.

3. _B_ Throughout the paragraph, the writer metaphorically describes New York as if it were (a) a hospital (b) a human body (c) a vast underground network (d) a disease

4. _B_ In the sentence, "the whole thing is implausible," the author means that New York is (a) an exciting, cosmopolitan city (b) so complicated that its survival should be impossible (c) miraculous in its efficiency (d) deceptively complicated in appearance. It should have been —

5. ___→ Write the phrase that acts as a coherent device to hold many of the supporting sentences together.

6. Vocabulary: Look up the best definition for each italicized word, and write your choice in the space provided.

(a) some deep *labyrinthine* short circuit _complicated, puzzling_
(b) an *insoluble* traffic snarl _unsolvable_
(c) its *myriad* cells _indefinite in number_
(d) the fearful *pall* _Covering that darkens_

* (New York: Harper & Row, Publishers, 1949), pp. 24–25.

VI.   First the embryo bursts through the seed coat and a pallid eager primary root thrusts out, and dives into the earth.[1] As it goes it jerks the seed that way and this;[2] just when the seed seems most ignominiously upended, out gush the fat, juvenile seed leaves, uncrumpling and unfolding their palms, holding them to the sunlight.[3] Soon above them rises the first shoot.[4] While the seed leaves surrender their nourishment to its hungry needs, they writhe and wither.[5] Indifferent to their death, the demanding shoot reaches for the air and light, gesticulating, spiraling, contorting.[6] The buds swell; something living seems to shoulder within them; the scales fall from its eyes, and the light-perceiving true leaves expand.[7]

Description of a process

DONALD CULROSS PEATTIE, from
*Flowering Earth**

1. _____ What method of paragraph development does the author use?
2. _____ What kind of paragraph order does the author follow? (a) deductive order (b) variation of deductive order (c) inductive order (d) implied main idea.
3. _____ This paragraph describes (a) the growth of a plant (b) the the pollination of a plant (c) the formation of a leaf (d) the growth of a sapling tree.
4. _____ The author describes the roots, seeds, and buds as if they were (a) the human heart (b) a flower (c) a human being (d) a young animal.
5.   Find five examples of strong, colorful verbs and write them in the spaces provided. The first is already done for you.

   gesticulating
   spiraling
   contorting

   (a) bursts   dives   (d) ___jerks___
   (b) thrusts   swell   (e) ~~surrendered~~
   (c) ___gush___   (f) writh wither

6.   Vocabulary: For each italicized word, look up the best definition and write it in the space provided.

   (a) a *pallid* primary root ___pale___
   (b) *ignominiously* upended marked by disgrace
   (c) they *writhe* and wither twist & turn in pain
   (d) reaches for the air, *gesticulating* gestures thru meaning
   (e) seems to *shoulder* within them to push

VII.   England is not the jeweled isle of Shakespeare's much-quoted passage, nor is it the inferno depicted by Dr. Goebbels.[1] More than either it resembles a family, a rather stuffy Victorian family, with not many black sheep in it but with all its cupboards bursting with skeletons.[2] It has rich relations who have to be kowtowed to and poor relations who are horribly sat upon, and there is a deep conspiracy of silence about the source of the family income.[3] It is a family in which the young are generally thwarted and most of the power is in the hands of irresponsible uncles and bed-

* (New York: The Viking Press, Inc., 1939), p. 42.

ridden aunts.[4] Still, it is a family.[5] It has its private language and its common memories, and at the approach of an enemy it closes its ranks.[6] A family with the wrong members in control—that, perhaps, is as near as one can come to describing England in a phrase.[7]

GEORGE ORWELL, from "The Lion and The Unicorn" *

1. __1, 7__ Write the number of the sentence (or sentences) that expresses the main idea.

2. _____ What method of paragraph development does the author use?

3. _____ In your own words, describe what the author means in the second sentence by "cupboards bursting with skeletons."

4. __a/b__ The author's main point is to show that, despite their problems, English people remain (a) closely knit and unified (b) rich and powerful (c) corrupt and powerless (d) cut off and isolated from the rest of the world.

5. __C__ The last sentence in the paragraph represents (a) a justification of Shakespeare's and Goebbels' theories mentioned in the first sentence (b) proof that Goebbels' theory was more accurate than Shakespeare's (c) a clever way of redefining the main idea: England's internal political and social order (d) a clever way of redefining the main idea: England's political relationship with other nations.

6. __A__ The reader can infer from the paragraph that (a) England has a fairly strict class system (b) England has never been able to withstand an enemy attack (c) young people in England will eventually gain more power (d) England is socially and politically progressive (e) England's source of income is from her colonial holdings.

7. Vocabulary: For each italicized word, look up the best definition and write it in the space provided.

(a) nor is it the *inferno* _____

(b) *depicted* by Dr. Goebbels _____

(c) have to be *kowtowed* to _____

(d) a deep *conspiracy* of silence _____

(e) the young are generally *thwarted* _____

VIII. Physically speaking, wood has the qualities of both stone and metal:[1] stronger in cross section than is stone, wood resembles steel in its physical properties:[2] its relatively high tensile and compressive strength, to-together with its elasticity.[3] Stone is a mass:[4] but wood, by its nature, is already a structure.[5] The difference in toughness, tensile strength, weight, and permeability of various species of wood, from pine to hornbeam, from cedar to teak, give wood a natural range of adaptability to various purposes that is matched in metals only as a result of a long evolution of

* From *The Collected Essays, Journalism and Letters of George Orwell,* Volume 2 (New York: Harcourt Brace Jovanovich, Inc., 1968).

metallurgical skill:[6] lead, tin, copper, gold, and their alloys, the original assortment, offered a meagre choice of possibilities, and down to the end of the nineteenth century wood presented a greater variety.[7] Since wood can be planed, sawed, turned, carved, split, sliced, and even softened and bent or cast, it is the most responsive of all materials to craftsmanship:[8] it lends itself to the greatest variety of techniques.[9] But in its natural state wood keeps the shape of the tree and retains its structure:[10] and the original shape of the wood suggests appropriate tools and adaptations of form.[11] The curve of the branch forms the bracket, the forked stick forms the handle, and the primitive type of plow.[12]

LEWIS MUMFORD, from *Technics and Civilization**

1. _____ Write the number of the sentence (or sentences) that expresses the main idea.

2. _____ Which method of paragraph development does the author use?

3. _____ Which of the following best summarizes the advantage of wood over stone and metal? (a) its ready availability (b) its inexpensive cost (c) its adaptability and strength (d) its toughness and durability.

4. _____ In terms of physical properties, which of the following does wood most nearly resemble? (a) iron (b) metal (c) stone (d) steel (e) tin.

5. _____ Which of the following statements is an accurate inference? (a) wood is cheaper than metal (b) manufacturers use more wood than metal (c) primitive men realized that wood was useful for making tools (d) the author is a craftsman (e) all species of wood are equally strong.

6. Vocabulary: For each italicized word, look up the best definition and write it in the spaces provided.

   (a) high *tensile* strength _____
   (b) its *elasticity* _____
   (c) *permeability* of various species _____
   (d) a *meagre* choice _____
   (e) the most *responsive* of all materials _____

IX. Here at the age of thirty-nine I began to be old.[1] I felt stiff and weary in the evenings and reluctant to go out of camp; I developed proprietary claims to certain chairs and newspapers; I regularly drank three glasses of gin before dinner, never more or less, and went to bed immediately after the nine o'clock news.[2] I was always awake and fretful an hour before reveille.[3]

Here my last love died.[4] There was nothing remarkable in the manner of its death.[5] One day, not long before this last day in camp, as I lay awake before reveille, in the Nissen hut, gazing into the complete black-

* (New York: Harcourt Brace Jovanovich, Inc., 1962), pp. 78–79.

ness, amid the deep breathing and muttering of the four other occupants, turning over in my mind what I had to do that day—had I put in the names of two corporals for the weapon-training course? 6 Should I again have the largest number of men overstaying their leave in the batch due back that day? 7 Could I trust Hooper to take the candidates class out map-reading? 8—as I lay in that dark hour, I was aghast to realize that something within me, long sickening, had quietly died, and felt as a husband might feel, who, in the fourth year of his marriage, suddenly knew that he had no longer any desire, or tenderness, or esteem, for a once-beloved wife; no pleasure in her company, no wish to please, no curiosity about anything she might ever do or say or think; no hope of setting things right, no self-reproach for the disaster.9 I knew it all, the whole drab compass of marital disillusion;10 we had been through it together, the army and I, from the first importunate courtship until now, when nothing remained to us except the chill bonds of law and duty and custom.11 I had played every scene in the domestic tragedy, had found the early tiffs become more frequent, the tears less affecting, the reconciliations less sweet, till they engendered a mood of aloofness and cool criticism, and the growing conviction that it was not myself but the loved one who was at fault.12 I caught the false notes in her voice and learned to listen for them apprehensively; I recognized the blank, resentful stare of incomprehension in her eyes, and the selfish, hard set of the corners of her mouth.13 I learned her, as one must learn a woman one has kept house with, day in, day out, for three and a half years; I learned her slatternly ways, the routine and mechanism of her charm, her jealousy and self-seeking, and her nervous trick with the fingers when she was lying.14 She was stripped of all enchantment now and I knew her for an uncongenial stranger to whom I had bound myself indissolubly in a moment of folly.15

> EVELYN WAUGH, from *Brides-*
> *head Revisited**

1. _____ Which method of paragraph development does the second paragraph follow?

2. _____ The author implies that his life in the army was similar to (a) an unfaithful wife (b) a bad marriage to a woman no longer loved (c) an unhappy love affair (d) a middle-aged, nagging wife.

3. _____ The author discovered that the reason for his unhappiness was (a) his own inability to adjust to military life (b) the routine of military life (c) his approaching middle age and sense of disillusion with the army (d) the faults inherent within the military system itself.

4. _____ What kept the author from leaving the army? (a) a sense of patriotic duty (b) a sense of honor (c) a sense of law and obligation (d) a feeling of optimism, the idea that the future would be better.

* (New York: Little, Brown and Company, 1944), pp. 11–12.

5. _____ The author's attitude toward military life is essentially a feeling of (a) disrespect and rebelliousness (b) hatred and bitterness (c) disillusionment and disenchantment (d) indifference and apathy.

6. Vocabulary: For each italicized word, look up the best definition and write it in the space provided.

(a) I was *aghast* to realize _horror-stricken, appalled_
(b) no self-*reproach* for the disaster _to blame, rebuke_
(c) marital *disillusion* _to free, disenchant_   *deprive of illusion*
(d) the first *importunate* courtship _stubbornly, unreasonably resistant_
(e) a mood of *aloofness* _distant, indifferent_
(f) to listen *apprehensively* _anxious of future, uneasy_
(g) her *slatternly* ways _a woman untidy_

Reading Selection 4 George Orwell, from "The Lion and the Unicorn" *

Although George Orwell, the famous British novelist and essayist, wrote this passage in 1941 during World War II, the past three decades have proved his observations and predictions to be true. Underneath the fears and confusion caused by the war, Orwell displays a profound respect for English culture and its remarkable stability.

One of the most important developments in England during the past twenty years has been the upward and downward extension of the middle class. It has happened on such a scale as to make the old classification of society into capitalists, proletarians, and petit bourgeois (small property-owners) almost obsolete.

England is a country in which property and financial power are concentrated in very few hands. Few people in modern England *own* anything at all, except clothes, furniture, and possibly a house. The peasantry have long since disappeared, the independent shop-keeper is being destroyed, the small businessman is diminishing in numbers. But at the same time modern industry is so complicated that it cannot get along without great numbers of managers, salesmen, engineers, chemists, and technicians of all kinds, drawing fairly large salaries. And these in turn call into being a professional class of doctors, lawyers, teachers, artists, etc., etc. The tendency of advanced capitalism has therefore been to enlarge the middle class and not to wipe it out as it once seemed likely to do.

But much more important than this is the spread of middle-class ideas and habits among the working class. The British working class are now better off in almost all ways than they were thirty years ago. This is partly due to the efforts of the trade unions, but partly to the mere

* From *The Collected Essays, Journalism and Letters of George Orwell*, Volume 2 (New York: Harcourt Brace Jovanovich, Inc., 1968).

advance of physical science. It is not always realized that within rather narrow limits the standard of life of a country can rise without a corresponding rise in real wages. Up to a point, civilization can lift itself up by its boot-tags. However unjustly society is organized, certain technical advances are bound to benefit the whole community, because certain kinds of goods are necessarily held in common. A millionaire cannot, for example, light the streets for himself while darkening them for other people. Nearly all citizens of civilized countries now enjoy the use of good roads, germ-free water, police protection, free libraries, and probably free education of a kind. Public education in England has been meanly starved of money, but it has nevertheless improved, largely owing to the devoted efforts of the teachers, and the habit of reading has become enormously more widespread. To an increasing extent the rich and the poor read the same books, and they also see the same films and listen to the same radio programs. And the differences in their way of life have been diminished by the mass production of cheap clothes and improvements in housing. So far as outward appearance goes, the clothes of rich and poor, especially in the case of women, differ far less than they did thirty or even fifteen years ago. As to housing, England still has slums which are a blot on civilization, but much building has been done during the past ten years, largely by the local authorities. The modern Council house, with its bathroom and electric light, is smaller than the stockbroker's villa, but it is recognizably the same kind of house, which the farm laborer's cottage is not. A person who has grown up in a Council housing estate is likely to be—indeed, visibly is— more middle class in outlook than a person who has grown up in a slum.

The effect of all this is a general softening of manners. It is enhanced by the fact that modern industrial methods tend always to demand less muscular effort and therefore to leave people with more energy when their day's work is done. Many workers in the light industries are less truly manual laborers than is a doctor or a grocer. In tastes, habits, manners, and outlook the working class and the middle class are drawing together. The unjust distinctions remain, but the real differences diminish. The old-style "proletarian"—collarless, unshaven, and with muscles warped by heavy labor—still exists, but he is constantly decreasing in numbers; he only predominates in the heavy-industry areas of the north of England.

After 1918 there began to appear something that had never existed in England before: people of indeterminate social class. In 1910 every human being in these islands could be "placed" in an instant by his clothes, manners, and accent. That is no longer the case. Above all, it is not the case in the new townships that have developed as a result of cheap motor cars and the southward shift of industry. The place to look for the germs of the future England is in the light-industry areas and along the arterial roads. In Slough, Dagenham, Barnet, Letchworth,

Hayes—everywhere, indeed, on the outskirts of great towns—the old pattern is gradually changing into something new. In those vast new wildernesses of glass and brick the sharp distinctions of the older kind of town, with its slums and mansions, or of the country, with its manor houses and squalid cottages, no longer exist. There are wide gradations of income, but it is the same kind of life that is being lived at different levels, in labor-saving flats or Council houses, along the concrete roads and in the naked democracy of the swimming pools. It is a rather restless, cultureless life, centering round tinned food, *Picture Post*, the radio, and the internal combustion engine. It is a civilization in which children grow up with an intimate knowledge of magnetos and in complete ignorance of the Bible. To that civilization belong the people who are most at home in and most definitely *of* the modern world, the technicians and the higher-paid skilled workers, the airmen and their mechanics, the radio experts, film producers, popular journalists, and industrial chemists. They are the indeterminate stratum at which the older class distinctions are beginning to break down.

This war, unless we are defeated, will wipe out most of the existing class privileges. There are every day fewer people who wish them to continue. Nor need we fear that as the pattern changes life in England will lose its peculiar flavor. The new red cities of Greater London are crude enough, but these things are only the rash that accompanies a change. In whatever shape England emerges from the war, it will be deeply tinged with the characteristics that I have spoken of earlier. The intellectuals who hope to see it Russianized or Germanized will be disappointed. The gentleness, the hypocrisy, the thoughtlessness, the reverence for law, and the hatred of uniforms will remain, along with the suet puddings and the misty skies. It needs some very great disaster, such as prolonged subjugation by a foreign enemy, to destroy a national culture. The Stock Exchange will be pulled down, the horse plough will give way to the tractor, the country houses will be turned into children's holiday camps, the Eton and Harrow match will be forgotten, but England will still be England, an everlasting animal stretching into the future and the past, and, like all living things, having the power to change out of recognition and yet remain the same.

Reading Selection 4

COMPREHENSION

Do not refer to the article to answer these questions. Choose one of the items that best answers each question, and mark the letter in the space provided.

1. ___*D*___ Choose the statement that best expresses the main idea of the selection. Industrialization and advanced capitalism in England have (a) eliminated the differences between the rich and poor classes (b) created a new managerial and professional class (c) caused English society to become Americanized (d) increased the numbers of middle-class people and caused the working classes to adopt middle-class values.

2. ___*C*___ English society was formerly divided into three distinct classes. Which was not among those Orwell listed? (a) the capitalists (b) the proletarians or working classes (c) the aristocracy or royalty (d) the small landowners or petit bourgeois.

3. ___*B*___ In England, property and financial power are concentrated in the hands of (a) the government (b) very few people (c) the large middle class (d) the industrial leaders.

4. ___*C*___ Advanced capitalism in England has caused (a) a larger number of independent shopowners (b) a decline in the peasant class (c) an increase in the numbers of managers, salesmen, and technicians (d) improved public facilities, such as roads, sanitation, and police protection (e) all of the above (f) only b, c, and d.

5. ___*A*___ Orwell says that the British working classes were better off in 1941 than in the early 1900's because (a) trade unions were abolished (b) millionaires could no longer exploit workers for profit (c) technical achievement benefited the entire society, thereby making middle-class values more widespread (d) workers were freed from paying taxes.

6. ___*b+d*___ Public education improved because (a) the government spent large sums of money building new schools (b) teachers became more dedicated (c) students were required to attend school for a longer time (d) books became cheaper and more accessible.

7. ___*C*___ The gap between the rich and poor become narrower for several reasons. Which was *not* mentioned? (a) more free libraries (b) mass production of inexpensive clothes (c) elimination of nearly all slums (d) increased popularity of

books, movies, and radio programs (e) standardization of housing.

8. __B__ Manual laborers in heavy industry are now concentrated only in (a) large cities, especially London (b) northern England (c) rural areas (d) the new red brick cities.

9. __A__ After 1918 when the middle and working classes blended together, Orwell noticed that increasingly (a) accent, dress, and manners no longer determined class (b) all previous injustices to the working class were eliminated (c) people's life style became much more uniform (d) all of the above (e) only a and c.

10. __B__ Orwell predicted that after World War II was over, English society would (a) become another communist satellite (b) destroy all remaining class privileges and create a completely new culture (c) remain essentially the same destroying all remaining class privilege, but retaining the other, older traditions (d) be conquered by a foreign enemy like Germany.

VOCABULARY

From the lettered choices, find the best definition for each vocabulary item, and mark the appropriate letter in the space provided.

1. __C__ classification is *obsolete*
2. __F__ *tendency* of advanced capitalism
3. __J__ differences have been *diminished*
4. __D__ it is *enhanced* by
5. __M__ he only *predominates*
6. __L__ *indeterminate* social class
7. __N__ *squalid* cottages
8. __G__ an *intimate* knowledge
9. __H__ the gentleness, the *hypocrisy*
10. __K__ *subjugation* by an enemy

A. purpose; cause
B. very rich; splendid
C. out-of-date; outmoded
D. heightened; increased
E. slight
F. inclination; course
G. familiar; detailed
H. undemocratic
I. deceit; pretense of having qualities not actually possessed

J. lessened; decreased
K. control of; enslavement
L. indefinite; imprecise
M. prevails; exists in quantity
N. wretched; poverty-stricken
O. sincerity; honesty

COMPREHENSION   No. right _____ × 10 = _____ %

VOCABULARY   No. right _____ × 10 = _____ %

No. of words 1060 ÷ time in seconds _____ × 60 = _____ WPM

WPM × Comprehension % = Reading Efficiency Rate _____

Chapter 5

IMPROVING VOCABULARY
Using Context Clues

'Twas brillig, and the slithy toves
    Did gyre and gimble in the wabe:
All mimsy were the borogoves,
    And the mome raths outgrabe.

"Beware the Jabberwock, my son!
    The jaws that bite, the claws that catch!
Beware the Jubjub bird, and shun
    The frumious Bandersnatch!"

He took his vorpal sword in hand:
    Long time the manxome foe he sought—
So rested he by the Tumtum tree,
    And stood awhile in thought.

And, as in uffish thought he stood,
    The Jabberwock, with eyes of flame,
Came whiffling through the tulgey wood,
    And burbled as it came!

One, two! One, two! And through and through
    The vorpal blade went snicker-snack!
He left it dead, and with its head
    He went galumphing back.

"And hast thou slain the Jabberwock?
    Come to my arms, my beamish boy!
A frabjous day! Callooh! Callay!"
    He chortled in his joy.

> 'Twas brillig, and the slithy toves
>   Did gyre and gimble in the wabe:
> All mimsy were the borogoves,
>   And the mome raths outgrabe.
>
>   LEWIS CARROLL, "Jabberwocky" *

Can you make sense of this poem? Despite the nonsense words, the poem does follow the grammatical patterns and rhythms of English. The poem is clearly about a boy who was warned about the dreaded Jabberwock, a dangerous animal. He meets the Jabberwock in battle, kills him with his "vorpal" sword, and carries the head back in triumph. If you can get the *feel* of the poem, then you already know something about context clues. *Context* is the environment surrounding a word, the circumstance in which a word is used. A *context clue* is a word or a group of words near an unfamiliar word which may suggest its meaning.

Most of the words you use in speaking and recognize in reading, you learned from contexts in which you heard them used. Small children learn words by imitation. They duplicate the sounds they hear and give them meanings from their contexts. Consider these sentences.

Don't touch your sister's things. Those are her *personal* belongings.

She is too interested in her friends' *personal* lives.

John's *personal* problems cost him his job and ruined his marriage.

The child, overhearing these sentences, quickly relates *personal* to *person*, a word he already knows, and correctly deduces the meaning of the new word without asking.

Learning to use context clues is one way to improve your vocabulary. However, they should never be a substitute for looking up exact meanings in the dictionary, nor should they be used to make wild guesses. Nor will you always find context clues every time you come upon an unfamiliar word. But when they do occur, they are a good short-cut to more efficient reading.

There are four kinds of context clues:

(1) Synonyms
(2) Antonyms
(3) Examples and illustrations
(4) Opinion and tone

(1) Context Clues—Synonyms

The most frequently used context clue is a *synonym*, a word similar in meaning to the unfamiliar one you have encountered in your reading. The clue word may not have exactly the same meaning as the word for which

* From *Through the Looking Glass* (New York: Random House, Inc., 1946), pp. 18–19.

you seek a definition, but it may be close enough to give you an approximate definition. For example,

The student was so *reticent* about speaking before an audience that his (long silences) made everyone feel uncomfortable.

The phrase, *long silences,* is the context clue, and from that, you could determine that *reticent* means *unwilling to speak* or *habitually silent.*

Once you learn the meaning of *reticent* in one context, you can easily deduce the meaning of this synonym:

Calvin Coolidge was famous for his *taciturnity.* His (reticence to speak) more than five words at a time is legendary.

By now it should be obvious that once you learn to use context clues properly and prudently, your reading will become more efficient. Each word you determine in this manner will help you to learn a synonym and so on, like a chain reaction.

Sometimes the trial-and-error method is necessary before you can decide on one meaning.

The president's business *acumen* accounted for his (shrewd) decisions, which always (profited) the company.

Does *acumen* mean (a) sense, knack
                (b) stupidity
                (c) keenness of intellect, insight
                (d) unpredictability?

You can eliminate (b), *stupidity,* right away, and (d), *unpredictability,* doesn't fit the context. That leaves either (a) or (c), both of which could work. Now, consider the context clues again carefully—in this case, *shrewd* and *profited.* In this light (a), *sense* or *knack,* seems a bit vague. So, by process of elimination, (c) *keenness of intellect,* is the most accurate choice.

Here are four more examples. After you find the context clue, circle it and draw an arrow back to the italicized word. Then choose the definition which best fits the context.

1. The traditional American political vision does not deny the existence of *inequity,* injustice and unfairness in our society.

                            KENNETH KENISTON, from *Young Radicals**

inequity (a) inequality
         (b) evil practices
         (c) racial discrimination
         (d) political patronage

* (New York: Harcourt Brace Jovanovich, Inc., 1968), p. 127.

2. She spoke with great distinctness, moving her lips *meticulously* . . .

> DOROTHY PARKER, from "Arrangement in Black and White" *

meticulously (a) cleanly
               (b) precisely
               (c) carelessly
               (d) slowly

3. There is one subculture of poverty in the United States that at times is spirited, *ebullient*, enthusiastic. It is the only humorous part of the other America. Here live the people who are intellectuals, bohemians, beats.

> MICHAEL HARRINGTON, from *The Other America: Poverty in the United States*†

ebullient (a) hostile
             (b) stubborn
             (c) exuberant
             (d) happy

4. Although man's record as a steward of the natural resources of the earth has been a discouraging one, there has long been a certain comfort in the belief that the sea, at least, was *inviolate*, beyond man's ability to change and to despoil.

> RACHEL CARSON, from the Preface to *The Sea Around Us*‡

inviolate (a) impenetrable
             (b) indescribable
             (c) kept intact, not ruined
             (d) easy to manipulate

(2) Context Clues: Antonyms or Opposites

Occasionally a writer may use an *antonym*, a word meaning the opposite, to suggest the meaning of an unfamiliar word. Assuming that you know the antonym, the word in question is easy to define. For example,

> The twin sisters were different in every way. Sue had a pleasant disposition, but Sarah was *dour*. Sue was *garrulous*, but Sarah preferred to sit by herself and avoid talking.

The opposite of *pleasant* is *unpleasant*, and *dour* means just that—*ill-tempered*. The clue for *garrulous* is at the end of the sentence, which suggests the definition *talkative* or *social*.

---

* From *The Portable Dorothy Parker* (New York: The Viking Press, Inc., 1944) p. 44.
  † (New York: The Macmillan Company, 1962), p. 83.
  ‡ (New York: Oxford University Press, 1961), p. xi.

Try another:

Should a man choose between honesty or *duplicity* in his dealings with others? That is an ethical choice, but when a man begins to deceive himself, he is lost.

Does *duplicity* mean (a) frankness, candor
(b) deception
(c) contempt
(d) greed?

Several clues are provided: the antonym, *honesty;* the word, *or,* which sets up the contrast; the synonym, *deceive.*

(3) Context Clues—Examples and Illustrations

A writer may frequently suggest the meaning of an unfamiliar word by examples and illustrations. In this case, no one word implies the definition, but the examples taken together may provide several good clues. For example:

When I left the restaurant, I realized that I couldn't remember what the waitress looked like. It must have been her ordinary features that made her so *nondescript.*

Does *nondescript* mean (a) mediocre, average
(b) not distinctive enough to be described
(c) ugly, unattractive
(d) sullen, gloomy?

The situation and the word's form (non + descript) suggest that the correct answer is (b).

Here is another:

Where did man come from? Does life exist on other planets? What does the future hold? All these are *enigmas,* which have perplexed human beings for centuries.

Does *enigmas* mean (a) unimportant, trivial concerns
(b) questions
(c) baffling puzzles
(d) eternal truths?

In this case, (b) *questions* is not as precise an answer as (c), *baffling puzzles,* which is suggested by the questions themselves and by the second clue, *perplexed.*

This last example includes all three methods of direct context clues described so far:

As we learn more about the sea through the combined studies of many specialists a new concept that is gradually taking form will almost certainly be strengthened. Even a decade or so ago it was the fashion to speak of the *abyss* as a *place of eternal calm*, its *black recesses* undisturbed by any *movement* of water more active than a slowly creeping current, *a place isolated* from the surface and from the very different world of the *shallow sea.* This picture is rapidly being replaced by one that shows the *deep sea* as a place of movement and change, an idea that is far more exciting and that possesses deep significance for some of the most pressing problems of our time.

RACHEL CARSON, from the Preface to The Sea Around Us*

The meaning of *abyss* should be clear from the four italicized clues.

(4) Context Clues—Opinion and Tone

The last kind of context clue is indirect, and consequently, more difficult to rely on with accuracy. The writer's tone, his attitude toward his subject, and his opinions may provide a clue for an unfamiliar word. In this case, there may be no direct word clue to help you. This illustration was written during the 1968 Democratic Convention in Chicago:

> The only people who can possibly feel at ease at this convention are those who have been to a hanging. All the *macabre* trappings are here except the rope and the condemned . . .

RUSSELL BAKER from "A Morbid Spectacle" †

Does *macabre* mean (a) sensational
(b) gruesome, ghastly
(c) normal, ordinary
(d) important, essential?

The correct answer is (b), because *macabre* extends the metaphorical comparison of the convention to a hanging.

This example is more difficult:

> What a monstrous *spectre* is this man, the disease of the *agglutinated* dust, lifting alternate feet or lying drugged with slumber; killing, feeding, growing, bringing forth small copies of himself; grown upon with hair like grass, fitted with eyes that move and glitter in his face; a thing to set children screaming;—and yet looked at nearlier, known as his fellows know him, how surprising are his *attributes!*

ROBERT LOUIS STEVENSON, from "Pulvis et Umbra" ‡

* (New York: Oxford University Press, 1961), p. ix.
† From *The New York Times*, August 29, 1968.
‡ (New York: Charles Scribner's Sons, 1923), pp. 271–272.

Spectre usually refers to a ghost, but in this context, does it mean

(a) shadow
(b) spirit
(c) a horrible, fearful creature
(d) image, figure?

Does *agglutinated* mean (a) stuck together
(b) rotten
(c) weak
(d) stupid?

Does *attributes* mean (a) facial expressions
(b) qualities, characteristics
(c) weaknesses
(d) ideas, beliefs?

The correct answers are (c) and (a) and (b) respectively.

You can use context clues to their best advantage with uncommon words which may require only an approximate definition. Suppose, for instance, that you came upon this sentence in a short story:

> Madeline stepped to the *jalousies* and tugged at them gently, and as the sun came streaming through, outlining her slight figure, she turned to smile at her husband.
>
> HARVEY SWADOS, from "The Balcony" *

Jalousies could mean venetian blinds, curtains or window shutters. Although *window shutters* is actually the correct answer, you can still understand the sentence perfectly well with any of the three definitions. Because *jalousies* is an uncommon word, you could continue reading without missing anything important. It is important, too, to remember that a word may have different meanings in different contexts. Read these three sentences, and then decide which of the three definitions that follow best fits each context.

1. The man's *countenance*, unnaturally red and blotchy, and his trembling hands, suggested that he was on another drinking spree.

2. The clerk drew in his breath, bit his lip, silently counted to ten and managed to keep his *countenance* as the woman tried on pair after pair of shoes too small for her feet.

3. No one can *countenance* murder, even when the circumstances seem to justify violent death.

(a) approve, condone
(b) face, facial features
(c) self-control, temper

* From *A Story for Teddy and Others* (New York: Simon & Schuster, Inc., 1965), p. 172.

You should not consider context clues as an invitation to license. Simply to have a word suggest itself is no guarantee that it is an accurate definition. Many students stubbornly insist that a hastily-conceived definition "could" fit the context. But rather than guessing randomly, first try to reason out the meaning from context clues. But if you are unsure about your guess, or if you suspect the clue to be misleading, or if you need an exact definition to make sense of the passage—then you are safer using the dictionary. Using context clues is not a panacea, a cure-all, for your vocabulary ills. They should never be used as a substitute for an authoritative definition. But used intelligently, they can help increase your rate of comprehension, and even help you to read with greater ease. Like all good things, context clues must be used with discretion and in limited quantities.

EXERCISES

For the next exercise, circle the context clue for each italicized word. Then decide which of the four definitions best fits the context.

1. The *belligerent* relations between Israel and the Arab nations threaten to disrupt the balance of the power in the entire Middle East.

    belligerent (a) harmonious, beautiful
              (b) warlike, bellicose
              (c) economic
              (d) ethnic, religious

2. Psychologists contend that forcing children to *emulate* an older sibling's academic performance is potentially harmful.

    emulate (a) admire, praise
            (b) ridicule, make fun of
            (c) quarrel with, fight with
            (d) try to equal or surpass; imitate

3. The student's term paper was anything but *lucid*; his thoughts wandered and rambled aimlessly.

    lucid (a) correct, proper
        (b) clear, easily understood
        (c) provocative, controversial
        (d) intelligent, bright

4. The first witness on the stand *corroborated* the defendant's story, but the second declared it false.

    corroborated (a) contradicted, denied
                (b) elaborated; added details

(c) confirmed, supported
(d) challenged, questioned

5. To see a telephone pole in a film about the Roman Empire is an *anachronism.*

anachronism (a) something out of proper time or place
(b) harmless but amusing blunder
(c) effective device
(d) anticlimax

6. Most American soldiers find the climate in Southeast Asia *enervating.*

enervating (a) weakening
(b) bracing, brisk
(c) strengthening
(d) disease-producing

7. When the student looked up, he realized with dismay that the teacher had observed him copying test answers from his notes. He knew from her *grave* expression that he was in serious trouble.

grave (a) good-humored, pleasant
(b) ghastly, horrible
(c) stern, solemn
(d) hostile, angry

8. The robber made his way *furtively* down the alley; then he turned to see if anyone had observed him.

furtively (a) confidently, self-assuredly
(b) hastily, quickly
(c) slyly, stealthily
(d) careful, painstakingly

9. It is an *axiom* that human beings are seldom satisfied with what they have.

axiom (a) illusion, false belief
(b) moot point, debatable issue
(c) self-evident, universally-recognized truth
(d) strange phenomenon

10. The candidate conducted a bitter campaign by accusing his opponent of *nefarious* business practices.

nefarious (a) ingenious, clever
(b) wicked, vile
(c) secret, clandestine
(d) destructive, ruinous

The two exercises which follow will give you practice in using context clues in longer reading passages. The first selection describes George Orwell's experience as a white colonial officer in Burma. He must decide whether or not to kill an escaped elephant that has gone on a rampage. The context clue for each italicized word has been circled for you. After you read the selection, decide which of the definitions best fits the way the word was used.

But at that moment I glanced round at the crowd that had followed me. It was an *immense* crowd, two thousand at the least and growing every minute. It blocked the road for a long distance on either side. I looked at the sea of yellow faces above the garish clothes—faces all happy and excited over this bit of fun, all certain that the elephant was going to be shot. They were watching me as they would watch a *conjurer* about to perform a trick. They did not like me, but with the magical rifle in my hands I was momentarily worth watching. And suddenly I realized that I should have to shoot the elephant after all. The people expected it of me and I had got to do it; I could feel their two thousand wills pressing me forward, *irresistibly*. And it was at this moment, as I stood there with the rifle in my hands, that I first grasped the hollowness, the *futility* of the white man's dominion in the East. Here was I, the white man with his gun, standing in front of the unarmed native crowd— seemingly the leading actor of the piece; but in reality I was only an absurd puppet pushed to and fro by the will of those yellow faces behind. I perceived in this moment that when the white man turns tyrant it is his own freedom that he destroys. He becomes a sort of hollow, posing dummy, the *conventionalized* figure of a *sahib*. For it is the condition of his rule that he shall spend his life in trying to impress the "natives," and so in every crisis he has got to do what the "natives" expect of him. He wears a mask, and his face grows to fit it. I had got to shoot the elephant. I had committed myself to doing it when I sent for the rifle. A sahib has got to act like a sahib; he has got to appear *resolute*, to know his own mind and do definite things. To come all that way, rifle in hand, with two thousand people marching at my heels, and then to *trail* *feebly* away, having done nothing—no, that was impossible. The crowd would laugh at me. And my whole life, every white man's life in the East, was one long struggle not to be laughed at.

> GEORGE ORWELL, from "Shoot-
> ing an Elephant" *

You may refer to the selection to answer these questions.

1. an *immense* crowd (a) very large (b) angry (c) very small (d) threatening.
2. a *conjurer* about to perform a trick (a) hunter (b) circus animal trainer (c) magician (d) hypnotist.

* From *Shooting an Elephant And Other Essays* (New York: Harcourt Brace Jovanovich, Inc., 1950), pp. 6–7.

3. pressing me forward, *irresistibly* (a) forcibly (b) gently (c) seductively (d) incapable of being withstood or resisted.
4. the hollowness, the *futility* (a) harshness (b) unimportance, emptiness (c) injustice (d) vagueness
5. the *conventionalized* figure (a) standardized, conforming to a model (b) artificial (c) mechanized (d) ordinary.
6. figure of a *sahib* (a) judge (b) puppet (c) character (d) white master.
7. he has got to appear *resolute* (a) weak; compromising (b) determined; unflinching (c) stubborn (d) masterful.
8. to trail *feebly* away (a) bravely (b) humiliatingly (c) weakly (d) sickly.

Some, but not all, of the words in the following passage can be gleaned from direct context clues. Try to find a context clue for each italicized word; circle it and draw an arrow back to the italicized word. For the others, you will have to rely on the "tone" of the selection. Try to imagine yourself as an old person, lonely and resentful, who is no longer able to care for himself.

This is an Institution for the Aged. This is where they come when the other *alternatives* of their lives become unbearable. This is their choice when isolation, an apparently pointless struggle for bare maintenance, renders private life so unbearable that the alternative—a bed in a corner of a room in an Institution for the Aged—seems suddenly a *solace* and a relief.

It is indeed a relief. The applicant is relieved of the claims of his life which become more—not less—of a *tormenting* burden as they are not met, as life does not yield to them: the claim to love (particularly from children) on the grounds that love has been given; the claim to reward, somehow, for all the suffering, the patience, with which one has outlasted life's losses and troubles. And finally, the claim to happiness after all. As these claims are not met, they are, at long last, *bleakly* surrendered, except in the case of the rare individual who has preserved *autonomy*— whose *requisites* for happiness are neither love nor rewards from sources outside himself. But unless disabled by illness, few such people ever make their way into a Home. For so necessary to happiness is their autonomous pursuit of life, that its surrender is unimaginable, even in the names of security and *respite* from physical danger.

When the new resident arrives at the Home, his relief is as real as it is temporary. Gone are the *forays* into danger, the daily fear of going out to shop in the old neighborhood, where he is likely to have been one of the few remaining whites in an all-black community, where his fears of mugging and robbery limited his trips outside his apartment for groceries and a newspaper to the morning hours, where he stayed closeted in his apartment after three or four in the afternoon. Ironically, the very ghetto neighbors who seem so threatening in number to the lone, aged *alien* in their midst, may be his only source of concerned relationship. Frequently, the first signs that something is amiss or that illness has struck, are perceived by neighbors who have kept a *tacit,* almost unconscious eye out for the old isolate living among them. When the family, several communities removed, is finally aware that something is wrong, it is often discovered that these self-same neighbors have been tending to him, as a matter of course, for some time. It is also true, however, that the ghetto residents and their isolated neighbor tend to leave each other strictly alone, socially. But whether the *bar* is color, culture, or age, the lack of immediate friends or neighbors to talk with, to visit with, is the most bitter source of loneliness to the aged.

> Dorothy   Rabinowitz,   from
> "Among the Aged" *

Choose the best definition for each word. You may refer to the passage for help.

1. the other *alternatives* (a) problems (b) choices between two or more courses of action (c) decisions (d) dilemmas.
2. a *solace* and a relief (a) miracle (b) wise decision (c) remedy (d) comfort.
3. a *tormenting* burden (a) slightly bothersome (b) impossible (c) agonizing, miserable (d) unbearable.
4. *bleakly* surrendered (a) cheerlessly, drearily (b) ultimately (c) eagerly (d) reluctantly.
5. preserves *autonomy* (a) self-assurance (b) uniqueness (c) independence, self-determination (d) anonymity.
6. *requisites* for happiness (a) physical needs (b) requirements, indispensable necessities (c) reasons, causes (d) demands.
7. security and *respite* from danger (a) interval of relief, escape (b) safety (c) intimidation (d) postponement.
8. the *forays* into danger (a) searches (b) short trips, expeditions (c) temptations (d) wanderings.
9. the lone, aged *alien* (a) resident (b) close friend (c) outsider, stranger (d) foreign immigrant.
10. kept a *tacit* eye (a) wary, watchful (b) unspoken, silent (c) unconcerned, indifferent (d) obvious.
11. whether the *bar* is color (a) obstacle, barrier (b) gap, chasm (c) hostility (d) reason, cause.

Reading Selection 5 Marya Mannes, "Stay Young" †

> *Beauty aids, cosmetics, and diet salons are vastly profitable enterprises which cater to millions of middle-aged women trying to retain (or regain) their fading youth and allure. In this essay, Marya Mannes, an American journalist, examines the American dream of "perpetual youth" and its occasionally unhappy results.*

* From *Commentary,* March 1969, p. 61.
† From *More in Anger* (New York: J. B. Lippincott Co., 1958), pp. 35–37.

Again, you will answer comprehension and vocabulary questions. In addition, there is a second vocabulary exercise in determining accurate definitions from context clues.

Like all people in the middle span, I am aware of death and saddened by its advance forces of disintegration. I do not like the signs in flesh and muscle and bone of slow decline, even if they are yet unaccompanied by pain. To one in love with physical beauty, its inevitable blurring by years is a source of melancholy.

Yet I feel sure that while the flesh may retreat before age, the man or woman can advance if he goes towards death rather than away from it, if he understands the excitement implicit in this progression from the part to the whole. For that is, really, what it should be: a steady ascent from personal involvement—the paths and rocks and valleys and rises of the foothills—to the ultimate height where they fuse into one grand and complex pattern, remote and yet rewarding. It is like coming into clearer air. And if that air becomes in course too rare to breathe, the final breath is one of total purity.

It is because of these convictions that I protest against the American tyranny of youth. There is beauty and freshness in youth (if there is less and less innocence), but it is an accident of time and therefore ephemeral. There is no "trick" in being young: it happens to you. But the process of maturing is an art to be learned, an effort to be sustained. By the age of fifty you have made yourself what you are, and if it is good, it is better than your youth. If it is bad, it is not because you are older but because you have not grown.

Yet all this is obscured, daily, hourly, by the selling barrage of youth; perhaps the greatest campaign for the arrested development of the human being ever waged anywhere. Look young, be young, stay young, they call from every page and on every air wave. You must be young to be loved. And with this mandate, this threat, this pressure, millions of goods are sold and millions of hours are spent in pursuit of a youth which no longer exists and which cannot be recaptured.

The result of this effort is, in women, obscene; in men, pathetic. For the American woman of middle age thinks of youth only in terms of appearance and the American man of middle age thinks of youth only in terms of virility.

If obscene seems a strong word to use for old women who try to look young, I will be more explicit. It is quite true and quite proper that better eating habits, better care and less drudgery have made American women look ten years younger than their mothers did at the same age. One of the pleasing phenomena of our life is the naturally young and pretty grandmother, almost as lithe and active as her daughter. But I am talking of the still older woman, past her middle fifties, often alone, often idle, who has the means to spend the greater part of her leisure in beauty salons and shops and weight-reducing parlors, resisting age with desperate intensity. They do not know it, but the fact of this resistance nullifies the effects of the effort. The streets of American cities are full of these thin, massaged, made-up, corseted, tinted, overdressed women with faces that are repellent masks of frustration; hard, empty, avid. Although their ankles are slender and their feet perched on backless high-heeled slippers, they fool no one, and certainly no man. They are old legs and old feet. Although their flesh is clear and fairly firm in the visible areas, it is kneaded flesh, and fools no one. The hips are small indeed, but the girdle only emphasizes their stiff aridity. And the uplift bra, the platinum hair, the tight dress? Whom do they fool? The woman herself, alone. And the obscenity in all this is that she uses the outward techniques of sexual allure to maintain her youth when she is no longer wanted by men. And she does it because she has been told to do it by the advertising media. She has been sold a bill of goods.

Let me hastily say at this point that it is the solemn duty of all women to look as well as they can and to maintain through life the grooming that makes them pleasing to others. Towards this end, the advertisers have performed a signal service to Americans. But they have over-reached themselves, and us. Instead of saying "Be yourself," they say, "Be Young." Instead of saying "Relax," they say "Compete!" In doing this, they deprive the maturing woman of a great joy, an astounding relief: the end, not of sex, heaven knows, but of sexual competition. By the time a woman is fifty she is either wanted as a woman of fifty or not really wanted at all. She does not have to fool her husband or her lover, and she knows that competition with women far younger than she is not only degrading but futile.

It is also an axiom that the more time a woman spends on herself, the less she has for others and the less desirable she is to others. If this goes for young women—and I believe it does—it goes doubly for older women, who have—if they knew it—more to give.

When I go to Europe and see the old people in villages in France or Italy, for instance, I am struck at once by the age of all women who are no longer young, pitying their premature withering; and at the same time startled by the occasional beauty of their old faces. Lined and grooved and puckered as they may be, their hair grizzled or lank, there is something in their eyes and in their bones that gives age austerity and makes their glossy contemporaries at a bridge table here seem parodies of women. They show that they have lived and they have not yet found the means to hide it.

I remember also that as a child and a young girl I never thought of my mother in terms of age. Whatever it was at any time, she looked it; and nobody then told her to lose weight or do something about her hair because she was far too interesting a human being to need such "ameliorations." It would, indeed, have been an impertinence. My mother had no illusions of beauty: she was too concerned with music and her husband and her children to be concerned, in detail, with herself. I don't doubt that, given today's aids, she could have looked younger and smarter than she did. But she would have lost something. The time and effort spent in improving her looks would have been taken from music and from love. With her unruly eyebrows plucked to a thin line, her face made-up, her plump, small body moulded into girdles, an important part of her would have vanished: her identity.

It is this that the older women of America are losing. At club gatherings, at hotels, at resorts, they look identical. What lives they have led have been erased from their faces along with the more obvious marks of age. They have smoothed and hardened into a mould. Their lotions have done well.

It could be said that if they maintain the illusion of youth to themselves only, no harm is done and some good. But I wonder if all self-deceptions do not harm, and if their price is not loss of self.

I wonder too whether one of the reasons for wild, intemperate, destructive youth might not be this same hard finish, this self-absorption, of the women to whom they might otherwise turn. I cannot imagine going for counsel and comfort to a mother or aunt or grandmother tightly buttressed by lastex and heavily masked by makeup. Where is the soft wide lap, the old kind hands, the tender face of age?

None of us with any pride in person and any sense of aesthetics can allow ourselves to crumble into decay without trying to slow the process or at least veil its inroads. But that is not the major battle. The fight is not for what is gone but for what is coming; and for this the fortification of the spirit is paramount, the preservation of the flesh a trivial second.

Let the queen bee keep her royal jelly. Or so I keep telling myself.

READING SELECTION 5

COMPREHENSION

Do not refer to the article to answer these questions. Choose one of the items that best answers each question, and mark the letter in the space provided.

1. ___C___ The title of the selection, "Stay Young," refers to (a) the author's own convictions about middle-aged beauty (b) the natural desire for immortality (c) the message constantly implied in American advertising (d) the art of growing old gracefully.

2. ___Ba___ According to the author, old age and death are (a) the culmination of life, beautiful and rewarding in their own ways (b) a natural part of life which people should become resigned to (c) too frightening to think about (d) the most interesting, exciting part of life.

3. ___C___ It is apparent that the author (a) envies the beauty and innocence of youth (b) considers all beauty salons and weight-reducing salons a waste of time (c) dislikes the emphasis Americans put on youth (d) thinks middle-aged people should be concerned with their appearance.

4. ___CB___ Miss Mannes protests what she calls the "tyranny of youth" because (a) young people are too sophisticated and worldly (b) youth is merely an accident of time and doesn't last very long (c) young people dictate rules of beauty and fashion (d) advertisers appeal only to youthful consumers.

5. ___D___ Which maxim would best describe the main idea of the selection? (a) you are only as young as you feel (b) a stitch in time saves nine (c) beauty is only skin-deep (d) beauty is in the eye of the beholder.

6. ___A___ Miss Mannes gives several reasons why the pursuit of youth is obscene and pathetic. Which was not mentioned? (a) once gone, youth can never be recaptured (b) efforts to regain youth are obvious and fool no one (c) women delude themselves into thinking they are attractive (d) middle-aged women use the outward techniques of sexual allure when men no longer want them (e) women waste too much money buying beauty products that will not work.

7. ___C___ The author feels that advertisers do a disservice to middle-aged women by (a) over-emphasizing standards of hygiene and good grooming (b) misrepresenting their products (c) emphasizing the need for sexual competition with younger women to sell products (d) using only youthful models in their advertisements.

8. __B__ Miss Mannes recalls that her mother in middle age (a) also had illusions of beauty and youthful allure (b) was more concerned with music and her family than with her appearance (c) refused to accept suggestions to improve her appearance (d) should have lost weight and fixed her hair.

9. __A__ Miss Mannes is ultimately concerned with the American woman's (a) attempts to conform to a standardized model, thereby losing her identity and individuality (b) hope of finding beauty in a cosmetic jar or corset (c) preoccupation with her appearance rather than with her mind (d) hopeless attempts to compete with younger women.

10. __A__
    __C__ The last lines, "Let the queen bee keep her royal jelly. Or so I keep telling myself," is an amusing way of saying that (a) the author thinks all cosmetics are worthless (b) the author would secretly like to try cosmetics to see if they work (c) the author has to remind herself continually to resist the claims of cosmetics (d) the author thinks that queen bee royal jelly is a waste of money.

VOCABULARY

From the lettered choices, find the best definition for each vocabulary item, and mark the letter in the space provided.

1. __D__ youth is *ephemeral*
2. __N__ all this is *obscured*
3. __I__ selling *barrage* of youth
4. __L__ in terms of *virility*
5. __O__ *nullifies* the effects
6. __C__ their stiff *aridity*
7. __F__ gives age *austerity*
8. __G__ *parodies* of women
9. __M__ would have been an *impertinence*
10. __H__ fortification of the spirit is *paramount*

A. innocence; naiveté
B. emphasized; dwelled upon
C. barrenness; dryness
D. transitory; short-lived
E. permanence; continued existence
F. solemnity; simplicity
G. humorous or burlesque imitations; caricatures
H. chief in importance

I. overwhelming quantity of words or ideas
J. campaign
K. rejuvenation; process of regaining youth
L. masculinity; vigor
M. unwarranted boldness; insolence
N. hidden; covered
O. undoes; makes useless

COMPREHENSION   No. right ——— × 10 = ——— %

VOCABULARY   No. right ——— × 10 = ——— %

No. of words 1200 ÷ time in seconds ——— × 60 = ——— WPM

WPM × Comprehension % = Reading Efficiency Rate ———————————

This exercise does not count toward your vocabulary score, but it will give you additional practice in using context clues. From the context clue, determine the meaning for each italicized word, referring to the selection for help if necessary. Write your guess in the first blank. In the second blank, look up the word in the dictionary and write the best definition. The objective is to see how accurate your guess is.

	MEANING FROM CONTEXT	DICTIONARY MEANING
1. forces of *disintegration*	———	*seperation*
2. its *inevitable* blurring	———	*unavoidable*
3. source of *melancholy*	———	*depress / sad*
4. this *mandate*, threat	———	*command*
5. this effort is *obscene*	———	*offensive*
6. as *lithe* and active	———	*limber, supple*
7. *repellent* masks of frustration	———	*repulsive*
8. techniques of sexual *allure*	———	*attraction*
9. a *signal* service	———	*unusual*
10. it is an *axiom*	———	*truth*
11. hair *grizzled*	———	*mixed w/ gray*
12. to need such *"ameliorations"*	———	*improvements*
13. wild, *intemperate*, destructive youth	———	*immoderate*
14. tightly *buttressed* by lastex	———	*to support*
15. sense of *aesthetics*	———	*artistic beauty*

Chapter 6

IMPROVING VOCABULARY
Using the Dictionary

Let's suppose a student is asked to define *obsolete* in this sentence:

The human appendix is an *obsolete* organ. He opens the dictionary and finds these definitions:

ob·so·lete (ob′sə·lēt, ob′sə·lēt′) *adj.* **1.** Gone out of fashion; out-of-date; outmoded: an *obsolete* weapon. **2.** No longer used or practiced; not current: an *obsolete* word. **3.** *Biol.* Imperfectly developed; atrophied or vestigial: said of certain organs, parts, etc., no longer functional in living forms of the same species or sex. Abbr. *obs.* [< L *obsoletus* grown old, worn-out, pp. of *obsolescere.* See OBSOLESCENT.] **— ob′·so·lete′ly** *adv.* **— ob′so·lete′ness** *n.* **— ob′so·let′ism** *n.*

— Syn. 1. *Obsolete, obsolescent, archaic,* and *rare* are applied to words that are now seldom or never used. An *obsolete* word is no longer used either in speech or writing, usually because it has been supplanted by a different word; *oscitate,* meaning to yawn, is now *obsolete.* An *obsolescent* word, though still in use, is becoming *obsolete; mercaptan,* a former chemical term, is such a word. *Archaic* words were current at some time in the past, and appear in the works of Shakespeare, the Bible, etc., but unlike obsolete words they are still used for effect because they have an unmistakable flavor of their period or milieu, or are used by persons whose vocabularies were formed in a distinctively earlier era. *Rare* words may be *archaic* or current, but are little used; *trow* is an *archaic* word, and *obsecrate* is an example of a *rare* word.

From *Funk & Wagnalls Standard College Dictionary**

Because he has learned that the first definition is the most common, he writes *gone out of fashion* and continues the assignment. But what has happened? If he had thought for a moment, he would have realized that human organs don't depend on the whims of fashion, like hemlines or hair styles. Another student considers the list and writes *rare,* because it's the shortest definition requiring the least effort. A third student, trying to impress his instructor with his vocabulary, chooses *archaic,* again distorting the meaning.

You can avoid this kind of confusion if you use common sense, consider the context, read all the definitions carefully and discard those which

---

* (New York: Funk & Wagnalls, 1969), p. 933.

can't possibly work. In this case, the third definition is the most appropriate, for in this instance, *obsolete* means *no longer functional, vestigial.*

Using a dictionary blindly is as foolish as using an expensive, complicated camera without consulting the directions. This chapter will give you practice in using your dictionary to its best advantage.

The most important matter is to purchase a good dictionary. If a particular edition is not required, look over several kinds of unabridged dictionaries and choose a sturdy, complete edition that will last. For college courses, an unabridged dictionary (college edition) is best and there are several good ones available.

> *Random House Dictionary of the English Language* (College Edition), Random House, Inc., 1968.
>
> Funk & Wagnalls *Standard College Dictionary* (Funk & Wagnalls, 1969).
>
> *The American Heritage Dictionary of the English Language* (American Heritage Publishing Co., Inc. and Houghton Mifflin Company, 1969).
>
> *Webster's Seventh New Collegiate Dictionary* (G. & C. Merriam Company, 1967).

For best results, you should not rely on an inexpensive abridged paperback dictionary. Although they are cheap, the over-simplified definitions may be worthless for help in reading difficult prose. Abridged dictionaries are fine to carry to class or for looking up spellings; but for any serious vocabulary work, they are not recommended. Nor should you use an outmoded dictionary handed down by your parents from their college days. Language changes constantly, and an old dictionary may list definitions that are obsolete.

After you purchase a good dictionary, get acquainted with the front matter. Dictionaries contain much useful and interesting information in the beginning portions. If you are interested, you can read about the development of the English lanuguage, the variations in American dialects or about the dictionary's policy on usage. However, one essential section to read is the *guide* or *plan* to the dictionary, which describes how the dictionary orders its definitions.

Most dictionaries organize definitions by frequency of use, so that the first definition is the most widely used. But some, notably the Merriam Webster editions (*Webster's New Collegiate*), order definitions by "semantic evolution" or historically. In this way, the first definition is the earliest recorded definition; the last definition or two are the most commonly used now. Historical arrangement shows you at a glance the word's evolution. To demonstrate the difference, compare these two entries for the word *nice.*

A.

nice (nīs) *adj.* **nic·er, nic·est 1.** Agreeable; commendable; pleasing; respectable; suitable. **2.** Friendly; kind. **3.** Characterized by, revealing, or demanding discrimination, delicacy, or subtlety: a *nice* distinction. **4.** Precise, accurate, or minute, as an instrument or measurement. **— nice and** Gratifyingly; properly: *nice and* dry. [< OF, innocent, foolish < L *nescius* ignorant < *ne* not + *scire* to know] **— nice′ly** *adv.* **— nice′ness** *n.*

From *Funk & Wagnalls Standard College Dictionary**

B.

nice \'nīs\ *adj* [ME, foolish, wanton, fr. OF, fr. L *nescius* ignorant, fr. *nescire* not to know — more at NESCIENCE] **1** *obs* **a :** WANTON, DISSOLUTE **b :** COY, RETICENT **2 a :** showing fastidious or finicky tastes **:** REFINED **b :** SCRUPULOUS **3 :** marked by or demanding delicate discrimination or treatment ⟨~ distinction⟩ **4** *obs* **:** TRIVIAL **5 a :** PLEASING, AGREEABLE ⟨~ time⟩ ⟨~ person⟩ **b :** well-executed ⟨~ shot⟩ **6 :** most inappropriate **:** BAD ⟨a ~ one to talk⟩ **7 a :** socially acceptable **:** WELL-BRED **b :** VIRTUOUS, RESPECTABLE **— nice** *adv* **— nice·ly** *adv* **— nice·ness** *n*
syn DAINTY, FASTIDIOUS, FINICAL, PARTICULAR, SQUEAMISH: NICE implies fine discrimination in perception and evaluation; DAINTY suggests a tendency to reject what does not satisfy one's delicate taste or sensibility; FASTIDIOUS implies having very high and often capricious ethical, artistic, or social standards; FINICAL implies an affected often exasperating fastidiousness; PARTICULAR implies an insistence that one's exacting standards be met; SQUEAMISH suggests an oversensitive or prudish readiness to be nauseated, disgusted, or offended **syn** see in addition CORRECT

From *Webster's Seventh New Collegiate Dictionary*†

It is very important to know which method your dictionary follows; otherwise, you may look up a word and mistakenly choose an archaic definition.

Another feature of the dictionary is the etymology of words. Etymology is the study of word origins, the formation and derivation of words. While most English words are derived from Latin and Greek, or from the Romance languages like French or Italian, many words have more unusual origins. The etymology of a word is printed in brackets after the definitions as this entry for *illusion* shows:

il·lu·sion (i·lōō′zhən) *n.* **1.** A false, misleading, or overly optimistic idea; misconception; delusion: to outgrow one's youthful *illusions*. **2.** A general impression not consistent with fact: Red gives an *illusion* of heat. **3.** *Psychol.* A sensory impression that results in misinterpretation of the true character of an actual object: an optical *illusion*: distinguished from *hallucination*. **4.** A delicate, transparent, netted fabric used as veiling, trimming, etc. **5.** *Obs.* The act of deceiving or misleading by means of false appearances. **— Syn.** See DELUSION. [< OF < L *illusio, -onis* mocking, deceit < *illudere* to make sport of < *in-* toward, against + *lu-dere* to play] **— il·lu′sion·al** (-əl), **il·lu′sion·ar·y** (-er·ē) *adj.* **◄** etymology

From *Funk & Wagnalls Standard College Dictionary.*‡

The symbol (<) means "derived from." *Illusion* was derived from Old French (OF), which in turn was originally derived from Latin (L). The original meaning was *mocking, deceit*, formed by the Latin word, *illudere* ("to make sport of"), which in turn was formed by the combination of

* (New York: Funk & Wagnalls, 1969), p. 912.
† (New York: G. & C. Merriam Company, 1967), p. 569.
‡ (New York: Funk & Wagnalls, 1969), p. 668.

the Latin prefix, *in-*("toward, against") and (+) *ludere* ("to play"). Notice how different the contemporary definitions are from the derivations. Using the key to abbreviations from the inside of your dictionary's front cover, look up the derivations (the originating language), original meanings and contemporary meanings of these words. The first example has been done for you.

WORD	DERIVATION	ORIGINAL MEANING	CONTEMPORARY MEANING
1. *piranha* (fish)	Portuguese (Brazilian) < *Tupi*	toothed fish	small, carnivorous fish
2. *maudlin*	French Latin	tearful repentance	effusively sentimental
3. *asinine*	Latin	asinus - ass	stupid or silly
4. *bedlam*	English	asylum madhouse	noisy uproar + confusion
5. *gloat*	Scandivaian	to smile scornfully	great pleasure or satisfaction
6. *hassle*	uncertain South.U.S.	trouble, bother	argument or fight
7. *beatnik*	English	rejection of convent. forms	disregard dress of proper
8. *jazz*	uncertain	Big Band music	rhymic music
9. *lunatic*	English Latin	wildy foolish	lunacy insane
10. *luscious*	English	sweet cloying	sweet + pleasant to taste or smell

One other feature of the dictionary is essential for good reading—the pronunciation guide. Students often avoid pronouncing unfamiliar words from their phonetic spelling because the symbols look so forbidding and complicated. The phonetic description is always printed in parentheses after the word; the pronunciation guide at the bottom of each right-hand page shows you how to pronounce the symbols. Each sound is darkened in a familiar word for easy reference. Here is the word *hypocrisy* spelled phonetically:

(hi pok′ rə sē)

Using the pronunciation guide opposite, you will find that

—in *hi*, the *i* is pronounced as in *if;*
—in *pok*, the *o* sounds like the vowel in *hot;*
—the peculiar looking symbol (ə) is the schwa, pronounced *uh* in any unaccented syllable; *rə*, then, is pronounced *ruh;*

—and in *sē*, the *ē* is pronounced like the first sound of *equal*, or like the word *see*.

Notice that the stress mark (′) *follows* the syllable to be accented: (hi *pok*′ rə sē) or hy*poc*risy.

Try these two pronunciations of *obsolete*. The first is the preferred.

(ob′ sə lēt′, ob′ sə lēt′)

In the first phonetic spelling, the first syllable receives the heavier stress, and the last syllable gets only light stress (ob′ sə lēt). While in the second pronunciation, the first syllable gets light stress, and the last receives the heavier stress (ob sə lēt).

If you want to read more accurately and at the same time improve your vocabulary, try to sound out difficult words you look up. Chances are, even if you've never read the word before, you may have heard it spoken. Students occasionally either skip over unfamiliar words or pronounce them sloppily, even confusing them with another, similar word. If you put off looking up words until "later," the danger is that you may put it off forever, and so the word, its pronunciation, and definition remain a mystery.

Using the pronunciation guide for reference, sound out these words, not from the word itself, but from the phonetic spelling in parentheses. Be sure to pay attention to stress marks. You might cover the first word with an index card to see how well you can apply the symbols.

CONCISE PRONUNCIATION KEY: a*ct*, ā*ble*, dâ*re*, ä*rt*; e*bb*, ē*qual*; *if*, ī*ce*; *hot*, ō*ver*, ô*rder*, *oil*, bŏŏ*k*, ōō*ze*, *out*; *up*, û*rge*; *chief*; *sing*; *shoe*; *thin*, *that*; *zh* as in *measure*. ə = *a* as in *alone*, *e* as in *system*, *i* as in *easily*, *o* as in *gallop*, *u* as in *circus*; ᵊ as in *button* (but′ᵊn), *fire* (fīᵊr), *cradle* (krād′ᵊl). See the full key inside the front cover.

Pronunciation Guide, *Random House Dictionary of the English Language.*

Some of these words are commonly mispronounced; others may be entirely new.

PRONUNCIATION	WORD
1. (shûr′ bit)	sherbet
2. (noo′ klē ər, nyoo′ klē ər)	nuclear
3. (as′ pə rin, as′ prin)	aspirin
4. (feb′ roo er′ ē, feb′ yoo er′ ē)	February
5. (nōm)	gnome
6. (bô′ dē)	bawdy

  * (New York: Random House, Inc., 1966).

PRONUNCIATION	WORD
7. (ə plom′) ~~vostless~~	aplomb
8. (vap′ id)	vapid
9. (si kā′ də, si kä′ də)	cicada
10. (en vī′ rən ment)	environment
11. (im′ pə tənt)	impotent
12. (ə lōō′ mə nəm)	aluminum
13. (sen trif′ yə gəl)	centrifugal
14. (in ûr′ shə)	inertia
15. (fi nom′ ə non′)	phenomenon
16. (är′ ki tīp′)	archetype
17. (om nish′ əns)	omniscience
18. (pûr sev′ ə rā′ shən)	perseveration
19. (mə lev′ ə lənt)	malevolent
20. (ə poth′ ē ō′ sis, ap′ ə the̱′ ə sis)	apotheosis
21. (in kō′ it)	inchoate
22. (im brōl′ yō)	imbroglio
23. (som nam′ byə liz′ əm)	somnambulism
24. (ə vänt′ gärd′)	avant-garde
25. (mə tas′ tə sis)	metastasis

Here is another exercise for further practice in reading phonic symbols. For each word on the left written in phonic symbols, look through the four choices on the right, and select the one that matches exactly. To make the exercise more challenging, try to do the ten items in less than thirty seconds.

Example:

(pə ten′ shəl) (a) potentate (b) potentiate (c) potentially (d) <u>potential</u>

1. (gal′ ek sē) (a) galactic (b) glacial (c) <u>galaxy</u> (d) jealousy
2. (ek′ splə rā′ shən) (a) exploratory (b) expurgation (c) <u>exploration</u> (d) exploitation
3. (tô tol′ ə jē) (a) tautonym (b) <u>tautology</u> (c) totally (d) tautologism
4. (neb′ yə ləs) (a) nebulize (b) <u>nebulous</u> (c) nebula (d) nemesis
5. sangk′ tə mō′ nē) (a) ceremony (b) <u>sanctimonious</u> (c) sanguinary (d) sanctimony
6. (pri kō′ shəs) (a) precarious (b) <u>precocious</u> (c) precondition (d) precipitous
7. (kal′ kyə ləs) (a) calculate (b) callous (c) careless (d) <u>calculus</u>
8. (in′ si kyōōr′) (a) uncertain (b) incident (c) insecurity (d) <u>insecure</u>
9. (ə pos′ trə fē) (a) apostle (b) apostrophe (c) apothecary (d) apostolical
10. (sof′ ə môr′ ik) (a) <u>sophomoric</u> (b) soporific (c) sophistry (d) sophomore

Of course, the most important function of a dictionary is its definitions. But as the illustration at the beginning shows, the objective is to choose the best definition for the context. It is necessary to keep in mind that the first definition, or the most common definition, may not always be appropriate. After you read the following passage, decide which definition *best* fits the context. All definitions are from the dictionary, but their order has been scrambled.

> Public attitudes toward the poor today are a *mosaic*. The poor are viewed with some *compassion* but are also frequently seen as immoral, unmotivated, and *childlike* in their behavior. There is still a public lack of appreciation of the *debilitating* effects of poverty and the *stresses* that result from a lack of *adequate* resources. *Hostility* and racial prejudice may be directed toward some of the poor. In some cases, these attitudes *permeate* the leadership *elites* of communities, making the task of poverty reduction more difficult. In truth, history has widened the social distance between the poor and the affluent since life in suburbia makes it possible for the affluent to carry on day-to-day activities with little *intimate* awareness of the poor or their problems in the crowded urban ghettoes.
>
> Louis A. Ferman, Joyce L. Kornbluh and Alan Haber, eds., from the preface to *Poverty in America**

1. public attitudes are a *mosaic* (a) inlaid work composed of bits of stone, glass, forming a pattern (b) an intricate, complex design (c) a collection of aerial photographs (d) a virus disease of plants.
2. viewed with *compassion* (a) mercy (b) commiseration, condolence (c) deep sympathy, pity; quality of sharing another's suffering (d) tenderness.
3. *childlike* in their behavior (a) childish, juvenile (b) trusting (c) innocent, meek (d) artless, natural.
4. the *debilitating* effects (a) causing listlessness, boredom (b) enfeebling, weakening (c) enervating, exhausting (d) relaxing.
5. the *stresses* that result (a) emphases, significances (b) emotional strains, tensions (c) resistance of a body to external forces (d) mechanical pressures, forces.
6. lack of *adequate* resources (a) suitable, fully sufficient (b) equal (c) barely suitable, sufficient (d) reasonably sufficient for legal action.
7. *hostility* and racial prejudice (a) act of war (b) animosity, enmity (c) resistance, opposition to a plan (d) fighting, conflict.
8. these attitudes *permeate* (a) diffuse through; spread out (b) saturate (c) pass through physical substance or mass (d) penetrate, pervade.
9. the leadership *elites* (a) highest social classes (b) group of persons

* (Ann Arbor: University of Michigan Press, 1968), p. xvii.

having major share of authority (c) most skilled part of a particular group (d) narrow, powerful clique.

10. little *intimate* awareness (a) having illicit sexual relations (b) essential, intrinsic (c) characterized by informality and privacy (d) closely familiar; first-hand.

After you read the next paragraph, look up each italicized word in an unabridged dictionary and write the best definition for the context in each space provided.

On any person who desires such *queer* prizes, New York will *bestow* the gift of loneliness and the gift of privacy. It is this *largess* that accounts for the presence within the city's walls of a considerable section of the population; for the residents of Manhattan are to a large extent strangers who have pulled up *stakes* somewhere and come to town, seeking *sanctuary* or fulfillment or some greater or lesser *grail*. The capacity to make such *dubious* gifts is a *mysterious* quality of New York. It can destroy an individual, or it can fulfill him, depending a good deal on luck. No one should come to New York to live unless he is willing to be lucky.

E. B. WHITE, from *Here Is New York**

1. such *queer* prizes _odd, eccentric, strange_
2. will *bestow* the gift _to present, to give, to apply_
3. it is this *largess* _liberality in giving, generosity_
4. pulled up *stakes* _to conclude ones affairs + move on_
5. seeking *sanctuary* _rest, refuge, amunity from punishment_
6. some greater or lesser *grail* _prolonged endeavor_
7. such *dubious* gifts _doubt to validity, or quality_
8. a *mysterious* quality _difficult to explain or account for_

After you read the next passage, which contains more difficult words, try to guess from the context what each of the first set of words means. Then verify your answer using an unabridged dictionary to see how accurate you were.

Certain other aspects of American love, though not so fully *portrayed*, are *illuminatingly* touched upon in magazine advertisements. For it is apparent from any careful *scrutiny* of the ads that Americans require the *stimulus* of *exotic*, remote, or uncomfortable surroundings, in order to experience the real *transports* of delight. Here is an advertisement showing a couple on a wild, chilly-looking beach at sundown (how *did* they get that automobile down there without making tracks in the sand?); here is another couple deep in the forest *primeval*, smoking cigarettes and hugging each other; here is a third exploring a wild stream bank in their good clothing, *undaunted* by steep *declivity* or tangled underbrush. Oasis Cigarettes *render* continual reports of lovers cozily *nestled*

* (New York: Harper & Row, Publishers, 1949), pp. 9–10.

on a desert cactus, moodily *bussing* each other in some dim alley of the Vieux Carré of New Orleans, or *perching* together in a high window overlooking Monte Carlo. They never *wax* romantic in Middletown, U.S.A.; they never grow fond in a middle-class living room. Wind-swept Alpine *crags*, the slippery decks of heeled-over *yawls*, castles without plumbing, streams in the heart of a jungle—these would seem to be the typical *loci* of love, rather than the sofa, bed, or park bench. How all this may be possible—since most people are forced to spend their lives at or near home—is a nagging question; perhaps the meaning of it all is that love, in the twentieth century, is an *actuality* for the wealthy, but still only a dream for the poor and the middle class.

Morton M. Hunt, from "Love According to Madison Avenue" *

WORD IN CONTEXT	DEFINITION FROM CONTEXT	DICTIONARY DEFINITION
1. not so fully *portrayed*	pictured	to depict/represent
2. careful *scrutiny*	examination	close observation
3. steep *declivity*	hill	descending slope
4. *render* continual reports	announce	submit/present
5. cozily *nestled*	close together	snugly/comfortably
6. moodily *bussing* each other	hugging	to kiss loudly
7. *perching* in a window	sitting	resting/sitting place
8. Alpine *crags*	cliffs	mass of rock
9. heeled-over *yawls*	boats	sailing vessels
10. the typical *loci* of love (plural of *locus*)	place	a place

For the remaining words, look up the most appropriate definition for the context in the dictionary, and write your answer in the blank.

1. *illuminatingly* touched upon — to understand - enlighten
2. requires the *stimulus* — causing a response
3. *exotic*, remote surroundings — intriguing, unusual & beautiful
4. the real *transports* of delight — to carry one place to another
5. the forest *primeval* — earliest age = original
6. *undaunted* by steep declivity — resolute, fearless
7. they never *wax* romantic (verb) — being full - to grow
8. an *actuality* for the wealthy — being actual, reality

To vary the next exercise, the italicized words in the selection are already defined for you. Find the italicized word in the passage that fits each definition and write your answer in the space. Note: there are five more definitions than words.

* From *Horizon*, November 1959.

Columbia University in the City of New York is in some respects a strange place for a revolution yet, in others, a likely breeding ground for student unrest. Unlike many large schools such as Berkeley, and many small schools such as Swarthmore, Columbia has little *cohesion* as a community, for there is little to differentiate it from New York City. There are few trees, and the buildings are cramped onto a six-square-block campus. Columbia is *diffused* into New York. And in the process something happens that *transforms* it from the Ivy League school that its alumni and administrators imagine it to be to the urban university that it is in reality. As Columbia flows into the streets of New York, so the society of the streets flows into Columbia. *Medieval* attempts to keep reflective thought separated from reality only prove *futile*. New York is life. Its dirt, congestion, motion and art force people to respond; its physical environment has *generated* a mental climate of liberality and social consciousness, which has *permeated* the urban campus.

Universities have only recently begun to respond to rapid changes in society and the resulting changes in the psychology and attitudes of their students. One would expect Columbia, because of its location, to be in the *vanguard* of institutional change. Instead it lags far behind most American universities. Operating under conceptions that were perhaps *valid* ten years ago, it offers part of its new gymnasium in a gesture of *benevolence* to a black community that today wants no gifts from white institutions. And with similar lack of understanding, it expects its students to uphold the values of law and order over morality, when those students have seen "law and order" distorted to provide a *cloak* for white racism and for American involvement in Vietnam.

Today, when students seek to engage themselves actively with society, Columbia is still clinging to the funnel theory of education, trying to protect its students for four years and then channeling them into professional life. This concept of a university as a degree factory with an *ovipositor* in society is one great source of *disillusionment* to thousands of students, who on the one hand resist being processed into that society, and on the other refuse to be *shunted* off from that society during their *"incubation"* period. So, at Columbia, some students cut classes to get arrested at anti-draft demonstrations, and others devote their hours to community action programs. Their desire to act springs from a deep sense of morality and frustration—frustration that they have no say in shaping the decisions that shape their lives and their world.

JERRY AVORN, et al., from *Up
Against the Ivy Wall* *

DEFINITIONS (Match with italicized words from the passage)

1. upset, antagonized _____
2. penetrated, passed through ___*permeated*___
3. moved to one side; cut ___*shunted*___
4. a disguise, cover ___*cloak*___
5. disengagement; withdrawal _____

* (New York: Atheneum Publishers, 1969), p. 4.

6. kindliness; disposition to do good ___benevolence___
7. belonging to an earlier age ___Medieval___
8. caused, brought into being ___generated___
9. changes the character or nature of ___transforms___
10. depositor of eggs; in this sense, that which produces educated people in vast quantities ___ovipositer___
11. disenchantment ___disillusionment___
12. modern, contemporary _____
13. prohibited; denied _____
14. forefront of a movement ___vanguard___
15. a period before maturity is reached ___incubation___
16. influence; power _____
17. useless; done in vain ___futile___
18. sound; acceptable ___valid___
19. unity; tendency to hold, stick together ___cohesion___
20. scattered widely; spread out in all directions ___diffuse___

Which two words in the passage carry out the metaphor of the "breeding ground" mentioned in the first sentence?
___incubation___, ___diffused___ ___ovipositer___

Generally, we speak of two kinds of vocabulary skills:

(1) *active* or *sight vocabulary*—those words you understand and use without difficulty;

(2) *passive* or *recognition vocabulary*—those words you recognize but which you cannot define precisely.

Rather than trying to memorize every word you look up, it is much more sensible to begin working on your recognition vocabulary. Begin using a systematic approach on those words you've seen a hundred times, but which you have trouble defining. When you feel more confident about these troublesome words you usually avoid, then you can go on to learning completely new words.

What should you do when you come to an unfamiliar word when you're reading? If context clues don't work, and if you really can't understand the passage without a definition, then stop and look it up. Otherwise, make a light check mark in the margin next to the word. When you finish, look up all the checked words. If you interrupt your reading too often by running to the dictionary, you may either lose track of the content, or even worse, you may never get back to the book at all.

Another way to use the dictionary to improve your vocabulary is the three-dot method. It works like this: every time you look up a word, put a small dot in the dictionary next to the entry. The second time, put a second dot. When three dots have accumulated, you should write the word and its definition and learn it for good.

Another practice students find helpful is to keep a notebook or a set of index cards of important vocabulary words. You might use a form like this:

```
The mayor's assistant was an obvious

sycophant.   -----------------------   -- CONTEXT


         SYCOPHANT   --------------   -- WORD TO BE
                                         DEFINED
```

```
              REVERSE SIDE

SYCOPHANT—servile flatterer; self-
              seeking or fawning
              parasite   -----------   -- DEFINITION

   NOUN       (sik'ə fənt)   --------   -- PART OF SPEECH
                                          AND PRONUNCIATION
```

It doesn't matter so much which system you use, but that you use one regularly. The best way is to learn each set of new vocabulary words every day and review at the end of each week. Vocabulary words collected over many months simply can't fit into your head at once—at least not if you really want to remember them.

READING SELECTION 6 Paul Chevigny, "Abuses of Police Power" *

Paul Chevigny graduated from Harvard Law School in 1960. After working for a New York law firm, he did legal work for the Congress of Racial

* From *Police Power* (New York: Pantheon Books, Inc., 1969), pp. 139, 140–142.

Equality (CORE). In 1966, he studied complaints of police abuses in New York City for the New York Civil Liberties Union. This excerpt is from Chevigny's discussion of false arrest and police cover-ups.

The apparently irrational and sometimes provocative behavior of the police in street conflicts has often raised the question whether the police deliberately encourage violence or at least disorderly behavior from a troublemaker in order to show that he really is an offender and to provide grounds for removing him from the street by arrest. This is one of the unresolved questions about police behavior, and one that is central to an understanding of police abuses. If the police react in a rough manner to provocation from citizens, if they in fact themselves behave in a rude and hamhanded fashion, that is one problem, but it is quite another if the police deliberately provoke to violence people they believe to be troublemakers.

The consensus among the authorities who have studied the problem is that the police do sometimes try to provoke violence in order to make an arrest. It is logical to think that policemen will try such things with outcasts, whom they fear and dislike and would prefer to see in jail. One young Negro in a ghetto neighborhood in Brooklyn, who had the reputation of being a "cop fighter," complained that the police would not let him alone. Whenever they saw him on the street they slowed down their cars and asked him if he wanted to fight. In New York City, however, I think that the challenge by a policeman to physical combat, or even to a public disturbance, is the exception. In most cases, even if a policeman wanted to use such crude tactics, they would not be necessary. The New York police are sophisticated enough in drawing charges and making them stick not to need an actual act of physical violence to arrest anyone. If they feel that a man is a troublemaker, they can, unfortunately, charge him with resisting arrest, without the necessity of risking injury to an officer.

The worst problem in street-corner incidents is not that of police quarreling with citizens. Most such quarrels, while never admirable, are at least understandable; they are much like quarrels between private citizens. The worst abuse is not even the police hitting people in such quarrels; pugnacious citizens hit others in private disputes every day. The root problem is the abuse of power, the fact that the police not only hit a man but arrest him. Once they have arrested him, of course, lying becomes an inevitable part of the procedure of making the quarrel look like a crime, and thus the lie is the chief abuse with which we must come to grips. If the police simply hit a man and let him go, there would be an abuse of the authority conferred by the uniform and the stick, but not the compound abuse of hitting a man and then dragging him to court on criminal charges, really a more serious injury than a blow. One's head heals up, but a criminal record never goes away. There is no more embittering experience in the legal system than to be abused by the police and then be tried and convicted on false evidence.

Police abuse and consequent conviction on false evidence are a combination which feeds the impulse to riot; once respect for the legal process is gone, grievances can be expressed only by force. Despite these obvious repercussions upon community relations, it is rare that anyone is abused without being criminally charged, not only because of the rationale for such abuses ("he was guilty anyhow") but because the policeman is likely to get into trouble if he lets an abused person go free. There is nothing to cover a later accusation of abuse if an arrest has not been made.

There can be no doubt that police lying is the most pervasive of all abuses. In most cases we studied, there was a lie whenever there was a criminal trial. If the charge was disorderly conduct, officers lied to create a breach of the peace where none existed. If the charge was assault or obstructing an officer, they supplied blows by the defendant when none had been struck. In the police canon of ethics, the lie is justified in the same way as the arrest: as a vindication of police authority, by proving that defiance of the police is a crime in fact if not in law. A member of a pariah group, or anyone who defies the police, being guilty at heart and sometimes potentially guilty in fact, deserves to be punished out of hand. Besides, the police dislike such people so much that they consider them unworthy of the protection of the law. By lying, the police enforce these folkways of their own, while preserving the shell of due process of law. Not surprisingly, police lying is a problem on which little reliable research has been done.

READING SELECTION 6

COMPREHENSION

Do not refer to the article to answer these questions. Choose one of the four items that best answers each question, and mark the letter in the space provided.

1. _C_ The selection describes the problems of (a) law enforcement agencies which officially condone abuses of police power (b) police attitudes toward outcasts or members of pariah groups (c) police who deliberately provoke disorder to make arrests and who cover their abuses by making false charges (d) increased public criticism of and resistance to police misuse of authority.

2. _A/B_ Chevigny limits his discussion of police abuses to (a) apprehension of suspects (b) streetcorner incidents involving quarrels between citizens (c) crimes actually committed by outcasts (d) domestic quarrels which disturb the peace.

3. _B_ The author states that police often provoke violence or disorderly conduct because (a) police have authoritarian personalities (b) police feel they must stop potential offenders before they actually commit a crime (c) police know that brutal tactics prevent crime (d) police must work under tense conditions.

4. _C_ Chevigny claims that few police in New York City actually need to resort to physical violence because (a) the suspect usually becomes violent first (b) such practices are deplored by the police department (c) police have sophisticated enough techniques to make their charges look believable (d) the suspect usually remains calm and does not resist arrest.

5. _A_ In the example of the Negro youth in Brooklyn who was harassed by police, Chevigny implies that (a) the police seldom forget a person's reputation once it is established (b) people with past police records usually commit more crimes (c) the example was isolated, for such harassment seldom occurs (d) the youth actually was a troublemaker.

6. _C_ In streetcorner incidents, when police intervene, they frequently (a) become violent if they are insulted, for they have tempers like anyone else (b) try to settle the dispute politely but firmly (c) quarrel with the citizens and make the quarrel look like a crime by pressing false or trumped-up charges, usually disorderly conduct (d) use of physical force but seldom make arrests.

111

7. _____ The author listed three unfortunate results of police abuses. Which was *not* mentioned? (a) disruption of community relations (b) the stigma of police records that prevents the convicted from finding jobs (c) fostering riots because police abuses, when openly tolerated, can only be stopped by the citizens' rebelling (d) disrespect and distrust of civilian review boards which are ineffectual in controlling police abuses (e) loss of community respect for the legal process.

8. _____ Police often rationalize their arresting a potential trouble-maker by saying "he was guilty anyhow." Another reason stated for such arrests is that (a) police fear their authority will be questioned if they don't act tough (b) police think they can get away with abuses because law-abiding citizens seldom question police authority (c) police have to protect themselves against possible complaints from those they arrest (d) police know that most troublemakers are indeed guilty when they defy police authority.

9. _____ According to the author, police get away with lying about their arrest charges because (a) legally, defying or questioning police authority is a crime (b) police view citizens who defy their authority as criminals who do not deserve police protection (c) most citizens are law-abiding, supporting anything the police do as correct or necessary (d) they know that the police department encourages such lying.

10. _____ At the end, when the author states that little reliable research has been done about police lying, he implies that (a) most people think such research is unnecessary: if a person is arrested, he probably is in fact guilty (b) police chiefs refuse to believe that police lying exists (c) police are careful not to abuse their powers when researchers observe them (d) police departments do not allow outside observers to investigate police practices (e) none of the above can accurately be inferred.

VOCABULARY

From the lettered choices, find the best definition for each vocabulary item, and mark the letter in the space provided.

1. _____ the *irrational* behavior
2. _____ *provocative* behavior
3. _____ police are *sophisticated* enough
4. _____ *pugnacious* citizens hit others
5. _____ authority *conferred* by the uniform
6. _____ *grievances* can be expressed
7. _____ these obvious *repercussions*

8. ___H___ most *pervasive* of all abuses
9. ___N___ members of a *pariah* group
10. ___C___ *potentially* guilty

A. quarrelsome
B. after-effects; indirect results
C. possibly, but not actually
D. serving to stir up anger, resentment
E. harmful actions; injuries
F. cruel; unjust
G. altered by experience so as to be worldly-wise

H. widespread; thoroughly penetrating
I. bestowed; granted
J. senseless; contrary to reason
K. advised; counseled
L. stimulating sexually
M. powerfully; forcefully
N. social outcast
O. wrongs; causes for complaints

COMPREHENSION No. right ___ × 10 = ___ %

VOCABULARY No. right ___ × 10 = ___ %

No. of words 750 ÷ time in seconds ___ × 60 = ___ WPM
WPM × Comprehension % = Reading Efficiency Rate _____

Chapter 7

DENOTATION
AND CONNOTATION

In the last two chapters you learned about the meaning of words in context. In this chapter you will learn that words can suggest meanings beyond their dictionary definitions.

DENOTATION

One of the functions of language is denotation. A word denotes when it points or refers to something—an object, idea, event—which is called its *referent*. A word is not the same as its referent; it only stands for it. *Chair* is the spoken and written symbol for ⊓, its referent is the real world. This object, ⊓, might have been named differently—karba or cheeseburger or xzplka—but only if every speaker of English agreed on what that sound meant. Language, then, results from agreement. Native speakers of English have no trouble identifying the referent of words like *money* or *president, pencil* or *book,* even when these words appear in different contexts. You can easily imagine the mess society would be in if everyone spoke his own private language.

The most common uses of purely denotative language are scientific writing and straight, factual, and objective reporting. Every scientist in the world understands the symbols Au or O or H_2SO_4 or the Latin generic label for human beings, *homo sapiens.* Your objective in reading denotative language is to understand exactly what referents the writer's words stand for. The following passage about the world's population in the future illustrates denotative language because the writer's only intention is to inform and explain, not to arouse the emotions.

> Barring nuclear warfare or some other global cataclysm, the world population will continue to increase for several decades at least, in affluent as well as in underdeveloped countries. This will happen even if contraceptive techniques achieve universal acceptance. With the low

mortality rates now prevalent in all countries that have introduced modern public health practices, the population can be stabilized only if the number of children is less than 2.5 per couple. There is no evidence that family control will soon reach this drastic level anywhere. It can therefore be taken for granted that the world population will greatly increase in the immediate future and will indeed probably double within less than a century. As a consequence, the largest percentage of human beings will be born and develop, and their children will be born and develop, within the confines of large urban agglomerations. Whatever individual tastes may be, mankind will thus be shaped by the urban environment.

> René Dubos, from *So Human an Animal* *

Here is another example of denotative language in which James Harvey Robinson describes the phenomenon of curiosity:

> Curiosity is as clear and definite as any of our urges. We wonder what is in a sealed telegram or in a letter in which someone else is absorbed, or what is being said in the telephone booth or in low conversation. This inquisitiveness is vastly stimulated by jealousy, suspicion, or any hint that we ourselves are directly or indirectly involved. But there appears to be a fair amount of personal interest in other people's affairs even when they do not concern us except as a mystery to be unraveled or a tale to be told. The reports of a divorce suit will have "news value" for many weeks. They constitute a story, like a novel or play or moving picture. This is not an example of pure curiosity, however, since we readily identify ourselves with others, and their joys and despair then become our own.
>
> James Harvey Robinson, from
> *The Making of the Mind* †

The word *curiosity* is a good example of denotation which points to an intangible referent. That is, no one has ever touched curiosity, but everyone has experienced the sensation or has felt its effects. In the same way, you cannot point to *evil*, but you can point to its effects. Abstract words like *evil, liberty, terror* or *peace* are denotative because everyone generally agrees on what they mean. But everyone may disagree on how these abstractions are made real. As a result, communication may break down because the referents are confused. The Paris Peace Talks are a good illustration. Each delegation, American, South Vietnamese, North Vietnamese and Viet Cong, wants *peace* or a *peaceful settlement* to the war. But each delegation has quite different notions about how that peace should be accomplished in reality. In reading, the same is true. You may misinterpret the author's words by not paying strict attention to the context. To carry the same example further, if you read two articles on ways to achieve peace in Vietnam, one by a North

---

* (New York: Charles Scribner's Sons, 1968), pp. 54–55.
† (New York: Harper & Row, Publishers, 1921), p. 50.

Vietnamese and the other by an American, you must be aware that each writer may mean something different by the abstract word *peace.*

For your purposes, however, you can consider denotation as the literal meaning or the dictionary definition, which *most people* agree on. But you must also be aware that a writer may have a different referent in mind when he uses abstract words. This you must try to determine from the subject matter, the context, the writer's point of view, and so forth.

Recognizing connotative language is an important skill for better reading comprehension. We call a word *connotative* because it carries emotional suggestions and implications with it, in addition to its purely denotative meaning. Denotation is the literal meaning of a word; connotation describes the attitudes that colorful, figurative, or evocative language calls up. These words illustrate the difference between connotation and denotation.

Compare the denotative word, *walk,* which carries almost no emotional response, with these more figurative variations:

(1) *lumber*—denotative meaning: to walk heavily
        connotation: suggests a bulky, clumsy, awkward person
   Example: The man *walked* into the china shop.
        The man *lumbered* into the china shop.

(2) *sneak*—denotative meaning: to move in a stealthy, furtive manner
        connotation: suggests a suspicious person, trying to hide his real intentions.
   Example: The man *walked* into the bank.
        The man *sneaked* into the bank.

(3) *saunter*—denotative meaning: to stroll, to walk in a leisurely manner
        connotation: may suggest either smugness, arrogance, or laziness, depending on the context.
   Example: The young man *walked* down the street, eyeing every girl who passed.
        The young man *sauntered* down the street, eyeing every girl who passed.

These sentences show why connotative words are more colorful and suggestive than ordinary denotative words. *Lumber, sneak,* and *saunter* suggest something about the subject that the first sentences lack.

Connotative words may suggest either a favorable or an unfavorable response. In these two sentences, which word has an unfavorable connotation? Which suggests a favorable connotation?

(1) Her teachers considered the girl *childish.*
(2) Her teachers considered the girl *childlike.*

Although the dictionary lists these two words as synonyms, their connotations are quite distinct. *Childlike* suggests innocence, but *childish* suggests immature, selfish behavior—the unpleasant side of children. In the same way, the words, *naked* and *nude,* denote the same physical state of undress, but their connotations again are different.

> The English language with its elaborate generosity distinguishes between the naked and nude. To be naked is to be deprived of our clothes, and the word implies some of the embarrassment most of us feel for that condition. The word nude, on the other hand, carries in educated usage, no uncomfortable overtone. The vague image it projects into the mind is not of a huddled and defenseless body, but of a balanced, prosperous and confident body: the body reformed. In fact, the word was forced into our vocabulary by critics of the early 18th Century to persuade the artless islanders that the naked human body was the central subject of art.
>
> LORD KENNETH CLARK, from
> *The Nude: A Study in Ideal Form**

In the King James Version of the Bible, Adam and Eve's shame after disobeying God is described like this: "And the eyes of them both were opened, and they knew that they were *naked;* and they sewed fig leaves together, and made themselves aprons." (Genesis 3:7). Theater reviewers often refer to the new trend in entertainment as "nudity in the theater," which suggests, as Clark does, that disrobing before spectators is artistic. But critics of the trend may well use the phrase "nakedness in the theater" to emphasize the offense to public standards of decency.

Consider these two hypothetical statements made by an American president seeking re-election on a nationally televised speech:

(1) I am asking you to put me *into power* for another four years.
(2) I am asking you to elect me to another *term of office.*

The phrase, *into power,* in the first sentence suggests authoritarianism, and the electorate might well bristle at the implication. A politician seeking votes would probably use the less offensive phrase, *term of office.*

The next illustration is interesting, for the writer describes in denotative language the emotional effects (connotations) of simple words:

> Simple words such as air, water, soil, and fire evoke in most human beings deep emotions that recall the past; just as they did for primitive people, these words stand for the very essence of the material creation. Despite much knowledge of the physical and chemical properties they represent, they still convey to most people a sense of eternal and essentially irreducible value. Fire, for example, remains a great reality with mystic undertones, probably because human life has been organized around it for ages. Fire as a concept has progressively disappeared from

* (Princeton: Princeton University Press, 1956), p. 3.

science during the past few decades; the chapters devoted to it in textbooks of physics and chemistry are becoming shorter and shorter, when they exist at all. But the words flame and fire remain just as deeply meaningful for real human life—including the life of physicists and chemists.

RENÉ DUBOS, from *So Human an Animal* *

One difficulty students have with reading prose is that they read only for the literal or surface meaning. In other words, they read prose, especially fictional prose, as if it were strictly denotative. But most good prose is a mixture of connotative and denotative words. And connotation is particularly important because the writer wants the reader to see the world as he sees it. To be an "active reader," to recreate in your mind the writer's descriptions and moods, you have to "tune in" to his wave length by paying attention to both context and connotation. The following describes the most common ways that connotative language is used.

Connotation: Metaphors and Figurative Language

A metaphor is a comparison between two unlike ideas for effect. Turn back for a minute to Christopher Rand's analogy on page 57. His metaphorical comparison of Los Angeles to a complicated machine is much more effective then if he had simply described the city in literal terms. These simple sentences illustrate the favorable and unfavorable metaphorical uses of the word *dog.*

(1) He worked like a *dog* to support his wife's demands for luxury.
(2) The poor boy *dogged* his girlfriend's trail, but she still refused to marry him.
(3) He worked like a *dog* to satisfy his greed for power.
(4) He acts like a sad-eyed puppy *dog* around his fiancée, to the amusement of his friends.

Compare the effect of these two sentences.

(1) Her eyes, *lost* in the *fatty ridges* of her face, looked like *two small pieces* of *coal* pressed into a *lump of dough* . . .

WILLIAM FAULKNER, from "A Rose for Emily" †

(2) Her eyes, lost in her shapeless, gray face, were small and beady.

* (New York: Charles Scribner's Sons, 1968), p. 114.
† From *The Collected Stories of William Faulkner* (New York: Random House, Inc., 1957).

The first sentence is obviously more effective, because Faulkner *shows* by metaphor instead of telling the reader as in the second example.

This paragraph describes an adult's memory of discovering water as a child. The metaphors are italicized for you.

> The scullery was a mine of all the minerals of living. Here I discovered water—a very different element from the *green crawling scum* that stank in the garden tub. You could pump it in *pure blue gulps* out of the ground; you could swing on the pump handle and it came out *sparkling like liquid sky.* And *it broke and ran and shone* on the tiled floor, or *quivered in a jug,* or *weighted your clothes with cold.* You could drink it, draw with it, froth it with soap, swim beetles across it, or fly it in bubbles in the air. You could put your head in it, and open your eyes, and *see the sides of the bucket buckle,* and *hear your caught breath roar,* and *work your mouth like a fish,* and smell the lime from the ground. Substance of magic—which you could *tear or wear, confine or scatter,* or *send down holes, but never burn or break or destroy.*
>
> LAURIE LEE, from *The Edge of Day**

Connotation: Sensory Words

Another kind of connotation appeals directly to your sense of taste, smell, sight, hearing, or touch. *Glossy,* for instance, appeals to your sense of touch and sight; *horseradish* appeals to (or perhaps offends) your senses of smell and taste. Which senses do these words appeal to? *sputter, hay, satin, plastic, glue, mustard, lisp, furry, coffee, brittle, cobweb, detergent, antiseptic, dust.*

Here is the remainder of Laurie Lee's description of the scullery. Which senses do the italicized words appeal to?

> The scullery was water, where the old pump stood. And it had everything else that was related to water: thick *steam* of Mondays, edgy with *starch; soapsuds boiling, bellying* and *popping, creaking* and *whispering, rainbowed with light* and *winking with a million windows.* Bubble, bubble, *toil* and *grumble, rinsing* and *slapping* of sheets and shirts, and *panting* Mother rowing her *red arms* like oars in the *steaming waves.* Then the linen came up on a stick out of the pot, like *pastry,* or *woven suds,* or *sheets of moulded snow.*
>
> LAURIE LEE, from *The Edge of Day**

These short passages will give you more practice in recognizing and interpreting connotative language. The first is by Mark Twain, who describes an approaching storm that Huck Finn and Jim, the escaped slave, watch as they hide on an island.

---

* (New York: William Morrow & Co., 1959), pp. 11–12.

We spread the blankets inside for a carpet, and eat our dinner in there. We put all the other things handy at the back of the cavern. Pretty soon it darkened up, and begun to thunder and lighten; so the birds was right about it. Directly it begun to rain, and it rained like all fury, too, and I never see the wind blow so. It was one of these regular summer storms. It would get so dark that it looked all blue-black outside, and lovely; and the rain would thrash along by so thick that the trees off a little ways looked dim and spider-webby; and here would come a blast of wind that would bend the trees down and turn up the pale underside of the leaves; and then a perfect ripper of a gust would follow along and set the branches to tossing their arms as if they was just wild; and next, when it was just about the bluest and blackest—*fst!* it was as bright as glory, and you'd have a little glimpse of tree-tops a-plunging about away off yonder in the storm, hundreds of yards further than you could see before; dark as sin again in a second, and now you'd hear the thunder let go with an awful crash, and then go rumbling, grumbling, tumbling, down the sky towards the under side of the world, like rolling empty barrels down-stairs—where it's long stairs and they bounce a good deal, you know.

MARK TWAIN, from *The Adventures of Huckleberry Finn**

Underline all the words that evoke the sounds, colors, and smells of the storm.

In *Let Us Now Praise Famous Men,* James Agee described how poor white tenant farmers subsisted in the South during the Depression. As you read, let your senses turn on to recapture the remarkable variety of odors the author found in one tenant house.

The Gudgers' house, being young, only eight years old, smells a little dryer and cleaner, and more distinctly of its wood, than an average white tenant house, and it has also a certain odor I have never found in other such houses: aside from these sharp yet slight subtleties, it has the odor or odors which are classical in every thoroughly poor white southern country house, and by which such a house could be identified blindfold in any part of the world, among no matter what other odors. It is compacted of many odors and made into one, which is very thin and light on the air, and more subtle than it can seem in analysis, yet very sharply and constantly noticeable. These are its ingredients. The odor of pine lumber, wide thin cards of it, heated in the sun, in no way doubled or insulated, in closed and darkened air. The odor of woodsmoke, the fuel being again mainly pine, but in part also, hickory, oak, and cedar. The odors of cooking. Among these, most strongly, the odors of fried salt pork and of fried and boiled pork lard, and second, the odor of cooked corn. The odors of sweat in many stages of age and freshness, this sweat being a distillation of pork, lard, corn, woodsmoke, pine, and ammonia. The odors of sleep, of bedding and of breathing, for the ventilation is poor. The odors of all the dirt that in the course of time can accumulate in a

* (New York: Harper & Row, Publishers, 1896), pp. 67–68.

quilt and mattress. Odors of staleness from clothes hung or stored away, not washed. I should further describe the odor of corn: in sweat, or on the teeth, and breath, when it is eaten as much as they eat it, it is of a particular sweet stuffy fetor, to which the nearest parallel is the odor of the yellow excrement of a baby. All these odors as I have said are so combined into one that they are all and always present in balance, not at all heavy, yet so searching that all fabrics of bedding and clothes are saturated with them, and so clinging that they stand softly out of the fibers of newly laundered clothes. Some of their components are extremely "pleasant," some are "unpleasant"; their sum total has great nostalgic power. When they are in an old house, darkened, and moist, and sucked into all the wood, and stacked down on top of years of a moldering and old basis of themselves, as at the Ricketts', they are hard to get used to or even hard to bear. At the Woods', they are blowsy and somewhat moist and dirty. At the Gudgers', as I have mentioned, they are younger, lighter, and cleaner-smelling. There too, there is another and special odor, very dry and edged: it is somewhere between the odor of very old newsprint and of a victorian bedroom in which, after long illness, and many medicines, someone has died and the room has been fumigated, yet the odor of dark brown medicines, dry-bodied sickness, and staring death, still is strong in the stained wallpaper and in the mattress.

> JAMES AGEE and WALKER EVANS,
> from *Let Us Now Praise Famous
> Men**

You may have the habit of skipping descriptive passages in novels or short stories because "nothing ever happens in them." Quite the contrary, a good deal happens. The author's carefully chosen words suggest the mood he wants you to feel, and the descriptions provide the setting for the characters' actions and conflicts. This illustration from the beginning of John Cheever's *Bullet Park* sets the tone for the rest of the book.

> Paint me a small railroad station then, ten minutes before dark. Beyond the platform are the waters of the Wekonsett River, reflecting a somber afterglow. The architecture of the station is oddly informal, gloomy but unserious, and mostly resembles a pergola, cottage or summer house although this is a climate of harsh winters. The lamps along the platform burn with a nearly palpable plaintiveness. The setting seems in some way to be at the heart of the matter. We travel by plane, oftener than not, and yet the spirit of our country seems to have remained a country of railroads. You wake in a pullman bedroom at three a.m. in a city the name of which you do not know and may never discover. A man stands on the platform with a child on his shoulders. They are waving goodbye to some traveler, but what is the child doing up so late and why is the man crying? On a siding beyond the platform there is a lighted dining car where a waiter sits alone at a table, adding up his accounts. Beyond this is a water tower and beyond this a well-lighted and empty street. Then you think

* (Boston: Houghton Mifflin Co., 1939), pp. 154–155.

happily that this is your country—unique, mysterious and vast. One has no such feelings in airplanes, airports and the trains of other nations.

JOHN CHEEVER, from *Bullet Park**

You may refer to the passage and a dictionary to answer these questions.

1. Cheever gives several illustrations of scenes one might see in the railroad stations of nameless towns. Which do his examples connote? (a) sadness, loneliness (b) despair, anxiety (c) happiness, joy (d) insecurity, instability
2. What does this sentence suggest? "Paint me a small railroad station, then, ten minutes before dark." What does that particular time of day suggest? How would the effect of the passage have changed if Cheever had "painted" a railroad station "ten minutes before noon"? "Ten minutes before dawn"?

This passage describes two contrasting qualities of the Great Plains:

The region of the Great Plains is a land of romance. Its most widely distributed product is fiction and movie plot, wild-west shows and Buffalo Bill, Indian fights, buffalo hunts, cowboy skill, round-ups and shoot-ups; has been stage hold-ups, escapes from prairie fires, wolves and rattlesnakes, wanderings in blinding blizzards, conquering bucking bronchos. The stories of these have gone far beyond the limits of the English language—and have raised the hair of youth in all continents.

The Great Plains region is a land of tragedy. For two and a half centuries the white man had marched westward, conquering the land, settling and making successful homesteads and building up communities. Thus he worked his triumphant way from the Atlantic to central Kansas and Nebraska. On westward, into the region of the Great Plains, marched this army of settlers, but here the battle turned against them and they were thrown back by hundreds of thousands. But this battlefield of their defeat, of the triumph of their enemies is not marked by tablets, monuments, and the usual signs of victory. A lion does not write a book, nor does the weather erect a monument at the place where the pride of a woman was broken for the want of a pair of shoes, or where a man worked five years in vain to build a home and gave it up, bankrupt and whipped, or where a baby died for the want of good milk, or where the wife went insane from sheer monotony and blasted hope.

J. RUSSELL SMITH, from *North America†*

1. The writer presents a contrast: the Midwest is both a land of *romance* and a land of *tragedy*. What do these words usually connote?

* (New York: Alfred A. Knopf, Inc., 1969), pp. 3–4.
† (New York: Harcourt Brace Jovanovich, Inc., 1925), p. 409.

2. What do the words *romance* and *tragedy* connote in this passage?
3. What is the effect of the passage? What devices does the author use to achieve it?

SLANTED LANGUAGE

Words have tremendous power. If you have ever read or listened to the speeches of Hitler, Martin Luther King, or Eldridge Cleaver, you know that words can move people to hatred, war, goodness, courage, mercy, or anything else the speaker intends. Unfortunately, connotation has another function besides those we have looked at. You may encounter language that is slanted, deliberately inflammatory and even irresponsible. Slanted writing usually attempts to arouse your emotions and appeal to your fears and prejudices. The Vietnam War, as an illustration, has spawned new sorts of slanted language. The most obvious labels, "hawk" and "dove," attempt to classify people automatically and without qualification according to their positions on the war. Other epithets like "peacenik," "fascist imperialist," "V. C. sympathizer," evoke a response, depending on the reader's political attitudes and the context. The danger with slanted language is that it blocks reason and discussion, because the writer forces conclusions on you. Slanted language is never a substitute for documentation or reasoned analysis, and when you encounter it in reading you must learn to question critically its use.

We shall consider only two basic kinds of slanted language. The first is the technique of *name-calling*, used to elicit an immediate response, usually unfavorable. Racial slurs fall into this category, as do stereotyped labels such as "fascist pig," "anarchist," and "liberal kneejerk." In the same way, slogans like "law and order," "anarchy in the streets," or "the silent majority" provoke an automatic and unthinking response.

A second technique is the *euphemism*. A euphemism is a nice way of saying something which otherwise might be harsh or offensive. Euphemisms, then, are favorable connotative words used to the extreme. *Death* is often referred to euphemistically as "passing away" or "meeting one's Maker," to disguise the harshness of death. However, if you look beneath the euphemism, the referent, *death*, is the same. On television, *sweat* is always called "perspiration" in deodorant advertisments because the latter "sounds nicer." A cleaning woman may call herself a "household technician"; a janitor a "building" or "maintenance engineer"; some banks now refer to their tellers as "money hostesses." The danger with euphemisms is that you may really believe that the euphemism makes the referent in question better than it really is. In this paragraph, Mary McCarthy illustrates the American use of euphemism in Vietnam.

> I confess that when I went to Vietnam early last February I was looking for material damaging to the American interest and that I found it, though often by accident or in the process of being briefed by an official.

Finding it is no job; the Americans do not dissemble what they are up to. They do not seem to feel the need, except through verbiage; *e.g.*, napalm has become "Incinderjell," which makes it sound like Jello. And defoliants are referred to as weed-killers—something you use in your driveway. The resort to euphemism denotes, no doubt, a guilty conscience or—the same thing nowadays—a twinge in the public-relations nerve. Yet what is most surprising to a new arrival in Saigon is the general unawareness, almost innocence, of how what "we" are doing could look to an outsider.

MARY MCCARTHY, from *Vietnam**

In this exercise, there are several groups of words with approximately the same referents. For each word, mark

(1)—if the word is a name-calling device or suggests an unfavorable connotation;

(2)—if the word is a euphemism which suggests an overly favorable connotation;

(3)—if the word is neutral.

The first set is done for you.

1. undertaker __3__
   funeral director __2 or 3__
   mortician __2__
   grievance counselor __2__
2. draft-dodger __1__
   draft-resister __2__
   anti-war protester __1__
   pacifist __2__
   peacenik __1__
3. policeman __3__
   cop __1__
   law enforcement officer __2 or 3__
   pig __1__
   fuzz __1__
   peace officer __2__
4. hippie __1__
   dirty, unwashed long hair __1__
   non-conformist __2__
   social dropout __1__

5. bum __1__
   homeless unemployed __1__
   derelict __1__
   tramp __1__
   panhandler __1__
   beggar __1__
6. war __3__
   holocaust __1__
   massacre __1__
   hostilities __2 or 1__
   military action __3__
7. garbage man __3__
   sanitation engineer __2__
   refuse worker __2__
   refuse collection agent __2__
8. student activist __3__
   student militant __1__
   student anarchist __1__
   student extremist __1__

The following editorial is an example of slanted writing. Written in 1969, the editorial refers to the Reverend William Sloane Coffin's conviction for conspiring to counsel men to avoid the draft, along with Dr. Benjamin Spock and five other men.

* (New York: Harcourt Brace Jovanovich, Inc., 1967), p. 3.

Yale President Kingman Brewster Jr. is such an able and perceptive man that for the life of us we can't see why in his annual freshman assembly address, he went out of his way to praise Yale Chaplain William Sloane Coffin.

Brewster cited two alumni—New York City Mayor John V. Lindsay and Coffin—as men "wholly unashamed of their high purpose," men who have not yielded to the "temptations to cynicism which pervade the country."

Forget that John Lindsay is at this very moment engaged in one of the most cynically opportunistic political campaigns in New York City history, and ponder the praise for Coffin.

Mr. Coffin was convicted last year in a federal court on charges of conspiring to counsel young men to evade the draft. And altho that conviction was sent back on a technicality for a new trial, the fact remains that Coffin is a symbol—because he wishes to be a symbol—of every campus militant and new leftist who believes it the greater part of nobility to destroy college campuses.

Indeed, just weeks after his conviction, Coffin praised change even if it comes in violent ways. And he compared Jesus' actions in throwing the money changers out of the temple with the activities of radical student leader Mark Rudd, the S. D. S.er who brought violence and bloodshed to the Columbia campus.

Is that any way to inculcate respect for law and order, by holding up Coffin as a symbol to freshman students? Is it any way to inculcate respect for reasoned debate and civilized behavior?

What President Brewster neglected to mention is that "high purpose" is not enough. What zealot or extremist isn't convinced that he is motivated by "high purpose"? What budding Hitler or Stalin doesn't believe he is the epitome of "high purpose"?

We are deeply distressed by President Brewster's praise of Mr. Coffin. We hope the Yale campus is spared the agony of its students acting on the bad advice so freely and often dispensed by its chaplain.

> "High Purpose?," *Arizona Republic**

1. Why does the writer put "high purpose" in quotation marks?
2. What phrase in the passage describes what the author really thinks "high purpose" should mean?
3. Underline any examples of slanted language.
4. What evidence does the writer present to defend his point of view?

One way, then, to improve both your comprehension and critical reading skills is to determine the way a writer uses his language. If you can discern the intended referent of denotative words, and if you can recreate the emotional attitudes that connotative words suggest, then your reading will become more intelligent and precise. Furthermore, you will begin to recognize subtleties and nuances of meaning of which you may not have been aware before.

* From *The Arizona Republic*, September 29, 1969.

READING SELECTION 7 George Orwell, "Some Thoughts on the Common Toad" *

For centuries, great poets and prose writers have revelled in the pleasures of spring. In this selection, written in 1946, George Orwell suggests a more serious interpretation of spring, and concludes with a defense for the enjoyment of nature which may help preserve mankind from the forces of destruction that threaten its existence.

Before the swallow, before the daffodil, and not much later than the snowdrop, the common toad salutes the coming of spring after his own fashion, which is to emerge from a hole in the ground, where he has lain buried since the previous autumn, and crawl as rapidly as possible towards the nearest suitable patch of water. Something—some kind of shudder in the earth, or perhaps merely a rise of a few degrees in the temperature—has told him that it is time to wake up: though a few toads appear to sleep the clock round and miss out a year from time to time—at any rate, I have more than once dug them up, alive and apparently well, in the middle of the summer.

At this period, after his long fast, the toad has a very spiritual look, like a strict Anglo-Catholic toward the end of Lent. His movements are languid but purposeful, his body is shrunken, and by contrast his eyes look abnormally large. This allows one to notice, what one might not at another time, that a toad has about the most beautiful eye of any living creature. It is like gold, or more exactly it is like the golden-colored semi-precious stone which one sometimes sees in signet rings, and which I think is called a chrysoberyl.

For a few days after getting into the water the toad concentrates on building up his strength by eating small insects. Presently he has swollen to his normal size again, and then he goes through a phase of intense sexiness. All he knows, at least if he is a male toad, is that he wants to get his arms round something, and if you offer him a stick, or even your finger, he will cling to it with surprising strength and take a long time to discover that it is not a female toad. Frequently one comes upon shapeless masses of ten or twenty toads rolling over and over in the water, one clinging to another without distinction of sex. By degrees, however, they sort themselves out into couples, with the male duly sitting on the female's back. You can now distinguish males from females, because the male is smaller, darker and sits on top, with his arms tightly clasped round the female's neck. After a day or two the spawn is laid in long strings which wind themselves in and out of the reeds and soon become invisible. A few more weeks, and the water is alive with masses of tiny tadpoles which rapidly grow larger, sprout hind legs, then forelegs,

* From *Shooting an Elephant and Other Essays* (New York: Harcourt Brace Jovanovich, Inc., 1950).

then shed their tails: and finally, about the middle of the summer, the new generation of toads, smaller than one's thumbnail but perfect in every particular, crawl out of the water to begin the game anew.

I mention the spawning of the toads because it is one of the phenomena of spring which most deeply appeal to me, and because the toad, unlike the skylark and the primrose, has never had much of a boost from the poets. But I am aware that many people do not like reptiles or amphibians, and I am not suggesting that in order to enjoy the spring you have to take an interest in toads. There are also the crocus, the missel thrush, the cuckoo, the blackthorn, etc. The point is that the pleasures of spring are available to everybody, and cost nothing. Even in the most sordid street, the coming of spring will register itself by some sign or other, if it is only a brighter blue between the chimney pots or the vivid green of an elder sprouting on a blitzed site. Indeed it is remarkable how Nature goes on existing unofficially, as it were, in the very heart of London. I have seen a kestrel flying over the Deptford gasworks, and I have heard a first-rate performance by a black bird in the Euston Road. There must be some hundreds of thousands, if not millions, of birds living inside the four-mile radius, and it is rather a pleasing thought that none of them pays a half-penny of rent.

As for spring, not even the narrow and gloomy streets round the Bank of England are quite able to exclude it. It comes seeping in everywhere, like one of those new poison gases which pass through all filters. The spring is commonly referred to as "a miracle," and during the past five or six years this worn-out figure of speech has taken on a new lease of life. After the sort of winters we have had to endure recently, the spring does seem miraculous, because it has become gradually harder and harder to believe that it is actually going to happen. Every February since 1940 I have found myself thinking that this time winter is going to be permanent. But Persephone, like the toads, always rises from the dead at about the same moment. Suddenly, toward the end of March, the miracle happens and the decaying slum in which I live is transfigured. Down in the square the sooty privets have turned bright green, the leaves are thickening on the chestnut trees, the daffodils are out, the wallflowers are budding, the policeman's tunic looks positively a pleasant shade of blue, the fish-monger greets his customers with a smile, and even the sparrows are quite a different color, having felt the balminess of the air and nerved themselves to take a bath, their first since last September.

Is it wicked to take a pleasure in spring, and other seasonal changes? To put it more precisely, is it politically reprehensible, while we are all groaning, under the shackles of the capitalist system, to point out that life is frequently more worth living because of a blackbird's song, a yellow elm tree in October, or some other natural phenomenon which does not cost money and does not have what the editors of the left-wing newspapers call a class angle? There is no doubt that many people think so. I know by experience that a favorable reference to "Nature" in one of my articles is liable to bring me abusive letters, and though the keyword in these letters is usually "sentimental," two ideas seem to be mixed up in them. One is that any pleasure in the actual process of life encourages a sort of political quietism. People, so the thought runs, ought to be discontented, and it is our job to multiply our wants and not simply to increase our enjoyment of the things we have already. The other idea is that this is the age of machines and that to dislike the machine, or even to want to limit its domination, is backward-looking, reactionary, and slightly ridiculous. This is often backed up by the statement that a love of Nature is a foible of urbanized people who have no notion what Nature is really like. Those who really have to deal with the soil, so it is argued, do not love the soil, and do not take the faintest interest in birds or flowers, except from a strictly utilitarian point of view. To love the country one must live in the town, merely taking an occasional week-end ramble at the warmer times of year.

This last idea is demonstrably false. Medieval literature, for instance, including the popular ballads, is full of an almost Georgian enthusiasm for Nature, and the art of agricultural peoples such as the Chinese and Japanese centers always round trees, birds, flowers, rivers, mountains. The other idea seems to me to be wrong in a subtler way. Certainly we ought to be discontented, we ought not simply to find out ways of making the best of a bad job, and yet if we kill all pleasure in the actual process of life, what sort of future are we preparing for ourselves? If a man cannot enjoy the return of spring, why should he be happy in a labor-saving Utopia? What will he do with the leisure that the machine will give him? I have always suspected that if our economic and political problems are ever really solved, life will become simpler instead of more complex, and that the sort of pleasure one gets from finding the first primrose will loom larger than the sort of pleasure one gets from eating an ice to the tune of a Wurlitzer. I think that by retaining one's childhood love of such things as trees, fishes, butterflies, and—to return to my first instance—toads, one makes a peaceful and decent future a little more probable, and that by preaching the doctrine that nothing is to be admired except steel and concrete, one merely makes it a little surer that human beings will have no outlet for their surplus energy except in hatred and leader-worship.

At any rate, spring is here, even in London, N.1, and they can't stop you enjoying it. This is a satisfying reflection. How many a time have I stood watching the toads mating, or a pair of hares having a boxing match in the young corn, and thought of all the important persons who would stop me enjoying this if they could. But luckily they can't. So long as you are not actually ill, hungry, frightened, or immured in a prison or a holiday camp, spring is still spring. The atom bombs are piling up in the factories, the police are prowling through the cities, the lies are streaming from the loudspeakers, but the earth is still going round the sun, and neither the dictators nor the bureaucrats, deeply as they disapprove of the process, are able to prevent it.

READING SELECTION 7

COMPREHENSION

Do not refer to the article to answer these questions. Choose one of the items that best answers each question, and mark the letter in the space provided.

1. _____ Which statement best expresses the main idea? (a) people no longer consider it fashionable to enjoy nature (b) the common toad's emergence is the first sign that spring has arrived (c) spring, the season of rebirth and growth, should be enjoyed for the lessons it offers human society (d) the pleasures of nature are free, accessible and possibly even helpful in making life a bit more bearable.

2. _____ What is the purpose of Orwell's description of the emerging toad? (a) it has no real purpose other than decoration for the rest of the essay (b) it tries to prove a point—that anyone can enjoy nature in unusual and unexpected ways (c) it tries to prove a point—that everything in nature revolves around the sexual instinct (d) it tries to prove a point—that the emerging toad is the most valid sign that spring has arrived.

3. _____ Aside from Orwell's admission that the toad particularly appeals to him, what other reason does he give for describing it? (a) the toad is so pathetically ugly that he feels sorry for it (b) the emerging toad is much easier to observe than other signs of spring (c) the emerging toad can be observed in the city as well as in the country (d) in describing spring, poets have ignored the lowly toad in favor of more beautiful creatures.

4. _____ When does the toad usually hibernate? (a) summer and autumn (b) autumn and winter (c) winter and spring (d) only in the winter.

5. _____ To Orwell, which of the following is the *most* impressive feature of spring? (a) its presence can be detected everywhere, even in the dirtiest city street (b) its miraculous reappearance every year even after the harshest winter (c) its ability to make everything seem better than it really is (d) its ability to make people kinder to one another.

6. _____ When Orwell makes a favorable reference to spring, he states that critics usually accuse him of (a) immaturity (b) naiveté (c) sentimentality (d) stupidity.

7. _____ Orwell lists several common arguments against appreciating nature which its detractors often cite. Which was *not* mentioned? An appreciation of nature (a) is inaccessible for

poor people (b) is a delusion for city dwellers who have no idea what nature is really like (c) is old-fashioned, backward-looking, and reactionary in the machine age (d) lessens people's awareness of social and political problems (e) violates the modern idea that people ought to be discontented and not enjoy those pleasures they already have.

8. __B__ Orwell defends his opinions by stating that (a) not all social ills can be solved by government and technology (b) the pleasures of nature may help people realize a decent, even a peaceful, future (c) without nature, people would soon become only machines (d) people may soon forget how to enjoy simple pleasures.

9. __D__ Orwell also submits that if people deny themselves the pleasures of nature, the result may be (a) societies dominated by machines (b) cities so filthy and sordid that nature may be obliterated (c) authoritarian governments that will forbid individuals from enjoying simple pleasures (d) frustrated human beings who lack healthy outlets for their leisure time, and, who in turn, will resort to hatred and leader-worship.

10. __D__ At the end Orwell says: "but the earth is still going around the sun, and neither the dictators nor the bureaucrats, deeply as they disapprove of the process, are able to prevent it." This statement implies (a) a criticism of government officials who would like to unite the world under one authority (b) that nature will persist despite men's efforts to control it or make it conform to technology (c) that science has failed to comprehend the mysteries of the universe (d) that nature will persist despite the petty efforts of politicians and bureaucrats to deny people its pleasures.

VOCABULARY

From the lettered choices, find the best definition for each vocabulary item, and mark the letter in the space provided.

1. __H__ his movements are *languid*
2. __K__ eyes look *abnormally* large
3. __B__ in the most *sordid* street
4. __F__ decaying slum is *transfigured*
5. __I__ *balminess* of the air
6. __A__ politically *reprehensible*
7. __D__ *abusive* letters
8. __C__ a *foible* of urbanized people
9. __G__ *utilitarian* point of view
10. __E__ wrong in a *subtler* way

A. capable of receiving blame, rebuke
B. filthy; dirty
C. weakness; failing
D. myth
E. more refined, discriminating
F. changed outward appearance of
G. feasible; practical
H. listless; lacking energy
I. mildness; soft warmth
J. mildly critical
K. unusually; irregularly
L. cured; remedied
M. serving material ends
N. more obvious, direct
O. insulting

COMPREHENSION   No. right _____ × 10 = _____ %

VOCABULARY   No. right _____ × 10 = _____ %

No. of words 1250 ÷ time in seconds _____ × 60 = _____ WPM
WPM × Comprehension % = Reading Efficiency Rate _____

Chapter 8

MAKING INFERENCES AND JUDGMENTS

These last chapters introduce the most crucial and most difficult elements of good reading—those which can't be reduced to simple principles and formulas. Besides getting the main idea and paying attention to the context, good reading requires sensitivity and active participation.

One of the most important reading skills is drawing inferences from a writer's words. An *inference* is a conclusion drawn from what is known or assumed. When a writer implies, he hints or states indirectly; from that hint, you must infer or draw conclusions. You might consider making inferences similar to the old saying, "reading between the lines."

Let's look at some simple examples.

1. Mrs. Smith cashed her Social Security check at the bank.
   INFERENCE: Mrs. Smith is retired. (If you keep in mind the definition of inference—a conclusion drawn from something implied but not directly stated, you can assume that anyone cashing such a check is retired.)
2. Novels in the twentieth century have become much more frank in their depiction of sex. One only has to read the novels of Henry Miller, Jean Genet or Philip Roth to see this phenomenon.
   INFERENCES: (a) Henry Miller, Jean Genet and Philip Roth are contemporary novelists who write about sex with candor.
   (b) Literature before this century was more restrained in its treatment of sex.
   (c) The author of the sentence is familiar with these contemporary authors' works.
3. During the 1950's, Germany and Japan prospered once again, because American aid helped them recover from the losses they suffered in World War II.
   INFERENCES: (a) Germany and Japan were prosperous before their defeat.

135

(b) America had sufficient money to give them foreign aid.

(c) Without American aid, they might not have regained prosperity.

4. Sam is failing history. He claims he never studied. He just looked over toward Sally's final exam; then he wrote something on his own paper.

Based on the information, these inferences are inaccurate because they cannot be verified.

(a) Sam cheated by copying from Sally's test. (From the evidence, you cannot say for certain that he actually copied a test answer. This is a judgment, based on inconclusive evidence.)

(b) Sam has difficulty studying history. (Based on the evidence in the second sentence, this is another inaccurate inference. The reasons for Sam's failure to study are not given.)

(c) Sally will pass the test. (Nothing in the evidence suggests Sally's scholastic abilities.)

These examples are simple and obvious enough. They show that you can make inferences in several ways—by drawing conclusions, by predicting the possible outcome, or by interpreting the writer's illustrations. In other words, inferences require you to do some detective work, so that you can accurately interpret the information you are given.

Notice, too, that an inference can only be safely made from the author's words, and so it must be fairly narrow. You should not go outside the limits of what you are told or what the writer implies. Inferences cannot always accurately be made from general knowledge or personal opinion.

In real life, however, the situation is different. You make inferences all the time when you observe people. Suppose you are driving down a freeway, and you observe ahead a car weaving dangerously over all the lanes. You immediately infer that the driver is drunk. But you haven't actually observed the driver himself, only the path his car makes. Perhaps the driver had a heart attack. Or perhaps his steering mechanism failed. Your original inference, then, would be based on a false assumption.

Or suppose that standing before you in a supermarket checkout line is a scruffily dressed, barefoot, long-haired boy. You infer that he is a hippie, and that perhaps he subsists by pan-handling. But suppose the same boy were to take from his pocket a thick wad of money, mostly twenties and fifties. Is he a drug dealer? A successful bank robber? A rich kid playing hippie? With no more information, you can't be sure. Even if you observe him later suspiciously exchanging goods for money with another person, you still couldn't infer that he is selling drugs, for you haven't seen exactly what was exchanged.

Making inferences when you observe people is a relatively harmless diversion. But in reading, the case is different. The thing to remember is to infer only from those clues the author gives you. Just because a writer favors the war in Vietnam in one piece of writing does not necessarily permit you to assume that he is opposed to peaceful anti-war dissent—unless he alludes to that in another piece of writing.

The exercises which follow begin with simple practice in making inferences and gradually become more challenging. To begin, a fable is a little story that illustrates a moral truth. After you read this fable by Aesop, decide which moral truth he intended the reader to infer.

A dispute once arose between the Wind and the Sun as to which was the stronger of the two. They agreed, therefore, to try their strength upon a traveler to see which should be able to take his cloak off first. The Wind began and blew with all his might and main, a cold and fierce blast; but the stronger he blew the closer the traveler wrapped his cloak about him and the tighter he grasped it with his hands. Then broke out the Sun and with his welcome beams he dispersed the vapor and the cold. The traveler felt the genial warmth and as the Sun shone brighter and brighter, he sat down, overcome with the heat, and cast his cloak on the ground. Thus the Sun was declared the conqueror.

"The Wind and the Sun" from
*Aesop's Fables**

(1) Force is more effective than persuasion.
(2) Persuasion is more effective than force.
(3) The mighty rule the world.
(4) The meek shall inherit the earth.
(5) Competition breeds avarice.

Here is another, more sophisticated fable.

There was a merchant in Bagdad who sent his servant to market to buy provisions and in a little while the servant came back, white and trembling, and said, Master, just now when I was in the market-place I was jostled by a woman in the crowd and when I turned I saw it was Death that jostled me. She looked at me and made a threatening gesture; now, lend me your horse, and I will ride away from this city and avoid my fate. I will go to Samarra and there Death will not find me. The merchant lent him his horse, and the servant mounted it, and he dug his spurs in its flanks and as fast as the horse could gallop he went. Then the merchant went down to the market-place and he saw me standing in the crowd and he came to me and said, Why did you make a threatening gesture to my servant when you saw him this morning? That was not a threatening gesture, I said, it was only a start of surprise. I was astonished to see him in Bagdad, for I had an appointment with him tonight in Samarra.

W. Somerset Maugham, from
"Death Speaks" †

* (New York: The Viking Press, Inc., 1947), pp. 17–18.
† From *Sheppey* (London: William Heinemann, Ltd. and A. P. Watt & Son, 1933), p. 112.

Based on the evidence in the fable, mark for each statement:

   T—if the statement is probably true or if it makes an accurate inference;
   F—if the statement is probably false or if it makes an inaccurate inference;
   X—if the statement is not verifiable or if there is insufficient evidence to warrant the inference.

1. __F__ Death is a man, disguised as a servant.
2. __X__ Death is a clever woman.
3. __X__ The merchant thought his servant was foolish to go to Samarra.
4. __T__ The servant thought he could outwit Death.
5. __X__ Fate determines the time and place of man's death at birth.
6. __T__ No man can escape death.
7. __X__ Some men consciously or unconsciously seek death.
8. __T__ Some men consciously or unconsciously try to avoid death.

The following excerpt is from an article describing the weaknesses inherent in modern education. After you read the passage, mark T, F, or X.

> There are two sections to almost every school's statement of educational objectives—one for real, and one for show. The first, the real one, talks about academic excellence, subject mastery, and getting into college or a job. The other discusses the human purpose of school—values, feelings, personal growth, the full and happy life. It is included because everyone knows that it is important, and that it ought to be central to the life of every school. But it is only for show. Everyone knows how little schools have done about it.
>
> In spite of this, the human objectives describe the things all of us cite when we try to remember what "made a difference" in our school careers: the teacher who touched us as persons, or the one who ground out our lives to polish our intellects; the class that moved with the strength and grace of an Olympic team, or the dozens of lessons when each of us slogged separately toward the freedom of 3 o'clock. What we learned, and what we became, depended to a significant degree on how we felt about ourselves, our classmates, and our teachers. The schools were right—the human purposes *were* important. But with the exception of those teachers who were so rare we never forgot them, the schools did little to put their philosophy into practice.
>
>   TERRY BORTON, from "Reach, Touch, and Teach" *

1. __X__ Schools do little about the "human" purposes of education because they are over-crowded and too bureaucratic.
2. __X__ Those students who manage to receive both the practical and human objectives of education are probably exceptions.

* From the *Saturday Review*, January 18, 1969.

3. _____ The human objective of education is talked about in schools more to impress than to put into effect.

4. _____ Most teachers are too overworked to worry about teaching anything besides the practical ends of education.

5. _____ School administrators have done little to fulfill the human objectives because they consider getting into college or getting a good job more important goals.

6. _____ The writer implies that schools would like to help children to become better people but they don't really know how to go about it.

7. _____ Most teachers stress only the practical objectives in the classroom.

8. _____ Schools would be better if parents demanded better education for their children.

By now it should be evident that making accurate inferences requires attention only to the author's words, and not to your personal opinions or general knowledge. Even though you may think that schools fail partly because they are over-crowded, the author nowhere implies it.

The following selection is more difficult. After you read it, choose the most accurate inference for each question. And in the space provided, write the words from the passage that imply the answer.

Abroad in the world today is a monstrous falsehood, a consummate fabrication, to which all social agencies have loaned themselves and into which most men, women and children have been seduced. In previous writings, I have called this forgery "the Eleventh Commandment"; for such, indeed, has become the injunction: You Must Adjust!

Adjustment, that synonym for conformity that comes more easily to the modern tongue, is the theme of our swan song, the piper's tune to which we dance on the brink of the abyss, the siren's melody that destroys our senses and paralyzes our wills. But this is something known only to the few who have penetrated its disguises and glimpsed the death's head beneath: for the many, adjustment is the only way of life they know, the only way of life permitted to them by the powers that govern their existences from cradle to grave.

ROBERT M. LINDNER, from *Must You Conform?* *

1. Besides individual people, which of the following accepts and even fosters the order to conform? (a) social institutions (b) one's peers (c) political leaders (d) schools

_____ all social agencies _____

* (New York: Holt, Rinehart & Winston, Inc., 1956), p. 167.

2. How do most people accept the order to conform? (a) willingly yet grudgingly (b) unwillingly (c) willingly, possibly even happily (d) not evident from the passage

---

3. When do most people accept the order to conform? (a) during their youth (b) during their early married life (c) during their middle age (d) during their whole lifetime

    men & women & children

4. What difference is there between older culture's notions of conformity and modern society's? (a) there is no difference at all; conformity is a fact of human nature (b) older cultures demanded even more conformity than we do (c) older cultures demanded less conformity than ours (d) not evident from the passage

---

5. What is the effect of conformity on the individual? (a) it is good because men set their goals to a higher standard (b) it is very harmful because it denies individuality (c) it is not measurable (d) it is good because without it, society would be chaotic.

    it is the only thing they know

   Satire is a form of humorous writing in which a writer pokes fun at social institutions or at human weaknesses. Satire involves deliberate exaggeration and overstatement, so that you must infer from the author's words the real point he wants to make. The following selection satirizes what happens when "adult" movies are taken too seriously.

   > Once upon a time there was a young lad named Horatio Alger, who was determined to struggle and persevere and somehow get himself a good education. A good sex education.
   > But the little lad faced many hurdles. The first was the local school board, which voted 5-4 against showing Horatio any sex education films. The second was Horatio's parents, who voted 2-0 against allowing Horatio to attend any Adult Movies.
   > "Adult movies," thundered Horatio's father, "are corrupting the morals of our youth and destroying our American way of life."
   > So Horatio was 18 and on his own before he saw his first Adult Movie. He didn't, of course, understand it. But he thrust forth his chin and vowed to persevere.

For two years, Horatio persevered. He saw Adult Movies thrice weekly and twice on Saturdays. "It was a hard struggle," he said proudly on reaching 20, "but at last I have won myself a good sex education."

It was then that he met Miss Penelope Trueheart and fell in love.

"All I desire on this earth," he said, falling to his knees one night in her apartment, "is to be the father of your child and spend the rest of my life as your husband."

"Oh, dearest," said Miss Trueheart ecstatically, "when will we be married?"

"As soon as we have a child," said Horatio, drawing on his good sex education. "For we can't have one afterward, you know. People never do."

"And how do we have a child?" she asked, blushing modestly.

"There are several ways," said Horatio. "The easiest, I believe, is for you to smoke a cigarette on the couch. I will pounce on you. Your hand will go limp and the cigarette will fall on the carpet. (We can use an ashtray, I suppose, if you worry about fire.) And then you will cry."

"I don't smoke," said Miss Trueheart.

"Then we'll have to throw our clothes on the floor," said Horatio, "though it isn't very tidy. But please turn up the heat first as we have to lie under just a sheet and talk. Then I will go for a drive and you will cry."

"Will you take me in your arms, dearest?" she asked hesitantly:

"Yes," said Horatio. "In the shower."

"I don't have a shower," said Miss Truehart, close to tears.

"Well, I guess we can skip that," said Horatio dubiously, as he threw his tie on the floor. "Come, my love, I can hardly wait."

So they threw their clothes on the floor, got under the sheet, talked, and then Horatio dressed and went for a drive while Miss Trueheart cried.

But, oddly enough, though they faithfully repeated this routine every night for seven years; they never did have a child.

With his good sex education, Horatio privately blamed Miss Trueheart for neither smoking nor having a shower. But he was too gallant to say so.

Moral: Adult Movies may, indeed, destroy our way of life. And the human race along with it.

ARTHUR HOPPE, "Is Sex Old-
Fashioned?" *

Based on the evidence in the selection, decide if these conclusions are justified (J) or not justified (NJ).

1. __NJ__ Adult movies harm children because they depict sex too realistically.

2. __J__ Adult movies depict sex artificially, because they show the

* From the *San Francisco Chronicle*, September 15, 1968.

"before" and "after," which only gives the illusion that sex has
taken place.

3. _NT_ Children would not get silly, false notions about sex if their
parents did not avoid the subject.

4. _NO_ If children have formal sex education courses in school, they
will be encouraged to experiment with their new-found knowledge.

5. _NJ_ Children should not be taught sex formally, because they will
learn it naturally as adults.

6. _NT_ A child would probably not be harmed by seeing a typical
Hollywood romance movie.

7.   When Horatio tells Penelope they can't be married until they
have a child, because "people never do," the author implies
(mark all three):

   (a) _J_ some movie viewers interpret behavior on the
   screen as true-to-life

   (b) _NJ_ notions of morality presented in movies have
   degenerated so much in recent years, that youth has
   been corrupted

   (c) _NJ_ producers insist on depicting sex in adult
   movies because they know that viewers expect it

8. _NJ_ If parents prevent a child from learning about sex naturally,
he may be damaged in later years.

There is another kind of inference essential to good reading called a
judgment. The author's point of view toward his topic and the judgment
he tries to impart may not always be obvious. In fiction, especially, writers
usually describe a character's appearance and actions, leaving his judgment for you to infer. Connotation, context, and metaphors all come into
play in making judgments. Again, you have to look beneath the literal,
surface level to determine if the character is to be judged good or evil,
virtuous or cruel, immature or wise. This paragraph from the beginning
of a short story describes the main character, a parson, in detail:

> He was a short, very heavy man—obese, although oddly thin in the face
> and with square hands, flat-tipped fingers, no flesh between the knuckles.
> A narrow, flat forehead that with the years grew higher, although he
> never appeared to become bald; eyebrows that jutted out enormously
> long, curly and wiry, and small eyes beneath all this tangle as sharp as
> terriers', but blue. They were never tender or glazed with sentiment.
>
> His nose became larger and bonier as his forehead grew higher. As he
> grew older, as his face sank away from it, this nose was like the prow
> of Methodism rising out of a receding sea. The eyes might blaze, the
> eyebrows bristle, the forehead soar ever more lofty, but the nose was of
> chapel and sin. Around the bridge, it had a pinched look of virtue and
> condemnation.

A long upper lip, which might have been taken off a comedian; and a mouth that changed with time more than any other feature, starting off wide and broad-lipped and ending as a thin line, an opening slit for food or, almost nonexistent, clamped round a cigarette.

All this head, with its contradictions and discrepancies, rode too large for the short, heavy body. His back view, in suspended gray flannels and shirtsleeves, digging, weeding, mowing a lawn, was the rear of a squat old elephant—the same vast, solid gray folds ending in short, tubular legs, the same lumbering quality.

And yet he was deft. Until he became ill and lazy and clumsy, he could make or mend most things. He played chess in a series of vicious jabs, pouncing the pieces down, grunting, puffing great blasts of smoke, and usually winning—his one intellectual achievement.

He was a clergyman for one reason only—there was nothing else he could possibly have been.

PENELOPE MORTIMER, from "The Parson" *

Which of these descriptive statements best fits the author's judgment of the character?

(1) he is congenial and attractive to others despite his shortcomings;
(2) he is ugly and despicable despite his cleverness and intelligence;
(3) he is so pathetic and unattractive that he deserves sympathy and compassion rather than scorn.

In this paragraph, E. M. Forster describes a peculiar idiosyncracy of T. E. Lawrence, better known as the famed Lawrence of Arabia:

T. E. Lawrence, that desert hero, once told me that he did not think highly of the sea. He considered it overrated. He enjoyed teasing sailor-men and found them easy game, and when on board would make such remarks to them as, "I've been sitting upstairs on the verandah. I think I'll go now and rest in my room." Their infuriated reactions amused him. He never crossed the line, I think, but he would have regarded that ordeal as an opportunity for experiencing vulgarity. He was the aggressive landlubber—a refreshing type and a modern one. The landlubber gets covered with tar and chucked overboard, he turns green and is sick, but he has had his laugh and his say. He has made fun of the sea. Sacrilege!

E. M. FORSTER, "The Enchafed Flood" †

How does Forster judge Lawrence's attitude toward the sea?

(1) Lawrence was witty and irreverent; he loved to poke fun at things people took seriously;

* From *The New Yorker*, July 20, 1957, p. 20.
† From *Two Cheers for Democracy* (New York: Harcourt Brace Jovanovich, Inc., 1951), p. 265.

(2) Lawrence was cruel and merciless in his joking, unnecessarily hurting people's feelings;

(3) Lawrence was silly and juvenile and undoubtedly deserved to be thrown overboard.

The following passage is a bit more difficult.

> Flory had been fifteen years in Burma, and in Burma one learns not to set oneself up against public opinion. . . .
>
> He was not quite twenty when he came to Burma. His parents, good people and devoted to him, had found him a place in a timber firm. They had had great difficulty in getting him the job, had paid a premium they could not afford; later, he had rewarded them by answering their letters with careless scrawls at intervals of months. His first six months in Burma he had spent in Rangoon, where he was supposed to be learning the office side of his business. He had lived in a "chummery" with four other youths who devoted their entire energies to debauchery. And what debauchery! They swilled whisky which they privately hated, they stood round the piano bawling songs of insane filthiness and silliness, they squandered rupees by the hundred on aged Jewish whores with the faces of crocodiles. That too had been a formative period.
>
> From Rangoon he had gone to a camp in the jungle, north of Mandalay, extracting teak. The jungle life was not a bad one, in spite of the discomfort, the loneliness, and what is almost the worst thing in Burma, the filthy, monotonous food. He was very young then, young enough for hero worship, and he had friends among the men in his firm. There were also shooting, fishing, and perhaps once in a year a hurried trip to Rangoon—pretext, a visit to the dentist. Oh, the joy of those Rangoon trips! The rush to Smart and Mookerdum's bookshop for the new novels out from England, the dinner at Anderson's with beefsteaks and butter that had traveled eight thousand miles on ice, the glorious drinking bout! He was too young to realize what this life was preparing for him. He did not see the years stretching out ahead, lonely, eventless, corrupting.
>
> GEORGE ORWELL, from "Burmese Days" *

1. Which statement most accurately describes Flory? (a) a hard, dedicated worker unfortunately led astray by the wrong sort of friends (b) a callow, ne'er-do-well who is undisciplined and ungrateful toward his parents (c) an immature, selfish fool whose intentions are nevertheless basically good.
2. Which of the following is probably an *inaccurate* inference? Flory's parents (a) have enough money, but are not excessively rich (b) try to protect their son (c) blind themselves to Flory's disgraceful behavior (d) bought Flory a job (e) are disappointed in Flory's excesses.
3. How does Orwell intend you to respond to Flory? (a) with contempt (b) with admiration (c) with pity (d) with humor.

* From *The Orwell Reader* (New York: Harcourt Brace Jovanovich, Inc., 1956), p. 20.

This following exercise is difficult, but it will show you the kind of interpretation you will be asked to do in Part II. After you read the passage, mark the first seven questions with T, F, or X as before.

In our own time practices marked as obscene have been beaten down only to rise again. New methods, from photography to the paint-spray can of the New Graffiti, have quickly been pressed into service. If in the course of time occasional words have disappeared from the language, force from above is hardly to be credited with a kill; new ones rose to take their place, and the principal old words lived on. Today, with monosyllables referring to sex and excretion forbidden in newspapers and on television, they are nevertheless displayed and available at low cost in the paperback book racks of drugstore and airport, and there are specialized centers for such books near Times Square in New York City and doubtless somewhere in every city in the United States. They are part of the regular fare of today's theater and are finding their way into movies labeled "for adults only" (sometimes even "for mature adults only"). Movies and still pictures in magazines, especially those accessible in price and content to the relatively uneducated poor, seem to be the principal current targets of the censors. We live, to be sure, in an age that is surely corrupt if not depraved, but causes and effects are intermingled, and actual damage done by so-called obscenity is yet to be measured.

THEODOR ROSEBURY, from *Life on Man**

1. __F__ Notions of what is obscene and what is not have remained the same within our culture.

2. __T__ Obscene words and practices often disappear spontaneously to be replaced by new forms.

3. __T__ Enforcement of anti-obscenity laws is hypocritical and arbitrary.

4. __X__ A national board of censors should be established to enforce laws against obscene materials.

5. __X__ Obscenity directed toward rich, educated audiences is sometimes ignored by censors.

6. __X__ It is irrational to ban some words from television and newspapers when they are commonly found in books, magazines, and films.

7. __X__ There is sufficient evidence to prove that obscenity, when openly available, harms the individual, especially those with latent criminal inclinations.

8. __d__ Which of these four statements best describes the author's judgment of obscene words? (a) he is exceedingly tolerant and feels obscene material should be accessible to anyone who wants it; (b) he is dismayed more by the lack of intelligent and sensible enforcement than by obscenity itself; (c) he

* (New York: The Viking Press, Inc., 1969), pp. 87–88.

is exceedingly critical of public lenience toward obscenity because he feels our society is corrupt enough without making it worse; (d) his judgment is not evident from the passage.

READING SELECTION 8 A. J. Liebling, "R. I. P.—John Lardner" *

Until his death in 1963, A. J. Liebling was one of America's finest journalists, whose articles on "The Wayward Press" were famous for their wit and candor. In this short eulogy, which appeared in "The Talk of the Town," Liebling relates his fondness for John Lardner in his characteristically unsentimental but nostalgic manner.

John Lardner once wrote, "You may have noticed that these playwrights who are not afraid of emotion tend to write things for the stage that explain all too clearly why other writers *are* afraid of emotion." He was one of the other writers. His style reminded a reader of a jockey riding a race with something in hand; he never scrubbed or whipped. Yet it is hard to write with any restraint at all about his death at forty-seven.

The style accorded with the man. As a man and as a writer, Lardner was reserved. His humor was direct without being blunt, his use of understatement graceful without being soft. He was as easy to like as he was hard to know. We had the pleasure of his benevolent acquaintance from the time he was a boy. His first piece for *The New Yorker* appeared on December 26, 1931, when he was nineteen. The last that he read the proofs on ran on March 19 this year, a week before he died. Oddly, both were about broadcasting—the first, a slight bit of straight-faced humor about a radio storyteller; the last, one of the numerous television departments he wrote during the past two and a half years.

In the time between, Lardner wandered far and wrote about most things under the sun. A younger brother, David, was a *New Yorker* war correspondent when he was killed at Aachen in 1944. In the following year, John wrote for us accounts of the fighting on Iwo Jima and Okinawa that were as good as J. W. De Forest's reporting of combat in the Civil War, which in our opinion is almost perfect. David's death may have brought emotion closer to the surface, but without troubling the medium or dulling the eye. John was naturally brave; when he saw blinding bomb flashes by night, he used to walk *toward* them to see better. After the war, Lardner substituted for the late Wolcott Gibbs as drama critic of *The New Yorker*, during Gibbs's long absences, and did so with a felicity of which the quotation at the beginning of this notice is sufficient evidence. Then he chose to devote himself to writing about television.

John grew up in the shadow of a father who was a great writer. This is

* From *The Most of A. J. Liebling* (New York: Simon & Schuster, Inc., 1963), pp. 313–14.

a handicap shared by only an infinitesimal portion of any given generation, but it did not intimidate him. He made his own way. As a humorist, reporter, sportswriter, and critic, he found his style—a mixture, unlike any other, of dignity and gaiety, precision and surprise. He was a funny writer, and, though he would never have admitted it, an artist. In one of his last pieces, he wrote that his father "struggled constantly to make his stuff as good and as true as it could be." He might have been writing about himself.

Through all the years we knew him, John remained outwardly the same: handsome, grave, and equable, only the corners of his mouth, and of the eyes behind the thick lenses, betraying occasionally his private amusement with what he thought about. If he was sad—and there was much in his life that might have made him so—he never talked about it. He was often for long hours a tall, vertical silence in front of a bar with a cigar in his hand, dominating by his dignity a saloonful of noisy newspapermen, yet there was nobody idiot enough to resent this withdrawal. He did not mind jokers who suggested that he must be an Indian. At long intervals, he would look down at the floor and, after another long interval, up at the ceiling and blow a smoke ring. He had not worked for the *Herald Tribune*, his first employer, since 1933, but to the last he maintained a sentimental affiliation with the saloon next door. We think we will never enter it without turning our head to the right, by reflex, to look in his favorite corner, or know a night that we won't be sad not finding him.

READING SELECTION 8

COMPREHENSION

Do not refer to the article to answer these questions. Choose one of the items that best answers each question, and mark the letter in the space provided.

1. __B__ During his career, John Lardner wrote (a) only for *The New Yorker* (b) for both *The New Yorker* and the *Herald Tribune* (c) for both *The New Yorker* and *The New York Times* (d) for *The New Yorker,* the *Herald Tribune* and other major daily newspapers in New York.

2. __C__ Which was specifically *not* mentioned as one of Lardner's journalistic assignments? (a) drama reviews (b) television reviews (c) horse racing analyses (d) sportswriting.

3. __C__ Because Lardner's father was also a great writer, the son (a) felt insecure and inferior around him (b) competed fiercely and bitterly to emulate him (c) took after his father and was successful in his own right without becoming jealous or hostile (d) always felt intimidated.

4. __a__ When Lardner died, his last assignment for *The New Yorker* was writing (a) television and broadcasting reviews (b) drama reviews (c) retrospective pieces on famous Civil War battles (d) humorous anecdotes about journalists.

5. __B__ The quotation from one of Lardner's drama reviews states: "You may have noticed that these playwrights who are not afraid of emotion tend to write things for the stage that explain all too clearly why other writers *are* afraid of emotion." This implies (a) a harsh criticism of playwrights who write with too little feeling (b) Lardner's humorous way of admitting his own faults as a writer (c) a clever way of poking fun at bad playwrights who indulge in excessive emotion (d) a tongue-in-cheek criticism of the then current state of Broadway plays.

6. __b/c__ With reference to the same quotation, Liebling says that Lardner was one of the "other writers," which suggests (a) that Lardner was always unemotional and objective in his viewpoint (b) that Lardner was a precise, truthful yet witty writer (c) that Lardner was restrained in his writing style and shied away from emotion (d) that Lardner's style was emotional and flamboyant.

7. __b__ Leibling implies that Lardner's friends considered him admirable as a writer (a) but difficult to get along with (b)

but difficult to get close to (c) but unapproachable and stern (d) but arrogant and haughty.

8. ___*a*___ After Lardner's younger brother, David, was killed in 1944, Lardner's reports from Iwo Jima and Okinawa were (a) a bit more emotional perhaps, but still written with calmness, courage, and lack of sentimentality (b) much more emotional, often bordering on bitterness and irrationality (c) unchanged because Lardner was wholly realistic about the realities of war (d) not quite as good as deForest's reports of the Civil War.

9. ___*C*___ Lardner's friends at his favorite saloon often jokingly called him an Indian because of (a) his impassive, inscrutable face (b) his habit of blowing smoke rings from his cigar (c) his habit of standing silently and with dignity for long hours at a time (d) his habitual silence.

10. ___*b*___ Which of the following best describes this selection? (a) a sentimental piece, bordering on the maudlin (b) a thoughtful, sympathetic eulogy—a dignified lament for an esteemed journalist (c) an impartial, objective recounting of a great journalist's career (d) a restrained yet witty comment on contemporary journalism as practiced by one writer.

VOCABULARY

From the lettered choices, find the best definition for each vocabulary item, and mark the letter in the space provided.

1. ___*F*___ direct without being *blunt*
2. ___*K*___ his *benevolent* acquaintance
3. ___*D*___ without troubling the *medium*
4. ___*G*___ did so with a *felicity*
5. ___*C*___ only an *infinitesimal* portion
6. ___*M*___ John remained handsome, *grave*
7. ___*I*___ did not *intimidate* him
8. ___*B*___ *betraying* his private amusement
9. ___*E*___ a sentimental *affiliation*
10. ___*L*___ without turning, by *reflex*

A. pleasant, effective style
B. revealing; giving away
C. insignificantly small
D. instrument; agency of communication
E. association; connection
F. abrupt; unpleasantly frank
G. happiness; blissfulness

H. unending; interminable
I. make fearful; threaten
J. filled with danger
K. good; kind
L. involuntary movement; habit
M. solemn; dignified
N. deceiving; being a traitor to
O. environment; condition of life

COMPREHENSION No. right ——— × 10 = ———%

VOCABULARY No. right ——— × 10 = ———%

No. of words 600 ÷ time in seconds ——— × 60 = ——— WPM

WPM × Comprehension % = Reading Efficiency Rate ———————

Chapter 9

OPINION AND PERSUASION

How many times have you wanted to read accurate background information about a controversial topic only to find that every article expresses a different opinion? How do you know which writers are reputable or which opinions are correct interpretations of the facts? The problem is aggravated because so much material is written that you naturally may come away bewildered and confused. Because you are likely to confront these problems in your efforts to be informed, it is essential that you establish some critical standards for evaluating what you read.

To begin with, you should know the difference between *fact* and *opinion*. A fact is a statement about something that actually exists or that has actually occurred. More important, a fact can be verified—either by personal observation or by checking with authoritative sources. These are facts:

Water freezes at 32° Fahrenheit at sea level.
A yard equals three feet or thirty-six inches.
New York City's population is more than eight million.
Britain has done away with the death penalty.

An opinion is a conclusion or judgment that is maintained with confidence, but which *falls short of positive knowledge*. That is, an opinion cannot be verified as a fact can be. These are opinions:

Sally is tall. (How tall is tall?)
We should destroy all chemical and biological weapons.
San Francisco is a better city to live in than Los Angeles.
Television entertainment is mediocre.

There is nothing at all wrong with a writer expressing his opinion or offering an interpretation, for you are free to accept or reject his conclusions. But as you probably know from composition courses, a writer must support

153

his opinions, not with other opinions, but with facts, statistics, personal observations, pertinent illustrations, and so forth. A writer who feels that the Mafia is a threat to legitimate business does not adequately support that opinion merely by saying they are big-time crooks. That is only another opinion, an allegation, rather than verifiable proof. Here are two examples of conflicting opinions supported by other opinions.

(1) The death penalty is just. If a murderer takes a life, he should have to pay with his own life.

(2) The death penalty is unjust. Men have no moral right to take a man's life, even a murderer's. Besides, the death penalty does not deter potential criminals.

Although both these opinions are honest, as stated, they still fall short of *positive* knowledge. In fact, this topic would be extremely difficult to support with facts, because even if reliable research had been done, one could still question the interpretation of the evidence. The real difficulty with reading materials that express an opinion is that two writers may interpret the same set of facts entirely differently. Two writers visiting Vietnam during the same time may observe the same events, yet their reports may conflict in nearly every way. One writer may conclude that the war is senseless and immoral; the other that the war is truly helping the South Vietnamese to achieve a stable political future. Are both right; are both wrong? Before you can form an intelligent opinion, you have to read many more articles, for two accounts of a complex situation are not sufficient.

Experience, then, is one solution. But you can also evaluate individual articles by establishing critical criteria in the form of these questions:

(1) Who is the writer? What authority does he have to comment on his subject? Is he qualified? Is the man dressed in a white coat in the aspirin commercial really a "doctor"? Is the book he refers to really an "authoritative medical report"? Is a veterinarian qualified to offer an opinion on human heart transplants?

(2) Are his opinions based on first-hand knowledge and personal observation or only on hearsay, allegations, or on other people's opinions?

(3) Does he support his opinions with facts and illustrations or merely with other opinions? Is his evidence reasonable and convincing?

(4) What are his motives? Does he stand to gain (or lose) anything from readers accepting (or rejecting) his opinion?

(5) Does he anticipate questions which the intelligent reader might raise, or does he ignore possible critical questions? Is his evidence complete, or are there loopholes, inconsistencies or ambiguities left unresolved?

(6) Are his opinions honest and objective—that is, are they drawn from the facts and information presented? Or are they subjective, based only on

his own feelings, prejudices and emotions? Are his conclusions independent from his own motives?

The last critical question needs further explanation. No man can ever
be totally objective. When a writer examines a situation, he naturally
passes judgment—by the words he chooses in particular. Most good persuasive writing combines and balances objectivity and subjectivity to
effect. But you should guard against persuasive devices that appeal only
to your emotions or that rely on flimsy evidence. You might keep in mind
the illustration of a scientist who discovers after extensive research that
his original hypothesis was wrong. Should he doctor his findings to fit his
original theory, or should he redo the theory? Writers must interpret the
world as they see it; the point is, however, that some writers offer more
substantial evidence than others.

A good bit of the reading you will do is persuasive in intent. With the
exception of textbooks and fiction, most writing offers an opinion or an
interpretation that the writer hopes is convincing. Persuasive writing is
an attempt to move you to action, to question your ideas and possibly to
change them, or perhaps merely to give you another, less popular point of
view. Every time you pick up a magazine or turn on the television, you
are confronted with exhortations to buy a particular brand of mouthwash,
to change your brand of cigarette or to stop smoking, or whatever. But
these attempts to persuade are not the same as propaganda. Propaganda
intends to manipulate your thinking by deliberate and conscious methods.
Propaganda relies on half-truths, distortions of reality, inflammatory or
slanted language—in other words, it appeals to fears and irrational prejudices. Persuasive writing, on the other hand, attempts to convince through
appeals to reason and understanding. But an effective writer may choose,
as a legitimate device, appeals to your emotions—to your sense of injustice,
anger, pity, outrage—without trying to manipulate or coerce you into
changing your beliefs.

The exercises for this chapter will give you some guided experience in
reading passages that are persuasive in intent. The first two articles discuss
the problem of hunger. The first is by TRB, who has written editorials for
The New Republic for several years. This article was written in early 1969
during the Senate hearings on malnutrition and worm-infestation in the
United States. To answer the questions, you may refer to the selection.

> Skip this piece if you have a weak stomach. It's about worms. Worms in
> people. Poor people. By almost common consent Americans shun it. I
> notice reporters who cover Sen. George McGovern's hearings on hunger
> sidestep it. Facts are facts. Here they are.
>   Charles Fraser is a quiet-voiced executive of a private resort area in
> South Carolina with tennis and golf and some of the finest beaches in the
> world. A lot of local blacks have parasite infections and Mr. Fraser

thought it could be eradicated. To his surprise he found that in the entire *US Cumulative Index Medicus,* 1961–67, there is no article on mass eradication. There are 224 articles on symptoms and side effects of roundworms (Ascaris) and whipworms (Trichuris) but nothing on mass control.

Mr. Fraser knew that farm journals abound in pieces on worm control in cattle—in pigs. If your dog has worms you know it's sick and you do something. Mass infestation in people, it appears, is different.

The Fraser group checked further. The *Index* showed 18 articles on community parasite control in Russian medical journals; also in Japan and other far-off places. But these weren't translated.

Well then, the group asked, is infection prevalent in the US? Spot tests by doctors astonished them. In some impoverished areas three out of four had either roundworms or whipworms. Not just in South Carolina, it appeared, but among low-income people in 153 similar counties in seven states. Maybe one to three million people. (No government survey has been made.)

The McGovern subcommittee heard disgusting clinical details. Sen. Ellender (D., La.), a well-meaning conservative, acted as a kind of straight man. He told a harrowing personal experience. "When about eight, I remember running to my mother because of the worms coming out of my mouth. . . ." The matter was brought to medical attention, he said. Then "a campaign of all of the people" stamped it out. Why don't "local people" (blacks) act here, Ellender asked?

Doctors explained patiently that "personal hygiene" is difficult in the near-animal conditions of some areas. Blacks and some whites live in shanties without running water; in many cases without privies. People use the woods. The parasite ova contaminate the soil. Ignorance is such, they testified, that many actually believe the worms "come from sugar." How about kindergarten-type educational leaflets to inform them? The government prints none. How about films? HEW has a library of 480 films for national distribution on child-rearing; not one on worm infestation.

Officially, worms don't exist. Actually, some witnesses guessed "about a million" children are infested. "It is our firm conclusion," Mr. Fraser testified, "that nothing of any substance is presently being done in the US to eradicate the continuing heavy worm infestation of low-income families."

Mrs. Landon Butler, a trim, slender white volunteer worker in Beaufort County, S.C., said, "I found entire families existing on rice, sweet water and bread, often rationed in small amounts." When individual children are treated for worms, she said, they go home and are immediately reinfected. Others noted that a poor family might, perhaps, borrow $1,500 to build a new pigsty under OEO programs, but not to install a pump, a well, or a hygienic bathroom.

Dr. James Carter, nutritionist from Vanderbilt University, has worked in Guatemala, Nigeria and Egypt, and said hunger symptoms in children here are about the same; in samples he found "distended stomachs in 41 percent," attributed to secondary effects of roundworms.

In bald terms, when food is swallowed it's a question who gets it, child or worm. Between 1960–64 the US sent over $392 million abroad, he said, to help underdeveloped countries get "water supplies and waste disposal systems." It would have been nice, he said mildly, to have had some of that money here.

Sen. McGovern is pushing his astonishing inquiry. He has beat a Senate effort to cut his funds. He has won astonishing support from Sen. Hollings (D., S.C.). He has even got assistance from the Department of Agriculture. Hunger, it is now believed, causes irreversible brain damage in children. And these children, McGovern notes, are not merely hungry from birth; they are hungry before birth, in their mother's womb.

Dr. Robert Coles of Harvard had trouble controlling his anger. Fresh from surveys, he and a team of doctors tried to get aid from the Department of Agriculture. But spokesmen said they feared Congress—the chairmen of agriculture committees particularly. After all, the billions spent are to support farm prices, not feed the hungry. Rep. Jamie Whitten is chairman of the House Appropriations subcommittee on agriculture. Coles charges Whitten's Mississippi district "has an infant mortality that rivals any place in the world—including India."

Once in the intestine, an ascaris worm grows to 6 to 14 inches. In the normal life cycle the immature worm migrates from the bloodstream to the intestines by way of the lungs (often causing pulmonary symptoms or bleeding). Fifty worms of this size in a child are classed as "moderate" in medical articles, Mr. Fraser said.

It is hard, of course, to teach a hungry child. Sen. Ellender, age 78, appeared nonplussed that areas in Louisiana are still heavily infested. Apparently, he thought it was all ended when he was eight. He said he would visit the communities. "This has been kept under cover," explained Dr. E. J. Lease, University of South Carolina, "for reasons that you can guess as well as I. This matter has not ever really been taken before the public."

"If I brought in a jar of some child's roundworms," Mr. Fraser said, "a great many people would be thoroughly nauseated. It is the sort of thing that is left unsaid, undiscussed and unreported throughout the US."

A good note to close on! Let's not disturb folks. The thought of that jar upsets refined people. Things should be kept in their place, in the . . . well, let's skip it. Sleep well, good people—only a few million kids are affected.

TRB, "Sleep Well" *

1. Is the writer qualified to comment on the subject of malnutrition? Does he appear to be well-informed?

2. Is his opinion based on first-hand information and personal observation?

3. How does TRB support his opinions? What sort of evidence does he use to warrant his conclusions?

4. Are his opinions subjective, objective, or an effective combination of both?

5. Is this article convincing or not? How can you justify your answer?

* From *The New Republic*, March 8, 1969, p. 6.

6. Are his opinions motivated by self-gain or by honesty and compassion for hungry children?

7. What is the effect of the last line? "Sleep well, good people—only a few million kids are affected."

8. Which best describes TRB's organization of the evidence? (a) a description of poor rural areas in the South and a criticism of government spending in irrelevant areas (b) a description of the Senate hearings, statistics to support the incidents of hunger and worm-infestation, and a criticism of foreign aid and farm subsidies (c) a comparison of the amounts of money spent on foreign aid and on government subsidies to farmers; a description of sanitary conditions in Southern rural areas.

9. What is TRB's attitude toward his subject? (a) he is indignant and outraged that a rich country ignores the problems of hunger (b) he is sarcastic and bitter about both public and governmental apathy (c) he is confident that changes will result from public exposure and publicity of the Senate hearings (d) both a and b (e) a, b, and c.

Edward Keating was one of five Americans who went to Biafra in early 1969 as an observer for the American Committee to Keep Biafra Alive. Although the Biafran war is over, Keating's description of a feeding station for starving refugees could have taken place in any country ravaged by war and famine.

> When I think of Biafra, I think of a small wicker basket I bought in the refugee camp at Umunwamma. It cost five shillings; it took an old man three days to make; it costs that old man ten shillings to buy food for one day.
>
> The economy is insane. There is almost no currency in circulation. Farmers are the major cash earners and since they don't believe in banks, they bury whatever they receive, thus further restricting available currency.
>
> Just as there is almost no currency, there are almost no commodities to buy—a few fruits and vegetables, snails or stock fish.
>
> In the market place, a cup of salt costs $5.50. Meat, when there is any, costs 12 shillings a pound; a two-and-a-half-pound chicken sells for $14.40.
>
> We were frequently asked if we had a cigarette. They sell for $7.20 a pack in Biafra.
>
> In any community you enter, 85 per cent of the people are refugees. Many go to communities due to the vast food shortage. And so not only are they no longer producing any food, they are adding to numbers which must be fed on meagre supplies. The supply of locally grown produce, such as yams, casavas, bananas, greens, spices and peppers, had to be stretched far beyond its ability to stretch.
>
> Now the people are kept alive through the feeding centers run by Caritas (the Catholic Welfare Agency) and the World Council of Churches.

And yet, the Biafrans are serene. They smile readily, are of long endurance, and are extraordinarily polite, not just to foreigners but, more importantly, among themselves.

Daily life for everyone is directed at one thing: survival. We lived as guests of the state and subsisted on virtually starvation rations.

Very early one morning—in order to avoid creating ready targets for bombers—we visited a feeding station at Nguru, run by the Holy Ghost fathers. Four thousand women were fed there.

"It is the only food most of them get," a priest told us. "We feed them six days a week. We have Mass on Sunday. Not that we place Mass over food," he insisted grimly, "it's just . . . there isn't enough for every day."

The women sat everywhere; some had walked many miles and then sat patiently waiting for their daily meal. Each woman carried her own little dish or pail into which was poured an orange flecked liquid (high protein and vitamins known as formula two), a ball of garri and maybe half an ounce of stock fish.

Several hundred yards away 3000 children were being fed the same diet. Among them were hundreds of older boys with sticks to keep the children in order and to prevent the bigger children from taking food from the smaller.

Although there were thousands of small children, hungry, exhausted, many cut off from their mothers, there was almost no crying. I was told that African children cry only under unendurable circumstances.

Six months ago the protein shortage was so acute that only drastic and immediate aid saved most of Biafra from dying. The protein crisis is over.

In its place, however, rises a new crisis that is virtually insoluble. In their desperate need, the people have eaten not only all the yams and garri throughout the entire country, they have also eaten the plant seeds. Planting season has arrived and there is no seed to plant.

Within 60 to 90 days Biafra faces its greatest crisis. Carbohydrates on a massive scale must be brought in.

Planes can't handle the job. While 100 tons per night of proteins can stabilize one crisis, it would require a minimum of 2500 tons per night to solve the carbohydrate problem. There is neither enough landing strip nor enough planes.

And while the relief agencies try to solve the insoluble thousands of Biafrans continue to die daily.

In a refugee camp at Oboro, I saw an infant perched on the edge of a slat bed, staring silently and sightlessly ahead. She was not yet two years old. Curled up beside her was a figure, small, inert, its hair turned blond, a sure sign of advanced starvation. You could not tell the sex or age of the figure.

"What is it, a boy?" I asked the sister in charge.

"No, she is the child's mother."

EDWARD M. KEATING, "The Face
of a Starving Nation" *

* From the *San Francisco Chronicle*, February 13, 1969.

1. What are the writer's qualifications?
2. Is his opinion based on first-hand information and personal observation?
3. How does the author support his opinions?
4. Are Keating's opinions directly stated or merely implied, leaving the reader to draw his own conclusions?
5. Are the writer's opinions subjective, objective, or effectively balanced between the two?
6. This article can best be described as (a) an historical account of the Biafran war, especially its effect on the food supply (b) a statistical analysis of the Biafran economy and a description of the welfare agencies' efforts to help the refugees (c) a description of the Biafran people and their ordeal with a failing economy, food shortages, and poor conditions in the refugee camps.
7. At the end, Keating describes a mother whom he mistook for a small child. What is the effect of this illustration? (a) he shocks the reader into realizing the severity of starvation (b) he criticizes the refugee centers for not doing more to help (c) he illustrates an alarming experience which the reader will not soon forget (d) both a and c (e) a, b, and c.

The following two editorials describe and interpret the so-called "Siege of Chicago" by the Weatherman faction of the S.D.S. during the Chicago Eight conspiracy trial in late 1969. Although the demonstration was planned as an anti-war protest, the result was far different. Both editorials attack the demonstration, but each offers a different opinion of its significance. After you read both editorials, answer the questions for analysis, referring to the selections if necessary.

In the standard lexicon of Communists and revolutionaries the enemy [capitalism "imperialism"] is characterized as "running dogs." The young scum who brought madness to the streets of the near north side Wednesday night have a variant. They refer to the whole constituted order, from government thru the military and law-enforcing arm down to the huge majority of law-abiding citizens, as "pigs."

Wednesday night these mobsters, rioters, vandals, and pillagers were the running dogs. They behaved worse than any pig ever could, for pigs, at least, are self-respecting animals. Animals these people were—fighting police, injuring 18 of their number, overturning cars, breaking windows, beating motorists and passers-by.

This hoodlum conduct was mindless and meaningless. What ideological point or intellectual position could be registered by such behavior?

Moreover, this rabble went out of the way looking for trouble. The revolutionaries evidently sought what they call a "confrontation" with police when they assembled in Lincoln park. When the police refused to oblige, the mob spilled into the streets. When the main force was turned back, it split into what the organizers call "guerrilla" formations, and began an advance, between trot and run, on shops, restaurants, high-rise buildings, and other targets at hand. The windows of hundreds of parked cars were smashed and the bodies of the cars marred and dented.

The weapons employed in this senseless destruction and in attacks on police and civilians were poles, boards, baseball bats, crowbars, rocks, bottles, and potatoes studded with razor blades.

We read with astonishment in some segments of the press that the perpetrators of this carnival of violence could appropriately be described as "radicals," or, even more mildly, as "kids," and that what they were doing was "demonstrating" or "protesting." This is equivalent to describing the enforcers of the Mafia as instructors in adult education.

It is difficult these days to tell the splintered elements of the hoodlum left without a program. To most citizens the whole kit and caboodle— S. D. S., Progressive Labor, hippies, the "Conspiracy"—represent distinctions without a difference. The current onslaught against Chicago is supposedly under the direction of the "Weatherman" faction of Students for a Democratic Society. It operates on the wishful thought that a worldwide revolution is under way, spearheaded by black, brown, and yellow "Third World" peoples with the communist North Vietnamese in the lead.

If so, the abstention of the Black Panthers and other Negro militants from Wednesday night's mob action hardly signifies solidarity. The Black Panthers can hardly be regarded as a moderate and reasonable organization, but even they had no inclination to join the white syndicate gangsters who tried to reenact the street brawling at the Democratic national convention in August, 1968.

Mayor Daley moderately observed at his press conference yesterday that he hoped that those who were so critical of the city and its police in the 1968 incidents might be disposed to revise their thinking. We doubt if that is going to happen, for once a professional carper is caught with his fiction he is unlikely to reform. But even those most inclined to tear down Chicago's reputation will be hard put to find that the conduct of the police Wednesday night was less than professional and restrained.

"Mad Dogs in the Streets" *

Never having covered a real revolution before, I got to Lincoln Park early so I wouldn't miss a thing.

I knew that if the revolution was successful, it would be my last, since it is customary for revolutionary governments to shoot newsmen. I didn't want to miss anything that important, especially with a weekend coming up.

The size of the SDS crowd surprised me. At most, 300 people huddled around a bonfire, or paced nervously amid the trees.

Now, 300 people might seize the principality of Monaco, or even a dean's office. But that didn't seem like enough to overwhelm 11,000 policemen, plus 3,000,000 or so unfriendly citizens.

And, frankly, the people in the park did not look like they could seize a geriatrics ward without a good tussle.

* Editorial, from the *Chicago Tribune*, October 10, 1969, p. 18.

They were talking tough, as always, using a lot of Negro slang and greaser jargon, mixed in with Marxist slogans, which is not an easy way to talk if you have a master's degree in anthropology and your father is a stockbroker.

But like most SDS'ers, they grew up in such rough-and-tumble jungles as Glencoe and Lake Forest, where they had knock-down brawls with their baby-sitters, which they probably lost.

History tells us, of course, that most revolutions are started by intellectuals and members of the upper classes. But they usually goad the peasants and workers into doing the fighting.

So, while a pretty young lady led everybody in a love chant for Che, I looked around the park for any peasants or workers who might be hidden away.

A middle-aged man was sitting on a bench, but he said he wasn't part of the revolution. "I'm just watching. I hope the cops kill those fairies."

That's the SDS's biggest problem. Nobody wants to join. Most college students think they are noisy bores. Militant blacks think they are suicidal loonies. And the white working man, whose alleged unhappiness the SDS wants to exploit, would be less unhappy if he could stomp on the SDS.

This is why the SDS is the fastest shrinking revolutionary force around.

So it appeared that the 300 in the park would have to do it alone. Being outnumbered, they used surprise as a tactic.

One minute they were chanting slogans. The next, somebody shouted: "To the Drake," and they began running out of the park.

The Chicago revolution was on. At first I was confused about the destination. The Drake is probably the city's most aristocratic old hotel. I wondered if they had suddenly abandoned the revolution and were rushing to meet their parents for dinner and dancing in the Camellia House.

But no. The Drake was to be the symbol of wealth, luxury and all the other things they know, from experience, but are not as good as work and sweat, which they have read about.

As they jogged from the park, they began protesting the war in Vietnam by breaking windows in the Chicago Historical Society, a notorious arm of the military-industrial complex.

And they dealt a blow to racial injustice, caving in the windows of a barber shop, an antique shop and the Red Star Inn.

Moving down Clark St., they smashed the windows of car after car, store after store. The idea seemed to be that society would collapse from the sniffles if you broke all its windows.

For several blocks, they were unhindered. The police, surprised at first, were forming ahead.

That would be the big moment of the Revolution. And as they approached the police, the SDS'ers swaggered, just as they had seen the tough kids do when they drove through city neighborhoods.

At Division St., they met the police. They charged. A moment later they ran the other way and took off down side streets, resuming their window-breaking.

The police had pulled a sneaky trick. Instead of flailing anything that moved, as they did during the Democratic National Convention, they acted coolly, professionally, made quick arrests, and kept the head-busting to a minimum. It was the most remarkable personality change since Mr. Hyde.

The SDS found itself scattered all over the Near North Side. And it is harder to be brave, and charge police lines, in groups of four or five. The rear rank is too near the front.

By midnight, the student warriors were either in jail, an emergency ward, or straggling back to the pad.

By Thursday morning, they had shamelessly resorted to sending the SDS girls out to confront the police in Grant Park.

Most of the girls, incidentally, didn't wear bras, which is probably just as good a way to get the boys home from Vietnam as breaking windows.

They flung themselves at the police lines, so the police arrested Celeste and Kathie, Judy and Suzie, Linda and Dee, and even Phoebe. The other girls surrendered their clubs and lead pipes, burst into tears, and gave up for the day.

Although the broadcasts and headlines have made it sound like the Battle of the Bulge, the revolution hasn't been much by modern standards of urban whoopee.

If the mini-revolution proved anything, it is only that the SDS doesn't have many members left, and those who remain couldn't fight their way into a Polish wedding.

By Thursday night, they had retreated to the suburbs and were last reported boldly occupying some churches in Evanston.

I think it is safe for us to come out now.

MIKE ROYKO, "S.D.S. 'Tigers' A
Sorry Sight" *

1. What kinds of evidence do the writers use to support their opinions?

2. What opinions of the "Weatherman" rampage do each of the editorials offer? Are they convincing?

3. Are there any examples of inflammatory or slanted language in either editorial? If so, underline them.

4. Is each editorial's approach to the incident subjective, objective, or balanced in its point of view?

The following editorial appeared in the *Wall Street Journal* the day Apollo 11 was launched, the first successful manned expedition to the moon. It is a fine example of a balanced, well-reasoned editorial that lacks the emotional impact of the two editorials on hunger, yet it makes the reader consider the space program with caution.

---

* From the *Chicago Daily News,* October 10, 1969.

If this morning's scheduled launch of the Apollo 11 is a source of vicarious adventure for most Americans, it should serve as a cause for reflection as well. A successful attempt to land a man on the moon is a space age milestone; it also may mark the end of an era on earth when the benefits of advancing technology could be taken for granted.

For more perceptive observers, the awareness has grown recently that technological advance is at best a mixed blessing. Achievements in the name of human progress may open the way to human disaster as well. Thus, tapping the fantastic energy locked in an atom's nucleus makes possible nearly limitless power to light homes and run machines—or to destroy entire nations. Less obviously, widespread advances in medical science save or prolong millions of human lives—but also make possible a chaotic population explosion.

This ambiguity is understandable, if distressing. Not only are human beings often unprepared to accept the responsibilities of terrible new powers liberated by scientists or engineers. Even plainly beneficial technical advance may tend to complicate rather than ease social problems. New super-productive seeds and fertilizers, for example, won't feed the hungry in developing nations without first posing agonizing problems for their economies.

Speculation on the human disasters that could result from space exploration can only be grim. In the past, man has turned his efforts to control new environments—the sea and the air—to military advantage first, with more constructive uses resulting later.

If for centuries nations have sought to rule the seas for military reasons, only now that population pressures threaten resources on land do men look seriously to the possibility of developing the ocean's resources.

Thus the prospect of bringing the moon and nearby space under human control seems hardly promising for the social and political future, whatever new scientific knowledge and resources this mastery of a new environment may eventually yield, and whatever elements of space technology may be "spun off" to make life on earth more comfortable.

We don't share Bertrand Russell's acerbic attitude, expressed elsewhere on this page, toward the U.S. space program. But we tend to agree that it is naive to suggest that men could overcome their differences in the exploration of space. The technology that lifts men to the moon may also lift nuclear warheads from one nation to another. The artificial satellites that were the earliest space experiments now routinely spy on national enemies.

The Soviet Union's plainly political launch of a moon sampling craft— to offset some of the prestige the U.S. might gain from a successful moon flight—hardly encourages the thought that space exploration might result in greater brotherhood on earth.

Advancing technology, then, can have mixed or negative results, in this case a costly and dangerous international competition for the control of nearby space and the moon. Yet it may also be inevitable.

Scientific and engineering knowledge cannot be repealed. To a certain extent, new ideas give birth to realities. If men can conceive of ways to travel in space, some of them will do so.

Still, the perhaps unexpectedly widespread tendency to question the value of the moon venture indicates a necessary shift in the American tendency to cherish ingenuity. This may be a central preoccupation for many thoughtful Americans over the coming weekend: That however cleverly man has learned to master new environments and technologies, he has not yet mastered himself, and the new forces liberated by his ingenuity may, unpredictably, either help him or destroy him.

This awareness is a healthy development. We do not share the view of some that the billions spent for space should have been spent on social programs; money alone is not the answer to social ills. But surely the experience of the U.S. in this decade, in Vietnam and in its own cities, has exposed a vulnerability to social problems that practical ingenuity cannot conquer. Without claiming to have an answer to the social problems, we feel it is important to recognize that technology itself may often be as much a source of problems as of solutions, and that however astonishing its achievements, there are some problems it cannot solve.

Americans should be proud of the pictures that will flash on their television screens during this space voyage; the view of an American standing on the moon will mark a brilliant climax of American ingenuity. At the same time, justifiable pride should not be permitted to obscure the more significant message from the moon: That a new technical age requires a humble new perspective on what man can and cannot do.

"Message from the Moon" *

1. The main idea of the editorial is that scientific technology (a) has successfully explored what was previously the unknown, and has confirmed the American talent for ingenuity (b) may someday solve our most urgent social problems (c) may result in good or evil, and we should be aware of both possibilities.

2. The editorial's opinion is that the Apollo 11 project is (a) a foolish waste of money and effort, which would be better spent correcting problems on earth (b) a source of both pride and caution, at least until we see how the knowledge will be used (c) a marvelous example of what a nation can accomplish (d) a potentially harmful and destructive weapon, which may extend man's wars to other planets.

3. How does the editorial support its opinion? (a) by analyzing the destruction which technology has already caused, thereby appealing to fear and suspicion (b) by citing examples of technological achievements that have been misused and by forecasting the possible consequences of the Apollo project (c) by citing statistics on the project's economic problems (d) by praising the Apollo's designers and technicians, thereby appealing to pride and patriotism.

4. The editorial's opinion about the Apollo mission's future implications is (a) cautiously optimistic (b) cautiously pessimistic (c) exceedingly optimistic (d) exceedingly pessimistic (e) both a and b (f) both c and d.

* From the *Wall Street Journal*, July 16, 1969, p. 12.

5. The editorial states at the end that "a new technological age requires a humble new perspective on what man can and cannot do." This suggests that there are (a) legal (b) economic (c) moral and ethical (d) scientific limits on man's scientific achievements in the future.

As you saw in Chapter 8, satire is one of the most effective kinds of persuasive writing. Two more short satirical selections follow. The first by Arthur Hoppe satirizes the disparity between white and black opinions of the police.

One of the grave problems in providing equal education for all citizens is the lack of adequate textbooks for children of the black ghettoes.

Take, for example, that well-known work for beginning readers, "Your Friend, The Policeman." In clean-cut illustrations, it depicts a kindly, beaming police officer guiding and protecting a golden-haired little girl and her apple-cheeked little brother.

Now this certainly instills the proper attitude toward the law in golden-haired little girls and apple-cheeked little brothers. But what about the ghetto child?

To rectify this oversight, I've been working on a beginning textbook for ghetto children, "Your Friend, The Fuzz."

This is the Fuzz. He is very big. He is very white. He has a gun. He shoots people with his gun.

The fuzz come in pairs. They ride in a patrol car. They hunt for suspects. Blacks are suspects. You are black. You are a suspect. The fuzz hunts for you.

If the fuzz catches you, do not run. Stand very still. Do not move. The fuzz will shoot you if you move.

But you are just a little boy. Maybe the fuzz will not shoot you if he knows you are just a boy. The fuzz knows you are a boy. He calls you, "Boy." He calls you, "Boy," as long as you live.

Call him, "Boss." Say, "Yassuh, Boss," or "Nossuh, Boss." This sounds dumb. The fuzz does not like smart suspects. Smart suspects are uppity. Uppity suspects get shot. It is smart to sound dumb.

Once you have said, "Yassuh, Boss," you can move. You can shuffle your feet. You can scratch your head. Do not smile. Only uppity suspects smile. But you have shown who is boss. He is boss. Now he will not shoot you. He will put you in jail.

You have rights. You have equal rights. All suspects are equal under the law. Sometimes the fuzz will shoot the wrong suspect. Sometimes the fuzz will put the wrong suspect in jail. It does not matter. All suspects are equal under the law.

The fuzz wears a badge. It is a pretty badge. It is shiny. It has a number on it. If the fuzz shoots you, try to remember the number. You can tell the NAACP. The NAACP will demand a trial. Then you will learn that the fuzz is your friend.

The fuzz will say he did not want to shoot you. He shot you in the

line of duty. It is his duty to protect the people. He protects the people
from suspects like you. It is his duty to shoot you.

And you can always count on your friend, the fuzz, to do his duty.

Just as "Your Friend, The Policeman" helps the white, middle-class child
grow up alive to his responsibilities as a citizen, so, too, will "Your
Friend, The Fuzz" help the black ghetto child grow up alive.

And that, after all, should be the first goal of any educational system.

ARTHUR HOPPE, "Your Friend,
The Fuzz" *

1. What is Hoppe's opinion of police treatment of Negroes? Of the policeman's duty to "serve and protect"? Of the way that duty is carried out in
ghettos?
2. Even though the editorial deliberately overstates the situation for satirical effect, is the evidence convincing or not?
3. To what extent does your answer to the second question depend on your
personal opinion? On your personal experience? On other reading you
have done? On the mass media's coverage of the problems of police
abuses?
4. What emotions, if any, does the author appeal to?

The following selections illustrate a different sort of satire—the take-off,
or burlesque. Michael Arlen, the former television critic for *The New
Yorker,* describes the plots of five hypothetical television shows.

WALDO

"Frankly, we tried to capture some of the honest-to-Christ *tendresse*
that still exists in the world, in the form of a boy's love for his pet" is the
way veteran producer Harry J. Frost describes his new outdoor-adven-
ture series *Waldo,* the story of what happens when a towheaded nine-
year-old boy called Biff Magowan saves an anopheles mosquito (Waldo)
from drowning in a bowl of won-ton soup and then is unable to "give him
up," despite the good-natured remonstrances of Biff's mother that Waldo
is a "wild thing" who ought to be "making his family with other wild
things," and the good-natured reminders of Biff's father, Biff Magowan,
Sr., deputy insect-control warden for the area, that one nip from Waldo
nets you about fifteen and a half months of 109-degree fever, plus a
long, lingering recovery, and "other attendant side effects." In an episode
last week, Biff, Waldo, and his mother have been left alone in the house,
when they are suddenly set upon by a Killer Gnat. Thereupon ensues
what veteran producer Frost has described as "one of the most dramatic
semi-authentic fights-to-the-finish between an anopheles mosquito and
a Killer Gnat ever filmed." Biff, Sr., returns several days later, in time
to put a comradely arm around Waldo and deliver a brief lecture on the
various pros and cons of forest fires.

* From the *San Francisco Chronicle,* April 4, 1969.

BLAKE

Blake is the personal story of Gil Blake, tough, dedicated, and hard-driving, one of the "new breed" of investigative dentists who have been shaking up the whole dynamics of the dental profession in recent years. Blake's offices are in a sleek little building in the fashionable Trumpington Hills section of Los Angeles, where, with a couple of old drills, a few X-rays, and his associate, Wally Sheinbaum (played by Negro actor Henry Woodlawn), he appears to be running a comfortable society practice. Inwardly, though, Blake is seething. "Filling! Polishing! It's not enough!" he seethes. "When I see a pair of upper canines walk in here, I want to know: What made those upper canines the way they are? A lousy, no-good marriage? A crummy, stinking childhood? A couple of rotten pieces of gravel?" In a recent episode, "The Tides in the Sargasso Run Deep," Blake is trapped in his office by a homicidal maniac and is forced to give him a free gum massage. Later, Blake remembers a "peculiar discoloration" on a lower left molar, and sets off on a search for the young killer that takes him through eight Western states, Canada, Mexico, Greece, and Mexico again, and ends up in a chase through the back corridors of the Vandivert Tooth Sanitarium in Lausanne.

THE ARNOLD NEWQUIST SPECIAL

Arnold Newquist, chief electrician at CBS for the past thirty-six years, patiently waited his turn for his own Special, and the result, which was shown live and in color last Tuesday night, was a relaxed, understated, deceptively casual performance that amply demonstrated Mr. Newquist's instinctive grasp of the new medium. In the first part of the show Mr. Newquist, informally attired in an old sweater and some underwear, sang a number of Indiana U. fraternity songs, hummed a little from Gilbert and Sullivan, and participated in a comedy skit with special guest star Mimmsey Mommeier (Cindy Paragon in *Annabelle Rattoon*) about defrosting ice trays. In the second part Mr. Newquist reappeared, more relaxed than ever, in bathrobe and pajamas, and did imitations of Warner Baxter, Millard Fillmore, and somebody he thought might be Count Ciano or might not be, and then sang "Stardust" several times. A musical dance number based on the Repeal of the Corn Laws was superbly executed by the Julian Grigsby Dancers.

POMFRET

"You just couldn't have made a show like this eleven or twenty-three years ago," says W. Loring Brickhouse, executive producer of *Pomfret*, the daring new series that attempts to deal head on with the "racial crisis." Henderson Pomfret, a Negro, is a brilliant young assistant professor of history at Hanford University, a Rhodes Scholar, a squash champion, beautifully mannered, not really too dark, who finds one day that his path to the chairmanship of the department is being blocked by the undisguised animosity of elderly Professor Jocko Lee. Professor Lee claims that his disapproval of Pomfret (played with great sensitivity by Toshira Okada) is based on nothing more than that Pomfret is only twenty-three years old, has published only one book—a personal attack on Dred Scott—and "looks a little funny, or something, although I can't quite put my finger on it." Pomfret, however, suspects that Lee "knows" he is a Negro and is out to get him. In a recent episode, "I Dreamt I Dwelt in Marble Halls," Lee accuses Pomfret of cheating at squash.

DISGUSTING WIFE

"Frankly, what with Vietnam and the pill and everything, I think the public is ready for something a little more sophisticated and contemporary in its comedy shows," says Pia Paxton, the vivacious, serious young actress who plays Millie Wentworth, the "disgusting wife" in the new adult-comedy series of that name, which studio executives describe as a "sort of hippie, up-to-the-minute, fun treatment of the way young adults really live today." In the first episode of the show, Millie's husband, W. Gardner Wentworth (Bruno Ilg), a handsome, hip young rent-a-car executive, goes down to the corner for a pack of Gauloises and, when he returns, finds Millie upstairs in the broom closet with Farraday Cleveland, the raffish young student activist from nearby Densher College. Cleveland hastily explains that he came over to ask Gardner's advice about a new ad-hoc committee on double parking and just "bumped into" Millie in the broom closet, but Gardner is too much of a swinger to be jealous, and laughingly suggests that they all go downstairs and sniff glue. To make Gardner mad, Millie threatens to adopt a couple of children.

MICHAEL ARLEN, from "The Ten
Most Shows" *

1. What characteristics and weaknesses of real television programs does Arlen poke fun at in his scenarios?
2. What common clichés does Arlen satirize?
3. What is the author's opinion about most "dramatic" television programs? About variety or musical shows? About shows that attempt to show a "relevant" view of American life as it really is?

In this chapter, you have been introduced to the criteria for evaluating what you read. Until you learn to read critically as a matter of habit, you are not really reading; you're only looking at black scribbling on a white page.

READING SELECTIONS 9 (A AND B) Erich Wise and Andrew Schlesinger, and Sanford D. Garelik, "When, If Ever, Do You Call In the Cops" †

During the spring of 1969, Harvard College witnessed its first student demonstration. The following two selections express divergent points of view about the demonstration and its possible origins. The first is by Sanford D. Garelik, formerly the police Chief Inspector for New York City. He is now President of the City Council in New York. The second

* From *Living-Room War* (New York: The Viking Press, Inc., 1969), pp. 123, 124–25, 127, 128.

† From *The New York Times Magazine*, May 4, 1969.

excerpt is by Andrew Schlesinger and Erich Wise, students at Harvard College. For these two selections, compute and record your scores separately.

(A) *Sanford D. Garelik*

By its very definition a university is a sanctuary for all shades of opinion. On our country's campuses, the right to dissent is historic.

We must give the widest latitude to dissent, but at the same time we should bear in mind the rights of others. One thing is certain: The campus is *not* a sanctuary for crime and lawlessness. Threats of violence, actual physical assaults, bombings and arson have no place in a society that lives under a rule of law. The campus is no exception.

Generally the responsibility for controlling campus activity rests with university authorities. Where a crime is committed—such as a shooting, a bombing or arson—the police are bound by law to enter the campus to take action. In fact, if they fail to do so, they would themselves be guilty of violating the law.

However, there are times when certain acts do not rise to the level of a crime *unless* a complaint is made by the university. A good example would be a sit-in which is a trespass on private property. Here, the police cannot, and should not, come on a campus until requested by the university.

To try to determine a specific point at which police should be called in by university authorities is unrealistic. You cannot create inflexible generalizations from the past as a basis for rigid responses in the future. No two campus disorders have been or will be parallel.

Police power is a matter of extraordinary sensitivity in our society, and must be used with restraint. Just as the judgment of the university must be flexible—so should be the techniques of police response.

Rather than make the crucial decisions in the midst of campus crises without any advance planning, we need guidelines for campus activity, and they should be the product of thinking and participation by university administrators, faculty and the students themselves. Then those who ignored the guidelines would be fully aware of the consequences.

One should also remember that a confrontation with the police is often the goal of many demonstrations and protests. This kind of confrontation requires a great deal of professionalism on the part of the police. They must be aware and trained in the nature of confrontation politics and action.

The years spent in colleges are a time for young men and women to search for their own personal identities. For young people, it is a time of freedom and idealism and of strong desires to improve civilization. Their education should flourish and develop constructively. Lawlessness and anarchy are not only destructive to the educational process but will dim the light of liberty.

Reading Selection 9A

COMPREHENSION

Do not refer to the article to answer these questions. Choose one of the items that best answers each question, and mark the letter in the space provided.

1. __D__ Choose the statement that best expresses the main idea. (a) student protests should be stopped with immediate police action (b) the university should set up rigid rules for student behavior, but should discipline offenders without police interference (c) the college should establish such lenient standards for behavior that students would have nothing to protest (d) if police are used on campus, they should act with restraint, although student lawlessness should never be tolerated.

2. __C__ Garelik emphasizes that (a) dissent in any form should never be allowed (b) dissent is healthy and should be encouraged (c) some dissent is acceptable, but only if others' rights are respected (d) the right to dissent is historic.

3. __D__ The author states that campus protests should be controlled by (a) only the police (b) only the administration (c) only the students (d) both the police and the administration depending on the seriousness of the crime.

4. __E__ According to the author, police should enter a campus only for (a) sit-ins which involve trespassing on private property (b) the bombing of a building (c) the burning of a building (d) the theft of files or other confidential materials (e) only b and c (f) all of the above.

5. __C__ The author suggests that the authority of both police and the administration be (a) sensitive to the students' needs (b) inflexible so that all protests are controlled uniformly (c) flexible and restrained because force often only encourages more violence (d) respect the students' right to protest legitimate grievances.

6. __B__ Garelik recommends that administrators solve the problem of campus disorders by (a) establishing rigid rules and punishments so there would be no temptation to rebel (b) consulting both faculty and students to define unacceptable behavior, so that protesters would know the consequences of their actions (c) stopping all protests at the same time in the same way (d) waiting until a crisis develops before deciding on control measures.

7. __D__ The police should respond to student-provoked confronta-

tions by (a) ignoring them (b) reacting so forcibly that students will be afraid to repeat the offense (c) refraining from the use of force until the situation becomes uncontrollable (d) acting professionally and with restraint.

8. ___B___ The author implies that some demonstrators (a) have no particular political philosophy (b) often deliberately provoke violence or confrontations with police (c) are simply immature delinquents and trouble-makers (d) actively promote lawlessness and anarchy as a prelude to revolution.

9. ___D___ Which statement best expresses the author's opinion of the radical student movement? (a) radical students are simply a small minority whom no one takes seriously (b) radical students should be excused for their actions because they are only idealistic but misguided do-gooders (c) radicals are so dangerous to society that they should be expelled automatically (d) radicals often use extreme means to protest, which endangers everyone's freedom.

10. ___D___ Judging from the author's tone, to whom does he seem most sympathetic? (a) the faculty (b) the majority of students whose studies are interrupted by demonstrations (c) the radical students (d) the author is objective, so that no particular sympathy is evident from the selection.

VOCABULARY

From the lettered choices, find the best definition for each vocabulary item, and mark the letter in the space provided.

1. ___F___ the university is a *sanctuary*
2. ___C___ the right to *dissent*
3. ___H___ actual physical *assaults*
4. ___O___ inflexible *generalizations*
5. ___N___ extraordinary *sensitivity*
6. ___E___ used with *restraint*
7. ___M___ university must be *flexible*
8. ___A___ the *crucial* decisions
9. ___D___ in the midst of campus *crises*
10. ___J___ lawlessness and *anarchy*

A. critical; severe
B. rigid; immovable
C. express strong disagreement with majority
D. critical turning points
E. control; restriction
F. place of refuge

G. criminal offenses
H. violent attacks
I. unlimited freedom; license
J. chaos; political disorder
K. unimportant; trivial
L. conform; agree
M. easily bent; adaptable

N. state of being easily irritated   O. conclusions based on insuffi-
    or inflamed   cient facts

COMPREHENSION   No. right ———— × 10 = ————%

VOCABULARY   No. right ———— × 10 = ————%

No. of words 450 ÷ time in seconds ———— × 60 = ———— WPM

WPM × Comprehension % = Reading Efficiency Rate ————————————

(B) *Andrew Schlesinger and Erich Wise*

Early in the morning of April 10, Harvard called the cops. The immediate result was the effective radicalization of much of a student body that had looked with little enthusiasm upon the protesters and with little interest upon their demands.

The administration's reaction to the seizure of University Hall showed a painful deficiency of coolness, integrity and rationality. Brute force was used with little caution or finesse; as in Vietnam, Chicago, the ghetto, it took the place of reason and free discussion. And the administration, instead of forming a broad consensus against the radicals, played right into their hands.

Probably S.D.S. itself could empathize most with the agony of the administration. Both were acting to support political goals and were sensitive to the interests and power threatened by the occupation; both saw it as a symbol, either of a new order or a new terror. The seizure was thus the first part of a war of conflicting ideas, philosophies, ways of life. The administration and the radicals, however, both overly conscious of, and sensitive about, their own rhetoric and the ideal positions they stubbornly upheld, overlooked the implications of their actions upon a community of peace, pragmatism and truth. Lines drawn so quickly and clearly allowed no room for compromise; the fight for political power forced both sides to sacrifice the humanity of their desires for a cause.

Unfortunately, President Pusey had misconstrued reality as badly as the radicals. In a community not at war, the tactics and brutality of war are not condoned. Stupidly, stubbornly, Pusey, blinded by his fears for Harvard, ignored the lessons of Columbia and Brandeis, sacrificed the opportunity to educate the community to the meaning of the seizure, alienated the moderate students by overlooking their advice and preempted the faculty who should have been called in on such a drastic and unprecedented decision. Reacting to the crisis in a desperate panic, Pusey fell back upon his ancient prejudices, furtively attempted to secure his position and status, and fortified himself against discussion and compromise.

The students, faculty and administration of any university, particularly of a traditional private institution like Harvard, look upon their community as somewhat of a sanctuary. Like a religious institution, the university should stand timelessly apart from any specific political issue. That is not to say Harvard is not or should not become an active force in today's society, but it does mean the university should act on moral principle rather than political interest. The Vietnam war, and therefore R.O.T.C.; the tearing down of low-income homes, and therefore university expansion—these are political issues that imply a certain moral stance. The students of S.D.S. see the university take what it construes as immoral actions (retention of R.O.T.C., expansion, use of police) for political reasons (protection of élitist interest). The administration sees S.D.S. take what it construes as immoral actions (takeover of a building and an effort to deny students their academic freedom to join R.O.T.C.) for political reasons (a revolutionary move to gain power through coercion). Each side sees the issues and actions of the other as purely political, outside the traditional realm of a free and moral university. Both sides, moreover, feel morally justified in their political actions.

Once students were in the building at Harvard, the administration saw only two alternatives—that the police be called or "nothing be done." If, on the other hand, the administration had been committed on moral grounds to the preservation of academic freedom, rather than on political grounds to the retention of R.O.T.C. and expansion, they probably could have waited out any sit-in, convinced a majority of students the sit-in was an immoral action and maintained a moral stance in the eyes of the community. Instead they violated the concept of a university sanctuary by the use of police.

The administration claims private files in University Hall were endangered by the occupation, and even the most radical faculty members admit to that fear. But the files are not priceless works of art or irreplaceable books. The question becomes whether it is worth jeopardizing the lives of students by clubbing and stampeding them out of the building to protect certain files. It may be argued that the lives and livelihood of administrators and faculty members were likewise jeopardized by the possibility that such files be revealed to the public. But still the files are in the realm of ideas; they can be argued out and explained. A girl's broken back or a boy's cracked skull are a little more difficult to justify.

By allowing excessive force to be used against students who had no means of protecting themselves or physically harming others, nor any intent to do so, the administration went far beyond its task of protecting a free university. Seduced by what it believed to be political necessity, the administration overreacted to the occupation, destroying in the process its own credibility and forfeiting the community's confidence in it.

READING SELECTION 9B

COMPREHENSION

Do not refer to the article to answer these questions. Choose one of the items that best answers each question, and mark the letter in the space provided.

1. ___C___ Choose the statement that best expresses the main idea of the selection: (a) the administration was correct in summoning the police to protect Harvard (b) the college community lost confidence in the administration because it did not discipline the protesters quickly enough (c) the administration reacted too harshly, for reasonable discussion and compromise would have solved the problem (d) the administration was correct in calling the police, but it also should have prevented them from using unnecessary force.

2. ___A___ The administration hoped that by calling police to University Hall, the majority of students would (a) ignore the radical students' demands (b) support the police (c) support the radicals' demands (d) join the protest.

3. ___A___ The moderate students reacted to the police tactics by (a) ignoring the brutality (b) becoming radicalized themselves (c) approving of the brutality (d) damaging private files.

4. ___A___ Both the S.D.S. and the administration considered the seizure of the building as (a) a war between conflicting political and moral philosophies (b) a symbol of a new kind of terror tactics (c) an opportunity for reasonable discussion (d) an end to the concept of the university as a sanctuary.

5. _____ One can accurately infer that (a) the faculty was not consulted before the administration summoned the police (b) the students destroyed private files (c) the radical faculty did not support the students' actions (d) the students were not concerned with the administration's political actions.

6. _____ The authors state the fight for political power between radicals and the administration caused each side to (a) sacrifice the humanity of their separate ideals for a cause (b) respond by reason rather than by prejudice (c) become more fearful of the other's motives (d) resort to rhetoric and inflammatory speeches.

7. ___A___ Schlesinger and Wise state because Harvard was not in a state of war, (a) warlike tactics were inappropriate (b) warlike tactics should have been used anyway to teach the radicals a lesson (c) the protest would have disappeared naturally (d) the university should not be closed.

8. _____ The S.D.S. had criticized all but one of the following uni-

versity actions. Which *one* was not mentioned? (a) university expansion into poor areas (b) retention of the ROTC
program (c) permitting the military to recruit new members on campus (d) using police to stop the protest.

9. _____ The authors are evidently sympathetic to (a) the faculty (b)
the administration (c) the students who were protesting the
university's immoral activities (d) the students who did not
participate and whose studies were interrupted (e) not evident from the selection.

10. _____ The authors feel that the administration could have avoided
the violence by (a) allowing the radicals to get their demands (b) convincing the moderate students that the seizure
was an immoral action (c) letting the faculty and students
vote on a solution (d) making the police use even more
violent, repressive tactics.

VOCABULARY

From the lettered choices, find the best definition for each vocabulary
item, and mark the letter in the space provided.

1. __J__ a painful *deficiency*
2. __B__ a broad *consensus*
3. __F__ *implications* of their actions
4. __O__ Pusey had *misconstrued* reality
5. __L__ tactics of war are not *condoned*
6. __A__ *alienated* the moderate students
7. __M__ in a *desperate* panic
8. __E__ move to gain power through *coercion*
9. __N__ *jeopardizing* the lives
10. __H__ destroyed its *credibility*

A. made hostile; estranged	H. trustworthiness; believability
B. general agreement; majority	I. condemned
opinion	J. lack; shortage
C. causes; reasons	K. authority; power
D. cooperation	L. overlooked; forgiven
E. exercise of force	M. almost hopeless
F. suggestions; results	N. exposing to injury, danger
G. abundance; large supply	O. interpreted wrongly

COMPREHENSION   No. right _____ × 10 = _____%

VOCABULARY   No. right _____ × 10 = _____%

No. of words 850 ÷ time in seconds _____ × 60 = _____ WPM

WPM × Comprehension % = Reading Efficiency Rate _____

Chapter 10

TONE AND STYLE

In addition to recognizing the author's opinion and the persuasive devices he employs to make his opinion palatable, interpreting the author's tone is equally important. The term *tone* is sometimes confusing, because it has three distinct meanings. *Tone* refers to:

(1) the writer's attitude and sentiments toward both his subject and his audience;

(2) in reading a particular work, the mood or feeling, or possibly the atmosphere, created in the reader's awareness by the work, that ideally is equivalent to the writer's attitude;

(3) the unusual characteristics, style, and quality of the writing, which distinguish one writer from another.

To decipher the tone of a selection, you must be sensitive to language. You must consider the writer's opinion, connotation of words, the level of vocabulary, the subject itself, and the audience addressed. You probably have, for example, no trouble "psyching out" an instructor or interpreting his attitude. Such characteristics as facial expressions, voice inflection, or peculiar gestures quickly suggest whether an instructor is enthusiastic or indifferent toward his material and his students. And critical reading requires the same kind of appraisal from the printed page.

All prose, fiction, or non-fiction, persuasive or didactic, has a characteristic tone. The writer's tone may be serious, stern, gloomy, somber, ironic, facetious, satiric, angry, indignant, bitter—in other words, any emotional attitude you can name. In the same way, the mood you feel when reading a passage should reflect what the author intended you to feel. And the writer's tone must be appropriate for the situation and for the audience for whom he writes. In this way, communication between the writer and reader is direct and both must participate equally.

This matter of appropriateness can best be illustrated by having you consider from various points of view a single topic, "the new student activists." Assuming the speaker or writer is qualified to comment on the topic intelligently, how might these audiences determine the content and tone? Which groups might require more background or explanatory information? Which would require more comprehensive and more carefully documented analysis?

(1) a speech before the Board of Education of a large urban school district;

(2) a speech before a group of suburban high school instructors;

(3) a speech before some students at a major European university;

(4) a personal letter to the writer's grandmother;

(5) a speech before a group of small-town businessmen;

(6) an informal question-and-answer session before a suburban women's bridge club;

(7) an article to appear in a major city's newspaper;

(8) an article to appear in a widely circulated "underground" newspaper;

(9) a letter to rich alumni, the real purpose of which is to solicit funds;

(10) a speech before the members of a plumbers' union.

These situations suggest that the writer (or speaker) must consider carefully just who makes up his audience. He must consider how much background information they are likely to have, their prejudices and opinions, whether the subject involves them directly, and so on. This is not to suggest that the writer's opinion toward his topic changes; but he must take into account these factors to be sure his level of diction, vocabulary, and kinds of detailed information are appropriate.

Most of the reading required in college, however, is informative or didactic in tone. Textbook authors view their subject objectively, for their intention is solely to instruct and inform. Here is an example of expository prose that is instructive in tone:

> Microbes are a pervasive part of the living world. They are present on land and in water, in soil, on healthy plants and animals, and in the carcasses of both. It is the microbes, as you must know, that do the work of returning plant and animal remains into the cycles of nature, breaking down the dead tissues so that plants can use their components again. Microbes are also found in the air, but mainly as they are spewed into it by the activities of animals, especially man. It was Pasteur who showed us that as we go up mountains into higher air the bacteria get fewer and fewer. The ultraviolet rays in sunlight tend to kill them. Above the ozone layer of the atmosphere, high above the clouds, the concentration of

short-wave radiation is much greater, and microbial life is probably entirely absent.

THEODOR ROSEBURY, from *Life on Man**

It is evident that the author describes microbial life directly and factually. He doesn't pass judgment nor does he invite you to pass judgment on his ideas. Do you suppose that the passage is intended for the general audience that is relatively unfamiliar with microbiology, or for knowledgeable research scientists?

In the following example, the writer's intention is quite different. H. L. Mencken, a famous American journalist and essayist, was admired for both his command of English and for his irreverence toward established, popular notions. Here, he seeks to instruct, but in a more philosophic and disturbing way.

> All democratic theories, whether Socialistic or bourgeois, necessarily take in some concept of the dignity of labor. If the have-not were deprived of this delusion that his sufferings in the sweat-shop are somehow laudable and agreeable to God, there would be little left in his ego save a belly-ache. Nevertheless, a delusion is a delusion, and this is one of the worst. It arises out of confusing the pride of workmanship of the artist with the dogged, painful docility of the machine. The difference is important and enormous. If he got no reward whatever, the artist would go on working just the same; his actual reward, in fact, is often so little that he almost starves. But suppose a garment-worker got nothing for his labor: would he go on working just the same? Can one imagine him submitting voluntarily to hardship and sore want that he might express his soul in 200 more pairs of pantaloons?

> H. L. MENCKEN, from "The Worker" †

1. Mencken's chief virtue was his ability to cut away to the truth which most people find unpleasant. What does Mencken imply about why workers work? ~for a reward~
2. Why do people delude themselves with the notion of the "dignity of labor?"
3. Which best describes Mencken's tone? (a) bitter and resentful (b) subtly irreverent and wry (c) self-congratulatory (d) informative; didactic.

The next two passages might be considered illustrations of "interpretative journalism." While this kind of journalism is not really new, the label now refers to writers who both describe and interpret the facts. Be-

---

* (New York: The Viking Press, Inc., 1969), p. 32.
† From *Prejudices: Third Series* (New York: Alfred A. Knopf, Inc., 1922), pp. 268–269.

fore you read the first example, you should understand the concept of
irony. Irony is a figure of speech in which the expected outcome is replaced by the unexpected. A boy walking down the street, eager to see
more closely the beautiful girl approaching him, might well be dismayed
to find that the "girl" is actually a long-haired boy wearing bell-bottom
pants. This passage is by Berton Roueché, a popular medical writer. His
account describes a deathly fog which covered Donora, a small mining
town in Pennsylvania in 1948, from which twenty people died. In this
excerpt, Roueché describes Donora's physical environment as it normally
is:

The Monongahela River rises in the middle Alleghenies and seeps for
a hundred and twenty-eight miles through the iron and bituminous-coal
fields of northeastern West Virginia and Southwestern Pennsylvania to
Pittsburgh. There, joining the Allegheny River, it becomes the wild Ohio.
It is the only river of any consequence in the United States that flows
due north, and it is also the shortest. Its course is cramped and crooked,
and flanked by bluffs and precipitous hills. Within living memory, its
waters were quick and green, but they are murky now with pollution,
and a series of locks and dams steady its once tumultuous descent, rendering it navigable from source to mouth. Traffic on the Monongahela is
heavy. Its shipping, which consists almost wholly of coal barges pushed
by wheezy, coal-burning stern-wheelers, exceeds in tonnage that of the
Panama Canal. The river is densely industrialized. There are trucking
highways along its narrow banks and interurban lines and branches of
the Pennsylvania Railroad and the New York Central and smelters and
steel plants and chemical works and glass factories and foundries and
coke plants and machine shops and zinc mills, and its hills and bluffs
are scaled by numerous blackened mill towns. The blackest of them is
the borough of Donora, in Washington County, Pennsylvania.
   Donora is twenty-eight miles south of Pittsburgh and covers the tip of
a lumpy point formed by the most convulsive of the Monongahela's many
horseshoe bends. Though accessible by road, rail and river, it is an extraordinarily secluded place. The river and the bluffs that lift abruptly from
the water's edge to a height of four hundred and fifty feet enclose it on
the north and east and south, and just above it to the west is a range of
rolling but even higher hills. On its outskirts are acres of sidings and
rusting gondolas, abandoned mines, smoldering slag piles, and gulches
filled with rubbish. Its limits are marked by sooty signs that read, "Donora.
Next to Yours the Best Town in the U.S.A." It is a harsh, gritty town,
founded in 1901 and old for its age, with a gaudy main street and a
thousand identical gaunt gray houses. Some of its streets are paved with
concrete and some are cobbled, but many are of dirt and crushed coal. At
least half of them are as steep as roofs, and several have steps instead
of sidewalks. It is treeless and all but grassless, and much of it is slowly
sliding downhill. After a rain, it is a smear of mud. Its vacant lots and
many of its yards are mortally gullied, and one of its three cemeteries is an
eroded ruin of gravelly clay and toppled tombstones. Its population is

12,300. Two-thirds of its men, and a substantial number of its women, work in its mills. There are three of them—a steel plant, a wire plant, and a zinc-and-sulphuric-acid plant—all of which are operated by the American Steel & Wire Co., a subsidiary of the United States Steel Corporation, and they line its river front for three miles. They are huge mills. Some of the buildings are two blocks long, many are five or six stories high, and all of them bristle with hundred-foot stacks perpetually plumed with black or red or sulphurous yellow smoke.

BERTON ROUECHÉ, from "The Fog" *

To answer these questions, you may refer to the passage.

1. In the first paragraph, what do these phrases connote? "murky with pollution"; "wheezy, coal-burning stern-wheelers."
2. In the second paragraph, what is the total connotative effect of these phrases? "a lumpy point," "smoldering slag piles," "a harsh, gritty town," "gaudy main street," "identical gaunt gray houses," "a smear of mud."
3. What is ironic about the signs, covered with soot, which read: "Donora. Next to Yours the Best Town in the U.S.A.?"
4. Which of the following best describes the tone, the author's attitude, toward Donora? (a) disgust and loathing (b) gloom and alarm (c) somberness, yet with sympathy and compassion (d) sentimentality and nostalgia.
5. What does Roueché's description of Donora seem to be? (a) exaggerated; harsher than the town probably is; (b) mild, less sordid than the town probably is; (c) more romantic and idealistic than the town probably is; (d) realistic and objective, with a trace of sadness.

In the next passage, Albert Goldman describes the scene at The Electric Circus, a famous New York discothèque. These paragraphs, from the beginning of an essay on rock music, set the mood vividly for the rest of the discussion.

To experience the Age of Rock full-blast and to begin to grasp its weird complexities, one can't do much better than spend a Saturday night at The Electric Circus, the most elaborate discothèque in New York. Located on St. Marks Place, the main nexus of East Village otherness, The Electric Circus is up a flight of stairs from The DOM (one of the early landmarks of the rock scene which has since evolved into a "soul" club). One makes his way through a gaggle of very young hippies sprawled on the porch steps, and enters a long, narrow alcove where the faithful, the tourists, and those somewhere in between wait in line for admission in a mood of quiet expectancy, like people waiting to get into one of the more exciting exhibits at the World's Fair. Once inside, the spectator moves along

* From *Eleven Blue Men* (Boston: Little, Brown and Company, 1953), pp. 173–174.

a corridor bathed in ultraviolet light in which every speck of white takes on a lurid glow, climbs a steep staircase, and passes through a dark antechamber. Here the young sit packed together on benches and, already initiated into the mysteries beyond, stare back at the newcomer with glazed, indifferent expressions as though they had been sitting there for days. Then, suddenly, there is a cleft in the wall, and the spectator follows the crowd pressing through it into a gigantic hall that suggests a huge bleached skull. Its dark hollows are pierced by beams of colored light that stain the walls with slowly pulsing patterns and pictures: glowing amoeba shapes, strips of home movies, and giant mandalas filled with fluid colors. The scream of a rock singer comes at one, the beat amplified to a deafening blast of sound. Housed within this electronic cave are hundreds of dancers, a number of them in exotic, flowing garments, their faces marked with phosphorescent insignia, hands clutching sticks of incense. Some of the dancers are gyrating frantically, as if trying to screw themselves down through the floor; others hold up their fists, ducking and bobbing like sparring partners; while others wrench their heads and thrust out their hands as if to ward off evil spirits. For all of its futuristic magic, the dance hall brings to mind those great painted caves such as Altamira in Spain where prehistoric man practiced his religious rites by dancing before the glowing images of his animal gods.

Magnetized by the crowd, impelled by the relentless pounding beat of the music, one is then drawn out on the floor. Here there is a feeling of total immersion: one is inside the mob, inside the skull, inside the music, which comes from all sides, buffeting the dancers like a powerful surf. Strangest of all, in the midst of this frantic activity, one soon feels supremely alone; and this aloneness produces a giddy sense of freedom, even of exultation. At last one is free to move and act and mime the secret motions of his mind. Everywhere about him are people focused deep within themselves, working to bring to the surfaces of their bodies their deep-seated erotic fantasies. Their faces are drugged, their heads thrown back, their limbs extended, their bodies dissolving into the arcs of the dance. The erotic intensity becomes so great that one wonders what sustains the frail partition of reserve that prevents the final spilling of this endlessly incited energy.

If one withdraws from the crowd and climbs to the gallery overlooking the dance floor, he soon succumbs to the other spell cast by this cave of dreams. Falling into a passive trance, his perceptions heightened perhaps by exhaustion or drugs (no liquor is served here), the spectator can enjoy simultaneously the pleasures of the theater, the movies, and the sidewalk cafe. At The Electric Circus the spectacle of the dancers alternates with the surrealistic acts of professional performers. An immaculate chef on stilts will stride to the center of the floor, where he looms high above the dancers. They gather around him like children, while he entertains them by juggling three apples. Then, taking out a knife, he slices the fruit and feeds it to his flock. High on a circular platform, a performer dressed to look like a little girl in her nightie struggles ineffectually with a Yo-Yo. A blinding white strobe light flashes across her body, chopping her absurd actions into the frames of an ancient flickering movie. Another girl comes sliding down a rope; someone dressed as a gorilla seizes her and carries her off with a lurching gait. Sitting in the dark gallery, one watches the crepitating spectacle below; the thumping music now sinks slowly through his mind like a narcotic; eventually he closes his eyes and surrenders to a longing for silence, darkness, and rest.

ALBERT GOLDMAN, from "The
Emergence of Rock" *

1. _____ Which of the following best describes Goldman's attitude toward The Electric Circus? Does he seem (a) overly enthusiastic (b) condescendingly amused (c) overly critical (d) bewildered, fascinated, and slightly amused?

2. _____ From the passage, what can you infer about the audience to whom Goldman appeals? (a) the general readers of a large urban newspaper (b) educated adults interested in learning more about the rock music phenomenon (c) classical musicians who probably loathe rock music (d) young readers of an underground newspaper who know about places like The Electric Circus first-hand? How can you justify your answer?

Style

The question of style is the most challenging, yet the most elusive of features of good prose. No one can exactly define what "good" style is, not to mention how one achieves or describes it. One thing is certain: prose should be clear, precise and effective. Any style which meets those requirements can be considered good. But what is style? It might be defined tentatively as the effective arrangement of words in a way that expresses both the writer's individuality and the ideas and intentions in his mind. It's pretty vague, and it certainly doesn't establish any criteria for measuring good or bad style. Nevertheless, ideally, the ideas in the writer's mind should transfer directly to paper in the same way they were conceived. But this would suggest that style is unconscious and spontaneous, and in reality, good style is achieved by deliberate means, usually by extensive revision.

Like the tone the writer imparts to his work, the style must be appropriate for both the subject and the audience. In this way, form (style) and content (subject) are inseparable. The style should be so closely wedded to the subject that it should never intrude consciously in the reader's mind. If a writer's style is good, then the reader should not be aware of stylistic devices used by the writer. And because there is no

* From *New American Review*, No. 3 (New York: New American Library Inc., 1968), pp. 118–120.

formula for style, one must simply "feel" that it is there. Here is an excellent illustration of a clear prose style by Winston Churchill. In a short biographical sketch, he describes Adolf Hitler's early life and his frustrations as a young man. First read the passage silently; then read it aloud, and try to listen to his arrangement of words, the length of his sentences, and his choice of words.

In October, 1918, a German corporal had been temporarily blinded by chlorine gas in a British attack near Comines. While he lay in hospital in Pomerania, defeat and revolution swept over Germany. The son of an obscure Austrian customs official, he had nursed youthful dreams of becoming a great artist. Having failed to gain entry to the Academy of Art in Vienna, he had lived in poverty in that capital and later in Munich. Sometimes as a house-painter, often as a casual labourer, he suffered physical privations and bred a harsh though concealed resentment that the world had denied him success. These misfortunes did not lead him into Communist ranks. By an honourable inversion he cherished all the more an abnormal sense of racial loyalty and a fervent and mystic admiration for Germany and the German people. He sprang eagerly to arms at the outbreak of the war, and served for four years with a Bavarian regiment on the Western Front. Such were the early fortunes of Adolf Hitler.

As he lay sightless and helpless in hospital during the winter of 1918, his own personal failure seemed merged in the disaster of the whole German people. The shock of defeat, the collapse of law and order, the triumph of the French, caused this convalescent regimental orderly an agony which consumed his being, and generated those portentous and measureless forces of the spirit which may spell the rescue or the doom of mankind. The downfall of Germany seemed to him inexplicable by ordinary processes. Somewhere there had been a gigantic and monstrous betrayal. Lonely and pent within himself, the little soldier pondered and speculated upon the possible causes of the catastrophe, guided only by his narrow personal experiences. He had mingled in Vienna with extreme German Nationalist groups, and here he had heard stories of sinister, undermining activities of another race, foes and exploiters of the Nordic world—the Jews. His patriotic anger fused with his envy of the rich and successful into one overpowering hate.

When at length, as an unnoted patient, he was released from hospital still wearing the uniform in which he had an almost schoolboyish pride, what scenes met his newly unscaled eyes? Fearful are the convulsions of defeat. Around him in the atmosphere of despair and frenzy glared the lineaments of Red Revolution. Armoured cars dashed through the streets of Munich scattering leaflets or bullets upon the fugitive wayfarers. His own comrades, with defiant red arm-bands on their uniforms, were shouting slogans of fury against all that he cared for on earth. As in a dream everything suddenly became clear. Germany had been stabbed in the back and clawed down by the Jews, by the profiteers and intriguers behind the front, by the accursed Bolsheviks in their international conspiracy of Jewish intellectuals. Shining before him he saw his duty, to save Germany from these plagues, to avenge her wrongs, and lead the master race to their long-decreed destiny.

WINSTON CHURCHILL, from "Adolf Hitler" *

To show you the difference between good and bad style, consider this original sentence from Churchill's sketch and these three revisions.

CHURCHILL: Fearful are the convulsions of defeat.
REVISIONS: (1) Defeat brings convulsive fear with it.
(2) Fearful is defeat in its convulsions.
(3) Fearwise, defeat is unbearable.
(4) Defeat is a terrible thing, because it is so fearful.

What is wrong with these revisions? They say essentially the same thing, yet Churchill's is pleasing to the ear and the rewritings are not. Consider number three. Aside from the colloquial or substandard use of -wise as a suffix, the sentence is two words shorter than the original, yet the rhythm of the words is heavy and cumbersome. Churchill's sentence is as concise and precise as a line of poetry. Perhaps recognizing good style, then, is really a matter of having a good ear. If you can *hear* that the original version sounds better, then you already have some inkling of what style ought to be.

In the following passage, Tom Wolfe humorously describes the complicated mechanisms in a New York Hilton Hotel room. Why is Wolfe's style so appropriate to his topic? What stylistic devices does he use to duplicate the effects of the alarm system?

. . . I still might have gotten some writing done if it hadn't been for the automated electric signs. These signs were stacked up on top of the combination TV set-bureau-desk-dressing table counter up against one wall, a remarkable object designed in the style known as Two Guys From Harrison Danish. The bottom sign, "PRESS BUTTON TO TURN OFF ALARM," was connected to a complicated alarm system involving the telephone, a tape recorder, an IBM machine or something, an unbelievable buzzer, and the sign itself. This alarm system got to me very quickly. The first night I was there, I wanted to wake up at nine in the morning, so I did the usual thing, you know. I dialed the operator and asked her to ring me up at nine in the morning. She told me to "read the directions," then switched me onto "memory hole" if that is the right terminology for it. All right. There were some directions on the phone there, and they said that to get yourself waked up in the morning, you dial 1 and then dial the time you want to be waked up—nine o'clock was 9-0-0—then you start listening for instructions. A terrific woman—with a kind of detention-home matron's baritone—comes on and says, "This is a recording. For your nine o'clock call, wait for the tone, then repeat clearly your name and room number." Then came the big beep and I said, "This is Mr. Wolfe

* From *The Gathering Storm* (Boston: Houghton Mifflin Company, 1948), pp. 52–53.

in Room 1703." Sure enough, at nine o'clock the next morning, all hell broke loose in the room. The alarm went off on the TV set-bureau-desk-etc., in shock waves like one of those incredible diesel claxons the New York Fire Department has now, and the big electric sign started flashing: "PRESS BUTTON TO TURN OFF ALARM," "PRESS BUTTON TO TURN OFF ALARM!" Pow! Flash! Pow! Flash! Get yo' mouldy shanks up on the flo'! Gawd, I roar up out of bed, throw my heart into fibrillation, and press button to turn off alarm. Relief! But then the whole thing began to bother me. There I had been, the night before, sitting down on the bed and talking into a set of machines and saying, "This is Mr. Wolfe." Mister! Massah! So the next night I dialed 9–0–8—and the voice came on and said, "For your 9:15 call . . ."—Gawdammit, I wanted to get up at 9:08, whathell was going on!—and then the beep sounded, and I said, "This is Mr. Wolfe in Room 1703 . . . a great human being!"—and then I hung up fast before they could catch me. The next morning, however, it was the same, the same madhouse alarm, that was all. The next couple of nights I made short speeches into the machine when the beep came, such as, "You! Slaves in the electronic bowels of the Hilton! This is Wolfe, the great organizer, in Room 1703. Cop out!" But nothing happened; same wildman alarm, with the electric sign flashing.

> TOM WOLFE, from "The Auto-
> mated Hotel" *

Unfortunately, few writers are as good as Churchill or as conscious of appropriateness as Wolfe. Modern technocratic society is particularly guilty of bad writing. Much of what you read, whether in textbooks, magazines or newspapers, is muddy, imprecise, pedantic and pretentious. As part of your critical reading skills, you should learn to recognize good as well as bad style.

One particular weakness of modern writing is the use of *jargon*. Jargon is the specialized vocabulary and language of a particular group or profession. Thieves have their jargon, students another, English teachers and sociologists theirs. The trouble with jargon is that people outside the group usually can't understand it; indeed, sometimes it is unintelligible to members in the group. Jargon is at its worst in social scientific writing, although it is by no means confined to that discipline. Jargon is characterized by the use of big words instead of simple ones; by the use of neologisms (new words introduced into the language, usually intended to make the style sound more "impressive"); and by the use of pseudo-scientific terms rather than ordinary layman's language. The following paragraph humorously describes the sociologists' penchant for making up neologisms:

> In addition to being abstruse, the language of the sociologists is also
> rich in neologisms. Apparently they like nothing better than inventing
> a word, deforming a word, or using a technical word in a strange con-

* From *The Pump House Gang* (New York: Farrar, Straus & Giroux, Inc., 1968), pp. 268–269.

text. Among their favorite nouns are "ambit," "extensity" (for "extent"), "scapegoating," "socializee," "ethnicity," "directionality," "cathexis," "affect" (for "feeling"), "maturation" (for both "maturing" and "maturity"), and "commonalities" (for "points in common"). Among their favorite adjectives are "processual," "prestigeful," and "insightful"— which last is insightful to murder—and perhaps their favorite adverb is "minimally," which seems to mean "in some measure." Their maximal pleasure seems to lie in making new combinations of nouns and adjectives and nouns used as adjectives, until the reader feels that he is picking his way through a field of huge boulders, lost among "universalistic-specific achievement patterns" and "complementary role-expectation-sanction systems," as he struggles vainly toward "ego-integrative action orientation," guided only by "orientation to improvement of the gratification-deprivation balance of the actor"—which last is Professor Talcott Parson's rather involved way of saying "the pleasure principle."

> MALCOLM COWLEY, from "Sociological Habit Patterns in Linguistic Transmogrification" *

Cowley's title itself suggests the same sort of nonsensical jargon which no one pretends to understand. There follows another illustration of jargon, this time from a sociological study of class structure:

> The identification of the peer group society as a class phenomenon makes it possible to suggest some propositions about the working class that will distinguish it both from the lower and middle classes. These propositions rest on a specific definition of class.
>
> Class can be defined in many ways, depending on the theoretical, methodological, and political orientation of the researcher. Some sociologists have argued that class is a heuristic concept, nominalist in nature, which serves as a methodological device to summarize real differences between people in income, occupation, education, and related characteristics. Other sociologists have viewed classes as real aggregates of people who share some characteristics and group interest, who favor each other in social relationships, and who exhibit varying degrees of group consciousness. In the latter category, one school of sociologists has explained class mainly on the basis of occupational characteristics, on the assumption that work determines access to income, power, and status, and that it has considerable influence on an individual's behavior patterns.
>
> Others see classes as more than occupational aggregates, that is, as strata in the larger society, each of which consists of somewhat—but not entirely—distinctive social relationships, behavior patterns, and attitudes. The strata thus are composed of subcultures and subsocial structures. For the sake of brevity, however, I shall henceforth describe them only as subcultures. While occupation, education, income, and other such factors help to distinguish the subcultures, the exact role of these factors is thought to be an empirical question. The strata are defined as subcultures on the assumption that relationships, behavior patterns, and

* From *The Reporter*, September 20, 1956, p. 42.

attitudes are related parts of a social and cultural system. The word
"system" must be used carefully, however, for many similarities and
overlaps exist between them. Moreover, these systems are quite open,
and movement between them is possible, though—as I shall try to slow
—not always easy. Considerable variation also exists within each stratum,
for social mobility and other processes create innumerable combinations
of behavior patterns.

The heuristic conception of class, not being very productive for social
theory, need not concern us here. The two remaining ones each have
some advantages and disadvantages. The occupational conception is
most useful for understanding societies in the early stages of industrialization, when unemployment is great, and when an individual's job is both
a determinant of and an index to his way of life. But in a highly industrialized society with considerable occupational variation and much freedom of choice in jobs—as well as in other ways of life—too great a concern with occupation, or any other single factor, is likely to lead the re-
searcher astray. For instance, when a blue-collar worker earns more than
a white-collar one, and can live by the values of the middle class, it would
be a mistake to classify him as working class. Similarly, when a white-
collar worker lives like a blue-collar one, even in a middle-class neighborhood, one should not consider him middle class.

HERBERT J. GANS, from "Sub-
cultures and Class" *

You needn't feel foolish or ignorant if you couldn't understand the passage.
The author takes three paragraphs to say what one sentence would state
more clearly. In effect, the author says the obvious: that different social
classes and subclasses exist, that classes are sometimes defined by common interests, but that generalizations about classes are often inaccurate.
Three paragraphs to make the obvious into gibberish!

If you are required to read this kind of prose, the best solution is to
skim the selection quickly, find the key ideas, translate them into normal
English, and most important, not be concerned about the rest. This in-
dictment of jargon should not lead you to believe, however, that all
lengthy or difficult prose is bad. Sometimes a complicated idea cannot be
stated in a simple prose style. But jargon is meaningless because the
writer tries too hard to make his writing impressive, when the result is
only obscurity.

Another fault of modern writing is *gobbledygook*. Like jargon, gobbledygook refers to an unnecessarily pretentious, wordy or imprecise
style. The term was coined by a U.S. Congressman named Maverick who
found that no government officials were able to write a clear sentence.
Gobbledygook might be defined as the art of using fancy words to say
nothing. These two letters to the *San Francisco Chronicle* by a young
conservationist are marvelous parodies of this art:

* From *The Urban Villagers* (New York: The Free Press of Glencoe, 1962), pp.
242–243.

IN A NUTSHELL . . .

Editor—In light of the fantastic nature of the most recent development to arise from the compromised situation in which we find ourselves, I think it behooves us to re-evaluate the entire state of affairs. Considering the fact that the seriousness of the problem is somewhat disguised by our own lack of critical perception, perhaps one solution might be in a full-blown inquiry by an appropriate authority. On the other hand given the time factor, and since it is rather likely that an in-depth investigation will open a whole new can of worms, the obvious course of action is to make it perfectly clear that we shall waste no time in reassessing the entire situation.

Tom Turner Berkeley

ON THE CONTRARY . . .

Editor—I must take serious issue with Mr. Turner's letter which appeared in these columns July 21.

It is not, as he implies, incumbent upon us to exercise our full discretion and/or competence with respect to the situation confronting us— quite the contrary. We must pursue with all the energy at our disposal the proper course without which action our very diligence is no longer incommunicado.

R. J. Bleauhard Berkeley
Letters to the Editor*

A final element that contributes to a bad style is the *cliché*. A cliché is a tired, worn-out, hackneyed expression. Metaphors like "peaches-and-cream complexion," "he's off his rocker," or "hard, cold cash" (or "facts") are obvious examples. The cliché is not original, and therein lies the fault. People who use clichés in writing or speaking only restate what is no longer an original idea.

Pick up a newspaper or listen to the news and count the number of times you hear that the U. S. is involved in a "massive build-up." Why must a build-up always be massive? Why does an army "mount" an offensive? Why don't people ever get hurt anymore? They always "sustain injuries." The point is that we read these insidious little phrases and incorporate them into our language unquestioningly. Flann O'Brien, whose pen-name was Myles na Gopaleen, was for years the leading columnist for Dublin's *Irish Times* until his death in 1966. Here is his definition of a cliché:

> A cliché is a phrase that has become fossilised, its component words deprived of their intrinsic light and meaning by incessant usage. Thus it appears that clichés reflect somewhat the frequency of the incidence of the same situations in life. If this be so, a sociological commentary could be compiled from these items of mortified language.
>
> Is not the gun-history of modern Ireland to be verified by the inflexible terminology attaching to it? A man may be shot dead but if he survives a shot, he is not shot but sustains gun-shot wounds. The man

* From the *San Francisco Chronicle*, July 21 and 29, 1969.

who fires the shot is always his assailant, never his attacker or merely the gun-man. The injured party is never taken to hospital but is removed there (in a critical condition). The gun-man does not escape, even if he is not caught; he makes good his escape.

Oddly enough—unnecessary phrase—a plurality of lawbreakers behave differently; they are never assailants but armed men. When they are not caught, they do not make good their escape; they decamp. If there be defenders on the scene, shots are *exchanged.* And the whole affair is, of course, a shooting affray. You see, there is no other kind of affray. If it is not a shooting affray, it is not an affray at all. But it might be a fracas.

> FLANN O'BRIEN, from "The Myles na Gopaleen Catechism of Cliché" *

O'Brien had a real sense of language, and in his "tireless campaign" (another cliché) against muddy prose, he wrote many columns satirizing these stale metaphors. In these parodies, he carried on an imaginary dialogue, in the form of questions and answers, between himself and his readers. For fun, use an index card to cover the answer to each question and see how many clichés you can answer.

CATECHISM OF CLICHÉ

What, as to the quality of solidity, imperviousness, and firmness, are facts?
Hard.
And as to temperature?
Cold.
With what do facts share this quality of frigidity?
Print.
To what do hard facts belong?
The situation.
And to what does a cold fact belong?
The matter.
What must we do to the hard facts of the situation?
Face up to the hard facts of the situation.
What does a cold fact frequently still do?
Remain.
And what is notoriously useless as a means of altering the hard facts of the situation?
All the talk in the world.
Is this killing you?
It certainly is.

CLIS É. A CHARA!

Of what colour is that horse?
Another.

* From *The Best of Myles* (New York: Walker & Co., 1968), p. 227.

To what should you put your shoulder?
The wheel.
What will your man some day come into?
His own.

Last week I had a long (almost, indeed, a protracted) conversation with an important foreign personality who was passing through Ireland on his way elsewhere. The conversation performed that curious act known as ranging over a wide field. Perfect agreement was reached on many points and it was felt that the relationship between the two countries had (much to gain) (from this frank exchange of views). It had been intended also to exchange notes but owing (to pressure of time) it was only found possible to exchange views. Afterwards a short visit was paid to the Zoological Gardens.

Who this person was and what we talked about, of course, I am (not in a position to disclose). A (prominent spokesman) would probably call what we were doing (intense diplomatic activity). It is necessary to emphasize, however, that the whole thing was entirely unofficial. It is unlikely that any announcement will be made.

Farther than this I regret I cannot go. I know better than to shoot (off) my mouth when tipped (off) to keep it shut. Remember that lovely thing by Goethe?

"Kommst du in des Königs Haus
Geh blind hinein und stumm heraus." *

Not that it was that particular party, of course.

THERE IS NO END TO THIS

What does it behove us to proclaim?
Our faith.
In what does it behove us to proclaim our faith?
Democracy.
From what vertiginous eyrie does it behove us to proclaim our faith in democracy?
From the house-tops.
At what time should we proclaim our faith in democracy from the house-tops?
Now, more than ever.
What action must be taken in relation to our energies?
They must be directed.
In what unique manner?
Wholeheartedly.
In what direction?
Towards the solution of the pressing post-war problems which the armistice will bring.
How will the armistice bring these problems?
In its train.
By what is the train hauled?

* [When you go into a king's house, go in blind and come out mute.]

A 2–4–2 compound job with poppet valves and Pacific-style steam chest.

YES, MORE OF IT

What happens to blows at a council meeting?
It looks as if they might be exchanged.
What does pandemonium do?
It breaks loose.
Describe its subsequent dominion.
It reigns.
How are allegations dealt with?
They are denied.
Yes, but then you are weakening, Sir. Come now, how are they denied?
Hotly.
What is the mean temperature of an altercation, therefore?
Heated.
What is the behaviour of a heated altercation?
It follows.
What happens to order?
It is restored.
Alternatively, in what does the meeting break up?
Disorder.
What does the meeting do in disorder?
Breaks up.
In what direction does the meeting break in disorder?
Up.
In what direction should I shut?
Up.

> FLANN O'BRIEN, from "The
> Myles na Gopaleen Catechism of
> Cliché." *

In each of the essays in Part II, you will have more practice in interpreting the author's attitude and tone.

READING SELECTION 10—Cynthia N. Shepard, "The World Through Mark's Eyes" †

In recent years, members of minority groups have attacked America's educational system for imposing white middle-class culture and values uniformly on all children, regardless of ethnic background. In this selection, Cynthia Shepard, Director of the Teacher Corps at the University of Massachusetts, takes a different approach. She describes the faults of modern education through her child's experiences—the confusion and frustration a little black child had to confront.

* From *The Best of Myles* (New York: Walker & Co., 1968), pp. 208–209, 214, 218, 219–220.
† From the *Saturday Review*, January 19, 1960, p. 61.

I would like you to know my son Mark, who is now five years old. Although he has not yet attended kindergarten, he can both read and write, and can accurately identify colors and forms with an acuity beyond his years. He collects American flags, and pictures and ceramics of our national emblem, the eagle. He learned from somewhere on his own initiative the Pledge of Allegiance, which he recites with deep fervor. He only asked me the definitions of those difficult words: *indivisible, liberty, justice.* My precious, precocious Mark is very proud of his white, Anglo-Saxon heritage. But, he's black: a beautifully carved and polished piece of black American earth.

You may debate with me whether I should have taught him from birth that he is black. Instead, I invite you to see the world through Mark's eyes. Mark learned to read when he was three years old—books based on the white American style of life with pictures of blond, blue-eyed suburbia, with decent interspersing of browns and brunets—but no blacks. He watched the "educational" newsreels on television, which for him reinforced the rightness of whiteness. The man in the white hat—beating the black man with a billy club and then kicking him into insensibility—was the good guy. He was the protecter of our individual rights. The books said so.

Black is the night which Mark fears, vanquished by the white of day. White is the knight on the white horse charging the black stains of daily living, and they all vanish. Black is unwanted; black is weak and easily defeated; black is bad.

I took Mark South with me and placed him in an all black nursery school while I taught during the day. The first evening, when I brought him home, he was in tears, writhing and retching in painful confusion. "Why did you make me go to school with all those Negroes?"

Then, just like NOW, I dig! Intellectuality had blocked my insight, creating of me a blind broad and of my black son a white racist. In his innocence—or highest sophistry, you see—he had intuitively perceived race not as a color, but as an attitude that he did not exemplify. My arguments to the contrary were completely hushed by his own words: "You said I could be anything I choose, and I choose to be white. I am white."

I returned North and searched both public and university libraries for literature with both pictures and narrative with which he might relate. *Little Black Sambo?* Oh no, dear God! Where are the black men of history, the Nat Turners, the Veseys, the Prossers? The uncompromising, unprecedented, unheralded warriors for true democracy?

I found a book about John Henry, with all the usual legendary verbiage. But it had pictures—pictures of John Henry as a big, black and beautiful baby; pictures of a handsome, adventurous black youth; and then, a picture of a dynamic, virile, muscle-bound black man. John Henry, the steel-driving man: a beautiful portrayal of black maleness, bared to the waist, swinging that hammer with all his might. It is with *that* picture that my son finally identified: an uncompromising image of black masculinity. That's what it's all about, baby.

I doubled my search for books that pictured black and white children running and laughing together, while black and white mothers shopped and lunched together, while black and white fathers worked and played together. I found a few. Mark had no difficulty identifying me in the pictures, but only recently could he find himself. Eventually, I overheard him speak of himself as a little brown boy, and I rejoiced—deeply, I say—that he was finding his way out.

Now, I have brought him East and have enrolled him in a kindergarten where all the other children are white. But I have not yet been able to send him to that school, although soon legally I will have to send him. What can be done to save my child from a plunge into utter confusion? What can be done to help my little black boy?

What can the world of education do to alleviate his pain—and mine? Must he grow like Topsy: confused, angry, alienated, lighting chaotic fires from the burning bitterness within? By America's guilt-ridden permissiveness, will he be ignored to become a black-helmeted, black-booted, black-bigoted replica of the swastika? Will my son see the necessity of asserting his blackness, his maleness, militantly and insensitively, riding roughshod over all who might in any manner oppose? Or, can the world of education, with all its demonstrated expertise, utilize the precociousness of my little black boy for the building of a better world for all people? How? When? *Now* is the answer.

Today Mark told me he is going to be an eagle and fly high above the earth where nobody will be able to stop him. That speaks to me. I gaze into Mark's face as he lies peacefully sleeping. With all the normal pains of growing, what utter, needless trauma I know he must also face tomorrow—unless change is *made* to happen.

Bitterness wells up within me, too, and I wretchedly whisper into his unheeding ear the words of a writer who must also have known deep human agony over the inhumanity of man to man:

> O pardon me, thou bleeding piece of earth,
> That I am meek and gentle with these butchers.

Reading Selection 10

COMPREHENSION

Do not refer to the article to answer these questions. Choose one of the items that best answers each question, and mark the letter in the space provided.

1. __C__ Which of the following best describes the author's purpose? (a) she criticizes the communications media for catering only to white children (b) she describes her child's confusion and bewilderment, and his eventual discovery of what it means to be black (c) she compassionately describes her child's confusion over race, and makes an effective plea for an end to racism in education (d) she argues for realistic books and television programs which depict all races equally and for immediate integration in public schools.

2. __D__ Why does the author choose to describe the problem of racism from her child's point of view? (a) to elicit the reader's sympathy for her topic; a small child is innocent, and ought not to be hurt by adult prejudices (b) to emphasize how severely racist attitudes affect a small child (c) to instruct the reader about the fears and confusion black children must endure from everything they read and see (d) all of the above.

3. __B__ The author directly and implicitly criticizes (a) black mothers who fail to instruct their children properly about their race (b) children's books and television programs geared solely to white audiences (c) the inability of American education to cope with and understand black children's problems (d) militant blacks who assert their masculinity aggressively (e) all of the above.

4. __E__ Whom does Miss Shepard blame directly for her son's confusion about his race? (a) various media which represent white as good and black as evil (b) her own ignorance, for not correctly perceiving why Mark was confused (c) his teachers (d) all of the above (e) a and b only.

5. __C__ Why did Mark not understand why he was different from white children? (a) because he was raised around only white children (b) because he failed to see that being black is only a state of mind and a set of attitudes (c) because he considered race, not as a color, but as an attitude which he did not exemplify (d) because he could not identify with black masculinity.

6. __A__ What irony does the author intend when she relates Mark's

fervent recitation of the Pledge of Allegiance and his curiosity about the words "indivisible," "liberty," and "justice"? The irony is that (a) Mark is innocent: it is difficult to explain to a child that these abstract concepts are not always applied to all people equally (b) these abstract concepts are meaningless to a small child (c) all children, black and white, should learn and believe in these abstract concepts, even if they are later proved untrue (d) Mark's teachers should have explained the meanings of the words.

7. __F__ At the end of the essay, the author asks several questions about her son's future. Basic to all her questions is the fear that (a) he will never understand what it means to be black, and will be angry and frustrated all his life (b) he will become meek and accept racial injustice as inevitable (c) his precociousness as a child will be stifled and killed, rather than developed and encouraged (d) he will assert his blackness militantly and instinctively (e) only b and c (f) a, c, and d.

8. __A__ According to the essay, what should the objective of education be? (a) to utilize everyone's talents, no matter what his racial background is, to build a better future (b) to offer all children courses in ethnic history and culture so that existing prejudices are broken down at an early age (c) to teach the practical goals which young people must confront when they become adults (d) to teach children to respect others' rights.

9. __E__ The author's tone in this selection is (a) gentle and meek (b) bitter and frustrated (c) compassionate and pleading (d) arrogant and disdainful (e) a combination of b and c.

10. __B__ The couplet at the end: "O pardon me, thou bleeding piece of earth,/ That I am meek and gentle with these butchers" suggests (a) that black people are justified in their bitterness and resentment of white people (b) that black people have been meek and gentle too long toward their oppressors (c) that black people are human and deserve respect like everyone else (d) that black people have no future but despair.

VOCABULARY

From the lettered choices, find the best definition for each vocabulary item, and mark the letter in the space provided.

1. __E__ on his own *initiative*
2. __J__ with deep *fervor*
3. __A__ precious, *precocious* Mark

4. __M__ *vanquished* by the white of day
5. __H__ he had *intuitively* perceived
6. __B__ he did not *exemplify*
7. __O__ the normal legendary *verbiage*
8. __F__ to *alleviate* his pain
9. __K__ black-*bigoted* replica
10. __C__ utter, needless *trauma*

A. unusually developed, advanced
B. illustrate; represent
C. severe emotional shock
D. imitate; copy
E. without compulsion or instruction; freely
F. make lighter; relieve
G. nonsense; foolishness
H. quality of learning without conscious attention or reasoning

I. intensify; make worse
J. great warmth; ardor
K. narrow-minded; intolerant of others
L. excuses; pretexts
M. defeated; conquered
N. inaccurately; incorrectly
O. excess of words

COMPREHENSION   No. right _____ × 10 = _____ %

VOCABULARY   No. right _____ × 10 = _____ %

No. of words 875 ÷ time in seconds _____ × 60 = _____ WPM
WPM × Comprehension % = Reading Efficiency Rate _____

Chapter 11

READING TEXTBOOKS

When you are assigned to read a textbook chapter, do you respond in any of these ways?

—you read it dutifully, but at the end, you can't remember a thing;

—you glance over the chapter, count the pages and the pictures, then decide to see a movie;

—you put off reading it, along with your other reading assignments until the night before the exam, so it will be fresh in your mind;

—you underline nearly everything, so you can go back and memorize your underlinings before the test;

—you make a perfectly detailed outline, put it away and never look at it again.

If you were honest, and if you answered yes to any of these, you are probably wasting a good share of your reading time. The key to efficient studying is to learn the material at once and to spend your study time only in reviewing what you've already learned. In this chapter, you will learn a simple but systematic way to read and study textbook material. The four steps in this study method are outlined here. Read them over thoroughly.

STEP 1 SURVEY AND QUESTION

Before you read, survey and make questions from

Book as a whole   { —the table of contents
  —preface and introduction

Each
individual
chapter

$\left\{\begin{array}{l}\end{array}\right.$

—chapter title
—introductory paragraphs
—main headings and sub-headings
—concluding paragraphs
—discussion questions and/or outline of chapter contents

STEP 2 READ: Read the material, keeping your questions from the first step in mind.

STEP 3 TAKE NOTES: Jot down notes to answer your questions after reading the material.

STEP 4 REVIEW: Look over your questions and notes immediately *after* completing an assignment and just *before* an examination.

STEP 1: SURVEY AND QUESTION

Most students make the fatal mistake of opening a book at page one and reading diligently until they have completed the assignment. But no matter how thoroughly you read, you are still reading haphazardly, because you lack a plan or a framework. The important point, *before you begin to read,* is to establish a framework, to get an idea of how the author organizes his subject. The first step, then, is to survey and ask questions from the prefatory material. Once you know how the subject is organized, you will have an overall pattern into which separate topics will fit. Let's say, for example, that you are assigned to read a supplementary book on Greek civilization. First, ask yourself what you already know about the Greeks, and more important, what you expect to find out from reading. Then, survey the table of contents to find out the overall plan for the book's organization.

CONTENTS

H. D. F. Kitto, from *The Greeks**

* (Middlesex: Penguin Books Ltd., 1962), p. 5.

After surveying the chapter titles, you will see that there are three basic divisions within the text:

I. Chapters 1–4: Introduction; origins of the Greek race and geography of the Greek islands.
II. Chapters 5–9: Detailed account of the Greek political system; important events in Greek history through its decline.
III. Chapters 10–12: Social and religious customs; the important achievements of Greek civilization.

Further, ask yourself what you are likely to find in each chapter. Refer to the table of contents if necessary and write the number of the chapters where you would expect to find these topics discussed:

1. A description of the geography of Greece and its surrounding islands. _____
2. An analysis of the Greek political system. _____
3. The mythic beginnings of the Greek race. _____
4. The role of women in Greek society. _____
5. Early Greek mythology and Greek religious customs. _____
6. An analysis of Homer's *Iliad* and *Odyssey*. _____

Read the following table of contents and then determine the three basic divisions of the subject, environmental conservation. Describe each division briefly in your own words.

RAYMOND F. DASMANN, *Environmental Conservation**

* (New York: John Wiley & Sons, Inc., 1968), p. xiii.

FRAMEWORK

Part I: Chapters _____ to _____: _____

_____

Part II: Chapters _____ to _____: _____

_____

Part III: Chapters _____ to _____: _____

_____

Next, mark the number of any pertinent chapters where you would expect to locate this information.

1. What man has done to his environment in the past. _____
2. A definition of environment and ecology. _____
3. Crop rotation and soil erosion. _____
4. Regional climates and sources for important natural resources. _____
5. Irrigation and water supply systems. _____
6. Major pollutants of cities. _____
7. A prediction for the future of the environment. _____

From these two examples, it should be readily clear why having a framework in mind before you read is so important. Rather than thinking of each chapter as a separate little box, you should see how each topic relates to the overall plan of the book. In addition to surveying the table of contents, be sure to read carefully through both the preface and the introduction. There you will find the author's purpose, the main ideas he will discuss, and very likely, his particular point of view.

To survey-question each chapter, here are the items you should pay attention to:

—the chapter title
—introductory paragraphs
—main headings
—sub-headings
—concluding paragraphs
—outline, summary and/or discussion questions.

To make correct questions, simply turn the information into a question which cannot be answered by yes or no. For example, consider this heading from a sociology textbook: "the culture of affluence." You might ask the question "what is the culture of affluence?" or "what are the main characteristics of an affluent culture?"—*not* "is there a culture of affluence?" For this heading from an American history textbook: "The Economic Effects of World War II on Germany," you might ask "what were the war's effects on Germany's economy?" or something similar. Remember that these questions give your reading a purpose, so they should be simple enough to keep in mind when you actually begin to read.

As you survey and question, jot your questions down on a sheet of paper, being sure to leave enough space after each one for notes. And be sure to survey carefully the introductory and concluding paragraphs, for there you will find the main ideas in capsule form.

The first selection for practice is from an introductory psychology text-book. The specific subject is *conformity*. To see how the topic relates to the entire section, here is the pertinent extract from the table of contents.

PART 8   The Child, The Adult, and Society

JEROME KAGAN and ERNEST HAVEMANN, *Psychology: An Introduction**

STEP 1: SURVEY AND QUESTION—Before you read through the passage, write your questions in the appropriate spaces. You should find four questions.

Question 1 _____

_____

_____

Question 2 _____

_____

_____

* (New York: Harcourt Brace Jovanovich, Inc., 1968), pp. xiii–xiv.

Question 3 _____

_____

_____

Question 4 _____

_____

_____

STEP 2: As you READ the passage through, keep your four questions in mind.

STEP 3: TAKE NOTES from the material you read, putting them into your own words as much as possible. Use the space provided after each question.

STEP 4: REVIEW your questions and notes before taking the short quiz.

CONFORMITY

Up to this point, the discussion has been mostly about norms—first the general standards for behavior and attitudes that are set by the particular society, culture, and social class, then the more specific expectations that are attached to different positions and roles in society. As has been mentioned briefly, society enforces its norms both through law and formal punishment and through the informal methods of social disapproval and praise. Let us enlarge upon this point now by considering some of the findings that have been made on the subject of *conformity*—which is defined as the yielding by an individual to pressures from another person or, more usually, a group.

Conformity, Counterconformity, and Independence

The word *conformity* has been a highly popular one in recent years. Many philosophers and social observers feel that we live in what might be called an "age of conformity"—in which all of us tend to dress alike, live in the same kind of houses, watch the same television shows, eat the same frozen TV dinners, hold the same kind of opinions, conduct the same kind of conversations, and in general behave meekly and imitatively like a flock of sheep. The leaders of the flock are not apparent; indeed there do not seem, according to this view of our present society, to be any leaders. We all seem to follow the lead of one another, trying to be alike and inconspicuous, taking up any new fad that appears, keeping up with the Joneses, staying in step.

There has also been a rebellion against this kind of conformity by some of the youth of America, expressed in such varied forms as beards, the wearing of sandals, campus protest meetings, picketing, new intellectual movements and new forms of music and literature, and sometimes experimentation with drugs.

It is difficult to make comparisons between different periods in history, and we have no scientific evidence to support or refute these views of our present society. People may or may not in truth conform more today than in previous times. The rebellion against conformity may be a real rebellion or, as some observers think, just a new way of conforming to some new norms. There is, however, considerable evidence about the tendency to conform and the factors that influence it.

Before going into the evidence, it is necessary to clarify some of the concepts that must be used in talking about this subject.

Conformity is a process that takes place only when there is a conflict between the individual's own desires, values, or opinions and the norms that society attempts to enforce. The individual who conforms abandons his own wishes and attitudes—or never dares develop any—and instead accepts the norms held by the people around him. There is a distinction between what have been called *true conformity* and *expedient conformity*. In true conformity the individual actually modifies both his behavior and his attitudes in accordance with the group pressure. For example, a working-class man who has been strongly in favor of labor unions may, after moving up into a conservative circle of upper-class businessmen, become actively and genuinely opposed to unions. In expedient conformity the individual only pays lip service to the norms, inwardly retaining his own attitudes. For example, a man who planned to vote for candidate A in a forthcoming election but found himself at a party where everyone else was strongly for candidate B might pretend to go along with the group simply to avoid argument.

Counterconformity is a sort of blind rebellion against society, engaged in by the kind of person who says, "If everybody else is for it, then I'm against it." Although the counterconformist may seem like the most rugged sort of individualist, actually he too is conforming—but in a negative direction. He disagrees with society automatically, no matter what position society takes.

Independence is the opposite of conformity; it describes a tendency to make up one's own mind and decide upon one's own behavior, taking society's norms into account but not giving them slavish devotion. One of the facts that make sweeping statements about conformity difficult is that the independent person may seem on the surface to be quite conventional. To preserve an orderly society every individual must observe a great many norms. Thus the independent person may dress, live, work, and play like everybody else but show a large amount of independence in making up his own mind, regardless of social pressures, on such issues as politics, religion, civil rights, and what kind of values to teach his children.

Milgram's Experiment on Conformity

One of the most dramatic experiments on conformity—in many ways a frightening experiment—was performed by Stanley Milgram at Yale. Like many persons interested in human nature, Milgram found himself haunted by the events in Hitler's Germany, where a great many ordinary sorts of people, presumably with ordinary social backgrounds and moral standards, took part directly or passively in a program that resulted in the mass execution of millions of European Jews. How, Milgram wondered, could such a thing happen? What in the human personality or in the structure of society could account for the willingness of so many people to take part in or at least go along with a slaughter of such magnitude?

In search of clues, Milgram devised the following experiment. Eighty men of various ages and occupational backgrounds were chosen as subjects and asked to take part in what they were told was an important experiment in learning. Each subject was assigned to a group of four people, the other three of whom, unknown to him, were Milgram's assistants. One of the assistants was the "learner" in the make-believe experiment; he was assigned to learn a laboratory task. The other two assistants and the subject were the "teachers," given the job of instructing the learner by punishing him with an electric shock when he made an error. The subject was put at controls that regulated the amount of shock, from mild to extremely intense and painful. Actually no electricity was hooked up to the controls and no learning took place; the learner deliberately made mistakes and only pretended to feel a shock when punished.

The purpose of the experiment was to learn to what levels the subjects would raise the amount of electric shock. Forty of the subjects were considered a control group and were not placed under group pressure. The other forty were urged by the other members of the team to raise the amount of electricity higher and higher, on the ground that this was essential to the experiment. The results were startling. The control subjects generally stopped at levels of shock intensity marked 3 or 4. But many of the other subjects, urged on by their fellow teachers, continued to raise the level even when the learner screamed and begged for mercy. Many of them showed signs of doubt and distress but went along anyway with the suggestions of their companions. On the average, they went all the way up to a shock level of 14 (23). Such can be the effect of social pressure and the tendency to conformity.

KAGAN and HAVEMANN, from
*Psychology: An Introduction**

REVIEW QUIZ

Do not refer back to either the passage or to your notes to answer these items.

1. Briefly define conformity. _____

_____

_____

* (New York: Harcourt Brace Jovanovich, Inc., 1968), pp. 593–595.

2. What is the main prerequisite for conformity? _____

_____

_____

3. How does one distinguish between *true* and *expedient* conformity?

_____

_____

_____

4. What is *counterconformity?* _____

_____

_____

5. Summarize briefly the results of Milgram's experiments with conformity. _____

_____

_____

Note: the italicized sub-heading, "Conformity, Counterconformity, and Independence," should have required three separate questions, because each is defined in three separate paragraphs. The alternative might have been to ask only one question, and when taking notes, you could have labeled each term carefully and defined them separately.

Here is a second practice selection from an introductory textbook in American history. Again, look at the table of contents first to see how the passage fits into the whole section. Follow the four steps in order, just as you did before.

33

The American People After the War   827

Population trends. Economic changes. Wealth and poverty. The Negro revolution moves left. The ordeal of the city.

The Culture of Affluence   833

A middle-class society. The homogenized society? Mass culture. The boom in religion. The uncommitted generation. Stirrings under the surface. The cultural boom. The tumultuous sixties. The new theology. The revolt of the young. The darkling future.

JOHN BLUM et al., from *The National Experience**

STEP 1: SURVEY AND QUESTION—Make questions from the two sub-headings and write them in these spaces.

Question 1 _____

_____

_____

Question 2 _____

_____

_____

STEP 2: READ the passage through, keeping your questions in mind.

STEP 3: TAKE NOTES, writing them under each question.

STEP 4: REVIEW your questions and notes.

THE AMERICAN PEOPLE AFTER THE WAR

   Population trends. In the years after the Second World War, an unexpected spurt in population increased the strain on the inherited institutions of American society. The fall in the birth rate during the Depression had led demographers to predict that the nation's population would soon level off. Instead, the return to prosperity in the war years produced a swing to earlier marriages and larger families. At the same time, medical advances—the introduction of penicillin and other antibiotics, of antipolio vaccines, and of new surgical techniques—brought about a steady drop in the death rate. Between 1935 and 1957 the birth rate rose from 16.9 to 25 per thousand, the death rate fell from 10.9 to 9.6, and life expectancy rose toward 70. Furthermore, about 2.25 million immigrants entered the country in the fifties—more than in any decade since the twenties. The nation's population had grown only about 9 million in the thirties; it grew 19 million in the forties and 28 million in the fifties. The increase in the fifties alone was almost equal to the total population of

* 2nd Edition (New York: Harcourt Brace Jovanovich, Inc., 1968), p. xviii.

the country a century earlier and took place at about the same rate in the United States as in India. Though the birth rate somewhat declined in the sixties—from a high of 4.3 million births in 1957 to 3.75 million in the middle of the next decade—the net population increase in the sixties was still in the range of about 2.8 million per year.

By 1967 the United States had nearly 200 million people, of whom about 11 per cent were nonwhite. Forty per cent of the population were under 21, 46.5 per cent under 25, and more than half under 30. But the number of old people was also greater than ever before. A new-born baby, who in 1920 would have had a life expectancy of 54 years, could now look forward to living to 70. As for the distribution of the population, the most striking change was that 70 per cent of the people lived in urban areas. By the mid-sixties the farm population was down to 12.4 million, as against 30.5 million in 1940; it now represented one-fifteenth of the total population as against almost one-fourth twenty-five years earlier. The census of 1960 showed the greatest regional increase in the West; its rate of 38.9 per cent was more than double the national rate of 18.5 per cent. California alone grew 5.1 million, accounting for nearly one-fifth of the total growth and soon (by 1964) surpassing New York as the nation's most populous state. About 85 per cent of the increase before 1960 took place in cities of over fifty thousand and the suburban areas around them, and two-thirds of this—around 17.6 million—was in the suburbs themselves. The number of suburbanites increased from 36.8 to 54.4 million, a gain of 48 per cent. And mobility continued to mark American life: 19.9 per cent of Americans, about 31.5 million people, moved from one place to another in the year ending April 1960.

Economic changes. From 1961 to 1966 the average rate of increase in the gross national product at constant prices was 5.4 per cent. By 1967 the GNP was running at $775 billion a year ($664 billion in 1958 prices)—a gain of 50 per cent in uniform dollars over 1956. The civilian labor force was over 75 million persons, and the unemployment rate had fallen to around 6 per cent. Manufacturing capacity had doubled since 1951; as much new plant and machinery had been added to the nation's industrial equipment in this period as in the first one hundred fifty years of American history. Between 1947 and 1965, moreover, output per man hour rose at a rate of 3.2 per cent a year, which made it possible for total manufacturing output to increase 50 per cent during the fifties with only a 9 per cent increase in the number of workers.

A significant factor in this striking increase in productivity was the development of the industrial techniques summed up in the word "automation." The basis of automation was the electronic computer. The first electric digital computer was built in 1946; and in the years after the war Norbert Wiener and others explored the dazzling potentialities of "cybernetics," the science devoted to the study of communication and control mechanisms. The distinctive element in the industrial application of the computer was the introduction of self-regulating devices into the manufacturing sequence based on the "feedback" principle. The computer, once it had been programed, could absorb information that would enable it to continue, vary, or correct automatic operations.

By the sixties the computer promised to revolutionize every aspect of industry from production to marketing and to affect the methods of everyone from the engineer to the economist. In one aspect automation threatened to intensify problems of technological unemployment. Thus the largest synthetic-ammonia plant in the world, built in 1965 by the Olin-Mathieson Corporation, required a total of thirty-two employes, of whom eleven were supervisory, technical, and clerical. In the coal fields the so-called pushbutton miner could cut and load 266 tons of coal an hour in one continuous operation with a crew of three operating by remote control from a panel outside the mine shaft. Experts disagreed, however, on the longer-run impact of automation on employment. The President's National Commission on Technology, Automation, and Economic Progress declined in 1965 to reach pessimistic conclusions.

Automation and other technological miracles stemmed in part from heavy investment in research and development by both business and government. Total research and development expenditures almost quadrupled between 1953 and 1964. By the latter year, $19 billion was spent annually, of which 66 per cent was provided by the federal government —a larger sum in a single year than the government had expended for this purpose from independence through the Second World War. Many scientists, however, considered the outlay for basic research inadequate. Moreover, the stimulation of research and development through government contracts was bringing about subtle far-reaching changes in the structure and control of the national economy—a process that led some observers to speak of "the contract state."

Aerospace—a $25-billion industry by 1967—became a particular focus for new research and investment. President Kennedy's commitment of the nation to a manned landing on the moon initiated a historic undertaking for the exploration of space. Though some questioned the diversion of resources to this objective, arguing that the funds might better go to social improvement at home, others regarded the breaking of man's terrestrial bonds as the most exciting and historic event of the twentieth century. The radio telescope and the space probe, said the British astronomer Sir Bernard Lovell, could have the same effect on contemporary life and thought as Galileo's small telescope had had three and a half centuries before; together they could put humanity "on the point of answering the great problems of the initial condition and evolution of the Universe and the Solar System."

Kennedy himself believed that man grew by his determination to explore the unknown. He said in 1962,

> We choose to go to the moon in this decade and do the other things, not because they are easy but because they are hard; because that goal will serve to organize and measure the best of our energies and skills. . . . Many years ago the great British explorer George Mallory, who was to die on Mount Everest, was asked why did he want to climb it, and he said, "Because it is there." Well, space is there, and . . . the moon and the planets are there, and new hopes for knowledge and peace are there.

By 1967 the national space program required a budget of more than $7 billion. The Apollo project, as the lunar landing was called, had set in motion a vast technological effort with a multitude of indirect scientific and economic implications. Though Kennedy's hope of a joint lunar expedition with the Soviet Union had evoked no response, mankind was now well launched on the most incredible of human adventures.

JOHN BLUM et al., *The National Experience**

REVIEW QUIZ

Answer these questions without referring to your notes or to the passage.

1. List two reasons for the increase in population after World War II.

   (a) _____

   (b) _____

2. By 1967, approximately what percentage of Americans lived in the cities? _____

3. What was the general trend in the Gross National Product between 1956 and 1967? _____

4. What one development accounts for the tremendous rise in manufacturing production after the war? _____

   _____

5. List two technological advances which have changed both business and government spending since the war. (a) _____

   _____

   (b) _____

   _____

Occasionally, some textbooks may not have the standard divisions of headings and sub-headings. In this case, you can still use the four-step method with slight modification.

* 2nd Edition (New York: Harcourt Brace Jovanovich, Inc., 1968), pp. 827–830.

STEP 1: SURVEY AND QUESTION—chapter title
                                         —introductory paragraphs
                                         —concluding paragraphs
                                         —first sentence of every other
                                           paragraph (if material is very
                                           difficult)

This system won't always work with chapters of straight prose, but you can at least get a notion of the chapter's general idea. You may find that looking for italicized words will help too, for usually these are important concepts or definitions. This short passage from a text on environmental conservation has only a title and no subsequent divisions. As you read, keep the title in mind: "What are the patterns and special problems of urban areas?" In addition, stop to think how much you already know about this topic. Chances are, a good portion of the passage is already part of your general knowledge. Survey the first sentences of each paragraph, for this is a short passage, and then read it through.

URBAN PATTERNS AND PROBLEMS

It is impossible here to do more than give a sketchy outline of some of the problems involved in planning and developing new urban areas and improving the old. Most of our towns and cities grew originally with little overall planning or control. They reflect thousands of individual decisions and hundreds of partial plans. These have contributed in some areas to a rich texture of interesting urban diversity, in others to ugliness and confusion. Past efforts to achieve some order in the cities have to a large degree taken the line of separating urban functions through zoning. Zoning laws have separated the industrial areas where people work in producing goods; the commercial areas where people shop or work at office jobs; and the residential areas where people sleep and carry out much of their social life. The latter are further divided into areas of single-family detached homes and areas of multiple-family housing represented by high-rise apartments or other high-density housing. Such a separation of urban functions was inhibited originally by transportation facilities. In the 19th century and earlier, it was necessary to be within walking distance of work and shopping areas. With the development of individual transportation by private automobile, however, it became possible to separate these urban functions widely. Thus the development of residential suburbs, extending often in uniform patterns for many miles beyond the former city boundaries, occurred.

Cities, by their very nature, present problems of transportation. They are areas in which agricultural produce is processed or consumed and areas in which the various products of industry are manufactured. There must be a constant flow of goods into and out of the city. The modern industrial city consequently grew up around the railroad junction. The central railway station was the focus around which hotels, entertainment centers, stores, and offices were grouped. The railway line was the axis along which the city expanded into the countryside, the means by which city people travelled to seek recreation, the basis for the existence of satellite towns, resorts, and other urban-oriented developments. Within the city, public transportation systems, horsecars or, later, electric trolleys served to move people from the industrial or commercial centers to the residential districts. With the rise of the private automobile and the gasoline or diesel-powered truck, however, this old framework of the city was disrupted. New urban centers, more readily accessible by automobile, arose, and the area around the railway station disintegrated into a "skid row" or slum district. Highways, rather than rails, provided the new avenues for urban expansion into the countryside. Public transportation facilities disintegrated.

With ever-growing numbers of automobiles the traffic jam became a permanent part of the urban scene. The difficulties of reaching the city center and of parking when there, along with other factors, led to a breakdown of the central city. Business and industry followed the people to the suburbs. New centers of work and commerce, dispersed widely around the periphery of the urbanized area, began to replace the old centralized urban core. The central city became a place where the poor concentrated, where ethnic minority groups were forced to live, and where housing, schools, and all other urban facilities deteriorated. Cities, in the old sense of vital, thriving centers of human activity and interest, appeared to be dying.

The suburbs have been the subject of many sociological studies since the end of World War II and have been blamed for many of the ills of modern society. Yet there is little doubt that most people who have moved there from the central city have gained a marked improvement in living conditions. The suburbs have become the established center of the American middle-class family, since they offer security and space for the raising of children in congenial surroundings. They have been consistently rejected by the adolescent and young adult who find them restrictive and dull. They have little appeal to the intellectual. In one form or another, however, they are likely to remain as part of urbanized America.

RAYMOND F. DASMANN, *Environmental Conservation**

REVIEW QUIZ

1. How did towns and cities originally develop? _____

_____

_____

2. How have zoning laws helped separate urban functions? _____

_____

_____

* (New York: John Wiley & Sons, Inc., 1968), pp. 301–302.

3. What are three main reasons for the rapid growth of the suburbs?

(a) _____

(b) _____

(c) _____

4. Why has the railway system finally become obsolete? _____

_____

_____

5. What are the advantages and disadvantages of the suburbs?

(a) advantages _____

_____

(b) disadvantages _____

_____

The fourth step, REVIEW, is nearly as important as accurate surveying, for this step will determine your success or failure in taking examinations. Be sure to review twice: first, just after you complete an assignment, and second, just before an exam. If you learn the material well the first time, your reviewing time before the exam should be relatively painless. And there is no need to reread an entire textbook chapter or even your underlinings. If your notes are comprehensible and in good order, they should be an adequate study guide.

This four-step method of study works. It works as long as you remember to keep in mind a framework, so that the facts you learn can hinge on something definite. Once you get used to applying the method, it will become second nature. Even more important, your grades may improve from mediocre to very good, or from very good to excellent. The length of time you devote to studying is not important; it's what you do during that time that counts.

EXERCISE: For further practice, try the four-step method on several textbook chapters you are assigned to read. Begin your practice with your easiest textbook, and gradually work up to the most difficult. This process, combined with concentration, is what good studying is all about.

READING SELECTION 11—Harvey Cox, from "Sex and Secularization" *

Harvey Cox, associate professor of Church and Society at Harvard University's Divinity School, argues that the two hallmarks of our society are the rise of urban civilization and the collapse of traditional religion. In this excerpt from "Sex and Secularization," a chapter of his famous book, The Secular City, *Dr. Cox gives us a disturbing interpretation of* Playboy *and its philosophy.*

The Playboy, illustrated by the monthly magazine of that name, does for the boys what Miss America does for the girls. Despite accusations to the contrary, the immense popularity of this magazine is not solely attributable to pin-up girls. For sheer nudity its pictorial art cannot compete with such would-be competitors as *Dude* and *Escapade*. *Playboy* appeals to a highly mobile, increasingly affluent group of young readers, mostly between eighteen and thirty, who want much more from their drugstore reading than bosoms and thighs. They need a total image of what it means to be a man. And Mr. Hefner's *Playboy* has no hesitation in telling them.

Why should such a need arise? David Riesman has argued that the responsibility for character formation in our society has shifted from the family to the peer group and to the mass-media peer-group surrogates. Things are changing so rapidly that one who is equipped by his family with inflexible, highly internalized values becomes unable to deal with the accelerated pace of change and with the varying contexts in which he is called upon to function. This is especially true in the area of consumer values toward which the "other-directed person" is increasingly oriented.

Within the confusing plethora of mass media signals and peer-group values, *Playboy* fills a special need. For the insecure young man with newly acquired free time and money who still feels uncertain about his consumer skills, *Playboy* supplies a comprehensive and authoritative guidebook to this forbidding new world to which he now has access. It tells him not only who to be; it tells him *how* to be it, and even provides consolation outlets for those who secretly feel that they have not quite made it.

In supplying for the other-directed consumer of leisure both the normative identity image and the means for achieving it, *Playboy* relies on a careful integration of copy and advertising material. The comic book that appeals to a younger generation with an analogous problem skillfully intersperses illustrations of incredibly muscled men and excessively mammalian women with advertisements for body-building gimmicks and foam-rubber brassière supplements. Thus the thin-chested comic-book readers of both sexes are thoughtfully supplied with both the ends and the means for attaining a spurious brand of maturity. *Playboy* merely continues the

---

* From *The Secular City* (New York: The Macmillan Company, 1965), pp. 199–205.

comic-book tactic for the next age group. Since within every identity crisis, whether in teens or twenties, there is usually a sexual-identity problem, *Playboy* speaks to those who desperately want to know what it means to be a man, and more specifically a *male*, in today's world.

Both the image of man and the means for its attainment exhibit a remarkable consistency in *Playboy*. The skilled consumer is cool and unruffled. He savors sports cars, liquor, high fidelity, and book-club selections with a casual, unhurried aplomb. Though he must certainly *have* and *use* the latest consumption item, he must not permit himself to get too attached to it. The style will change and he must always be ready to adjust. His persistent anxiety that he may mix a drink incorrectly, enjoy a jazz group that is passé, or wear last year's necktie style is comforted by an authoritative tone in *Playboy* beside which papal encyclicals sound irresolute.

"Don't hesitate," he is told, "this assertive, self-assured weskit is what every man of taste wants for the fall season." Lingering doubts about his masculinity are extirpated by the firm assurance that "real men demand this ruggedly masculine smoke" (cigar ad). Though "the ladies will swoon for you, no matter what they promise, don't give them a puff. This cigar is for men only." A fur-lined canvas field jacket is described as "the most masculine thing since the cave man." What to be and how to be it are both made unambiguously clear.

Since being a male necessitates some kind of relationship to females, *Playboy* fearlessly confronts this problem too, and solves it by the consistent application of the same formula. Sex becomes one of the items of leisure activity that the knowledgeable consumer of leisure handles with his characteristic skill and detachment. The girl becomes a desirable— indeed an indispensable—"Playboy accessory."

In a question-answering column entitled "The Playboy Adviser," queries about smoking equipment (how to break in a meerschaum pipe), cocktail preparation (how to mix a Yellow Fever), and whether or not to wear suspenders with a vest alternate with questions about what to do with girls who complicate the cardinal principle of casualness either by suggesting marriage or by some other impulsive gesture toward a permanent relationship. The infallible answer from the oracle never varies: sex must be contained, at all costs, within the entertainment-recreation area. Don't let her get "serious."

After all, the most famous feature of the magazine is its monthly foldout photo of a *play*mate. She is the symbol par excellence of recreational sex. When playtime is over, the playmate's function ceases, so she must be made to understand the rules of the game. As the crew-cut young man in a *Playboy* cartoon says to the rumpled and disarrayed girl he is passionately embracing, "Why speak of love at a time like this?"

The magazine's fiction purveys the same kind of severely departmentalized sex. Although the editors have recently dressed up the *Playboy* contents with contributions by Hemingway, Bemelmans, and even a Chekhov translation, the regular run of stories relies on a repetitious and predictable formula. A successful young man, either single or somewhat less than ideally married—a figure with whom readers have no difficulty identifying —encounters a gorgeous and seductive woman who makes no demands on him except sex. She is the prose duplication of the cool-eyed but hot-blooded playmate of the fold-out.

Drawing heavily on the fantasy life of all young Americans, the writers utilize for their stereotyped heroines the hero's schoolteacher, his secretary, and old girl friend, or the girl who brings her car into the garage where he works. The happy issue is always a casual but satisfying sexual experience with no entangling alliances whatever. Unlike the women he knows in real life, the *Playboy* reader's fictional girl friends know their place and ask for nothing more. They present no danger of permanent involvement. Like any good accessory, they are detachable and disposable.

Many of the advertisements reinforce the sex-accessory identification in another way—by attributing female characteristics to the items they sell. Thus a full-page add for the MG assures us that this car is not only "the smoothest pleasure machine" on the road and that having one is a "love-affair," but most important, "you drive it—it doesn't drive you." The ad ends with the equivocal question "Is it a date?"

Playboy insists that its message is one of liberation. Its gospel frees us from captivity to the puritanical "hatpin brigade." It solemnly crusades for "frankness" and publishes scores of letters congratulating it for its unblushing "candor." Yet the whole phenomenon of which *Playboy* is only a part vividly illustrates the awful fact of a new kind of tyranny.

Those liberated by technology and increased prosperity to new worlds of leisure now become the anxious slaves of dictatorial tastemakers. Obsequiously waiting for the latest signal on what is cool and what is awkward, they are paralyzed by the fear that they may hear pronounced on them that dread sentence occasionally intoned by "The Playboy Adviser": "You goofed!" Leisure is thus swallowed up in apprehensive competitiveness, its liberating potential transformed into a self-destructive compulsion to consume only what is *à la mode*. *Playboy* mediates the Word of the most high into one section of the consumer world, but it is a word of bondage, not of freedom.

READING SELECTION 11

COMPREHENSION

Do not refer to the article to answer these questions. Choose one of the items that best answers each question, and mark the letter in the space provided.

1. _____ According to the author, one of the primary reasons for *Playboy*'s success and popularity is its appeal to (a) men who like pictures of nude women (b) male consumers who want to know what is correct to buy and wear (c) men who like to read tantalizing encounters of successful sexual encounters (d) insecure men who want to acquire a male image.

2. _____ The author states that *Playboy* is read mainly by (a) affluent college students between 17 and 22 years of age (b) married men over 35 years of age (c) mobile, affluent men between 18 and 30 years of age (d) men of all ages and incomes.

3. _____ At the beginning of the selection, Cox says that "*Playboy* does for the boys what Miss America does for girls." From this one can infer that earlier in the chapter, Cox (a) promoted the Miss America contest because each winner is a symbol of what every woman should be (b) criticized the contest for denying the American woman her sexual status (c) criticized the contest for promoting a false, empty image of American womanhood (d) criticized the contest for promoting the new morality of recreational sex (e) none of the above.

4. _____ Cox cites a problem in American society, a theory of David Riesman's, which helps explain *Playboy*'s appeal. Which is the most accurate statement of that problem? (a) the breakdown of religious morality and the disregard for law and order (b) the tendency to question traditional values and the individual's desire to live by his own moral system (c) the phenomenon of the "other-directed" person whose values come not from his family, but from peers and mass media (d) the instability of contemporary society and the individual's insecurity about the future.

5. _____ The author compares *Playboy* metaphorically to comic books for adults which suggests that the magazine (a) is as juvenile and silly as children's comic books (b) offers a questionable brand of maturity to adults who lack sexual identity (c) is only harmless fantasy and diversion (d) offers only a caricature of masculinity.

6. _____ *Playboy* prescribes the male image by demanding in a subtle way that (a) a man must adapt to new fashions and taste when old styles become outmoded (b) a man must be cool, casual and correct in all social situations (c) a man cannot get too attached to one item, whether it is a woman or a jazz group (d) a man must use the products advertised to guarantee a masculine image (e) all of the above.

7. _____ Cox states that the magazine's philosophy, represented by the question-and-answer columns, advertising, and fiction, is (a) tolerant and liberal (b) humorous yet compelling (c) authoritarian and dictatorial (d) sophisticated and worldly.

8. _____ *Playboy's* philosophy toward men's sexual involvement with women stresses that (a) women are only desirable accessories and that total involvement inhibits freedom (b) women are to be fully enjoyed, but discarded if they suggest a permanent relationship (c) women are for entertainment and recreation, not for entangling alliances (d) women should engage in casual but satisfying sexual relationships with men but without making demands (e) all of the above (f) only b and d.

9. _____ According to Cox, the Playmate of the month is a symbol of (a) lewdness and vulgarity (b) recreational sex (c) feminine grace and beauty (d) sophisticated cheesecake.

10. _____ In his concluding argument, the author's main criticism of *Playboy* is that it (a) dictates rather than frees, tyrannizes rather than liberates, by making slaves of its readers (b) cleverly manipulates its readers toward an amoral standard of behavior (c) gives a false image of masculinity by appealing to the superficial virtues of ruggedness and virility (d) denies men their natural instincts for love and security (e) all of the above.

VOCABULARY

From the lettered choices, find the best definition for each vocabulary item, and mark the letter in the space provided.

1. __E__ a highly *mobile* group
2. __B__ peer-group *surrogates*
3. __K__ *plethora* of mass-media signals
4. __H__ an *analogous* problem
5. __N__ a *spurious* brand of maturity
6. __A__ casual, unhurried *aplomb*
7. __C__ made *unambiguously* clear
8. __D__ the *infallible* answer

9. ___F___ ends with the *equivocal* question
10. ___M___ unblushing *"candor"*

A. assurance; self-confidence
B. substitutes
C. capable of only one meaning or interpretation
D. free from errors of judgment
E. free to move; versatile
F. having a doubtful meaning; ambiguous
G. dishonest; unjust
H. resembling or comparable in certain respects

I. equals; contemporaries
J. lack; scarcity
K. excess; abundance
L. unanswerable; impossible to ascertain
M. frankness; openness
N. false; not genuine
O. insecurity; instability

COMPREHENSION   No. right _____ × 10 = _____%

VOCABULARY   No. right _____ × 10 = _____%

No. of words 1325 ÷ time in seconds _____ × 60 = _____ WPM
WPM × Comprehension % = Reading Efficiency Rate _____

Chapter 12

IMPROVING READING SPEED

The matter of reading speed has purposely been saved for the last chapter of Part I. As you learned in Chapter 2, it is foolish to try to push your speed if your comprehension skills are weak. But because in college you must read, digest and study masses of reading material, you may find it necessary to do something to improve your rate of comprehension.

There are many misconceptions about "speed reading," perhaps because of the current fad for crash reading courses that guarantee to triple your reading speed. This chapter makes no claim to accomplish that. Instead, you should work toward a more realistic goal—a 20 to 30 per cent increase in reading rate over one term. For instance, if your rate at the beginning of the course was around 250 words per minute, you might well be pleased with a final rate of 300 or 325 words per minute. Looked at another way, you could read about four books instead of three in the same time.

There are three things to keep in mind before you begin to work on your speed.

(1) Speed and comprehension are interdependent. Speed techniques are useless without good comprehension skills; in other words, if you read very slowly, you will not necessarily comprehend more. Conversely, if your comprehension skills are quite good, they may even improve if you push your speed ahead slightly.

(2) Your reading rate must be *flexible*. Flexibility means that you must adapt your speed according to the difficulty of the material and your purpose in reading. You should read a newspaper column advising the lovelorn more quickly than you would read a short story to prepare for a literature examination.

(3) Concentration is more important than the number of hours you spend reading. You only waste time if you read an entire assignment, remember nothing and have to read it again. It makes more sense to read material accurately the first time and to use reading time efficiently.

To improve your concentration and flexibility skills, spend a short time each day reading various kinds of news articles. You might read such diverse items as the gossip column, lead editorials, important articles on foreign policy, film reviews, and so on. As you practice, concentrate on varying your speed according to the difficulty of the material. After a few days, you should begin to pace yourself unconsciously. The thing to remember is that good readers never have just one reading speed; they have several that are appropriate to the material and to their purpose.

This chapter will introduce you to some techniques designed to help you read more quickly, and at the same time, to build your comprehension. You should realize, however, that these techniques should be used only for non-fiction—textbooks, magazine and newspaper articles, and expository essays—which may comprise anywhere from 50 to 70 per cent of your required reading. You should not try to "speed read" poetry, short stories or novels, nor very complex material like physics or chemistry texts that require very careful and exacting attention.

Two of the most common causes of poor reading rates are word-by-word reading and regressive eye-stops. As you may recall from Chapter 2, a word-by-word reader is unable to take in groups of words in one glance. To see how this affects not only speed but comprehension as well, read these three paragraphs very slowly, concentrating on reading only one word at a time.

> Intense competition in the food industry results in intense cost-consciousness. A penny or two cut from the cost of producing a food item can bring great profit gains to the producer. The lure of this possibility leads to a constant testing of the elasticity of the rules governing the business. Nor is it always just a matter of testing; sometimes the rules are simply thrown away.
>
> In addition to the food seizure actions it carries out, which are not punitive but are only a matter of stopping the bullet in flight, the Food and Drug Administration brings criminal charges in numerous cases, month after month, of violations of the Food, Drug, and Cosmetic Act. In most cases these are not unwitting infractions of regulations designed to guard the purity of food. They are deliberate efforts to make more money by breaking the law. Involved in them are nationally known food processing and distributing companies as well as shady individuals with gangland connections.
>
> The crooks—for that is what they are—have developed many ways, some ingenious, some brutally simple, of defrauding customers and selling them food that is not fit for anyone to eat. FDA files are crammed with reports of fines assessed against firms or individuals for shipping sorghum syrup adulterated with other sugar syrup, cocoa adulterated with cottonseed flour, short-weight potato chips, substandard "enriched" flour, cottonseed oil labeled olive oil, and peanut butter containing soy and cottonseed oils (to give just a few recent examples).
>
> BOOTH MOONEY, from *The Hidden Assassins**

* (Chicago: Follett Publishing Co., 1966), pp. 169–170.

Next, try to answer these two questions without referring to the passage:

(1) What is the main idea?
(2) What is the role of the F.D.A.?

You should have felt a "dragging" sensation, as if the words were pulling you back. Very likely, your mind works much faster than this. The obvious result of holding yourself back is boredom. Now read the passage again, this time consciously pacing yourself to read a bit faster than you normally would. Which feels more natural?

The second hindrance to efficient reading speed is the problem of regressive eye stops. A special machine has been developed to detect and record a reader's tiny eye movements. And research has proved that most readers, including very good ones, make regressive eye stops, often as many as one per line of print. You may recall that eye stops are the fixations your eyes make as they move across a line. A regressive eye stop simply means that your eyes jump back to reread a word or phrase, or even a whole sentence. Some amount of regression is natural, especially with difficult prose. But if you make an excessive number of regressions, the reason may be lack of concentration or interest, poor lighting, eye strain or distracting noises, all of which you can remedy. Here is an illustration of regression. The numbers above each line denote the eye stops.

```
            1                    2  3 ←——————— 3              4
The American driver is increasingly vociferous in his demand for better
  5          6                    7              8   9 ←—————————— 9
cars. The two major complaints are mechanical deficiencies and lack of
     10            11               12           13  14 ←——————————— 14
adequate safety features. As a matter of course, automobile manufacturers
     15               16              17            18
now recall thousands of models annually for repairs.
```

This hypothetical reader made three regressive eye stops in six lines (see the arrows). The only solution is steady concentration and attention to the matter at hand.

Review of Two Techniques:
Phrase Reading and "Reading Between the Lines"

If you have forgotten the principles of phrase reading, turn back to page 15 ff. and reread the pertinent sections. Here are two more exercises for practice. The first two paragraphs are reprinted in phrases. As you read them, concentrate on taking in the group of words as a whole. The third and fourth paragraphs are reprinted without phrase divisions. Try to maintain the pattern you established in the previous two paragraphs as you read them.

Folsom Prison
June 25, 1965

Nineteen fifty-four, when I was eighteen years old, is held to be a crucial turning point in the history of the Afro-American— for the U.S.A. as a whole—the year segregation was outlawed by the U.S. Supreme Court. It was also a crucial year for me because on June 18, 1954, I began serving a sentence in state prison for possession of marijuana.

The Supreme Court decision was only one month old when I entered prison, and I do not believe that I had even the vaguest idea of its importance or historical significance. But later, the acrimonious controversy ignited by the end of the separate- but-equal doctrine was to have a profound effect on me. This controversy awakened me to my position in America and I began to form a concept of what it meant to be black in white America.

Of course I'd always known that I was black, but I'd never really stopped to take stock of what I was involved in. I met life as an individual and took my chances. Prior to 1954, we lived in an atmosphere of novocain. Negroes found it necessary, in order to maintain whatever sanity they could, to remain somewhat aloof and detached from "the problem." We accepted indignities and the mechanics of the apparatus of oppression without reacting by sitting-in or holding mass demonstrations. Nurtured by the fires of the controversy over segregation, I was soon aflame with indignation over my newly discovered social status, and inwardly I turned away from America with horror, disgust and outrage.

In Soledad state prison, I fell in with a group of young blacks who, like myself, were in vociferous rebellion against what we perceived as a continuation of slavery on a higher plane. We cursed everything American—including baseball and hot dogs. All respect we may have had for politicians, preachers, lawyers, governors, Presidents, senators, congressmen was utterly destroyed as we watched them temporizing and compromising over right and wrong, over legality and illegality, over constitutionality and unconstitutionality. We knew that in the end what they were clashing over was us, what to do with the blacks, and whether or not to start treating us as human beings. I despised all of them.

ELDRIDGE CLEAVER, from "On Becoming" *

As you read the next passage, move your eyes from one dot to the next along the white space above each line.

May 14th: Friday evening—night before last—I drove out to Amagansett at rush hour, and was made sharply aware of one of the newer phenomena of the affluent society: ten years ago, the "season" for weekenders began about July 1st; four or five years ago, it began for many of them as early as the Memorial Day weekend; this year, the Long Island Express-

* From *Soul on Ice* (New York: McGraw-Hill Book Company, 1968), pp. 3–4.

way was choked on May 12th with a metallic-rubbery-gaseous outpouring that did not thin out appreciably for nearly forty miles. On Friday evenings in the summer, this river of fugitives will flow solidly for seventy or eighty miles along the flat, monotonous roads of Long Island—the drivers tense, pale, and sweating, their eyes rigidly fixed on the tail-lights in front, their feet jerking back and forth from gas pedal to brake, their minds numbed by the thoughtless routine. It may be only a few years before Friday-evening traffic from April through October will be a dense, unbroken stream stretching from midtown Manhattan to Montauk Point, a hundred and twenty-nine miles away. Yet when I came to my own turn-off and reached my own house, it seemed as though the porous soil of Long Island could soak up any flash flood of people and be none the worse, for here, barely half a mile from the highway, the land, faintly visible in the last of twilight, lay darkly empty, its silent trees black-laced against the deepening sky, its air as pure and fresh as water from a mountain stream. Only two houses are visible from my property, and both were unlighted and quiet. Later that evening, I bicycled down the road to the ocean. The scattered houses along the way were mostly silent and asleep; the beach, in the starlight, was a spectral mist under my feet, and the ocean a resounding void of blackness out of which the wraithlike foam sped toward me, faltered, and expired with a sigh, dissolving back into nothingness.

MORTON HUNT, from "Annals of Agriculture—The Three-Hundred-and-Nineteenth Growing Season" *

Peripheral Vision

To phrase read efficiently, you must practice expanding your peripheral vision. You may have heard this term with respect to driving. In reading, peripheral vision means the same: how much you see at the extremities when you look at a fixed point. To see how this works, hold a pencil directly in front of you and look at it steadily. How much can you see clearly to either side? To test your peripheral vision in reading, place this book squarely before you and fix your gaze on the dot centered below. With two index cards, uncover one letter at a time on each side of the dot.

j   a   p   d ■ m   x   l   b

* From *The New Yorker*, November 1, 1969, pp. 62–63.

If you can see at least two letters clearly without straining your eyes, you probably have highly developed peripheral vision. Here is another exercise to help you see words in groups rather than singly. Again using an index card, uncover one phrase at a time. Keep your eyes fixed on the vertical line drawn through the center of each phrase, and see how clearly you can make out the peripheral words. Try not to read in a typical left-to-right fashion. As the phrases get longer, you may have to look at the center line for several seconds until the words come into focus.

in a movie

an old farm

for the cat

after dinner

a metal table

a bottle of ink

ice cream cones

large black dog

little white lies

coffee with cream

shiny new quarter

silver tea service

a rusty razor blade

a dreadful argument

the result of the poll

coming around the bend

floating on white clouds

the resolution of the problem

the gelft squigged the nelbs

Reducing the Number of Eye Stops

One way to develop flexibility and reduce regression is to vary the number of eye stops according to the width of the page and the number of phrases on each line.

For a line of print like this, you should probably make four eye fixations, although the number of phrases is the determining factor.

But if you read one word at a time, giving each word equal significance, you are wasting time and reading inefficiently.

If the words were omitted from a line of print, your eye fixations might be diagrammed like this:

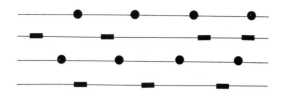

Notice that the fixations occur at different places on each line, which illustrates that they should correspond to natural phrasing. Here are two illustrations of phrasing. In the first, the eye stops are misplaced because they do not conform to natural phrasing.

Suffolk County's population has doubled in ten years, and is likely to double again by 1985; at that rate, twenty or thirty years from now houses and streets, industrial parks and golf courses, shopping centers and jetports, highways and parking lots will cover the land from end to end.

The second illustration is correct. Notice that the eye fixations occur slightly *before* the end of each phrase.

Suffolk County's population has doubled in ten years, and is likely to double again by 1985; at that rate, twenty or thirty years from now houses and streets, industrial parks and golf courses, shopping centers and jetports, highways and parking lots will cover the land from end to end.

MORTON HUNT, from "Annals of Agriculture" *

The advantage of making eye fixations slightly before the end of each phrase is that you can take in the remainder of the phrase with peripheral vision. Because your eye naturally inclines to read from left to right, your eye can read the remaining word clearly. To practice this, look at the phrases below and concentrate on the dot before the final word.

All the food
that people eat
will arrive
by truck or train
from hundreds
or thousands
of miles away
neatly wrapped
in plastic

*From *The New Yorker,* November 1, 1969, p. 85.

labeled, price-marked,
     sanitary, dead.

> MORTON HUNT, from "Annals of
> Agriculture" *

When reading a narrow column of newsprint, you should decrease the number of eye stops. For a normal line of print, three, four or even five eye stops may be required; but with a news column, two stops should be sufficient. As this diagram shows, you should be able to adjust your eye fixations so that you read a news column of average difficulty fairly quickly.

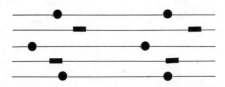

The following passage describes the problems faced by two conscientious objectors. The eye fixations are printed only in the first paragraph. As you read the second paragraph, try to maintain a constant speed even without the marks.

The problems encountered in trying
to present the S.C.O.'s position have
been exhibited in two well-publicized
trials of military officers—Army Capt.
Howard Levy and Air Force Capt.
Dale Noyd. Captain Levy, a derma-
tologist who drew three years' imprisonment for refusing to teach medics
of the Green Berets, argued that the
war in Vietnam was immoral and illegal. Captain Noyd, who refused either
to fly in Vietnam or to train others to
fly there, argued that the war was unjust; he was sentenced to one year in
jail. Levy was permitted at his court-
martial to produce testimony of atroci-
ties in Vietnam, but beyond that nei-

* From *The New Yorker*, November 1, 1969, p. 85.

ther he nor Noyd was allowed to
broach moral objections to the war;
these were judged irrelevant to the
charge of disobeying orders.

From all reports of these two courts-
martial, the officers who composed the
tribunals had difficulty in making head
or tail of the defendants. Levy was an
oddball Jewish doctor from Brooklyn
who wouldn't join the officers' club at
his base, waved back at enlisted men
when they saluted him, and busied
himself in off hours with voter-registra-
tion drives. Noyd must have seemed
even more mystifying. He was an
officer of a dozen years' impeccable
record, a recipient of the Air Force
Commendation Medal, who, it appeared, had gone wrong through reading *books*. By Albert Camus. One observer at his trial pointed out that his
fellow officers sitting in judgment had
scarcely heard of the American Civil
Liberties Union, which handled his
defense, much less of St. Thomas
Aquinas, on whose teachings a defense might have rested. Noyd was
willing to fly in Europe or in Korea or
to accept discharge as a conscientious
objector; but he balked at Vietnam.
To career officers, the notion of serv-
icemen not obeying a given order because they didn't care for a given war
can only have seemed bizarre, if not
cowardly, and since evidence bearing
on selective conscientious objection
was ruled irrelevant, the tribunals
were spared the exertion of having to
grapple with the problem at all, except to condemn the defendants for
the crime of disobedience which all
parites agreed had been committed.

WALTER GOODMAN, from
"Choose Your War; or the Case of
the Selective C.O." *

* From *The New York Times Magazine*, March 23, 1969, p. 128.

There is another way to reduce the number of eye stops. If a line is drawn about an inch from each margin, you can cut two fixations from each line of print: It works like this: rather than making the first eye stop at the very beginning of the left margin, begin at the left-hand vertical line, thereby eliminating one stop. And you can read the last word on the right-hand side peripherally. Try it on this paragraph which describes Long Island from an aerial view.

> After looking things over for a while, I headed west and flew most of the length of the island. The farther I went, the more my altitude lost its magical cleansing power; the air slowly became murky, and the land below became increasingly disfigured by the spreading cancer of urban sprawl. Here and there, the highways slash the land open; from them branch roads reach out through the green land and blossom into great eruptions of blight—the deadly grid of streets, the tedious parade formation of identical houses, battalion upon battalion, nameless and identical, stretching into the distance. The closer one gets to the western end of Nassau County, the more nearly the towns and areas of sprawl abut upon each other. Finally, they all but coalesce, conquering the land forever with concrete and macadam, gravel and metal, siding and shingles; the hills and valleys, meadows and brooks have been consumed and digested and lost for all time.
>
> MORTON HUNT, from "Annals of
> Agriculture" °

For the last exercise, try to incorporate both methods for reducing the number of eye stops as you read. See if you can feel any difference in your flexibility.

> One event that takes me by surprise every year is the announcement of a new Miss Rheingold. In her picture she looks so much like the old Miss Rheingold—in fact, like all the old Miss Rheingolds—that I can't believe it is not the same girl.
>
> And this is only one of many places where I see her. She is the stewardess in every American airliner, smiling away my fears. She is the girl in every television commercial, smiling away my cramps as she tells me of the pill that consumes thirty-eight times its weight in stomach acids. She is the TV weather girl, smiling that low-pressure area away from my door and assuring me that tomorrow will be fair and warmer. Her name is Miss Legion. She is the all-purpose face of modern America. It is not a face to launch a thousand ships, or even one. It is a face to beach a thousand ships and lull the sailors into a sleep of beautiful dreams.
>
> If there are smiles that make us happy, as the old song claims, there are smiles that make us sick, as the old song doesn't claim, and this smile is one of them. For it grins equally at good things (beer) and bad things (oven grease), serious things (a fire in engine 3) and trivial things (an electric toothbrush), and, in short, all things except funny things, which it wouldn't know if it met one on the street.

° From *The New Yorker,* November 1, 1969 p. 88.

Nothing so symbolizes the aggressive blandness of the times as this girl who is all smile and no substance. Don't give anything a second thought, she seems to be saying, or even a first thought. Just sing along with little Mary Sunshine and all the clouds will roll away. She does not, however, symbolize the real American woman. More than ever, the real American woman is a thinking creature. There is far more substance than smile in her concern for the world in which she lives today and in which her children will grow up tomorrow. She gives serious attention to the many different roles that she balances so adroitly from morning to night, and she knows that on the whole they are no laughing matter. The smiling girls don't realize this; they really think that they represent their sex. Obviously it is time for a new symbol—the American woman is taking a bum rap.

WILLIAM K. ZINSSER, "There Are Smiles" *

You may feel, and rightly so, that when you think about your reading rate you can't concentrate on the ideas. As you remember, slow reading is usually a bad habit which requires diligence to break. But rather than straining to read faster all the time, instead spend a short time each day— fifteen minutes of concentrated practice should be enough. You can practice any of the methods in this chapter which seem to work best. After a while, you may feel more comfortable and your comprehension should pick up. With consistent effort you may unconsciously absorb these methods into your regular non-fiction reading. And eventually, you may even develop an entirely new set of reading habits.

READING SELECTION 12—Nicholas von Hoffman, "18-Year-Old Vote— Nothing to It" †

> In the summer of 1970, the United States Senate passed a bill tied to the voting rights extension bill, giving citizens eighteen and older the right to vote. During the vote, few legislators fought against the amendment, and undoubtedly, popular sentiment was strong for the bill's passage. In this editorial, Nicholas von Hoffman argues, not against the amendment itself, but against the real motives of politicians who sponsored the bill.

A new effort is under way to give 18-year-olds the vote. But before you invest your enthusiasm and hope in this proposition, look around and see who's backing it.

Most prominent politicians are in favor of the idea. That's a warning signal. When members of both parties get behind a measure that means they're either hiding something from you (like the Tonkin Gulf resolution) or the idea is so insipid it's not worth the bother to oppose it.

* From *The Haircurl Papers* (New York: Harper & Row, Publishers, 1962), pp. 24–25.

† From the *Washington Post*, February 26, 1970.

Lyndon Johnson was for 18-year-olds voting, and if that doesn't make you wonder, then the fact that the present Administration has come out for it ought to make you question what's so good about the idea. Last week Richard G. Kleindienst, the deputy attorney general, told a senate subcommittee that "after careful study and consideration, the president has concluded that a constitutional amendment to permit 18-year-olds to vote is desirable."

According to present notions this is the last thing in the world this Administration should want if youth is as revolutionary and desirous of change as everybody's always saying. Why should Kleindienst recommend such a suicidal thing?

Maybe it's because he looked at what's happened in the states where younger people are allowed to vote and took comfort. In Georgia, 18-year-olds have been voting for years and they've got Lester Maddox, Herman Talmadge and Richard Russell.

There's no reason to think that lowering the voting age will change much except the electoral technicalities. During the campaign to give women the vote, there was much talk of how it would result in higher levels of honesty, greater sensitivity to human needs and even world peace. The last assertion was based on the assumption that mothers might be less likely to vote the death sentence on their sons.

None of it proved out here or abroad. Golda Meir in Israel is just as tough and warlike as the men who rule other countries. Women only got the vote nationally after it had been shown in states where they already had suffrage that their participation would make no measurable difference.

Lowering the voting age won't make any difference either, and that's why guys like Kleindienst aren't opposed to it. They know that the least effective and the least important form of political participation is voting. To most politicians we voters are nothing more than negligible, periodic nuisances.

If you want to see how unimportant voting is, compare Washington, D.C., which has no vote, no selfrule, with other large cities. The schools are rotten, the cops can't make the streets safe, the poor man's house is taken from him and given to the rich man through urban renewal; the grafters want to convert downtown into a superhighway cloverleaf. It's the same as any other city.

Washington's non-elected city officials make the same kind of vague and evasive speeches that the elected politicians give elsewhere. Their style and the results are the same because the electoral process has an almost accidental relationship to the making of public policy.

A more beneficial change in the voting laws, and one that wouldn't require a constitutional amendment would be to require every candidate for federal office to state where all his campaign money comes from. It would probably show that most of the big dough for opposing candidates comes from the same sources. This would be true of big corporations, trade associations and unions, outfits that can see through the superficial arguing over details and can apprehend the underlying sameness of parties and their spokesmen. It's the small contributors who think principles of great moment are won and lost in elections.

From a functional point of view the two parties are but a single, double-headed hybrid mulephant. True, from time to time men of great naiveté or strong conviction do attempt to rend this Reprocratic Party into two significant opposed bodies of opinion.

Senators Taft, Goldwater and McCarthy each threatened to inject serious disagreement into the charade.

Goldwater attempted to make our votes worth something, but he was a clumsy man, and his ideas not fully thought out; people laughed at him when he wasn't frightening them. He scared the big money men into running to Johnson, whose winning assured the continuance of the one-party system which so deflates the value of the vote that guys like Agnew are even willing to throw it away on long-haired hippie kids.

In many states the election laws make it next to impossible to establish and maintain third and fourth parties but occasionally it's happened and then the Reprocrats reveal their identity by running fusion candidates. This was the means used to beat the Populists and Socialists when they were strong and something of the same is going on in the South under pressure from Governor Wallace.

Instead of a three-party situation there, which would make the black vote important, the managers of the Reprocratic Party are switching labels on the bottles. The Democratic party will play the role that the Republicans used to play, but it's the same old people. Remember during the last election when the Reprocrats got so scared of how well Wallace might run that even the Nixon people were saying it was better to vote for Humphrey and save the two-party system?

By giving 18-year-olds the chance to vote, the politicians give themselves the opportunity to lecture the discontented with a new argument. They will be able to say, "behave yourselves. We've given you the vote so when we ship you off to war or practice apartheid or do other things you wrong-headedly oppose, remember you elected us. If you don't like what we're doing you can use legitimate channels of political activity to throw us out. Don't grouse, don't cut up on the streets. Register to vote, get politically active in the Reprocrat Party and hush up about not being allowed to participate."

Real political power is money and organization. This new constitutional amendment only confers the vote, and that will give the young the same power it has given black people and women.

Name _____   *Date* _____

Reading Selection 12

COMPREHENSION

Do not refer to the article to answer these questions. Choose one of the items that best answers each question, and mark the letter in the space provided.

1. _____ The main idea expressed in the editorial is that giving 18-year-olds the right to vote will (a) damage political institutions (b) improve political institutions (c) have no effect at all on political institutions and further disengage voters from real issues (d) help initiate other voting reforms for members of minority groups.

2. _____ Politicians favor the amendment primarily because (a) they want protesters to participate quietly through legal channels (b) they know it's a "phony" issue which will be meaningless in practice (c) they know it's a popular, vote-getting issue (d) they think young people will work constructively for political change.

3. _____ The author feels that voting is (a) the least effective way to change the political system (b) every citizens' inalienable right (c) meaningless because most voters are poorly informed (d) an important right made meaningless because of ineffectual candidates.

4. _____ Underneath von Hoffman's analysis of the amendment is the assumption that (a) politicians are evasive, mediocre, and self-seeking (b) political power is determined by money and organization (c) political parties are faceless, ridden with faults, and indistinguishable from one another (d) the two-party system prevents candidates with strong convictions from winning (e) all of the above.

5. _____ According to the author, the political system might improve if candidates were required to (a) disclose fully their personal financial condition (b) disclose fully the sources of campaign contributions (c) represent the voters' interests rather than those of large corporations or unions (d) put campaign speech promises into effect (e) all of the above (f) b and c only.

6. _____ The term *mulephant* suggests that in reality the country is run under a (a) two-party system (b) multi-party system (c) one-party system (d) two-party system with insignificant third and fourth parties.

7. _____ Von Hoffman compares the new voting amendment to the earlier bill that extended voting rights to (a) non-property

239

holders (b) minority groups, especially blacks (c) prisoners and illiterates (d) women.

8. _____ The author's attitude toward political institutions and government officials as they now operate is (a) favorable (b) indifferent (c) impartial (d) distrustful (e) belligerent.

9. _____ In the final analysis, the effect of the new voting amendment will be to (a) keep voters weak and powerless (b) provide an argument to silence dissenting voters (c) ensure the continuance of the Reprocratic Party (d) make young voters even more frustrated in their efforts to reform the system (e) provide an excuse to divert attention from true and serious issues (f) all of the above.

10. _____ One can most accurately infer that von Hoffman (a) favors the new amendment despite its disadvantages (b) opposes the new amendment because of its disadvantages (c) favors more substantive changes in political institutions rather than trivial changes in voting laws (d) is confused about the amendment's purposes.

VOCABULARY

From the lettered choices, find the best definition for each vocabulary item, and mark the letter in the space provided.

1. __F__ the idea is *insipid*
2. __J__ they already had *suffrage*
3. __C__ *negligible,* periodic nuisances
4. __O__ *evasive* speeches
5. __G__ a more *beneficial* change
6. __B__ the *superficial* arguing
7. __L__ a *hybrid* mulephant
8. __M__ *deflates* the value
9. __A__ men of great *naiveté*
10. __I__ practice *apartheid*

A. simple, unaffected nature; lack of worldly experience
B. not genuine; obviously lacking depth
C. too small to consider
D. mandatory; necessary
E. new species
F. lacking vitality; dull
G. advantageous; helpful
H. increases

I. official policy of segregation against non-whites
J. right to vote
K. tasteless; vulgar
L. having mixed origin; half-breed
M. reduces; causes to collapse
N. wretched condition
O. not direct, frank

COMPREHENSION   No. right _____ × 10 = _____%

VOCABULARY   No. right _____ × 10 = _____%

No. of words 1075 ÷ time in seconds _____ × 60 = _____ WPM
WPM × Comprehension % = Reading Efficiency Rate _____

PART II

ESSAYS FOR COMPREHENSION AND ANALYSIS

1

MICHAEL ARLEN

Television's War*

Of all the wars in American history, none has torn society apart so severely as the war in Vietnam. Michael Arlen, formerly television reviewer for The New Yorker, *questions both the medium's honesty in covering the war and the television viewers' gullibility in believing everything they see. His other reviews appear in a collection,* Living-Room War.

Summertime now, or very nearly. Kids already gabbling about the last day of school. Women walking down East Eighty-sixth Street in those jouncy cotton dresses. Connecticut suntans. Airconditioning in Schrafft's. *Daktari* reruns on the television. *Lassie* reruns. *Gilligan's Island* reruns. *Star Trek* reruns. Lots of baseball. (Not much doing on television in the good old, mythic old American summertime.) The other Saturday, just back from a trip, and for some reason conscious more pointlessly than ever of that miserable war, I made a mental note to watch, at five o'clock that afternoon, an NBC program called *Vietnam Weekly Review* for whatever it might have to offer, and went outside (it was a nice day—warm, sunny, full of the first hints of summer's dust and laziness, of all those hammocks one will never swing in), toward Fifth Avenue and the park, past which close to one hundred thousand men, women, and children were marching as part of a "Support Our Boys in Vietnam" parade. Lots of people in the streets. Lots of American Legion posts. Lots of those Catholic high-school bands. A flatbed truck went by full of teamsters, many of them holding aloft placards reading, "It's Your Country! Love It Or Leave It!" The Putnam County John Birch Society went by, singing "America the Beautiful." An American Legionnaire went by in a wheelchair, carrying a placard reading, "Victory over Atheistic Communism." The crowd applauded. Somewhere up toward Ninety-sixth Street a band was playing "The Yellow Rose of Texas." Children all around me clutched

* From the *Living-Room War* (New York, The Viking Press, Inc., 1969), pp. 80–85.

American flags and looked the way children usually do, with or without flags.

I went back home at ten to five, got out a beer, turned on the TV set. There was a baseball game in progress on NBC. (No *Vietnam Review* that week.) Not a bad game, either. Clendenon hit a long ball in the tenth and wrapped it up for Pittsburgh. I forget who was playing Pittsburgh, but you could look it up. From Fifth Avenue, two blocks away (you could hear it through the open window), a band was finishing up "The Marine Corps Hymn," then started "Sister Kate." Sometimes I wonder what it is that the people who run television think about the war. I'm sure they think about it. Everybody thinks about it. I'm sure they care a lot. (At times, I even picture them sitting around in the Communications Club after hours, brows furrowed in meditation, their tumblers of brandy and Perrier water barely sipped at. Finally a voice is raised. "Well, hang it, Fred. I think Tom Hayden speaks for all of us . . .") Perhaps one is unfair. Perhaps not. In any case, there are good men who work for television trying to tell us about the war. For example, the other Monday night, a little after seven, Walter Cronkite peered out at us pleasantly from the TV screen, said, "Today's Vietnam story in a moment," and then there we were, via film that had been taken twenty-six hours earlier, eighteen miles south of the DMZ, watching a Marine scout detail that had been sent out to look for North Vietnamese encampments. The film began routinely, with the CO briefing his patrol leaders (a sequence that always seems to be staged, although it probably isn't), and then we were watching a small group of men on their way up a thickly wooded hill ("They went up to investigate the distant voices," said the on-the-scene correspondent), and heard the sound of faraway small-arms fire, and suddenly men were running here and there in front of the camera, the small-arms fire became louder and more intense, and once again—in our living room, or was it at the Yale Club bar, or lying on the deck of the grand yacht *Fatima* with a Sony portable TV upon our belly?—we were watching, a bit numbly perhaps (we have watched it so often), real men get shot at, real men (our surrogates, in fact) get killed and wounded. At one point in the film, a mortar round fell near the cameraman, and for a couple of seconds the film spun crazily until it (and he) got straightened out again, and then we were looking, through the camera, at a young man—a boy, surely no more than nineteen or twenty—square-jawed, handsome, All-American, poised there on the side of the hill, rifle held in close to him, waiting on the side of the hill for the signal to move up to where the shooting was, and afraid. In the background, you could hear machine guns firing and the voice of the platoon sergeant, a deep-voiced Negro, calling, "Git on up there! Git! Git!" And the boy stayed there for several moments in the camera's eye, his own eyes staring straight ahead, his face so full of youth, fear, bravery, whatever else, until he finally moved up. One thinks of how one's memories of those other wars (wars one didn't fight in) exist for the most part frozen in the still photographs of the great war photographers —Robert Capa's picture of the Spanish Loyalist falling on the Catalonian hillside, Eugene Smith's Marine face down on the beach at Tarawa, Margaret Bourke-White's St. Paul's Cathedral against the blitz, David Duncan's Marines advancing through the Korean mud. Vietnam is different, to be sure. Not quite so "exciting." Not quite so photogenic. But it seems to me that Kurt Volkert, the man who held and worked that camera, who caught the meaning of that face, is one of the best journalists of the war, and one could probably say the same for many of the other cameramen covering Vietnam for the American networks.

Another afternoon not long ago, I watched a routine film clip, this one taken by Vo Huynh, a Vietnamese who works for NBC, about a military engagement in the South: scenes of men moving in to attack, and attacking—scenes, in fact, of men living close to death and killing—with one heart-rending sequence of a young soldier being carried out, his leg apparently smashed, screaming to his comrades, "It hurts! It hurts!" The special qualities of courage, energy, and strange, tough sensitivity that made men like Robert Capa so good at what they did—so good because so useful, so useful because they went in there (Capa's great pictures of the second wave at Omaha Beach were so blurred that you could barely make out the faces) and tried to show us what it was really like—are qualities that don't exist to any lesser degree in men like Kurt Volkert and Vo Huynh. They too seem to be trying to show us what it's like—at least, what the small, small corner allotted to them is like—and Lord knows there are mighty few other people on television who seem to be trying.

Vietnam is often referred to as "television's war," in the sense that this is the first war that has been brought to the people preponderantly by television. People indeed look at television. They really look at it. They look at Dick Van Dyke and become his friend. They look at a new Pontiac in a commercial and go out and buy it. They look at thoughtful Chet Huntley and find him thoughtful, and at witty David Brinkley and find him witty. They look at Vietnam. They look at Vietnam, it seems, as a child kneeling in the corridor, his eye to the keyhole, looks at two grownups arguing in a locked room—the aperture of the keyhole small; the figures shadowy, mostly out of sight; the voices indistinct, isolated threats without meaning; isolated glimpses, part of an elbow, a man's jacket (who is the man?), part of a face, a woman's face. Ah, she is crying. One sees the tears. (The voices continue indistinctly.) One counts the tears. Two tears. Three tears. Two bombing raids. Four seek-and-destroy missions. Six administration pronouncements. Such a fine-looking woman. One searches in vain for the other grownup, but, ah, the keyhole is so small, he is somehow never in the line of sight. Look! There is General Ky. Look! There are some planes returning safely to the *Ticonderoga*. I wonder (sometimes) what it is that the people who run television think about the war, because *they* have given us this keyhole view; we have given them the airwaves, and now, at this critical time, they have given back to us this keyhole view—and I wonder if they truly think that those isolated glimpses of elbow, face, a swirl of dress (who *is* that other person, anyway?) are all we children can really stand to see of what is going on inside that room.

Vo Huynh, admittedly, will show us as much of the larger truth of a small battle and of a wounded soldier as he is able to, and CBS, as it did some nights ago, will show us a half-hour special interview with Marine Corps General Walt, which is nice of CBS, but there are other things, it seems, that make up the Vietnam war, that intelligent men *know* make up the Vietnam war—factors of doubt, politics, propaganda, truth, untruth, of what we actually do and actually don't do, that aren't in most ways tangible, or certifiably right or wrong, or easily reducible to simple mathematics, but that, even so (and even now), exist as parts of this equation that we're all supposedly trying so hard to solve—and almost none of them get mentioned. It seems almost never to get mentioned, for example, that there's considerable doubt as to the effectiveness of the search-and-destroy missions we watch so frequently on television. (The enemy casualty figures seem to be arbitrarily rigged, and the ground we take isn't anything we usually plan to keep.) It seems almost never to get mentioned, for example, that there's considerable doubt as to the actual efficacy of many of the highly publicized (on TV, as elsewhere) sweeps into territory that, if you read the fine print, you realize the enemy has often already left, and presumably will come back to when we, in turn, have gone. It seems rarely to get mentioned that there has been considerable doubt as to the effectiveness of our bombing, or that an air force that can't always hit the right village certainly can't avoid killing civilians when it bombs power plants in Hanoi. It doesn't seem to get mentioned, for example, that we are using "anti-personnel" weapons such as the Guava and the Pineapple more than the military appears to want to admit, or that any people who drop their tortures from planes flying at five thousand feet are likely to be regarded as no less accomplices than if they had stood in person in some village square and driven little slivers of metal, at high velocity, into the flesh of other human beings. It doesn't seem to get mentioned, for example, that "anti-personnel," "delivering hardware," "pacification mission," and "nation building" are phrases, along with "better dead than Red," that only a people out of touch with the meaning of language could use with any seriousness. It doesn't seem to get mentioned, for example, that when a senior member of the administration states that he sees no reason for thinking we will have to send more troops to Vietnam this year he is probably not telling the truth, and that the fact of his probably not telling the truth is now more important than the fact of the troops. It doesn't seem to get mentioned— Well, enough of that. It is summertime now, or nearly. My kids were squabbling over bathing suits this morning, and who will learn to sail and who to ride. In summertime we cook outdoors a lot, play coronary tennis, drink, watch pretty sunsets out across the water. This summer, I will almost certainly perfect my backhand, write something beautiful (or very nearly), read *Finnegans Wake,* or something like it. This summer—already the streets outside seem quieter, more humane. A car rolls softly over a manhole cover—a small clank. All those quiet streets, all those brave middle-class apartments—and what lies beneath those manhole covers? Wires? Cables? Dying soldiers? Dying children? Sounds of gunfire? Screaming? Madness? My television set plays on, talking to itself—another baseball game, in fact. Juan Marichal is pitching to Ron Hunt. Hunt shifts his stance. Marichal winds up. The count is three and two.

Reading Selection 1: Arlen, "Television's War"

COMPREHENSION AND ANALYSIS

Do not refer to the article to answer these questions. Choose one of the items that best answers each question, and mark the letter in the space provided.

1. ___C___ Which of the following statements best describes the main idea of the review? Television's coverage of the Vietnam war has been for the most part (a) remarkably honest and frank compared with the medium's coverage of past wars (b) as unrealistic and fantastic as everything else on television (c) sadly lacking in honesty, realism, and critical appraisal (d) very poor because the medium has presented only the government's official position toward the war.

2. ___D___ At the beginning and end of the review, Arlen describes summer's arrival in New York and baseball games. His purpose is (a) to illustrate how far away and unreal the war is to most Americans (b) to illustrate that the war has not really affected people at home, who go about their business as usual (c) to illustrate the irony of a nation conducting a war in a distant country (d) all of the above.

3. ___B___ The author suggests in his review that an honest view of what war is really like has been attempted by (a) the majority of newsmen (b) very few newsmen (c) no newsmen (d) the majority of newsmen working for the major networks.

4. ___E___ Arlen states that television viewers "look at" the Vietnam War on television just as they "look at" Dick Van Dyke or automobile commercials. By this he suggests that (a) television viewers prefer to watch situation comedies and even commercials rather than serious newsreels of a war (b) viewers are so used to improbable, unrealistic programs on television that they can no longer distinguish between fantasy and reality on the screen (c) viewers only "watch" the images before them, no matter what they are, without really comprehending the realities (d) all of the above (e) b and c only.

5. ___B___ Arlen metaphorically compares television's coverage of the war with a child looking through a keyhole. By this he suggests that (a) even reporters don't know all the facts, for they look at the war through the same keyhole (b) viewers are entitled to see the whole truth, not just a shadowy, indistinct glimpse (c) that viewers are not mature enough to ac-

cept the truth because it might be too damaging (d) that most viewers regard television as a stupefying toy, as most children do.

6. ___C___ The review criticizes the television industry for "what doesn't get mentioned." From Arlen's list of items that are never mentioned, one can infer that (a) Arlen has serious doubts about the credibility of the statistics, the reports of bombing missions, and the truth of the government's position (b) Arlen believes most of the information which the government has released (c) Arlen believes the statistics, but dislikes the misuse of language from such euphemisms as "pacification missions" and "anti-personnel" weapons (d) Arlen thinks the military's statistics are convincing to most Americans.

7. ___E___ Arlen questions (a) the honesty and integrity of television newsmen for evading the truth (b) the government's unwillingness to clarify the facts of the war (c) the American public's indifference and apathy, to believe blindly everything they are told (d) what the men who run television really think about the war (e) all of the above.

8. _____ Based on the evidence in the review, mark T (true), F (false), or X (not verifiable) for the inferences that follow.

    A. ___X___ When Arlen wrote his review, there was an anti-Vietnam demonstration in New York.

    B. ___F___ Television networks always cancel programs such as sporting events for direct reports from Vietnam.

    C. ___F___ Arlen thinks that all briefings filmed in Vietnam are staged just for the audience.

    D. ___T___ Television gives a more honest, painful image of war than blurred photographs from earlier wars.

    E. ___X___ Most people are numbed by statistics about the war.

    F. ___X___ The author has traveled to Vietnam.

9. _____ Based on the evidence in the review, mark J (justified) or NJ (not justified) for the conclusions that follow.

    A. ___NJ___ Some newsmen have been killed while filming battles in Vietnam.

    B. ___NJ___ The army censors all films of the war heavily before they are shown in the U.S.

    C. ___J___ The Vietnam War is unique because it is the first war in our history extensively seen on television.

    D. ___J___ The American public has not been given all the facts about what is really happening in Vietnam.

    E. ___NJ___ Arlen doubts the authenticity of statistics on the number of enemy casualties.

F. _NJ_ The search-and-destroy missions and bombing raids have been successful in combating the enemy.

10. _B_ The tone of the review, the attitude Arlen displays toward "television's war" can most accurately be described as (a) angry and contemptuous (b) critically honest and analytical about a war which disturbs him greatly (c) confused and bewildered over television's war reports, yet indifferent to the war itself (d) completely impartial and objective, but not indifferent.

VOCABULARY

From the lettered choices, find the best definition for each vocabulary item, and mark the letter in the space provided.

1. _Q_ *mythic*, old summertime
2. _I_ *furrowed* in meditation
3. _K_ the film began *routinely*
4. _B_ seems to be *staged*
5. _O_ a bit *numbly*
6. _G_ our *surrogates*
7. _A_ *preponderantly* by television
8. _L_ the *aperture* of the keyhole
9. _E_ one searches in *vain* (w/out result)
10. _J_ that aren't *tangible*
11. _C_ *certifiably* right or wrong
12. _S_ easily *reducible*
13. _H_ seem *arbitrarily* rigged
14. _M_ the actual *efficacy*
15. _C_ regarded as *accomplices*

A. predominantly; almost exclusively
B. arranged, planned as theatre
C. associates, partners in wrong-doing
D. allies; close friends
E. without purpose, use
F. verifiably; able to be vouched for
G. substitutes
H. based on one's opinion or prejudice; not determined by reason
I. deeply wrinkled as in confusion or thought
J. real; capable of being touched

K. regularly; normally
L. opening; hole
M. power to produce desired results
N. troubled
O. unable to feel pain or sensation
P. realistically; truthfully
Q. pertaining to traditional stories in a culture
R. unimpressively; dully
S. able to be changed to a simpler form
T. proud; conceited

COMPREHENSION   No. right _____ × 5 = _____ %

VOCABULARY   No. right _____

No. of words 1850 ÷ time in seconds _____ × 60 = _____ WPM
WPM × Comprehension % = Reading Efficiency Rate _____

2

PETER COLLIER

Uneasy Rider: The Unilateral Withdrawal of Private Weise*

The Vietnam War has spawned an active resistance movement among young men. Some have applied for selective conscientious objector status; others have gone into exile in Canada or Sweden. In this essay, Peter Collier, a member of the editorial board of Ramparts, *relates the story of an army private whose life as a fugitive from military courts was a nightmare of anonymity, fear, and paranoia.*

The person who arranged our meeting told me to look for a short, stocky fellow with blond hair and mustache and a long scar cutting vertically down the bridge of his nose. I was told that he would meet me in a local coffee shop at nine in the morning, that he was a fugitive and that he would answer to the name "Marvin."

He came in without a jacket, his hands jammed down into his pants pockets and his eyes watering from the cold. He looked sleepy and slightly disoriented, but otherwise ordinary, like an undergraduate caught somewhere in limbo between fraternity and bohemia. He sat down, younger than I had imagined, and we made halting conversation for a few minutes. Then he began to talk about his life over the last two years. It was hard work for him: his forehead knotted when he groped after illusive concepts; a brief smile occasionally passed over his mouth, pulling it downward in self-deprecation; and his eyes, feral and haunted, roamed constantly around the room checking out the alien faces. There was a brutal fascination in his story, and I didn't think to ask what his real name was until we had talked for awhile. Even then it was as a sort of afterthought. "David," he replied. "David Weise." Then he shook his head vaguely. "Sometimes it sounds strange to me. I don't hear it very often."

He chain smokes, exhaling each lungful of smoke harshly. He goes through a half-pack of stomach mints in an hour. He picks at his breakfast,

---

* From *Ramparts*, February, 1970, pp. 4–10.

apologizing that it is hard for him to eat these days and that he sleeps only three hours a night. He admits to being paranoid. But the pressure he is under makes it all understandable. For the last two years he has been a deserter from the U. S. Army, on the run in a one-man underground.

A young man leaving a small town, setting out on the road, having a series of adventures, and finally coming to stand on the threshold of discovering who and what he is. This is a familiar and timeless American theme, the pattern for some of our best fiction. It also describes what has happened to David Weise, although his odyssey has taken place in a contemporary reality more nightmarish than a novelist could conjure up.

Weise describes his background willingly, but feels it had little impact on what he has gotten into. His family moved from Missouri when he was 11 years old and came to Oregon, settling down in a small town 40 miles outside of Portland. His mother left home when he was 12; his father left shortly thereafter. He grew up with a succession of aunts and uncles, foster parents, and finally his grandparents, who have functioned as the closest thing he has to a real family. He saw his four brothers and sisters only rarely, but maintained as firm a relationship with them as he could. All this is recollected with tranquility, not pain. It would be an appropriate cause for his desertion only to Army psychiatrists, enmeshed in the jargon of their profession and looking for a lie.

Mostly, the images from his past evoke the uneasy coming of age that most young people suffer in Middle America. He smoked a little pot and drank some beer. He had a car in which he struggled with unconsenting pom-pon girls. He was an average student, and his ideas didn't extend much beyond the conservatism of the small town he lived in. He loved hiking and was a good athlete, going to the state wrestling championships three years in a row and finishing as runner-up in his weight class as a junior. When he graduated from high school in 1966, the University of Oregon offered him an athletic scholarship. He went there for a year and then dropped out because he didn't feel ready for college. Thinking that he would work for a year and then perhaps re-enroll, he took a job at Yosemite National Park. In 1967, the life flow that would normally have led to a job, a family, and a settled life back in Oregon was interrupted by an induction notice.

"I had a vague idea that something was wrong with the war," he says, "and I tried to become a conscientious objector after I was drafted. But the draft board denied it. Then I decided to just go ahead and do my two years, and avoid going to Viet-Nam by getting stateside duty. Seventeen weeks after I was drafted—after basic and advanced infantry training—I got orders to ship for Viet-Nam. At that point, I was really out of it. I hadn't had time to think since I went in. They wear you down physically in basic to get at you mentally. And with me they did OK. By the end of training, I was the perfect soldier. I'd won a couple of trophies in physical conditioning. I was a good shot on the range. I was pretty well brainwashed and probably would have marched right into the war except that they gave me a 20-day leave before I was supposed to report."

He went back to Yosemite alone, assuming that his next hiking trip would be in the jungles of Southeast Asia. "While I was up there," he recalls, "I started wondering about things—what to do and all. Then it suddenly occurred to me that there really wasn't any decision to make. I didn't have any alternative. I couldn't go. I guess fear of being killed played some part in it, but the thing was that I hadn't minded standing there in basic firing at targets—you knew that when they went over after getting hit, they'd pop back up again. It was something else to go over there and do it to men who would stay down. I said the hell with it."

He spent the rest of the summer in Yosemite. It was, as he looks back on it now, an "impulse"; the meaning of being a fugitive dawned on him only gradually. He learned that he could go to Canada as a draft dodger, but not as a deserter. He had to begin to forget his name, aware that he could be traced through it. He lived as anonymously as possible, going down to the popular Yosemite park floor a couple of days a week, where a sympathizer had arranged to get him work as an automobile tour guide. With his earnings, he would buy supplies—mainly rice and bouillon cubes; then he would return to the high country where he lived out of a sleeping bag and a back pack.

Summer passed. He began to feel isolated in his guilt and confusion, and hitch-hiked to the Bay Area. There he was surrounded by the most active branch of the anti-war movement in the country, but he himself felt strangely ambiguous about protest. "I wasn't what you'd call 'political,'" he says. "I didn't really understand why I'd deserted and wasn't able to keep up with what a lot of the Berkeley people were doing and saying." He talked to draft counselors about what he had done, and they told him to turn himself in and hope for the best from military justice. He remembers wanting very much to take this advice, but being afraid. Unable to act, he floated in the hedonism of the Berkeley underworld, forgetting temporarily the magnitude of what he had done. An abrupt and violent encounter with the law jogged his memory.

He told me about it as we walked down the street. He had gotten more and more nervous in the coffee shop because, as he put it, "the walls were closing in."

"I had met this girl, Susan," he recalled. "We'd been living together in Berkeley and we decided to hitch down to Monterey for the weekend. We got there late and stayed in this small town motel. For some reason, maybe because of the way we looked or something, the landlady got uptight. The next morning she called the police on us.

"It was grey, and I still remember standing there in front of this cop.

I had told Susan that if anything happened she should say she didn't know me, that we'd just met hitch-hiking. Anyway, the cop asked for my ID. He noticed that there wasn't any draft card and asked me about it. I couldn't say that they make you turn it in when you're drafted, but I didn't know what else to say. He must have suspected I was AWOL because we were so close to Fort Ord. After calling in, he said I'd have to come with him. I said there was no way he could make me, and turned and ran. He fired three shots over my head. I thought I was going to get one in the back of the head any second, but I kept running, down to the beach. I ran for a couple of miles, then came to a rock formation that went into the ocean and blocked my path. There were these three guys camping there. They looked OK, so I ran over and told them what was happening and asked for help. They put me in the back of their camper, laid a mattress over me, and then started off. They hadn't gotten 20 yards before the cop car pulled in. They stopped, got out, and yelled out that I was hiding in their car before the cop even asked them anything. The next thing I knew, there was a gun in my face and I was under arrest."

He was taken to the small town of San Luis Obispo. Then the Fort Ord MP's came to get him. They handcuffed him and put him in leg shackles. Weise remembers one of them saying, "Go ahead and run. Just remember one thing: I won't shoot over your head." They took him to Camp Roberts, a Marine summer training base near Fort Ord, and then to Ord itself.

"They thought I was just another AWOL soldier, I guess, and treated me as if I was back in the Army now. I told them that I wasn't going back to duty and that there was no way they'd get me to Viet-Nam, but they didn't pay much attention. They put me in this temporary stockade, a sort of processing center, and said I'd be taken to the permanent one the next day.

"That one day was enough. It scared the hell out of me. There were six guards and about 30 men, most of them 17 or 18-year-olds who'd gone AWOL to see their parents or girlfriends. It was an absolutely vicious scene. There were these small boxes on the floor. The guards made you sit in them and if your legs dangled over, they'd come by and hit them. There was this tiny cage in the middle of the compound. They put the prisoners they took a dislike to in it and let them stay there for hours, all curled up and tortured. The rest of the men they made stand at attention against the wall, holding a piece of paper on it with their noses. You learned not to let the paper slip.

"One of the prisoners, he stuttered badly. The guards really had it in for him for some reason. They kept teasing him. They told him that he stuttered because he screwed his mother. The more up-tight he got, the more he stuttered. Finally, when he was all red and could hardly talk, one of the guards said something like, 'You're pretty mad, aren't you? Well, come on, why don't you do something about it? Just you and me. Come on.' The guy swung at the guard, then all the other guards jumped on him and beat him to hamburger with their clubs. It was terrible. By the time the guard changed later in the afternoon, most of the prisoners, they just sank down on the floor and started to cry. I decided that I had to get out.

"The compound we were in had cyclone fencing over all the windows. But there was a door, and it had an upper part of glass that didn't have any wire on it for some reason. I stayed awake all night, watching that door. About five in the morning I realized that they'd be coming to take me in a couple of hours, and that if I didn't get out now there'd never be another chance. I jumped up, grabbed this fire extinguisher I'd been sleeping next to, and went charging across the room. I threw it through the glass and dove out after it, cutting the hell out of my legs. I got outside the building and started running. I went up one row of barracks and down another so they wouldn't have a clear shot at me running in a straight line. I made it to Highway 1, crossed over, and went down to the beach. I ran along the edge of the water for about six miles so I wouldn't leave any footprints. After a while, I heard a helicopter up above the fog, looking for me, I guess. I crossed an artichoke field and went back to Highway 1 again. I wrapped a field jacket I'd been wearing around my waist so nobody could see the blood on my legs, and started hitch-hiking. I'd wait in the bushes along the side of the road until the last minute so I could make sure that it wasn't an official car and then jump out with my thumb in the air. The third car that came by gave me a ride. He took me to Santa Cruz. I got to the bus station there and stood around for a while. Then I took a chance and asked this hip-looking girl to buy me a ticket to Oakland. She did. I didn't know how I ever made it. I still don't."

Weise stayed in the Bay Area for a few weeks, recuperating from the cuts on his legs (which have left bad scars) and from his brief glimpse of military justice. He tried to consider all the alternatives, but they kept boiling down to the same two choices that had existed from the day he deserted: giving himself up or leaving the country. His day in the stockade decided him against the first. The latter seemed too final; friends told him that the war would be over soon and that people like him could hope for amnesty. He wanted to believe it and so decided to hang on. But he wanted to get as far away from the Army as possible. He left for New York with Susan in hopes of adopting a new identity and beginning a new life. It was October 1968. He was 21 years old, and the six months he had been a fugitive seemed like a lifetime.

He remembers spending his first weeks in New York fascinated by the skyscrapers and repelled by the violence that hung palpable in the air. It was a small town boy's culture shock, and although he finally got over it, he often wished he were back in Oregon again, or in the mountains somewhere far from the urban cauldron. He took a new name and obtained identification through secret channels in order to get a job. He gave prospective employers the names of friends on the West Coast as references and then alerted them that they might be contacted.

"I started with a bookkeeping job," he says. "These people I gave as references lied and said I had all this white-collar experience, which I didn't have. I wound up working at a whole series of clerk-type jobs, using the first one as a reference. It was a way of surviving and it worked OK. I kept the jobs as long as I could stand them. Most of them were pretty bad and didn't pay much. It wasn't my thing, but we had to eat." He kept to himself and lived a model lower middle-class existence. He thought he might be able to declare a truce with the destructive ambiguity of his situation, but it worked at him in ways he couldn't control.

In February, 1969, Weise came back to California for a month's respite from New York. He went to Squaw Valley, where he got jobs shoveling snow and washing dishes in a ski resort, making as much money as he had in his various big-city clerking positions. Toward the end of his stay, he came down to the Bay Area to visit a friend whom he hadn't seen for a year. Once again he was forcefully reminded that he was a desperado.

"This friend, for some reason he told his mother about me. I guess he trusted her. Anyway, she knew where I was staying and she must have got to worrying about me being a bad influence. She called the cops. They came out to the apartment. They had an MP with them. I was shaving when they knocked at the door. I remember having the bathroom door open a crack and freezing when I saw who it was. My friend told them I wasn't there and asked for a warrant. They didn't have one, and for some reason didn't force their way in. They went down to the car to call in, and my friend went out to keep them busy. I crawled through the house on my hands and knees so they wouldn't see me in the windows. I got out the side door, and then I was running again, through back yards and over fences. I took the plane back to New York."

After this, the FBI began to periodically question his known Bay Area friends and made regular checks with his grandparents in Oregon. Weise never saw an agent, but he knew they were there, invisible and unrelenting, piecing together a trail that would some day lead to his doorstep. There were constant reminders that they were getting close. When he had stopped in Monterey, for instance, Susan had been carrying her roommate's purse by mistake and had offered the policeman the other girl's identification. That part of the episode was soon forgotten, and the roommate had since moved from Berkeley to the East Coast where she was in periodic contact with Weise and Susan. One day she telephoned to warn them that the FBI had called to grill her, thinking she was the girl who was with David Weise in Monterey.

He kept at his white-collar jobs for a few months, getting work from a series of employment agencies under the new name to which he was beginning to answer as if it were his own. Once he was robbed by two men whom he talked into not taking the identification he used for his new name. Toward the end of spring, he got a job driving one of New York's gypsy cabs. It kept him out of the offices he had grown to hate; it was fairly good money, unobtrusive, and secure. It was also a turning point. "I had money, a home, and a woman I wanted to marry," he says. "I was all set for life, except it didn't make any sense. It wasn't living. A year and a half of wondering if every cop I saw was going to grab me, looking at every person who was clean and crewcut as if he were FBI, using another name, having my heart jump every time there was a knock at the door—it all started to get to me. Also, this war was still going on, and it didn't seem to be any closer to getting over than when I deserted. I was driving this cab and going through the ghetto almost every day, seeing all that poverty and suffering which I knew could be cured forever by just a little part of what we're spending over in Viet-Nam. Things aren't getting any better for the country, and they aren't getting any better for me."

Our walk had taken us to the University of California. We sat down in a quiet place near the plaza from which countless mass protests against the war had been launched, and he said that he hoped someday to finish his education at a school like this one. He had been wavering between prison and exile for weeks, and was reaching a point of crisis. He had to leave to catch the plane back to New York, and we said good-bye.

At the beginning of December, I got a telephone call, the operator saying in a thin French accent that a Mr. David was calling from Montreal. A movement lawyer had told him if he turned himself in, he could expect a minimum eight-year sentence. "It was just too much," he said. "I wanted to, but I couldn't. That's too much of my life. Anyway, I'm here now. I went across at Vermont on Thanksgiving Day. I had taken two librium, but I went across the border shaking like a leaf."

He has been an uneasy rider for the last two years. Now he is working with the American Deserters Cooperative in Canada, and his life is seeking new dimensions. He has applied for status as a landed emigrant, and as soon as Susan joins him, they will head for the open mountain country in the Canadian Northwest.

After we had talked long distance for a few minutes, not really saying much, he hung up. I remembered the day we had met and talked for a couple of hours. He had been lighting a cigarette when we said good-bye and had fumbled clumsily with the matches to shake hands. It had been a bad moment for both of us. He probably had never talked about himself so much before and seemed upset by it. I had wanted to tell him that he was a hero and that the wrecked digestion and tangled nerves were part of an anonymous epic that might be celebrated someday when the times were better; but I couldn't because it would have embarrassed him.

READING SELECTION 2: COLLIER, "UNEASY RIDER"

COMPREHENSION AND ANALYSIS

Do not refer to the article to answer these questions. Choose one of the items that best answers each question, and mark the letter in the space provided.

1. _____ This essay describes David Weise's (a) escape from an army stockade and his subsequent arrest (b) desertion from the army after basic training and his subsequent flight to avoid prison (c) desertion from the army while serving in Vietnam (d) experiences while in Army basic training and confinement in the stockade.

2. _____ According to Collier, at their first meeting Weise appeared (a) very nervous, tense and apprehensive (b) very calm, sedate and relaxed (c) hostile and scornful (d) nervous, apprehensive and suspicious of the author.

3. _____ Weise made his decision to leave the army because (a) his girlfriend insisted (b) he hated the regimented life (c) he was afraid of getting killed and disliked the notion of killing other people (d) he was a sincere pacifist who opposed all wars.

4. _____ According to Collier, Army psychiatrists would believe that the cause of Weise's desertion was (a) Weise's criticism of the Vietnam war (b) Weise's incompetency as a soldier (c) Weise's lack of close family ties and unstable childhood environment (d) Weise's emotional problems (e) the mood of the nation's youth.

5. _____ Throughout the essay, one gets the impression that the two years of Weise's ordeal were filled with (a) terror and the constant fear of being caught (b) weariness from the constant running and hiding (c) the desire to marry and resume a normal life (d) all of the above.

6. _____ Weise finally realized that he had to make a choice between (a) hiding and running or exile to another country (b) prison or exile to another country (c) taking his case to court or prison (d) military service in Vietnam or exile to another country.

7. _____ The title "uneasy rider" suggests that Weise was (a) an insecure, cowardly deserter who was afraid of being killed (b) a lonely but uncompromising fugitive, the victim of unfortunate political circumstances (c) a courageous hero who sought publicity and glory (d) a pacifist who was misunderstood for his motives.

8. _____ The most important lesson that Weise learned was probably that (a) a fugitive can only rely on himself, not on
friends or acquaintances (b) a fugitive must be cautious
about relying on strangers and must live as anonymously as
possible (c) a fugitive must trust everyone, even strangers,
if he is to survive (d) none of the above.

9. _____ Sometime after Collier's meeting with Weise, he learned
that Weise had finally (a) been caught and sent to prison
for eight years (b) escaped to Sweden (c) escaped to Canada (d) returned to California to begin hiding again.

10. _____ Based on the evidence in the essay, mark T (true), F (false),
or X (not verifiable) for the inferences that follow.

    A. _____ Weise assumed a new name during his ordeal.

    B. _____ Weise's feelings about the war were carefully
thought out and clear-cut when he was drafted.

    C. _____ Prior to his desertion, Weise had not been ac-
tive in the peace movement.

    D. _____ Weise's feelings or paranoia were probably ex-
aggerated and certainly unjustified.

    E. _____ Several times Weise almost got caught due to
his own carelessness.

    F. _____ The cruelty of the guards at Camp Roberts
played an important part in Weise's decision.

    G. _____ Weise continually felt the presence of the FBI.

    H. _____ Weise at first dismissed the idea of leaving the
country because it seemed too drastic a solution.

    I. _____ It is apparent that Weise eventually regretted
his decision to desert from the army.

    J. _____ Weise and his girlfriend finally were married
after his exile.

    K. _____ The author greatly admired Weise for his cour-
age and determination.

VOCABULARY

From the lettered choices, find the best definition for each vocabulary
item, and mark the letter in the space provided.

1. _____ he was a *fugitive*
2. _____ caught in *limbo*
3. _____ admits to being *paranoid*
4. _____ *illusive* concepts
5. _____ in self-*deprecation*
6. _____ eyes, *feral* and haunted
7. _____ novelist could *conjure* up
8. _____ *hedonism* of the underworld

9. _____ *enmeshed* in the jargon
10. _____ forgetting the *magnitude*
11. _____ a *vicious* scene
12. _____ hope for *amnesty*
13. _____ violence was *palpable*
14. _____ the job was *unobtrusive*
15. _____ between prison and *exile*

A. unreal; deceptive; imaginary
B. enigmatic; puzzling
C. banishment; expulsion
D. ensnared; entangled
E. disheveled; messy
F. state of oblivion for the forgotten or unwanted
G. suggestive of the dead; deathly; ghostly
H. one who flees from pursuit, danger
I. general pardon for wrong-doing
J. suffering from delusion of persecution

K. destruction; ruin
L. obvious; readily perceived
M. size; extent
N. think up; produce as if by magic
O. immigrant
P. not sticking out; unobvious
Q. violent; maliciously fierce
R. easy; not demanding
S. self-indulgent pursuit of pleasure
T. disapproval; belittling

COMPREHENSION   No. right _____ × 5 = _____ %

VOCABULARY   No. right _____

No. of words 3100 ÷ time in seconds _____ × 60 = _____ WPM
WPM × Comprehension % = Reading Efficiency Rate _____

GEORGE WALD

A Generation in Search of a Future*

On March 4th, 1969, an audience of students and professors at M.I.T. gathered for a day-long conference on the misuse of science. However, they were disturbed by the lack of focus in the panel discussions and speeches. But one speech that electrified the audience was given by Dr. George Wald, Professor of Biology at Harvard College and a 1966 Nobel Prize winner. His words received a standing ovation, and a reporter for The Boston Globe *returned to his office and said, "I think I've just listened to the most important speech of my lifetime."*

All of you know that in the last couple of years there has been student unrest breaking at times into violence in many parts of the world: in England, Germany, Italy, Spain, Mexico and needless to say, in many parts of this country. There has been a great deal of discussion as to what it all means. Perfectly clearly it means something different in Mexico from what it does in France, and something different in France from what it does in Tokyo, and something different in Tokyo from what it does in this country. Yet unless we are to assume that students have gone crazy all over the world, or that they have just decided that it's the thing to do, there must be some common meaning.

I don't need to go so far afield to look for that meaning. I am a teacher, and at Harvard, I have a class of about 350 students—men and women—most of them freshmen and sophomores. Over these past few years I have felt increasingly that something is terribly wrong—and this year ever so much more than last. Something has gone sour, in teaching and in learning. It's almost as though there were a widespread feeling that education has become irrelevant.

A lecture is much more of a dialogue than many of you probably appreciate. As you lecture, you keep watching the faces; and information

* From *The Boston Globe*, March 8, 1969.

keeps coming back to you all the time. I began to feel, particularly this year, that I was missing much of what was coming back. I tried asking the students, but they didn't or couldn't help me very much.

But I think I know what's the matter, even a little better than they do. I think that this whole generation of students is beset with a profound uneasiness. I don't think that they have yet quite defined its source. I think I understand the reasons for their uneasiness even better than they do. What is more, I share their uneasiness.

What's bothering those students? Some of them tell you it's the Vietnam War. I think the Vietnam War is the most shameful episode in the whole of American history. The concept of War Crimes is an American invention. We've committed many War Crimes in Vietnam; but I'll tell you something interesting about that. We were committing War Crimes in World War II, even before the Nuremburg trials were held and the principle of war crimes stated. The saturation bombing of German cities was a War Crime. Dropping atom bombs on Hiroshima and Nagasaki was a War Crime. If we had lost the war, some of our leaders might have had to answer for those actions.

I've gone through all of that history lately, and I find that there's a gimmick in it. It isn't written out, but I think we established it by precedent. That gimmick is that if one can allege that one is repelling or retaliating for an *aggression*—after that everything goes. And you see we are living in a world in which all wars are wars of defense. All War Departments are now Defense Departments. This is all part of the double talk of our time. The aggressor is always on the other side. And I suppose this is why our ex-Secretary of State, Dean Rusk—a man in whom repetition takes the place of reason, and stubbornness takes the place of character—went to such pains to insist, as he still insists, that in Vietnam we are repelling an aggression. And if that's what we are doing—so runs the doctrine—anything goes. If the concept of war crimes is ever to mean anything, they will have to be defined as categories of acts, regardless of alleged provocation. But that isn't so now.

I think we've lost that war, as a lot of other people think, too. The Vietnamese have a secret weapon. It's their willingness to die, beyond our willingness to kill. In effect they've been saying, you can kill us, but you'll have to kill a lot of us, you may have to kill all of us. And thank heavens, we are not yet ready to do that.

Yet we have come a long way—far enough to sicken many Americans, far enough even to sicken our fighting men. Far enough so that our national symbols have gone sour. How many of you can sing about "the rockets' red glare, bombs bursting in air" without thinking, those are *our* bombs and *our* rockets bursting over South Vietnamese villages? When those words were written, we were a people struggling for freedom against oppression. Now we are supporting real or thinly disguised military dictatorships all over the world, helping them to control and repress peoples struggling for their freedom.

But that Vietnam War, shameful and terrible as it is, seems to me only an immediate incident in a much larger and more stubborn situation.

Part of my trouble with students is that almost all the students I teach were born since World War II. Just after World War II, a series of new and abnormal procedures came into American life. We regarded them as temporary aberrations. We thought we would get back to normal American life some day. But those procedures have stayed with us now for more than 20 years, and those students of mine have never known anything else. They think those things are normal. Students think we've always had a Pentagon, that we have always had a big army, and that we always had a draft. But those are all new things in American life; and I think that they are incompatible with what America meant before.

How many of you realize that just before World War II the entire American army including the Air Force numbered 139,000 men? Then World War II started, but we weren't yet in it; and seeing that there was great trouble in the world, we doubled this army to 268,000 men. Then in World War II it got to be 8 million. And then World War II came to an end, and we prepared to go back to a peacetime army somewhat as the American army had always been before. And indeed in 1950—you think about 1950, our international commitments, the Cold War, the Truman Doctrine, and all the rest of it—in 1950 we got down to 600,000 men.

Now we have 3.5 million men under arms: about 600,000 in Vietnam, about 300,000 more in "support areas" elsewhere in the Pacific, about 250,000 in Germany. And there are a lot at home. Some months ago we were told that 300,000 National Guardsmen and 200,000 reservists—so half a million men—had been specially trained for riot duty in the cities.

I say the Vietnam War is just an immediate incident, because so long as we keep that big an army, it will always find things to do. If the Vietnam War stopped tomorrow, with that big a military establishment, the chances are that we would be in another such adventure abroad or at home before you knew it.

As for the draft: Don't reform the draft—get rid of it.

A peacetime draft is the most un-American thing I know. All the time I was growing up I was told about oppressive Central European countries and Russia, where young men were forced into the army; and I was told what they did about it. They chopped off a finger, or shot off a couple of toes; or better still, if they could manage it, they came to this country. And we understood that, and sympathized, and were glad to welcome them.

Now by present estimates four to six thousand Americans of draft age have left this country for Canada, another two or three thousand have gone to Europe, and it looks as though many more are preparing to emigrate.

A few months ago I received a letter from the Harvard Alumni Bulletin posing a series of questions that students might ask a professor involving what to do about the draft. I was asked to write what I would tell those students. All I had to say to those students was this: If any of them had decided to evade the draft and asked my help, I would help him in any way I could. I would feel as I suppose members of the underground railway felt in pre-Civil War days, helping runaway slaves to get to Canada. It wasn't altogether a popular position then; but what do you think of it now?

A bill to stop the draft was recently introduced in the Senate (S. 503), sponsored by a group of senators that ran the gamut from McGovern and Hatfield to Barry Goldwater. I hope it goes through; but any time I find that Barry Goldwater and I are in agreement, that makes me take another look.

And indeed there are choices in getting rid of the draft. I think that when we get rid of the draft, we must also cut back the size of the armed forces. It seems to me that in peacetime a total of one million men is surely enough. If there is an argument for American military forces of more than one million men in peacetime, I should like to hear that argument debated.

There is another thing being said closely connected with this: that to keep an adequate volunteer army, one would have to raise the pay considerably. That's said so positively and often that people believe it. I don't think it is true.

The great bulk of our present armed forces are genuine volunteers. Among first-term enlistments, 49 per cent are true volunteers. Another 30 per cent are so-called "reluctant volunteers," persons who volunteer under pressure of the draft. Only 21 per cent are draftees. All re-enlistments, of course are true volunteers.

So the great majority of our present armed forces are true volunteers. Whole services are composed entirely of volunteers: the Air Force for example, the Navy, almost all the Marines. That seems like proof to me that present pay rates are adequate. One must add that an Act of Congress in 1967 raised the base pay throughout the services in three installments, the third installment still to come, on April 1, 1969. So it is hard to understand why we are being told that to maintain adequate armed services on a volunteer basis will require large increases in pay; that they will cost an extra $17 billion per year. It seems plain to me that we can get all the armed forces we need as volunteers, and at present rates of pay.

But there is something ever so much bigger and more important than the draft. That bigger thing, of course, is the militarization of our country. Ex-President Eisenhower warned us of what he called the military-industrial complex. I am sad to say that we must begin to think of it now as the military-industrial-labor union complex. What happened under the plea of the Cold War was not alone that we built up the first big peace time army in our history, but we institutionalized it. We built, I suppose, the biggest government building in our history to run it, and we institutionalized it.

I don't think we can live with the present military establishment and its $80 billion a year budget, and keep America anything like we have known it in the past. It is corrupting the life of the whole country. It is buying up everything in sight: industries, banks, investors, universities; and lately it seems also to have bought up the labor unions.

The Defense Department is always broke; but some of the things they do with that $80 billion a year would make Buck Rogers envious. For example: the Rocky Mountain Arsenal on the outskirts of Denver was manufacturing a deadly nerve poison on such a scale that there was a problem of waste disposal. Nothing daunted, they dug a tunnel two miles deep under Denver, into which they have injected so much poisoned water that beginning a couple of years ago Denver began to experience a series of earth tremors of increasing severity. Now there is a grave fear of a major earthquake. An interesting debate is in progress as to whether Denver will be safer if that lake of poisoned water is removed or left in place. (N.Y. Times, July 4, 1968; Science, Sept. 27, 1968).

Perhaps you have read also of those 6000 sheep that suddenly died in Skull Valley, Utah, killed by another nerve poison—a strange and, I believe, still unexplained accident, since the nearest testing seems to have been 30 miles away.

As for Vietnam, the expenditure of fire power has been frightening. Some of you may still remember Khe Sanh, a hamlet just south of the Demilitarized Zone, where a force of U. S. Marines was beleaguered for a time. During that period we dropped on the perimeter of Khe Sanh more explosives than fell on Japan throughout World War II, and more than fell on the whole of Europe during the years 1942 and 1943.

One of the officers there was quoted as having said afterward, "It looks like the world caught smallpox and died." (N.Y. Times, Mar. 28, 1968.)

The only point of government is to safeguard and foster life. Our government has become preoccupied with death, with the business of killing and being killed. So-called Defense now absorbs 60 per cent of the national budget, and about 12 per cent of the Gross National Product.

A lively debate is beginning again on whether or not we should deploy antiballistic missiles, the ABM. I don't have to talk about them, everyone else here is doing that. But I should like to mention a curious circumstance. In September, 1967, or about 1½ years ago, we had a meeting of M.I.T. and Harvard people, including experts on these matters, to talk about whether anything could be done to block the Sentinel system, the deployment of ABM's. Everyone present thought them undesirable; but a few of the most knowledgeable persons took what seemed to be the practical view, "Why fight about a dead issue? It has been decided, the funds have been appropriated. Let's go on from there."

Well, fortunately, it's not a dead issue.

An ABM is a nuclear weapon. It takes a nuclear weapon to stop a nuclear weapon. And our concern must be with the whole issue of nuclear weapons.

There is an entire semantics ready to deal with the sort of thing I am about to say. It involves such phrases as "those are the facts of life." No—they are the facts of death. I don't accept them, and I advise you not to accept them. We are under repeated pressure to accept things that are presented to us as settled—decisions that have been made. Always there is the thought: let's go on from there! But this time we don't see how to go on. We will have to stick with those issues.

We are told that the United States and Russia between them have by now stockpiled in nuclear weapons approximately the explosive power of 15 tons of TNT for every man, woman and child on earth. And now it is suggested that we must make more. All very regrettable, of course; but those are "the facts of life." We really would like to disarm; but our new Secretary of Defense has made the ingenious proposal that now is the time to greatly increase our nuclear armaments so that we can disarm from a position of strength.

I think all of you know there is no adequate defense against massive nuclear attack. It is both easier and cheaper to circumvent any known nuclear defense system than to provide it. It's all pretty crazy. At the very moment we talk of deploying ABM's, we are also building the MIRV, the weapon to circumvent ABM's.

So far as I know, the most conservative estimates of Americans killed in a major nuclear attack, with everything working as well as can be hoped and all foreseeable precautions taken, run to about 50 millions. We have become callous to gruesome statistics, and this seems at first to be only another gruesome statistic. You think, Bang!—and next morning, if you're still there, you read in the newspapers that 50 million people were killed.

But that isn't the way it happens. When we killed close to 200,000 people with those first little, old-fashioned uranium bombs that we dropped on Hiroshima and Nagasaki, about the same number of persons was maimed, blinded, burned, poisoned and otherwise doomed. A lot of them took a long time to die.

That's the way it would be. Not a bang, and a certain number of corpses to bury; but a nation filled with millions of helpless, maimed, tortured and doomed persons, and the survivors of a nuclear holocaust will be huddled with their families in shelters, with guns ready to fight off their neighbors, trying to get some uncontaminated food and water.

A few months ago Sen. Richard Russell of Georgia ended a speech in the Senate with the words: "If we have to start over again with another Adam and Eve, I want them to be Americans; and I want them on this continent and not in Europe." That was a United States senator holding a patriotic speech. Well, here is a Nobel Laureate who thinks that those words are criminally insane. (Prolonged applause.)

How real is the threat of full scale nuclear war? I have my own very inexpert idea, but realizing how little I know and fearful that I may be a little paranoid on this subject, I take every opportunity to ask reputed experts. I asked that question of a very distinguished professor of government at Harvard about a month ago. I asked him what sort of odds he would lay on the possibility of full-scale nuclear war within the foreseeable future. "Oh," he said comfortably, "I think I can give you a pretty good answer to that question. I estimate the probability of full-scale nuclear war, provided that the situation remains about as it is now, at 2 per cent per year." Anybody can do the simple calculation that shows that 2 per cent per year means that the chance of having that full-scale nuclear war by 1990 is about one in three, and by 2000 it is about 50–50.

I think I know what is bothering the students. I think that what we are up against is a generation that is by no means sure that it has a future.

I am growing old, and my future so to speak is already behind me. But there are those students of mine who are in my mind always; and there are my children, two of them now 7 and 9, whose future is infinitely more precious to me than my own. So it isn't just their generation; it's mine too. We're all in it together.

Are we to have a chance to live? We don't ask for prosperity, or security; only for a reasonable chance to live, to work out our destiny in peace and decency. Not to go down in history as the apocalyptic generation.

And it isn't only nuclear war. Another overwhelming threat is the population explosion. That has not yet even begun to come under control. There is every indication that the world population will double before the year 2000; and there is a widespread expectation of famine on an unprecedented scale in many parts of the world. The experts tend to differ only in the estimates of when those famines will begin. Some think by 1980, others think they can be staved off until 1990, very few expect that they will not occur by the year 2000.

That is the problem. Unless we can be surer than we now are that this generation has a future, nothing else matters. It's not good enough to give it tender loving care, to supply it with breakfast foods, to buy it expensive educations. Those things don't mean anything unless this generation has a future. And we're not sure that it does.

I don't think that there are problems of youth, or student problems. All the real problems I know are grown-up problems.

Perhaps you will think me altogether absurd, or "academic," or hopelessly innocent—that is, until you think of the alternatives—if I say as I do to you now: we have to get rid of those nuclear weapons. There is nothing worth having that can be obtained by nuclear war: nothing material or ideological, no tradition that it can defend. It is utterly self-defeat-ing. Those atom bombs represent an unusable weapon. The only use for an atom bomb is to keep somebody else from using one. It can give us no protection, but only the doubtful satisfaction of retaliation. Nuclear weapons offer us nothing but a balance of terror; and a balance of terror is still terror.

We have to get rid of those atomic weapons, here and everywhere. We cannot live with them.

I think we've reached a point of great decision, not just for our nation, not only for all humanity, but for life upon the Earth. I tell my students, with a feeling of pride that I hope they will share, that the carbon, nitrogen and oxygen that make up 99 per cent of our living substance, were cooked in the deep interiors of earlier generations of dying stars. Gathered up from the ends of the universe, over billions of years, eventually they came to form in part the substance of our sun, its planets and ourselves. Three billion years ago life arose upon the Earth. It seems to be the only life in the solar system. Many a star has since been born and died.

About two million years ago, man appeared. He has become the dominant species on the Earth. All other living things, animal and plant, live by his sufferance. He is the custodian of life on Earth. It's a big responsibility.

The thought that we're in competition with Russians or with Chinese is all a mistake, and trivial. Only mutual destruction lies that way. We are one species, with a world to win. There's life all over this universe, but in all the universe we are the only men.

Our business is with life, not death. Our challenge is to give what account we can of what becomes of life in the solar system, this corner of the universe that is our home and, most of all, what becomes of men—all men of all nations, colors and creeds. It has become one world, a world for all men. It is only such a world that now can offer us life and the chance to go on.

READING SELECTION 3: WALD, "A GENERATION IN SEARCH OF A FUTURE"

COMPREHENSION AND ANALYSIS

Do not refer to the article to answer these questions. Choose one of the items that best answers each question, and mark the letter in the space provided.

1. __C__ Which of the following best describes the purpose of Dr. Wald's speech? (a) a description and criticism of America's military-industrial-labor union complex (b) an explanation and defense of student discontent (c) a definition of the issues which most concern students and a warning for mankind's future (d) an alarming attack on America's foreign policy and educational system.

2. __b__ Dr. Wald states that throughout our history, American foreign policy has followed a gimmick, the doctrine of (a) repelling alleged aggressions to disguise our war crimes (b) preserving our political and economic interests by any means possible (c) repressing people who fight against military dictatorships (d) playing off neutral nations one against the other.

3. __A__ According to the speech, the Vietnam War is (a) both the immediate and underlying cause of student uneasiness (b) only a symptom of a much greater, more dangerous situation which has caused student discontent (c) hardly a cause at all of student discontent (d) only an excuse for social turmoil.

4. __E__ Dr. Wald says that America's military complex is the fundamental wrong in our society because (a) it is incompatible with what America used to stand for (b) it is a temporary necessity which has become permanent (c) to justify its existence, it needs to find outlets, like Vietnam (d) it is corrupting the life of the whole country (e) all of the above (f) only a, b, and d.

5. __B__ From the speech, one can assume that Dr. Wald would favor (a) a worldwide buildup of nuclear weapons and defense systems (b) total worldwide disarmament (c) development of nuclear defense systems but an end to building any additional nuclear weapons (d) only American and Russian disarmament.

6. __C__ According to the speech, by 1990, if the present trends are not reversed, we will witness (a) the destruction of the entire solar system (b) a terrible famine in many parts of the

world (c) a one-in-three chance of nuclear war (d) all of the above (e) b and c only.

7. ___D___ Dr. Wald emphasizes that the only real issue we must confront is (a) a generation of students who is unsure that it even has a future (b) the prospect of a population explosion and worldwide famine (c) the threat from Russia and China (d) the assurance of prosperity and security (e) none of the above.

8. Based on the evidence in the speech, mark T (true), F (false), or X (not verifiable) for the inferences that follow.

A. ___X___ Student unrest has been only an American phenomenon.

B. ___F___ Although Vietnam is the most shameful episode in American history, it was a natural, inevitable result of our foreign and military policies.

C. ___T___ After World War II, the military complex was unwilling to relinquish its new-found strength.

D. ___T___ The draft lottery is an important step toward establishing an all-volunteer army.

E. ___X___ The ABM (Sentinel) system is only another excuse to prolong the so-called "balance of terror."

F. ___X___ Although Wald sympathizes with his students' uneasiness, he deplores their violent tactics.

9. Based on the evidence in the speech, mark J (justified) or NJ (not justified) for the conclusions that follow.

A. ___NJ___ Despite the military establishment's strength, America will never get involved in another war like Vietnam.

B. ___NJ___ The adult population is as guilty of its indifference to what is happening as the American government is for fostering death.

C. ___J___ Students are justifiably concerned with the threat of extinction from nuclear warfare.

D. ___NJ___ As this generation of students grows older, they will undoubtedly become as apathetic to the world's problems as their parents are.

E. ___NJ___ Most adults' anxieties over Communism and student unrest are both misguided and irrelevant.

F. ___J___ Pollution of the earth's environment is the single most important issue we face.

10. ___C___ In his conclusion, Dr. Wald states that only "a world for all men" can offer "a chance to go on." This view is (a) frightening and alarming, expressing no hope (b) cautiously optimistic, expressing a slight hope (c) cautiously pessimistic, expressing little hope (d) exaggerated, unreasonable, and impractical.

VOCABULARY

From the lettered choices, find the best definition for each vocabulary item, and mark the letter in the space provided.

1. ___D___ a *profound* uneasiness
2. ___P___ *repelling* an aggression
3. _____ established by *precedent*
4. _____ alleged *provocation*
5. ___L___ as temporary *aberrations*
6. ___F___ they are *incompatible*
7. ___C___ to *evade* the draft
8. ___I___ a force was *beleaguered*
9. ___A___ the *perimeter* of Khe Sanh
10. ___T___ to *deploy* missiles
11. ___N___ the *ingenious* proposal
12. ___H___ cheaper to *circumvent*
13. ___E___ we have become *callous*
14. ___K___ a nuclear *holocaust*
15. ___O___ the *apocalyptic* generation

A. boundary line; outer limits
B. interior; center
C. get out of; avoid
D. deep; penetrating
E. hardened in feelings; insensitive
F. not harmonious; incapable of coexisting
G. alternatives; choices
H. outwit; outsmart; thwart
I. surrounded; beset
J. convention; custom
K. total destruction (by fire)
L. deviations from the normal

M. inseparable; mutually dependent
N. clever; inventive
O. describing a revelation or disclosure about the future; that which fulfills predictions or warnings
P. forcing, driving back
Q. greedy; avaricious
R. incitement to action; stimulus
S. foolish; deceptively simple
T. put into effect; do according to a plan

COMPREHENSION   No. right _____ × 5 = _____ %

VOCABULARY   No. right _____

No. of words 3400 ÷ time in seconds _____ × 60 = _____ WPM
WPM × Comprehension % = Reading Efficiency Rate _____

ALFRED KAZIN

From Subway to Synagogue*

A Walker in the City is Alfred Kazin's autobiographical account of his life as a young man growing up in Brownsville, a neighborhood in Brooklyn settled by Jewish immigrants from eastern Europe. In "The Human Factory," Kazin describes with pathos his school and his teachers' attempts to transform their immigrant pupils into copies of model American youth.

All my early life lies open to my eye within five city blocks. When I passed the school, I went sick with all my old fear of it. With its standard New York public-school brown brick courtyard shut in on three sides of the square and the pretentious battlements overlooking that cockpit in which I can still smell the fiery sheen of the rubber ball, it looks like a factory over which has been imposed the façade of a castle. It gave me the shivers to stand up in that courtyard again; I felt as if I had been mustered back into the service of those Friday morning "tests" that were the terror of my childhood.

It was never learning I associated with that school: only the necessity to succeed, to get ahead of the others in the daily struggle to "make a good impression" on our teachers, who grimly, wearily, and often with ill-concealed distaste watched against our relapsing into the natural savagery they expected of Brownsville boys. The white, cool, thinly ruled record book sat over us from their desks all day long, and had remorselessly entered into it each day—in blue ink if we had passed, in red ink if we had not—our attendance, our conduct, our "effort," our merits and demerits; and to the last possible decimal point in calculation, our standing in an unending series of "tests"—surprise tests, daily tests, weekly tests, formal midterm tests, final tests. They never stopped trying to dig out of us whatever small morsel of fact we had managed to get down the night before. We had to prove that we were really alert, ready for anything, always in

* From *A Walker in the City* (New York: Harcourt Brace Jovanovich, Inc., 1951), pp. 17–25.

the race. That white thinly ruled record book figured in my mind as the judgment seat; the very thinness and remote blue lightness of its lines instantly showed its cold authority over me; so much space had been left on each page, columns and columns in which to note down everything about us, implacably and forever. As it lay there on a teacher's desk, I stared at it all day long with such fear and anxious propriety that I had no trouble believing that God, too, did nothing but keep such record books, and that on the final day He would face me with an account in Hebrew letters whose phonetic dots and dashes looked strangely like decimal points counting up my every sinful thought on earth.

All teachers were to be respected like gods, and God Himself was the greatest of all school superintendents. Long after I had ceased to believe that our teachers could see with the back of their heads, it was still understood, by me, that they knew everything. They were the delegates of all visible and invisible power on earth—of the mothers who waited on the stoops every day after three for us to bring home tales of our daily triumphs; of the glacially remote Anglo-Saxon principal, whose very name was King; of the incalculably important Superintendent of Schools who would someday rubberstamp his name to the bottom of our diplomas in grim acknowledgment that we had, at last, given satisfaction to him, to the Board of Superintendents, and to our benefactor the City of New York —and so up and up, to the government of the United States and to the great Lord Jehovah Himself. My belief in teachers' unlimited wisdom and power rested not so much on what I saw in them—how impatient most of them looked, how wary—but on our abysmal humility, at least in those of us who were "good" boys, who proved by our ready compliance and "manners" that we wanted to get on. The road to a professional future would be shown us only as we pleased *them. Make a good impression the first day of the term, and they'll help you out. Make a bad impression, and you might as well cut your throat.* This was the first article of school folklore, whispered around the classroom the opening day of each term. You made the "good impression" by sitting firmly at your wooden desk, hands clasped; by silence for the greatest part of the live-long day; by standing up obsequiously when it was so expected of you; by sitting down noiselessly when you had answered a question; by "speaking nicely," which meant reproducing their painfully exact enunciation; by "showing manners," or an ecstatic submissiveness in all things; by outrageous flattery; by bringing little gifts at Christmas, on their birthdays, and at the end of the term—the well-known significance of these gifts being that they came not from us, but from our parents, whose eagerness in this matter showed a high level of social consideration, and thus raised our standing in turn.

It was not just our quickness and memory that were always being tested. Above all, in that word I could never hear without automatically seeing it raised before me in gold-plated letters, it was our *character.* I always felt anxious when I heard the word pronounced. Satisfactory as my "character" was, on the whole, except when I stayed too long in the playground reading; outrageously satisfactory, as I can see now, the very sound of the word as our teachers coldly gave it out from the end of their teeth, with a solemn weight on each dark syllable, immediately struck my heart cold with fear—they could not believe I really had it. Character was never something you had; it had to be trained in you, like a technique. I was never very clear about it. On our side *character* meant demonstrative obedience; but teachers already had it—how else could they have become teachers? They had it; the aloof Anglo-Saxon principal whom we remotely saw only on ceremonial occasions in the assembly was positively encased in it; it glittered off his bald head in spokes of triumphant light; the President of the United States had the greatest conceivable amount of it. Character belonged to great adults. Yet we were constantly being driven onto it; it was the great threshold we had to cross. *Alfred Kazin, having shown proficiency in his course of studies and having displayed satisfactory marks of character . . .* Thus someday the hallowed diploma, passport to my further advancement in high school. But there—I could already feel it in my bones—they would put me through even more doubting tests of character; and after that, if I should be good enough and bright enough, there would be still more. *Character* was a bitter thing, racked with my endless striving to please. The school—from every last stone in the courtyard to the battlements frowning down at me from the walls—was only the stage for a trial. I felt that the very atmosphere of learning that surrounded us was fake—that every lesson, every book, every approving smile was only a pretext for the constant probing and watching of me, that there was not a secret in me that would not be decimally measured into that white record book. All week long I lived for the blessed sound of the dismissal gong at three o'clock on Friday afternoon.

I was awed by this system, I believed in it, I respected its force. The alternative was "going bad." The school was notoriously the toughest in our tough neighborhood, and the dangers of "going bad" were constantly impressed upon me at home and in school in dark whispers of the "reform school" and in examples of boys who had been picked up for petty thievery, rape, or flinging a heavy inkwell straight into a teacher's face. Behind any failure in school yawned the great abyss of a criminal career. Every refractory attitude doomed you with the sound "Sing Sing." Anything less than absolute perfection in school always suggested to my mind that I might fall out of the daily race, be kept back in the working class forever, or—dared I think of it?—fall into the criminal class itself.

I worked on a hairline between triumph and catastrophe. Why the odds should always have felt so narrow I understood only when I realized how little my parents thought of their own lives. It was not for myself alone that I was expected to shine, but for them—to redeem the constant anxiety of their existence. I was the first American child, their offering to the strange new God; I was to be the monument of their liberation from the shame of being—what they were. And that there was shame in this was a fact that everyone seemed to believe as a matter of course. It was in the gleeful discounting of themselves—what do we know?—with which our parents greeted every fresh victory in our savage competition for "high averages," for prizes, for a few condescending words of official praise from the principal at assembly. It was in the sickening invocation of "Americanism"—the word itself accusing us of everything we apparently were not. Our families and teachers seemed tacitly agreed that we were somehow to be a little ashamed of what we were. Yet it was always hard to say why this should be so. It was certainly not—in Brownsville!—because we were Jews, or simply because we spoke another language at home, or were absent on our holy days. It was rather that a "refined," "correct," "nice" English was required of us at school that we did not naturally speak, and that our teachers could never be quite sure we would keep. This English was peculiarly the ladder of advancement. Every future young lawyer was known by it. Even the Communists and Socialists on Pitkin Avenue spoke it. It was bright and clean and polished. We were expected to show it off like a new pair of shoes. When the teacher sharply called a question out, then your name, you were expected to leap up, face the class, and eject those new words fluently off the tongue.

There was my secret ordeal: I could never say anything except in the most roundabout way; I was a stammerer. Although I knew all those new words from my private reading—I read walking in the street, to and from the Children's Library on Stone Avenue; on the fire escape and the roof; at every meal when they would let me; read even when I dressed in the morning, propping my book up against the drawers of the bureau as I pulled on my long black stockings—I could never seem to get the easiest words out with the right dispatch, and would often miserably signal from my desk that I did not know the answer rather than get up to stumble and fall and crash on every word. If, angry at always being put down as lazy or stupid, I did get up to speak, the black wooden floor would roll away under my feet, the teacher would frown at me in amazement, and in unbearable loneliness I would hear behind me the groans and laughter: *tuh-tuh-tuh-tuh.*

The word was my agony. The word that for others was so effortless and so neutral, so unburdened, so simple, so exact, I had first to meditate in advance, to see if I could make it, like a plumber fitting together odd lengths and shapes of pipe. I was always preparing words I could speak, storing them away, choosing between them. And often, when the word did come from my mouth in its great and terrible birth, quailing and bleeding as if forced through a thornbush, I would not be able to look the others in the face, and would walk out in the silence, the infinitely echoing silence behind my back, to say it all cleanly back to myself as I walked in the streets. Only when I was alone in the open air, pacing the roof with pebbles in my mouth, as I had read Demosthenes had done to cure himself of stammering; or in the street, where all words seemed to flow from the length of my stride and the color of the houses as I remembered the perfect tranquillity of a phrase in Beethoven's *Romance in F* I could sing back to myself as I walked—only then was it possible for me to speak without the infinite premeditations and strangled silences I toiled through whenever I got up at school to respond with the expected, the exact answer.

It troubled me that I could speak in the fullness of my own voice only when I was alone on the streets, walking about. There was something unnatural about it; unbearably isolated. I was not like the others! I was not like the others! At midday, every freshly shocking Monday noon, they sent me away to a speech clinic in a school in East New York, where I sat in a circle of lispers and cleft palates and foreign accents holding a mirror before my lips and rolling difficult sounds over and over. To be sent there in the full light of the opening week, when everyone else was at school or going about his business, made me feel as if I had been expelled from the great normal body of humanity. I would gobble down my lunch on my way to the speech clinic and rush back to the school in time to make up for the classes I had lost. One day, one unforgettable dread day, I stopped to catch my breath on a corner of Sutter Avenue, near the wholesale fruit markets, where an old drugstore rose up over a great flight of steps. In the window were dusty urns of colored water floating off iron chains; cardboard placards advertising hairnets, Ex-Lax; a great illustrated medical chart headed THE HUMAN FACTORY, which showed the exact course a mouthful of food follows as it falls from chamber to chamber of the body. I hadn't meant to stop there at all, only to catch my breath; but I so hated the speech clinic that I thought I would delay my arrival for a few minutes by eating my lunch on the steps. When I took the sandwich out of my bag, two bitterly hard pieces of hard salami slipped out of my hand and fell through a grate onto a hill of dust below the steps. I remember how sickeningly vivid an odd thread of hair looked on the salami, as if my lunch were turning stiff with death. The factory whistles called their short, sharp blasts stark through the middle of noon, beating at me where I sat outside the city's magnetic circle. I had never known, I knew instantly I would never in my heart again submit to, such wild passive despair as I felt at that moment, sitting on the steps before THE HUMAN FACTORY, where little robots gathered and shoveled the food from chamber to chamber of the body. They had put me out into the streets, I thought to myself; with their mirrors and their everlasting pulling at me to imitate their effortless bright speech and their stupefaction that a boy could stammer and stumble on every other English word he carried in his head, they had put me out into the streets, had left me high and dry on the steps of that drugstore staring at the remains of my lunch turning black and grimy in the dust.

Reading Selection 4: Kazin, "From Subway to Synagogue"

COMPREHENSION AND ANALYSIS

Do not refer to the article to answer these questions. Choose one of the items that best answers each question, and mark the letter in the space provided.

1. ___B___ This essay describes (a) an adult's memory of growing up as an immigrant in America (b) an adult's autobiographical account of his childhood, his fears of a New York public school and its attempts to make him conform to an all-American image (c) an adult's recollection of his childhood teachers and their methods of drilling knowledge into him (d) an adult's reminiscences of childhood in New York.

2. ___B___ Throughout the essay Kazin makes it evident that he looked upon his school with (a) pride and reverence (b) fear and frustration (c) anger and bitterness (d) envy.

3. ___E___ The author did not associate school with learning, but rather with (a) the necessity to succeed (b) the necessity of making a good impression (c) achieving high test scores (d) development of one's character (e) all of the above.

4. ___C___ From his first experiences at school, Kazin felt that his teachers were (a) filled with unlimited wisdom and authority (b) poorly educated fools who could easily be outwitted (c) mistakenly dedicated to enforcing rules and regulations rather than imparting knowledge (d) dedicated people who had their pupils' best interests in mind.

5. ___B___ To Kazin, the epitome of the school's authority was represented by (a) the teacher's platform (b) the white record book (c) the endless tests (d) the attendance book.

6. ___A___ It is obvious from the selection that the Brownsville teachers treated their students with (a) distaste, as unrefined immigrants and potential criminals (b) respect, as bright, promising students who were the unfortunate victims of poverty (c) contempt, as stupid children who did not deserve time or attention (d) condescension, as inferior children who would never succeed.

7. ___D___ The most moving and pathetic part of the essay is Kazin's description of (a) his teacher's method of punishment for misbehavior (b) his difficulty with speaking English, his classmates' incessant teasing, and his misery at the speech clinic (c) the school's cold, factory-like appearance (d) his humiliation in speaking another language.

8. ___C___ Kazin's difficulties with speech were the result of (a) his

inability to speak refined English in front of others (b) a physical malfunctioning of his speech organs (c) his fear of being ridiculed by his teachers and classmates (d) his hatred of the speech clinic where he was sent for therapy.

9.　　　Based on the evidence in the essay, mark T (true), F (false), or X (not verifiable) for the inferences that follow.

A. __X__ Kazin's parents were poor and ashamed of their existence.

B. __X__ Kazin was his parents' only child.

C. __T__ Apparently Kazin never impressed his teachers very favorably.

D. __F__ To Kazin, his school building was beautiful, elegant and impressive.

E. __T__ Kazin felt his early years in school were filled with constant humiliation.

F. __X__ Some of Kazin's own classmates were sent to a reformatory.

G. __F__ Kazin's teachers disliked their pupils primarily because they were Jewish.

H. __F__ Kazin always stammered as a child, even when he practiced speaking in private.

I. __T__ In retrospect, Kazin feels that he was a good child, with a good character.

J. __F__ Kazin never outgrew his fear of his old school, even as an adult.

K. __X__ Kazin never realized how damaging conformity was until adulthood.

10. __E__ The chart describing the human digestive tract, "The Human Factory," is significant because Kazin realized (a) that his school was also a factory, which manufactured robots rather than happy, educated children (b) that his school had brought him to the brink of despair (c) that he would no longer allow himself to be molded into a model American boy (d) that the school demanded machine-like obedience and did not respect its students' individuality (e) all of the above.

VOCABULARY

From the lettered choices, find the best definition for each vocabulary item, and mark the letter in the space provided.

1. __N__ the *pretentious* battlements
2. __J__ the *façade* of a castle
3. __K__ *remorselessly* entered
4. __G__ anxious *propriety*

5. __P__ our *abysmal* humility
6. __M__ our ready *compliance*
7. __R__ standing up *obsequiously*
8. __E__ an *ecstatic* submissiveness
9. __A__ the *hallowed* diploma
10. __H__ the *aloof* principal
11. __I__ every smile was a *pretext*
12. __T__ I was *awed* by
13. __F__ every *refractory* attitude
14. __O__ the perfect *tranquillity*
15. __B__ the *infinite* premeditations

A. holy; sacred
B. unlimited; never-ending
C. false front which gives a favorable impression
D. grand; extravagant
E. rapturous; intensely pleasurable
F. obstinate; unmanageable
G. conformity to established standards of behavior
H. distant; cool
I. fictitious reason to conceal a real one

J. fearlessly; shamelessly
K. pitilessly; without compassion
L. frustration; confusion
M. obedience; consent
N. outwardly showy; ostentatious
O. calm; quiet
P. immeasurable; extreme
Q. dismal; abject
R. submissively; in a servile, slavish manner
S. unconfined to time or space
T. overwhelmed; impressed with fear

COMPREHENSION No. right _____ × 5 = _____ %

VOCABULARY No. right _____

No. of words 2300 ÷ time in seconds _____ × 60 = _____ WPM
WPM × Comprehension % = Reading Efficiency Rate _____

5   Skip

ELDRIDGE CLEAVER
The Black Man's Stake in Vietnam*

Eldridge Cleaver, Minister of Information for the Black Panther Party, has been in exile in Cuba and Algeria since 1968. Soul on Ice written from 1965 to 1967 while Cleaver served two prison terms in California, aroused a controversy because of his outspoken views on racial matters and his own experiences as a black man in a racist society. In this selection, written during President Johnson's term, Cleaver analyzes the Vietnam War and its significance to black Americans.

The most critical tests facing Johnson are the war in Vietnam and the Negro revolution at home. The fact that the brains in the Pentagon see fit to send 16 per cent black troops to Vietnam is one indication that there is a structural relationship between these two arenas of conflict. And the initial outrageous refusal of the Georgia Legislature to seat representative-elect Julian Bond, because he denounced the aggressive U.S. role in Vietnam, shows, too, the very intimate relationship between the way human beings are being treated in Vietnam and the treatment they are receiving here in the United States.

We live today in a system that is in the last stages of the protracted process of breaking up on a worldwide basis. The rulers of this system have their hands full. Injustice is being challenged at every turn and on every level. The rulers perceive the greatest threat to be the national liberation movements around the world, particularly in Asia, Africa, and Latin America. In order for them to wage wars of suppression against these national liberation movements abroad, they must have peace and stability and unanimity of purpose at home. But at home there is a Trojan Horse, a Black Trojan Horse that has become aware of itself and is now struggling to get on its feet. It, too, demands liberation.

What is the purpose of the attention that the rulers are now focusing

* From *Soul on Ice* (New York: McGraw-Hill Book Company, 1968), pp. 121–127.

on the Trojan Horse? Is it out of a newfound love for the horse, or is it because the rulers need the horse to be quiet, to be still, and not cause the rulers, already with their backs pressed to the wall, any trouble or embarrassment while they force the war in Vietnam? Indeed, the rulers have need of the horse's power on the fields of battle. What the black man in America must keep constantly in mind is that the doctrine of white supremacy, which is a part of the ideology of the world system the power structure is trying to preserve, lets the black man in for the greatest portion of the suffering and hate which white supremacy has dished out to the non-white people of the world for hundreds of years. The white-supremacy-oriented white man feels less compunction about massacring "niggers" than he does about massacring any other race of people on earth. This historically indisputable fact, taken with the present persistent efforts of the United States to woo the Soviet Union into an alliance against China, spells *DANGER* to all the peoples of the world who have been victims of white supremacy. If this sweethearting proves successful, if the United States is finally able to make a match with Russia, or if the U.S. can continue to frighten the Soviet Union into reneging on its commitments to international socialist solidarity (about which the Soviets are always trumpeting, while still allowing the imperialist aggressors to daily bomb the Democratic Republic of North Vietnam), and if the U.S. is able to unleash its anxious fury and armed might against the rising non-white giant of China, which is the real target of U.S. policy in Vietnam and the Object-Evil of U.S. strategy the world over—if the U.S. is successful in these areas, then it will be the black man's turn again to face the lyncher and burner of the world: and face him alone.

Black Americans are too easily deceived by a few smiles and friendly gestures, by the passing of a few liberal-sounding laws which are left on the books to rot unenforced, and by the mushy speechmaking of a President who is a past master of talking out of the thousand sides of his mouth. Such poetry does not *guarantee* the safe future of the black people in America. The black people must have a guarantee, they must be *certain,* they must be sure beyond all doubt that the reign of terror is ended and not just suspended, and that the future of their people is secure. And the only way they can ensure this is to gain organizational unity and communication with their brothers and allies around the world, on an international basis. They must have this power. There is no other way. Anything else is a sellout of the future of their people. The world of today was fashioned yesterday. What is involved here, what is being decided right now, is the shape of power in the world tomorrow.

The American racial problem can no longer be spoken of or solved in isolation. The relationship between the genocide in Vietnam and the smiles of the white man toward black Americans is a direct relationship. Once the white man solves his problem in the East he will then turn his fury again on the black people of America, his longtime punching bag. The black people have been tricked again and again, sold out at every turn by *mis*leaders. After the Civil War, America went through a period similar to the one we are now in. The Negro problem received a full hearing. Everybody knew that the black man had been denied justice. No one doubted that it was time for changes and that the black man should be made a first-class citizen. But Reconstruction ended. Blacks who had been elevated to high positions were brusquely kicked out into the streets and herded along with the masses of blacks into the ghettos and black belts. The lyncher and the burner received virtual license to murder blacks at will. White Americans found a new level on which to cool the blacks out. And with the help of such tools as Booker T. Washington, the doctrine of segregation was clamped firmly onto the backs of the blacks. It has taken a hundred years to struggle up from that level of cool-out to the miserable position that black Americans now find themselves in. Time is passing. The historical opportunity which world events now present to black Americans is running out with every tick of the clock.

This is the last act of the show. We are living in a time when the people of the world are making their final bid for full and complete freedom. Never before in history has this condition prevailed. Always before there have been more or less articulate and aware pockets of people, portions of classes, etc., but today's is an era of mass awareness, when the smallest man on the street is in rebellion against the system which has denied him life and which he has come to understand robs him of his dignity and self-respect. Yet he is being told that it will take time to get programs started, to pass legislation, to educate white people into accepting the idea that black people want and deserve freedom. But it is physically impossible to move as fast as the black man would like to move. Black men are deadly serious when they say *FREEDOM NOW*. Even if the white man wanted to eradicate all traces of evil overnight, he would not be able to do it because the economic and political system will not permit it. All talk about going too fast is treasonous to the black man's future.

What the white man must be brought to understand is that the black man in America today is fully aware of his position, and he does not intend to be tricked again into another hundred-year forfeit of freedom. Not for a single moment or for any price will the black men now rising up in America settle for anything less than their full proportionate share and participation in the sovereignty of America. The black man has already come to a realization that to be free it is necessary for him to throw his life—everything—on the line, because the oppressors refuse to understand that it is now impossible for them to come up with another trick to squelch the black revolution. The black man can't afford to take a chance. He can't afford to put things off. He must stop the whole show *NOW* and get his business straight, because if he does not do it now, if he fails to grasp securely the reins of this historic opportunity, there may be no tomorrow for him.

The black man's interest lies in seeing a free and independent Vietnam, a strong Vietnam which is not the puppet of international white supremacy. If the nations of Asia, Latin America, and Africa are strong and free, the black man in America will be safe and secure and free to live in dignity and self-respect. It is a cold fact that while the nations of Africa, Asia, and Latin America were shackled in colonial bondage, the black American was held tightly in the vise of oppression and not permitted to utter a sound of protest of any effect. But when these nations started bidding for their freedom, it was then that black Americans were able to seize the chance; it was then that the white man yielded what little he did—out of sheer necessity. The only lasting salvation for the black American is to do all he can to see to it that the African, Asian, and Latin American nations are free and independent.

In this regard, black Americans have a big role to play. They are a Black Trojan Horse within white America and they number in excess of 23,000,000 strong. That is a lot of strength. But it is a lot of weakness if it is disorganized and at odds with itself. Right now it is deplorably disorganized, and the overriding need is for unity and organization. Unity is on all black lips. Today we stand on the verge of sweeping change in this wretched landscape of a thousand little fragmented and ineffectual groups and organizations unable to work together for the common cause. *The need for one organization that will give one voice to the black man's common interest* is felt in every bone and fiber of black America.

Yesterday, after firmly repudiating racism and breaking his ties with the Black Muslim organization, the late Malcolm X launched a campaign to transform the American black man's struggle from the narrow plea for "civil rights" to the universal demand for human rights, with the ultimate aim of bringing the United States government to task before the United Nations. This, and the idea of the Organization of Afro-American Unity, was Malcolm's dying legacy to his people. It did not fall on barren ground. Already, black American leaders have met with the ambassadors of black Africa at a luncheon at UN headquarters. The meaning of this momentous event is lost on no one. The fact that it was the issue of Julian Bond, his denunciation of U. S. aggression in Vietnam, and the action of racist elements in the Georgia legislature which brought the leaders of black Africa and black America together is prophetic of an even clearer recognition by black men that their interests are also threatened by the U. S. war of suppression in Vietnam. This dovetailing of causes and issues is destined to bring to fruition the other dream which Malcolm's assassination prevented him from realizing —the Organization of Afro-American Unity, or perhaps a similar organization under a different name. Black Americans now realize that they must organize for the power to change the foreign and domestic policies of the U. S. government. They must let their voice be heard on these issues. They must let the world know where they stand.

It is no accident that the U. S. government is sending all those black troops to Vietnam. Some people think that America's point in sending 16 per cent black troops to Vietnam is to kill off the cream of black youth. But it has another important result. By turning her black troops into butchers of the Vietnamese people, America is spreading hate against the black race throughout Asia. Even black Africans find it hard not to hate black Americans for being so stupid as to allow themselves to be used to slaughter another people who are fighting to be free. Black Americans are considered to be the world's biggest fools to go to another country to fight for something they don't have for themselves.

It bothers white racists that people around the world love black Americans but find it impossible to give a similar warm affection to white Americans. The white racist knows that he is the Ugly American and he wants the black American to be Ugly, too, in the eyes of the world: misery loves company! When the people around the world cry "Yankee, Go Home!" they mean the white man, not the black man who is a recently freed slave. The white man is deliberately trying to make the people of the world turn against black Americans, because he knows that the day is coming when black Americans will need the help and support of their brothers, friends, and natural allies around the world. If through stupidity or by following hand-picked leaders who are the servile agents of the power structure, black Americans allow this strategy to succeed against them, then when the time comes and they need this help and support from around the world, it will not be there. All of the international love, respect, and goodwill that black Americans now have around the world will have dried up. They themselves will have buried it in the mud of the rice paddies of Vietnam.

Reading Selection 5: Cleaver, "The Black Man's Stake in Vietnam"

COMPREHENSION AND ANALYSIS

Do not refer to the article to answer these questions. Choose one of the items that best answers each question, and mark the letter in the space provided.

1. _____ According to Cleaver, how is the Vietnam War related to the black man's struggle for freedom in America? (a) both represent America's policy of suppression of national liberation movements (b) both represent the last state in the world-wide rebellion against white supremacy and the power structure (c) there is no direct relationship (d) both a and b.

2. _____ Cleaver says that America is finally paying attention to the black "Trojan Horse" because (a) America sincerely wants to help blacks achieve freedom (b) America has admitted that it can no longer deceive blacks with promises (c) America does not want to be embarrassed by black citizens' demands while they wage an unpopular war in Vietnam (d) America has admitted that more civil rights legislation is necessary for the country's stability.

3. _____ America's foreign policy, particularly toward Vietnam and the Soviet Union, is specifically intended to weaken the power of (a) the newly emerging African nations (b) mainland (Communist) China (c) all of Southeast Asia (d) the Communist "Iron Curtain" countries.

4. _____ Cleaver's primary concern about the aftermath of the Vietnam War is that (a) more black than white soldiers will have died for nothing (b) America will be free to intensify its repression of blacks (c) America will continue to pass liberal-sounding laws that will never be enforced (d) the black liberation movement will remain disorganized and powerless.

5. _____ The primary goals of the black movement in America, according to Cleaver, are both immediate freedom and (a) an end to the Vietnam War (b) a radical change in America's political and economic system (c) a guarantee that black people will be permanently safe from terror, repression, and racist policies (d) the guarantee that blacks will be able to form a separate state (e) the guarantee that blacks will achieve a better standard of living.

6. _____ Cleaver says that other nations consider black Americans

foolish for fighting in Vietnam because (a) they are letting themselves be used for slaughter (b) they lack the very rights at home that they are fighting for in another country (c) they are tacitly supporting America's policy of white supremacy (d) all of the above.

7. _____ Based on the evidence in the essay, mark T (true), F (false), or X (not verifiable) for the inferences that follow.

    A. _____ Cleaver fails to make recommendations for the black movement's future.

    B. _____ Julian Bond was denied his seat in Georgia's legislature because he was too outspoken on the Vietnam war.

    C. _____ Cleaver suggests that the only reason America sends blacks to fight in Vietnam is to kill off the best youths.

    D. _____ Of the blacks fighting in Vietnam, most are enlisted men.

    E. _____ Since the deaths of Martin Luther King and Malcolm X, the black movement has been without a leader.

    F. _____ Cleaver distrusts the motives and effectiveness of civil rights laws.

8. _____ Based on the evidence in the essay, mark J (justified) or NJ (not justified) for the conclusions that follow.

    A. _____ Recent events in the struggle for civil rights are directly related to the post-Civil War period.

    B. _____ To be successful, the black movement must become organized and united.

    C. _____ Some civil rights laws have been passed only for show, not to correct real injustices.

    D. _____ Black people should concern themselves with winning freedom at home and not with helping repressed people gain freedom in other colonial countries.

    E. _____ Black people now realize that they must organize to challenge racism in American society.

    F. _____ The amount of money spent in Vietnam should be used to help members of minority groups achieve a better standard of living.

9. _____ What is Cleaver's purpose and whom does he write for? He writes for (a) black Americans to support their demands for justice (b) white Americans to warn them that blacks can no longer be deceived (c) both a and b (d) neither his purpose or intended audience is evident.

10. _____ Which best describes the author's attitude toward his subject? (a) he is gentle and only mildly persuasive (b) he is forceful, moving, and relentless in his criticism (c) he

is argumentative, angry, and hostile (d) he is casual, off-hand, and only slightly concerned.

VOCABULARY

From the lettered choices, find the best definition for each vocabulary item, and mark the letter in the space provided.

1. _____ *denounced* the U.S. role
2. _____ wars of *suppression*
3. _____ *unanimity* of purpose
4. _____ doctrine of white *supremacy*
5. _____ *reneging* on its commitment
6. _____ *genocide* in Vietnam
7. _____ *brusquely* kicked out
8. _____ received virtual *license*
9. _____ *articulate* people
10. _____ *forfeit* of freedom
11. _____ colonial *bondage*
12. _____ *deplorably* organized
13. _____ *repudiating* racism
14. _____ on *barren* ground
15. _____ the *servile* agents

A. slavery; involuntary servitude
B. complete agreement
C. rudely; curtly
D. unproductive; unfruitful
E. systematic destruction of an entire race
F. praised; glorified
G. attacked; condemned openly
H. repression; deliberate crushing
I. wretchedly; sadly
J. sticking to; adhering to
K. failing to fulfill; backing out
L. liberation; disengagement

M. something given up or taken away
N. able to speak well and forcefully
O. fertile; productive
P. state of total dominance; superiority
Q. slavish; obedient
R. unrestrained liberty; abuse of freedom
S. anonymity
T. rejecting; refusing to accept

COMPREHENSION   No. right _____ × 5 = _____ %

VOCABULARY   No. right _____

No. of words 2050 ÷ time in seconds _____ × 60 = _____ WPM
WPM × Comprehension % = Reading Efficiency Rate _____

NOTES AND COMMENT

from "The Talk of the Town"*

In the late spring of 1970, President Nixon announced the American invasion of Cambodia to destroy enemy sanctuaries. The announcement was quickly followed by rioting, the deaths of students at Kent State and Jackson State, the regrouping of the nearly defunct peace forces, and frenzied peace activities on college campuses. This essay by a staff writer for The New Yorker *appeared in "The Talk of the Town," and uses the characteristically anonymous "we" form of address. It is a thoughtful and disturbing statement on the larger implications of America's penchant for victory in battle, whether the battle is fought in Indo-China, on college campuses or over the environment.*

Several months ago, the *Times* ran some remarkable stories about the unusual way in which an airline pilot dealt with a desperate armed hijacker and managed to bring his passengers, his crew, and his plane to safety. The pilot, whose name is Donald Cook, was on the way from Los Angeles to San Francisco when the hijacker, an A.W.O.L. marine named Raffaele Minichiello, appeared brandishing a gun and demanding that the plane fly to Rome. Captain Cook's first move was to persuade Minichiello to agree to his landing at Denver and letting the passengers off. When this was done and the plane was aloft again, Cook decided that the safest thing to do would be simply to land in New York, refuel, and then take Minichiello to Rome. Later, Robert C. Doty, of the *Times*, quoted Cook as saying that Minichiello "seemed to want to be met here by someone shooting" and wanted to "fight someone and die." Still later, when Cook was interviewed by Joseph Lelyveld, of the *Times*, he said, "We had arranged that there would be a minimum ground crew when we landed at Kennedy. . . . When we got there, there was the car with the replacement crew, but there were also many other vehicles and many

* From *The New Yorker*, May 23, 1970, pp. 27–29.

other men. Some of them were carrying weapons and wearing military-type flak jackets. . . . This boy was no dope. He was a very intelligent young man. He panicked and he started to scream, 'Get those people away from the airplane.' . . . I said, 'This boy is going to shoot us.'" Cook said that the agents ignored his plea and continued to move in on the airplane. He added, "We had seen him go from practically a raving maniac to a fairly complacent and intelligent young man with a sense of humor, and then these idiots from the F.B.I.—I don't know if 'idiots' is a word you want to use, but it's the way I feel—had irresponsibly made up their own minds about how to handle this boy on the basis of no information, and the good faith we had built up for almost six hours was completely destroyed." An Assistant United States Attorney whom Lelyveld also talked with explained that the F.B.I. agents had been trying to "crawl up through the belly of the plane either to get the drop on [Minichiello] or to get a shot at him." Eventually, the plane did take off for Rome, and on the way Minichiello at one point left his gun within Cook's reach, but Cook made no move to get it. When Minichiello asked him why he hadn't, Cook answered, "Raffaele, all of us have been in the service and all of us have had an opportunity to fight in wars and none of us want to fight in wars now or kill anyone. I couldn't consider it unless it was a mandatory thing. Besides, we've got to like you, and we really think we can bring this to a conclusion without our being killed and without your being killed." At the end of the flight, Minichiello apologized for giving the crew so much trouble, and Cook answered, "That's all right, we don't take it personally." And, with what we regard as a touch of the sublime, Cook told reporters that the crew wished they had met Minichiello "in other circumstances." Finally, Cook said of the dilemma he had faced, "The F.B.I. just thought they were playing Wyatt Earp and wanted to engage in a shoot-out with a supposed criminal. They would have wound up unnecessarily killing this boy, and, probably, completely destroying a seven-million-dollar airplane and wounding or endangering the lives of four crew members."

We believe that Captain Cook is an authentic hero of our times. Isn't his remark about the crew's wishing they had met Minichiello "in other circumstances" all the more to the point when one considers the police and National Guardsmen at Jackson State and Kent State and the students they killed, and when one considers the American soldiers now fighting in Cambodia and the people whose villages they are destroying? As we hear the calls to unleash American power in Indo-China and the calls to "untie the hands" of the American military, it strikes us that, generally speaking, America could use more of Captain Cook's instinct for protecting life and less of the F.B.I.'s eagerness to "get a shot" at its quarry regardless of who gets caught in the crossfire.

Traditionally, of course, mankind has had a special place in its heart for warriors who, with pure and single-minded devotion and unlimited courage, have plunged into battle with total abandon, withholding nothing. Some of the most shining deeds in history have been performed by men or by whole peoples who, for an ideal or in order to protect their countries, have cried "Victory or death!" and hurled themselves against overwhelmingly superior enemy forces. In the same way, we have all admired men who have seemed to pass beyond the normal limits of human endurance in struggles against the sea or against some other force of nature. It is also true, of course, that when these qualities of unlimited commitment and energy have been harnessed to personal ambition or to campaigns of territorial conquest they have brought about some of the darkest episodes in history. Yet, terrible as those episodes may have been, the scope and duration of the suffering they caused were limited by what seem to have been several natural checks. The passage of time, the diversity of mankind, and the sheer size of the globe were enough to defeat or transmute forces bent on unlimited conquest or destruction. Although it sometimes took centuries, the energy of the most powerful armies spent itself in the vastness of the populations they sought to conquer. Sometimes it was not men but nature that eroded the strength of invading forces. It is said that the Russian winter was as much responsible as the Russian Army for Napoleon's retreat from Russia. Until recently, nature and man were inexhaustible adversaries of the single-minded will of the conqueror and destroyer, but in our times the destructive power of man has gained the upper hand. Since the development of nuclear weapons, everyone has known that an international crisis could lead to the extinction of the human species, and since the discovery of the dangers of environmental pollution everyone has known that business as usual could bring the same result. Measured against our new powers of destruction, both man and nature are frail and vulnerable. Now we must learn to *protect* our old adversary the sea, and, what is more difficult, we must learn to protect our human adversaries—as well as those we regard as innocents—against the full power of our own wrath. In the light of this peril, it becomes plain that any single-minded and open-ended campaign, whether it is for military victory or for economic achievement, will lead us into the worst kind of trouble, and will, in the long run, keep us from reaching any goal that such a campaign might be aiming for in the first place. Our competitive instincts and our passion to win battles against other men have become suicidal. The more violence we unleash in order to annihilate our enemies, the closer we come to nuclear war, and to the annihilation of everyone, ourselves included. It used to be thought that men who wished to put an end to war were idealistic dreamers and that those who were willing to go to war were "realists." Now the reverse is true. Often in the past when the question of whether or not to go to war arose, the aim of preventing one's own people from suffering was considered a "reality" and the aim of preventing another people from suffering was considered an "ideal." Now, in a country such as ours, which possesses nuclear power, even if one accepts this callous view of what a reality is, it is those who call for victory who are the dreamers and those who call for restraint who are the realists. What used to be the question was whether men would continue waging wars as they always had or whether they would make a seemingly utopian dream of a world without war come true. Now, with the survival of man at stake, what used to be a dream has become a necessity. We can no longer emulate those who cry "Victory or death!" because in our times victory *is* death.

As we try to cope with this unprecedented situation, we cannot afford to let ourselves forget that there is still a deep and ancient instinct in all of us that wants to see issues shape up in the form of battles— that wants other people to commit themselves as our comrades-in-arms or as enemies and then fight to the death. It may be that it will prove particularly difficult for the American people to learn to temper this instinct. Our present leaders like to remind us that we have until now achieved victories, or at least been on the winning side, in all the wars we have entered. We have grown accustomed to victory, and it may come hard to many of us to learn that our appetite for victory has become deadly even to ourselves. And if this appetite is stronger in some Americans—our policemen, our soldiers, and our veterans among them—than it is in others, it may be in part because in the event of a battle they will have a chance to do what they have been trained to do and know how to do and what they have always been praised for doing. When the government sends the Army to perform such subtle and complicated tasks as keeping peace on the nation's campuses and building democracy in Vietnam, it should not be surprised if, almost unknowingly, the Army turns these tasks into the straightforward business of fighting conventional wars. If you give a man a gun with a bayonet and some ammunition, he is likely to stab and shoot.

It is true that from the start our policies in Indo-China have been haunted by a tendency to slip into the anachronistic idiom and inappropriate tactics of conventional wars, but in recent weeks it has begun to look as though the present Administration were entirely baffled by the shape and texture of the perilous realities we face, and had come to believe that through unilateral action we could force the world back into a less dangerous age. It looks as though the Administration believed that fighting the Indo-China war as a conventional war would transform it into a conventional war, with only conventional risks. Of course, the citizenry that rallies behind a government to give unshakable support to its war effort is as much a part of the conventional war as the army that fights to the limits of its resources in the field. In an attempt to stir up this kind of support, the President has raised the spectre of "humiliation and defeat" for America, and has told us that our willingness to support him is a test of our "courage" and our "character." But to believe that the

North Vietnamese Army challenges our courage in this way requires us to accept the enormous misconception that the strength of America is gravely threatened "both abroad and at home," in the words of the President, and that we can repel the threat only by calling on untapped reserves of energy and determination. Such demands, of course, have been the rallying cry of nations fighting for survival in the past, but how strange they sound coming in our times from the government of what the President himself calls "the richest and strongest nation in the history of the world" as it invades one of the poorest and most helpless nations in the world. The Administration speaks of the need to prove our "credibility." The truth is that the world is already well persuaded of our capacity for violence and our willingness to use it. As everyone knows, our capacity for violence is unlimited. God save us from ever *proving* it. When a call to support a policy that is moving in this direction is made, the citizens—who know somewhere in the back of their minds that their homes and families are threatened more directly by a wider war than they could be in any way by our present enemy—are likely to discover a worm of doubt inside them that makes them wonder whether this is what patriotism really does require, and tends to take the wind out of the warlike passion they are called on to display. Indeed, hawkish sentiment on the war has never really been very outspoken or very impassioned. Often its existence has been merely deduced, as is revealed by the phrase "the silent majority." When those with hawkish views *have* shown anger, they have vented it not on the North Vietnamese but on other Americans, such as demonstrators and the press. Even in what are regarded as the most hawkish quarters, there has been a reluctance to give strong support directly to the war. And when one looks for the kind of unity and resolves that governments ordinarily expect in support of their policies in wartime, one must turn to the anti-war movement to find it. It is in this movement—especially among the young, who have never learned the taste for military victory—that one finds the solidarity and the spontaneous determination of a people that is fighting for survival. But in this case it is the survival of the human race. It is generally recognized that the current generation of young people have lived their whole lives in the shadow of nuclear destruction. Surely Indo-China, being one of the places where the shadow falls most heavily, must loom preëminent in youth's struggle to insure that man will have a future. In this struggle, America's ability to impose its will on other nations by force is useless. And since it is compassion for our own people and for other peoples that keeps us from proving our character to the hilt, our government's indifference to the terrible fate it has decreed for the Cambodian people is alarming. It is profane that the first thing the American government told the American people about Cambodia was that American forces had begun to destroy it. One newspaper, limping along, like everybody else, to keep up with the President and the military, ran an article entitled

"Cambodia at a Glance," which informed its readers of such facts as that in Cambodia "most of the population is rural and farming is [its] major occupation," and that "mineral resources are undeveloped." The title seemed to suggest that if you wanted to learn anything about Cambodia you had better look quickly. Now, on television, Americans are getting their first look at Cambodians. Most of the Cambodians are lying dead in their shattered villages. On the evening of the invasion, when the President went to his map to show the American people where Cambodia is ("Here is South Vietnam, here is North Vietnam," etc.), we felt that we were being given a geography lesson by military invasion. We don't want to learn about our brothers on the earth in this way.

"Notes and Comment"

COMPREHENSION AND ANALYSIS

Do not refer to the article to answer these questions. Choose one of the items that best answers the question and mark the letter in the space provided.

1. ___A___ The main idea of the essay is that (a) America must curb its use of force and its appetite for victory if mankind is to survive (b) America must stop being the world's policeman and trying to protect all nations from enemy aggression (c) America has earned the fear and disrespect of the world from the war in Vietnam (d) the American government's policies in Indo-China are potentially destructive to our internal security (e) America's invasion of Cambodia ensures a nuclear war.

2. ___c___ The purpose of the story of the hijacked airliner is ultimately to (a) demonstrate the danger of such events (b) show that the FBI handled the case badly (c) praise Captain Cook's instincts for protecting the lives of people (d) prove that the incident is directly related to America's involvement in Indo-China.

3. ___e___ After describing the hijacking incident, the middle portion of the essay (a) contrasts early notions of war and victory with the terrible reality of modern warfare (b) describes man's awesome powers to destroy the environment as well as all mankind (c) redefines the concepts of patriotism and national unity (d) criticizes the American instinct for competition and victory in battle whatever the cost (e) a, b, and d only (f) a, c, and d only.

4. ___b___ The rallying cry nations have always used to elicit public support for wars, "victory or death!" is now outmoded because (a) people are indifferent to military conquests (b) modern warfare means that victory requires annihilation of the world (c) warring nations are kept in line by natural checks (d) there can be no more military victories, only political settlements.

5. ___a___ The author says that environmental pollution (a) if unchecked, will ensure the extinction of both mankind and nature (b) is not as dangerous to man's survival as nuclear war (c) is more dangerous to man's survival than nuclear war (d) is the price a strong nation pays to be economically and militarily superior.

6. ___e___ Which of the following events does the author *not* spe-

cifically mention in the essay? (a) the killing of students at Kent State and Jackson State (b) the Administration's way of appealing for public support for the war (c) the Army's practice of protecting campuses from disorder by resorting to violence (d) the American government's misconception that the Vietnam war could be contained by conventional military means (e) the Administration's method of silencing dissent against the war.

7. __B__ The author feels that most Americans, even the so-called "silent majority," (a) are confused and baffled by North Vietnam's military strength (b) are aware that a larger war is far more dangerous than any small present enemy (c) are afraid to voice their support of the war because they fear ridicule (d) secretly sympathize with the anti-war movement but are powerless to speak out.

8. _____ Based on the evidence in the essay, mark T (true), F (false), or X (not verifiable) for the following inferences.

A. __F__ Captain Cook was never able to calm the hijacker.

B. __T__ Traditionally, mankind has admired military bravery and successful exploits against the forces of nature.

C. __F__ Napoleon's defeat in Russia was accomplished only because of the severe winter.

D. __X__ The American government carefully prepared the public about Cambodian history before the invasion.

E. __T__ With respect to military victory, the roles played by "dreamers" and "realists" have completely been reversed.

F. __X__ America has had difficulty achieving victory in Vietnam because the government mistook a civil war for a conventional war.

9. _____ Based on the evidence in the essay, mark J (justified) or NJ (not justified) for these conclusions.

A. __J__ Americans must re-evaluate and redefine their concepts of patriotism, victory, and national strength if mankind is to survive.

B. __J__ America might have more "credibility" if the government persuaded other nations of its capacity for making peace.

C. __J__ The anti-war movement gained new strength after America's invasion of Cambodia.

D. __J__ There is little to be gained by proving our ability to use force to impose our will on other nations.

E. __J__ The world has become too small for nations to

rely on natural checks to prevent an enemy from achieving unlimited destruction.

F. ___I___ A government must be equally as concerned with maintaining military strength as it is with protecting human lives.

10. ___D___ Judging from the essay as a whole, and particularly from the last sentence, "we don't want to learn about our brothers on the earth in this way," the author's tone is best described as (a) argumentative and vehement (b) conciliatory and apologetic (c) nostalgic and sentimental (d) restrained, thoughtful, and persuasive (e) bitter and resentful.

VOCABULARY

From the lettered choices, find the best definition for each vocabulary item, and mark the letter in the space provided.

1. ___P___ *brandishing* a gun
2. ___S___ a *complacent* young man
3. ___H___ a touch of the *sublime*
4. ___K___ "get a shot" at its *quarry*
5. ___A___ with total *abandon*
6. ___R___ to defeat or *transmute* forces
7. ___J___ *eroded* the strength
8. ___F___ nature and man were *adversaries*
9. ___Q___ power of our *wrath*
10. ___B___ in light of this *peril*
11. ___N___ we can no longer *emulate*
12. ___T___ to slip into the *anachronism*
13. ___M___ the *spectre* of "humiliation and defeat"
14. ___C___ must loom *preëminent*
15. ___G___ it is *profane*

A. complete surrender to one's feelings without restraint or moderation
B. danger; risk
C. above all else; superior
D. pleasant; calm
E. the unconscious mind
F. enemies; opponents
G. vulgar; base; blasphemous
H. a sense of high purity; nobility
I. restraint; control
J. worn down; eaten away
K. game; prey
L. allies; partners
M. phantom; ghost, especially of a terrifying nature
N. try to equal or surpass
O. vindicate; clear from suspicion
P. waving menacingly
Q. violent anger; rage
R. transform; change in nature
S. arrogant; self-satisfied
T. event that is out of place, especially belonging to an earlier period

COMPREHENSION   No. right _____ × 5 = _____ %

VOCABULARY   No. right _____

No. of words 2430 ÷ time in seconds _____ × 60 = _____ WPM
WPM × Comprehension % = Reading Efficiency Rate _____

A. J. LIEBLING
Tummler*

A. J. Liebling, the late New York journalist, frequently wrote about one of his favorite haunts, the I. & Y. cigar store at Forty-ninth Street and Seventh Avenue owned by Izzy Yereshevky. In this essay, Liebling relates the story of Hymie Katz, a lovable and ingenious con man who frequented the I. & Y., entertaining its regulars with stories of his many nightclub adventures.

To the boys of the I. & Y., Hymie Katz is a hero. He is a short, broad-shouldered, olive-complexioned man who looks about forty-two and is really somewhat older. In his time he has owned twenty-five nightclubs.

"Hymie is a tummler," the boys at the I. & Y. say. "Hymie is a man what knows to get a dollar."

Hymie at present is running a horse-race tipping service in an office building on Longacre Square. "What is a nightclub made of?" he sometimes asks contemptuously. "Spit and toilet paper. An upholstered joint. The attractions get the money and the boss gets a kick in the pants." His admirers understand that this is only a peevish interlude. Soon he will open another nightclub.

The tipping service requires no capital. Hymie reads out-of-town telephone books for the names of doctors and ministers fifty or a hundred miles from New York. Then he calls them, one by one, asking the operator to reverse the charges. Hymie tells the operator, let us say, that he is Mr. Miller whom Dr. Blank or the Reverend Mr. Doe met at Belmont Park last summer. If the man accepts the call, Hymie knows he has a prospect. The man probably hasn't been at Belmont, and certainly hasn't met a Mr. Miller there, but thinks he is the beneficiary of a case of mistaken identity. Hymie tells him about a horse that is sure to win. All the doctor or minister has to do, Hymie says, is to send him the winnings on a ten-dollar

* From *The Most of A. J. Liebling* (New York: Simon & Schuster, Inc., 1963), pp. 106–115.

bet. Sometimes the horse does win, and the small-town man always remits Hymie's share of the profits. He wants to be in on the next sure thing. Doctors, Hymie believes, are the most credulous of mortals. Ministers never squawk.

Hymie picks his horses very carefully from the past-performance charts of the *Morning Telegraph*. He usually tips three or four entries in each race. Naturally, the physicians and clergymen who get bad tips send him no money, but the supply of small-town professional men is practically unlimited. Hymie says it is an ideal business for a man satisfied with a modest, steady income. Personally, he is resigned to opening another nightclub. "If I wasn't ashamed," he says, "I would put a couple of hundred dollars in it myself." The investment of his own money, according to Hymie's code, would be unethical.

All Hymie needs to open a nightclub is an idea and a loan of fifty dollars. There are fifteen or twenty basements and one-flight-up places between 45th and 55th Streets that cannot economically be used as anything but nightclubs. They have raised dance floors, ramps, numerous light outlets, kitchens, and men's and women's washrooms. Because they are dark during the day, or can be reached only by staircases, they are not adapted to ordinary restaurant use. Such a place may be worth $600 a month as a nightclub. Dismantled, it would bring only $100 or so as a store. The owner of a nightclub site makes out pretty well if his space is tenanted for six months of the year.

Hymie has been around Broadway since 1924. He is a good talker. In the past, some of his clubs actually have made money, although none of it has stuck to him. As a matter of ritual he always tells the owner of the spot he proposes to rent that he is going to spend $40,000 to fix it up. The owner does not believe this, but the sound of the words reassures him. If Hymie said less than $40,000, the landlord would sense a certain lack of enthusiasm. If more, the landlord would feel derided. It is customary to mention $40,000 when talking about redecorating a nightclub. If the owner appears to be hooked, Hymie goes out and spends the borrowed $50. He pays it to a lawyer to draw up a lease. The lawyer Hymie patronizes is the only man in the world Hymie has never been able to put on the cuff. But he draws a fine lease. It contains all sorts of alluring clauses, like "party of the first part and party of the second part agree to share equally in all profits above $10,000 a week, after reimbursement of party of the second part for outlays made in equipping the Dopey Club (said outlays for this purpose not to exceed $40,000)." It makes provision for profits of Aluminum Trust magnitude.

Hymie takes the lease to a hatcheck concessionaire. This is the really critical phase of the enterprise. He must convince the concessionaire that the place has a chance to do business ("Look at the figures in the lease, you can see what we're expecting"). He must fill the concessionaire with enthusiasm for the entertainers, who have not yet been engaged. For it is up to the concessionaire to provide the cash that will make the enterprise go—$3,000 in advance, in return for the hatcheck and cigarette concession for six months. Hymie is a great salesman. He does impersonations of his hypothetical acts. He tells about the Broadway columnists who eat out of his hand and will give yards of free publicity. While Hymie talks, the concessionaire distills drops of probability from his gallons of conversation. In his mind he turns Hymie's thousands of anticipated revenue into fifties and hundreds. If the club runs three months, the concessionaire knows, he will get his money back. If by some fluke it runs six months, he will double his money. If nobody financed nightclubs, there would be no concession business. So the concessionaire lets Hymie have the $3,000.

Hymie goes back to the landlord, signs the lease, and pays him a month's rent in advance—say $600. That leaves $2,400 for the other expenses. If possible, he saves himself from headaches by renting out the kitchen. The kitchen concessionaire provides the food, cooks up a stew on which all the nightclub help feed every night, and even pays half of the cost of the table linen. (Linen is rented, not bought.) The proprietor of the club gets from 12 to 20 per cent of the gross receipts for food. Since nightclub food is absurdly high, the food concessionaire, like the hatcheck man, is bound to make a good profit if the place lasts a few months.

The club may contain tables, chairs, and any amount of miscellaneous equipment abandoned by a former tenant in lieu of rent. If it doesn't, Hymie goes to a man named I. Arthur Ganger, who runs a Cain's warehouse of the nightclub business on West 45th Street. Ganger can provide out of used stock anything from a pink-and-onyx Joseph Urban bar to a wicker *smörgåsbord* table. Some of his silverware has been in and out of ten previous clubs. Usually Ganger will accept a 25 per cent down payment, which for one of Hymie's clubs amounts to a few hundred dollars. He takes notes payable weekly for the rest. Ganger is amenable to reason when the notes fall due. He has a favorite joke for customers like Hymie. "Your mother carried you only nine months," he says, "but I been carrying you all your life." The supply man retains title to his things until they are entirely paid for, and if the club folds, he carts them back to his warehouse. Ganger decorates some clubs, but Hymie would not think of hiring him for such a job. Hymie gets a girlish young man to perform a *maquillage* for $150, including paint.

Of the $3,000 received from the concessionaire, Hymie has now disbursed at most $1,200. He pays another $600 for a liquor license good for six months, and puts the rest of the money in the bank as profit in case the club flops. The remaining preparations are on the cuff. Hymie hires acts for his new club on the understanding that he will pay off a week after the place opens. He engages a band on the same terms. If there is to be a line of girls in the show, the girls rehearse free. But Hymie is not a bad fellow. He sends out for coffee and sandwiches for the girls during rehearsals. Once or twice he has been known to lend a girl $5 for room rent before a club opened.

Liquor is harder to buy on credit these days than before repeal. Mob credit was flexible, and if you bought from a bootlegger independent of the gangs, Hymie says, you never paid him at all. Wholesalers now are allowed to extend only twenty-one days' credit, according to the regulations of the State Liquor Authority. But matters sometimes may be arranged by paying a bill on the twenty-first day and then borrowing most of the money back from the wholesaler on the twenty-second.

A few days before the opening Hymie effects a deal that always puts him in especially good humor. He sells twenty waiters their jobs. The headwaiter pays $400, two captains pay $200 each, and ordinary waiters $50. Waiters like to work for Hymie because he lets them take what they can get. He wastes no time watching his employees. "Most of the stealing they do is from the customers, so what do I care?" says Hymie.

Despite all his forethought, exigencies sometimes arise which demand fresh capital. Perhaps an unusually stubborn landlord demands three months' security, or a police official must be heavily greased before he will let the club stay open after hours. In some places, especially black-and-tan or crudely bawdy spots, all the money comes in during the illegal early hours of the morning, after the bigger clubs have closed. In such emergencies Hymie sometimes has to take in partners. He usually bilks his partners for the principle of the thing. He is not avaricious. Dollars, Hymie thinks, are markers in a game of wits as well as a medium of exchange. He refuses to let his partners keep any markers.

Once he had to take a partner in a roadhouse he was running near Babylon. He sold the fellow 50 per cent of the place for one season. It happened to be a very good season, so Hymie built a sliding metal roof over a garden one hundred feet square, installed a swimming pool, and presented all his employees with a large bonus out of the receipts.

"I thought I would make some improvements and build up good will for next year, when Milton would be out," he says.

Some persons may wonder why even a concessionaire would trust Hymie with his money. But concessionaires know that he will not skip before the club opens, for he is under a compulsion as strong as the drive of a spawning salmon to swim upstream. His clubs satisfy his craving for distinction.

A week before an opening, Hymie gets out a mailing list of exhibitionists which he has accumulated through a decade of nightclub operation, and sends out his announcements. Then he makes the entertainers write letters to their friends inviting them to buy ringside tables. He insists on the attendance of every salesman who has ever sold him anything for the club, even if it all was on credit. The costumer who has dressed the show is expected to take part of his pay in trade. Since this may be the only part of it he will ever collect, the costumer usually brings a large party. It is a nice arrangement for Hymie, because he pays off on the costumer bill with Scotch at about 6 cents on the dollar. The costumer has made a profit of about 95 cents on the dollar, so this makes them both feel good. The band leader, if he has any considerable reputation in the trade, forces music publishers' pluggers to reserve tables. If the pluggers don't spend money, the leader slights their tunes.

A week after the opening, if it was profitable, Hymie gives his entertainers three days' pay. He tells them he is holding something back so they won't run out on him. Of course they never get it. If the opening has been bad, the entertainers and the concessionaire are likely to find the door locked the next night. In the event of a sour opening, Hymie takes the $1,000 or $1,500 of concession money remaining to him out of the bank and lays it on a ten-to-one shot at some obscure racetrack. He shares the weakness for betting common to most nightclub people, but he has it in an exaggerated form. He has never played a horse at less than eight-to-one in his life, because he is sure that every race is fixed. When a favorite wins, he attributes it to a double-cross. Hymie almost always loses.

Occasionally the personality of one of Hymie's entertainers catches on, or the *décor* hits the fancy of the Broadway high-life crowd, and the club begins to make money legitimately. Under these circumstances Hymie sells it to a corporation called Hymie-club, Inc. As manager for the corporation, he kicks out the hatcheck concessionaire and sells the concession over again for a higher price. The entertainer who draws the crowd gets a manager and demands more money. Hymie pays blackmail in the form of weekly raises. He spends a great part of his receipts in competitors' clubs to show how prosperous he is. He stalls off all creditors on general principles.

"Sometimes you can hold them off for six months," he says. "Meanwhile everything that comes in is profit."

Finally the creditors close in, or the entertainer either loses his brief vogue or goes on to a larger club. Hymie returns to the horse-tipping business. He has written one more chapter in his saga; he has been in the money again.

Hymie admits readily that it was vanity that drew him into the nightclub business in the first place, and that keeps him at it.

"Take a fellow who is born in Brooklyn," he says, "and he is a cloak-and-suiter or a shoe clerk, which he would feel honored even to talk to a trumpet player in a famous orchestra. He goes into this business and in two years celebrities like Rudy Vallee and Harry Thaw are calling him Hymie. It makes him feel wonderful. But it don't mean nothing."

Take, more specifically, Hymie Katz. He was born in Brooklyn, in the Williamsburg district. The record of his early days is shadowy, but he says that once he was a fur stretcher, and once he drove a taxi, and once he was married to a wealthy woman who died and cut him off with a dollar in her will because she didn't want him to spend anything on other dolls. Hymie got his start in the nightclub world as a singing waiter in a pseudo-Bavarian joint where people drank spiked near-beer at 50 cents a glass and sang "*Ja, das ist ein Schnitzelbank.*" He had not been there long before he had invented a new technique for reaming the customers. When one of the parties he was serving asked for a check, he would delay bringing it, if possible, until he had a similar request from another party of about the same size. One check might be for $16, say, the other for $12. Hymie would put the $12 check in the hip pocket of his leather pants and collect the $16 check from both parties, one after the other. The customers seldom became aware of the mistake.

After he got used to late hours, Hymie decided to open a nightclub for himself. That was in the winter of 1924, and many buildings between Longacre Square and Sixth Avenue had a joint on every floor. There would be a shabby nightclub at street level, a speakeasy-restaurant on the second floor, and two or three ratty bars on the levels above. Hymie picked a second-floor loft that had a dance floor ten by ten and forty tables with pink lampshades on them, left by a former proprietor who had not paid his beer bill. Hymie put down $200 for an option on the place—he could not then afford his present scruples against using his own cash. He dropped in at the I. & Y., where he was beginning to be known, and sold 20 per cent of the club for $1,000 to a fellow we will call Johnny Attorney. Johnny came from Attorney Street originally, but he was quite a big beer man by then, and had moved uptown.

Hymie and Johnny were able to sell the hatcheck concession for another $1,000 because Johnny was in on a couple of speakeasies where the hat-check man did business. Then they took in the no-good brother of a famous nightclub hostess who was the surest draw in town. They gave the brother 20 per cent, and all they asked was that he stay away from the place as much as possible. The hostess was working for a man named Denny Boylan, who had a large, elaborate club (for those days) about five doors up the block from their place. The Boylan club was on the street level, with a uniformed doorman and a marquee, and it had to close at two or three o'clock in the morning. Drawing her ermine wrap about her and jiggling her headdress of egrets two feet long, the hostess would then suggest to the best spenders present that they accompany her to a little intimate spot down the street, where the party could continue. Down the street they would stagger, and up the stairs to the Daylight Club, as Hymie and Johnny called their stuffy loft. After the second week the hostess demanded a share for herself, so Hymie sold her half of his 60 per cent for $5,000.

"The prices we got for liquor those days were brutal," Hymie recalls happily. "Twenty-five dollars for a bottle of champagne a guy made for us down on Mott Street. But the price didn't mean nothing. It was the bottles you could stab in on a customer's check that really counted. I mean the bottles you charged him for that he had never had at all. I remember a big patent-medicine man from Baltimore that used to come into the place that once paid me twenty-eight hundred dollars for one bottle of wine. He ordered the wine and then he fell asleep with his head on the table. I had the sense to have empty bottles in ice buckets put next to every table. When he woke up, I slipped him the check. 'What's this?' he says. 'Well,' I says, 'you ordered wine for everybody in the house. A hundred and twelve bottles at twenty-five a copy. The one on your table is on me.' He couldn't remember whether he had or not, but the money didn't mean nothing to him, so he paid."

After the Daylight Club was fairly launched, Hymie devoted late afternoons to the manufacturing department. Hymie doesn't mind work when it's fun.

"I made Black and White so good those millionaires wouldn't drink nothing else," he says. "There was a big towel man from North Carolina who would take cases of my Black and White home with him every time he come to town. Once a fellow in another joint gave him some of the McCoy straight from St. Pierre, and the towel man spit it out. 'You trying to poison me?' he says. 'This don't taste nothing like the genuine Black and White I buy from Hymie.' He would never go back to the joint."

Hymie thinks most of his customers in those days were temporarily insane. There was, for example, a wholesale whiskey exporter from Canada who, on his business trips to New York, had the quaint conceit of carrying only fifty-dollar bills. He would toss one of them on Hymie's bar and order drinks for everybody. If there were thirteen drinkers in the house, Hymie would charge him for about twenty-nine drinks at a dollar apiece. The Canadian never counted. He would leave his change for the bartender.

"When he come in," Hymie says, "I used to go behind the bar myself."

Hymie thinks that many of his former customers still have money, but have been afraid to throw it around in public since the depression. In a select spot like the Daylight Club, he says, "they knew they was among their own kind."

The end of the Daylight Club came when a squad of twenty prohibition agents raided the place and padlocked it.

"The reason you couldn't do nothing about them big raids," he says, "is that there was never twenty Feds who would trust each other. Each one would think one of the others in the squad was trying to put him in the bag, so you couldn't talk business. But when just one fellow or two or three come in, you knew they was on the shake. If you felt good-natured, you slipped them fifty. If you didn't, you kicked them down the stairs."

Hymie likes harness cops, but not detectives. He says the latter are like Feds, always on the shake.

"The cop on the block was a kind of doorman," Hymie explains. "When you threw a drunk out, the cop picked him up and walked him down to the corner to sober up, so he wouldn't remember where he was thrown out of." Each place on the block paid the policeman on beat from $2 to $5 a night, according to its volume of business. On a good block, Hymie estimates, it might have run to as much as $100 a night. He doesn't believe that the cop on beat was allowed to retain all this, but he says he never paid money to a police official higher up. His guess is that it was divided in the Department.

Hymie always enjoyed bouncing people in a nice way. When a big tough fellow heckled the hostess, Hymie would go to the cashier and get a roll of quarters. He would hold it in his right hand, with one end of the roll protruding, and he would lean over the fellow's table and slug him on the side of the jaw with it. Then a couple of waiters would carry the gentleman out and lay him on the sidewalk, where the cop would find him.

Mickey Finns, the pacifying pills slipped to obstreperous customers in many places, do not amuse Hymie. "Any fool can go into a drugstore for a dollar and buy a box of Mickeys," he says. Mickeys are purgative pills designed for horses, and act so drastically that one may kill a drunk with a weak heart. "But even with Mickeys, there is an art in the way to serve them," says Hymie. "Some fellows wait until the customer orders another drink, which may be too long, and others offer him a drink on the house, which maybe makes him suspicious. The best way is to tell the waiter, 'A little more ice in that glass, please.' The waiter has the ice on a spoon and the Mickey under the ice. He drops them in the drink together."

The Daylight Club ran fourteen months, during which, Hymie says, the partners earned about a quarter of a million dollars. The racetracks got most of Hymie's share. He remembers days when he went out to the track and lost $5,000 in an afternoon, then came back and delivered a case of bathtub gin to make $6. "Money don't mean nothing to me," he says. "Maybe I'm crazy."

After the Daylight was padlocked, Hymie and his associates opened a far more pretentious place on 50th Street, which he called the Club Chez Nous. He pronounced it the Club Chestnuts. The partners continued to make money. The place went out of existence because of the hostess's sense of humor. The adolescent son of a statesman then prominent came into the club drunk one night. She persuaded him to go out on the floor and do imitations of his father, who was flirting with a Presidential nomination. The father used his influence to have the place padlocked.

Hymie's third place, the Club Monastery, was a hard-lucker. It had been open only three weeks when a party of mobsmen dropped in and began shooting at Johnny Attorney and some friends. Two men were killed and Johnny Attorney disappeared. It is popularly supposed that his body was run through a rockcrusher and that he is now part of the roadbed of the Pulaski Skyway in New Jersey. The police, however, hadn't heard about this and thought that Hymie knew where Johnny was, so they gave him a terrific beating. Hymie was not the kind who would appeal to the American Civil Liberties Union. When the police let him go, some of the gangsters took him for a ride. Fortunately they forgot to gag him, and he talked so fast that they brought him back to his hotel and loaned him $20. It is one of his proudest memories. But the Monastery was "out on the street." Whenever there was a shooting in a speakeasy, the New York police closed it. That was the reason patrons about to shoot each other were always asked to leave.

The cares that might be expected to attend such a frenzied existence have left no mark on Hymie Katz. There are scars on his face from the beating the police gave him when they questioned him about Johnny Attorney, but no worry lines. He is not as handsome as he was twenty years ago, before he began to put on weight, but he has nice white teeth and pleasant features that wear a habitual unforced smile.

Hymie is unmarried at present. Wives, with Hymie, are symptoms of prosperity, like tailored shirts. His father is still living and owns a small jewelry shop on the Bowery near Canal Street. When Hymie visits him, the old man comes out to meet his son and locks the door from the outside. Then they talk on the sidewalk. Hymie is not offended by his parent's caution; he is flattered. Whenever he meets anybody new, he tells him about his father.

Hymie is living in a hotel on West 49th Street on a due bill. He pays the due-bill broker with due bills for entertainment at his next club, which he hasn't opened yet. When the club does open, the broker will sell the accumulated due bills for half their face value to couples who arrive via the bus lines and want to see New York night life.

Shortly before noon every day Hymie goes to his office, which he shares with a man who puts on stag shows, to see if any money has come in by mail. If there is any, Hymie spends the afternoon in a poolroom betting on races. If there is no money, he puts in a hard day at the telephone as Mr. Miller of Belmont Park. Generally he has dinner at an Italian Kitchen on Eighth Avenue, where he gets spaghetti, meatballs, and coffee for 25 cents. He smokes six cigars a day, five nickel ones and a 50-center, buying them all at I. & Y. He smokes the 50-center after his 25-cent dinner, so he will feel prosperous. Evenings he usually leans against a stack of cases in the cigar store and discusses his plans—never his real plans, of course, but vast enterprises like taking over the Paramount Theater and turning it into a nightclub with a ski slide and a $5 minimum. With ribald arguments he maintains the feasibility of projects which he improvises on the spot. The other habitués of the I. &. Y. listen with respect.

"You know who was in here?" Izzy asks friends who come in after Hymie has departed. "Hymie Katz." Izzy shakes his head admiringly. "He's a real tummler, that Hymie. He knows to get a dollar."

READING SELECTION 7: LIEBLING, "TUMMLER"

COMPREHENSION AND ANALYSIS

Do not refer to the article to answer these questions. Choose one of the items that best answers each question, and mark the letter in the space provided.

1. _____ When Hymie Katz's friends call him a "tummler," they mean he is (a) a cleaver criminal who never lets himself be caught (b) a shrewd con man who knows how to make a dollar (c) a harmless crank who pulls practical jokes (d) an unmerciful cheat who preys on innocent victims.

2. _____ Hymie's way of getting capital is to call small-town professional men and (a) sell phony insurance policies (b) give horse-racing tips to collect the winnings (c) ask for contributions to a non-existent charity (d) ask them to invest in a new scheme for a nightclub.

3. _____ After Hymie arranges for a new nightclub with borrowed money, he (a) bets the remainder on a sure horse (b) pays his waiter and musicians advance wages (c) deposits the remainder in a bank as sure profit (d) bribes officials to get a liquor license.

4. _____ The reason Hymie never has any money is his weakness for (a) buying expensive dinners and cigars (b) giving money away to destitute friends (c) betting high stakes on horses that always lose (d) spending money on extravagant pleasures and women (e) bribing the authorities to keep his clubs in business.

5. _____ According to Liebling, Hymie's most exciting, frenzied and dangerous time as a nightclub owner was (a) during Prohibition (b) before Prohibition (c) after Prohibition (d) after World War II.

6. _____ What reason does Liebling give for Hymie's stubborn insistence in staying in the nightclub business? (a) his vanity and pride (b) his need to rise above his Brooklyn background (c) his delight in knowing famous musicians (d) his need for distinction and respect (e) all of the above (f) only c and d.

7. _____ Hymie's many nightclub ventures were (a) always profitable (b) never profitable (c) usually profitable (d) occasionally profitable.

8. _____ Based on the evidence in the essay, mark T (true), F (false), or X (not verifiable) for the inferences that follow.

319

A. _____ The horse-racing tipping service is ideal for Hymie because it requires no money of his own.

B. _____ The reason Hymie never invests his own money in his nightclub schemes is probably that he never has any.

C. _____ Hymie's leases are specifically written with enough fancy-sounding clauses and loopholes to cover his losses in case a nightclub fails.

D. _____ To start a new club, the crucial step is getting an initial $50 loan.

E. _____ Hymie has been married at least three times.

F. _____ Hymie dislikes his waiters' habits of bilking the customers.

9. Based on the evidence in the essay, mark J (justified) or NJ (not justified) for the conclusions that follow.

A. _____ In view of Hymie's peculiar code of ethics regarding money, it is not surprising that he is so greedy.

B. _____ Hymie thinks of life as a continual game of wits with other con men.

C. _____ Hymie operates under the assumption that bilking suckers is fair, and that if he doesn't do it first, someone shrewder will.

D. _____ Hymie's one regret is his father's embarrassment over his son's notoriety.

E. _____ Hymie is modest in describing his nightclub successes.

F. _____ The author thinks of Hymie as an intriguing and ingenious character.

10. _____ Hymie was admired and respected by his friends at the I. & Y. cigar store for his ability to (a) conceive outlandishly extravagant but impressive schemes on the spot (b) give a convincing sales pitch (c) entertain them with wonderful stories of days gone by (d) make his victims feel that they might even profit from his schemes (e) turn a small loan into a profitable enterprise with a little clever manipulating (f) all of the above.

VOCABULARY

From the lettered choices, find the best definition for each vocabulary item, and mark the letter in the space provided.

1. _____ the *beneficiary* of
2. _____ *remits* his share
3. _____ the most *credulous*
4. _____ a *dismantled* place
5. _____ he would feel *derided*

6. _____ his *hypothetical* acts
7. _____ by some *fluke*
8. _____ *amenable* to reason
9. _____ *exigencies* sometimes arise
10. _____ *bawdy* spots
11. _____ he is not *avaricious*
12. _____ a strong *compulsion*
13. _____ his present *scruples*
14. _____ *obstreperous* customers
15. _____ the *feasibility* of projects

A. greedy; grasping
B. ridiculed; mocked
C. misfortune
D. capable of being persuaded; receptive
E. degraded; lowered in status
F. capability of being accomplished; practicality
G. one who receives benefits, advantages
H. noisy, boisterous
I. gullible; disposed to believe on slight evidence
J. profitable; successful
K. irresistible impulse
L. chance; lucky stroke
M. deviations; irregularities
N. indecent; obscene
O. doubts; uncertainties arising from moral questions
P. theoretical; imaginary
Q. sends; pays
R. skeptical; hard to convince
S. emergencies; crises
T. stripped; disassembled

COMPREHENSION No. right _____ × 5 = _____ %

VOCABULARY No. right _____

No. of words 4200 ÷ time in seconds _____ × 60 = _____ WPM
WPM × Comprehension % = Reading Efficiency Rate _____

8

PAUL JACOBS
The Welfare Bureau*

*In 1967, rioting, looting and burning took place in nearly every urban
ghetto. In the aftermath, Paul Jacobs, a widely recognized authority on
labor, went to the ghettos of Los Angeles to see life "at the bottom."
His book describes the institutions on which the victims of poverty depend
—medical services, employment offices, and welfare. Although this excerpt
describes the Bureau of Public Assistance in Los Angeles County, he emphasizes that every city's poor has within them the seeds for riot.*

I began to get some true perspective about welfare on the day I applied
for welfare myself, just to have the experience of being processed. I
sat in the waiting room for hours, along with a hundred other people,
mostly women with their children, who were crying, wriggling, restless
on chairs, or racing up and down aisles. Even I, just pretending to be in
need of help, felt humiliated, perhaps because the experience brought
back memories long suppressed of those days, years ago, when I too had
really needed help.

A few days later I went to lunch with the official who was then in
charge of the office and asked him about the processing, without telling
him that I had already been through it. He assured me that no one waited
very long, and as he took me on a tour of the building, kept pointing
out how businesslike an operation he was running. I asked him why he
didn't provide a little space for a nursery and find a couple of women to
take care of the children while their mothers were being interviewed. He
looked at me as if such a notion could never have occurred to a rational
person. Obviously, it hadn't occurred to him that applicants for welfare
might be humiliated by having to answer questions in front of their
children.

One afternoon a week later, when I was talking with a group of Negro

* From *Prelude to Riot: A View of Urban America from the Bottom* (New York:
Random House, Inc., 1967), pp. 61–74.

high school students and I asked how many of them had been arrested, almost every hand went up. But when I asked how many of them came from families getting welfare, not a single hand went up. And yet I knew that at least 75 per cent of the kids in that room were from families whose sole income was the twice-monthly check from the county.

People for whom humiliation is a condition of life find it hard to admit its existence or to organize themselves. Yet over and over in studying the welfare system, I saw that very few people in government have any notion of what effects their agencies are having on those unfortunate people, upon whom the constellation of separate government forces bears down inexorably.

Instead, each government agency operates under its own rules, impulses, and drives, responsible not so much to the citizens' needs as to its own internal organizational modes. These modes commit the staffs and especially the welfare staffs to never challenging the status quo, never taking risks, and never listening to voices that question.

Until recently the county agency administering the public welfare program in the city was called the Department of Charities. And the still implicit attitude of the department toward the program was explicit in that name: the welfare program is considered to be a "charity," something to be given only to the very poor and needy in Los Angeles who must first prove and then continue to demonstrate that they are "worthy" of being helped.

William Barr, County Superintendent of Public Charities, described the Bureau of Public Assistance as a "huge monster, an octopus, a monstrous thing which spreads out everywhere." *

He is correct.

Ellis (Pat) Murphy, who under Mr. Barr has direct responsibility for supervising the LA welfare department, says, "The police and the welfare system are the two agencies that touch the lives of the most people in the Los Angeles ghetto but the welfare system doesn't fit the needs of the people who are the recipients. The grants given by the bureau are cut off below the physical needs of the people, and the system is so involved in administrative detail that 50 per cent of the social workers' time is taken up with filling out papers instead of doing social work."

Mr. Murphy is correct, too.

But what neither Superintendent Barr nor Mr. Murphy says is that they, their subordinates, and the County Board of Supervisors to whom they are responsible are deeply involved in creating the situation they seem to deplore. If the administration of the "monstrous" welfare system is a source of tension in Los Angeles, and it is, a great deal of the fault must be attributed to the County Supervisors and officials. If the grants

---

* The bureau is now called the Department of Public Social Service and has been reorganized administratively. But nothing fundamental has been changed. Most recipients still describe it as the BPA or "the welfare."

are below the physical needs of the people, and they are, the County Supervisors and officials can be held accountable, for they have lobbied successfully for many years to keep those grants down. And if the system is as involved in administrative detail as they maintain, part of the blame rests directly on them.

A forty-year-old Negro woman, whose sole income is an Aid to Families with Dependent Children grant, is much more accurate than Barr or Murphy in her description of the program: "The main thing, too, is that from the very word go the income is based on the barest necessities. There is no such thing as an extra income, so say something—an accident or something else—happens that you've got to have extra transportation money; there's no such thing as there being a fund that can be an emergency fund that can be sent to you, you know, on the spur of the moment.

"Like, for instance, if you get a check on the first of the month, okay, that's our rent, utilities, phone, and so forth, and the kids have to have shoes. Then the next one is for the fifteenth—we get a little groceries on the first, enough that'll hold us until the fifteenth—then we do our heavy shopping. But you still got another bill or the kids need something or something is going on somewhere. You better believe there's always something, especially when it gets cold weather. And we can't live without necessities for ourselves—our personal necessities and our house necessities. Like I told my worker, my children have to take baths, my children have to have clean clothes to put on—and I can't clean up the house with the food I eat. All you can buy is food, and you can't buy much of a meal anyway because of the prices you got to pay.

"And another thing is that the caseworkers are falling under such a caseload that they don't have the time to give to the personal problems of the people that they're dealing with. They don't have time to listen a lot of times. This is where it is—a person will have a problem or a person will have a particular need to know something, and his social worker is sometimes his only contact with professional, educated-type people that could give him advice, and he's busy, and he's busy, he's had a lot of cases like this, he's tired, he's cranky, he doesn't want to be bothered. This causes quite a hassle, quite a feeling of insecurity."

The number of people in Los Angeles who suffer from a "feeling of insecurity" is staggering: the staff of the Los Angeles County welfare department is larger than that of many state governments; the number of family aid cases handled by just one office of the department is greater than similar caseloads of twenty-eight states; 40 per cent of all the welfare payments in California are made in Los Angeles County; the amount of money disbursed by the department just to families with dependent children in Los Angeles County is larger, by far, than the grants made in similar programs in forty-eight states. There are 7,500 people on the welfare staff; its total annual budget is half a billion dollars!

The sole or major source of income of 300,000 men, women and children in Los Angeles County is from public funds. More than 150,000 of these receive public funds through the Old Age Security, Aid to the Blind, Aid to the Needy Disabled, and General Home Relief programs, while nearly 175,679 families with a total of 218,425 children are the recipients of grants from the Aid to Families with Dependent Children program, the single most controversial program. But the average monthly payments to these AFDC families are only $174.55, nearly $1,000 per year below the federal government's poverty line; each recipient in an average family receives only $43.26 a month.

In August 1965, the month in which the events took place that shocked the country,* $5.5 million in public assistance payments of all kinds were made to nearly a hundred thousand people in the Negro ghettos, a population larger than that in thirty-six of California's fifty-eight counties. But while that monthly $5.5 million is portrayed as a tremendous sum by the taxpayers' associations and the supervisors, it averages out to only $55 per person per month—far, far below the barest minimum for the essentials of life.

In that same month the south-central Negro section of Los Angeles alone accounted for more than a third of all the payments made in the whole county to families with dependent children; BPA offices located in the ghetto areas account for nearly 68 per cent of all the cases aided and 84 per cent of the total AFDC expenditures. Forty-five per cent of all the Old Age Security program cases in the county and more than 60 per cent of the General Home Relief programs are also located in the ghetto. And despite the sanctimonious attitude of those who portray the $5.5 million as a drain upon the *local* taxpayers by lazy people who refuse to work, 84 per cent of the money comes from federal or state funds, and most of the people receiving it *cannot* work because of age, disabilities, or dependent children.

Other facts about the welfare population in Los Angeles must be emphasized, for they have generally been obscured and distorted, either deliberately or from ignorance. The commonly held notions about hordes of people coming to Los Angeles for the specific purpose of getting on welfare and then remaining on the welfare rolls for the rest of their lives are false. More than half the people who receive Old Age Security have lived in California for twenty-nine years before applying for help; more than half the families receiving Aid to Families with Dependent Children have lived in California for sixteen years before applying for help.

And while the size of the welfare population in Los Angeles may remain constant or increase, its individual components are changing continuously. Even such programs as Old Age Security, Aid to the Blind, and Aid to the Needy Disabled have changing populations as death cuts some off and age brings others to them. In the most controversial and, to the

* [The Watts riot]

taxpayer, most aggravating program—Aid to Dependent Children—the population is continually shifting. Families grow desperate and go "on the county," leaving when they can, to be replaced perhaps by ones who had been on it previously. On the average, families remain on public assistance for only two years. Thus, the welfare recipients are not a fixed population of the very poor who remain in that condition for the rest of their lives; instead, they are only part of a larger group of people who lead marginal lives, marked by periods of unemployment, underemployment, working at very low-paying jobs, and entering or leaving the welfare system.

So to the millions of poor whites, Negroes, Mexican-Americans, Indians, and Puerto Ricans in the U.S., the welfare system is only one element in the economic structure of their lives, albeit a far more disagreeable and abrasive one than the unemployment insurance office or the badly paying job as a dishwasher in a non-union restaurant. And it is not a lack of motivation that brings most families without fathers or with longtime unemployed ones to the welfare department offices for help: it is a lack of opportunity for the family head to get a job. But while the local authorities who control the program cannot be held responsible for creating an economy with no employment in it for the unskilled, they cannot evade their share of responsibility for *keeping* the unemployed and unskilled in their condition of dependency.

The Los Angeles County Board of Supervisors and their subordinates are not alone in this role, for the board seems to mirror accurately the sentiments of many people in the community. It is with generalized community approval that the welfare administration in Los Angeles forces humiliating, punitive, and tension-creating conditions of life upon the recipients as the price they must pay for receiving a meager amount of financial aid. The recipients, in turn, are forced to lie, to cheat, and to try to circumvent the rules of the administration in order to survive. One recipient writes about the amount of money allowed a family for rent and clothing:

SAFE, HEALTHFUL HOUSING

How can a welfare recipient have safe, healthful housing when the rent allowance is so low that it covers only about one-half of what he is now paying for rent—unless he lives in a housing project, and there, every time he gets an increase in his budget the rent is raised. He can not afford to move to a better residence because then he would use the food allowance—he can't afford the amount of rent he is now paying for the high-rent, run-down house or apartment he's in now, designed for three or four people, which he has to stick three or four children into each bedroom or bed, and if he's lucky, he ends up in the living room—if he is not lucky he sleeps in the bath tub or maybe the family sleeps in shifts . . . How! How can you rent a three or four bedroom house on a NO-bedroom rent allowance—$55 per month (monthly rent allowance for most welfare recipients—some even less). This large amount will get you an unfurnished single on the lower east side—NO CHILDREN—but CATS allowed; because the RATS come pretty BIG and the CATS aren't allergic to RAID and BLACK FLAG used to try to kill off the roaches. How can a sardine-can be safe and healthful????? For a sardine—yes—but he's dead and nothing matters then anyway . . .

MINIMUM CLOTHING FOR HEALTH AND DECENCY

For an example we shall take a six year old school student . . . $6.15 per month is allowed for clothing per child through age six (6) . . . $6.15 per month totals the grand sum of $73.80 per year. With this large amount you are able to purchase for this six year old the following items:

```
4 pair of shoes—(1 pair every 3 months) at $3.99 pair
($4.15 incl. tax) ....................................... $16.60
    Note: $3.99 shoes last three to four weeks, child without shoes seven
    to eight weeks before it is time to buy a new pair.
10 used dresses or pants at the "Good Will" for about ...... $20.00
5 shirts or blouses at $1.59 each on sale (IRR's) ............  7.95*
48 pairs of socks—4 pair per month if they are 4 for $1.00 ..... 12.00*
1 new—but cheap—coat at $10.00 (everything can't be used) .. 10.00*
1  sweater ...................................................  5.00*
                                                                 -------
                                                                  71.55
                                        *Sales Tax               2.25
                                                                 -------
                                                                 $73.80
```

Now let's see just what we have here—4 pairs shoes, 10 used (and I do mean used) dresses or pants—what is so healthy about USED clothing—I bet GOVERNOR BROWN thinks "Good Will" is an attitude and doesn't know it is a welfare recipient clothing store—5 shirts or blouses, 48 pairs of socks—you say why so many socks, well baby with those cheap shoes with those big holes after only a few weeks, the cardboard, book covers and sidewalk wear out the socks (and that weak bleach we use ain't going to get them clean), 1 coat, the nicest thing on the list, for it covers all those used things underneath, one sweater, it will last if it doesn't get lost—and that is all for that six year old. Oh, you say I forgot underwear? No I didn't, but as some people say, welfare recipients are usually second and third "welfare generations" and "illegitimacy is a way of life" so if this is the case underclothing would only get in the way . . .

Even though most of the money distributed by the county comes from federal and state sources, the welfare department exacts a heavy price for the funds it distributes. It demands, first, that anyone seeking help prove in detail that no other means are available; specifically, the administration of the program is based on the assumption that whatever the people seeking aid say about themselves must be checked, exhaustively. The parallel would be if the Bureau of Internal Revenue were to investigate, exhaustively, every single taxpayer's income tax return rather than make spot checks. The Internal Revenue Service assumes that most taxpayers tell the truth in their declarations of income, even when they ask for tax relief or refunds; the Department of Public Social Service assumes that most of the people asking for relief lie in their declarations of need.

Next, the county assumes that in exchange for the financial help it gives it has the right to determine the essential conditions of life for those who receive any assistance. It determines not only the amount of income for each recipient or family of recipients, it also says how much of that income shall be spent on rent, food, clothing, and furniture. And because of this policy it forces a family of recipients to pay a larger portion of its income in rent to a public housing project than would be paid to the same project for an identical apartment by an identical family with identical income derived from unemployment insurance! Yet the man drawing unemployment insurance who can spend his money as he pleases has not contributed a single penny directly to the fund—unemployment insurance is wholly paid for by the employer. And no one in government told a single person receiving assistance under the GI Bill how the monthly check was to be spent, although every penny of that money came from the same public funds that supply most of the money administered by the welfare department. In fact, the closest parallel to the way in which the local government operates the welfare department is Mr. Bumble, who beat Oliver Twist when he asked for more porridge. The department beats its recipients, too, and even though the beating is psychological rather than physical, the consequences are just as filled with hate and tension.

The analogy between the welfare department and Mr. Bumble is not so far-fetched, for public assistance programs in America have evolved basically from the English Poor Laws. These laws were fundamentally "paternal, custodial, coercive and punitive," as they are described by Jacobus TenBroek, an outstanding authority on the subject. Poor Laws were based on the assumption that only the indigent poor, those not physically capable of working at some job, were to be helped, for idleness was considered a vice. And the Poor Law tradition, still the basis of all public welfare in America, also assumes that in exchange for assistance given to them the recipients must give up control over their lives and subject themselves to a series of controls and regulations of any work they do, any movement or travel arrangements they make, their living arrangements, family relations, and how they spend the money they receive. Above all, too, the taxpaying public believes that the recipients must somehow demonstrate how "grateful" they are for what they get.

Yet, California's Welfare and Institutions Code asserts: "The purpose of this code is to provide for protection, care and assistance to the people of the State in need thereof, and to promote the welfare and happiness of all the people of the State by providing public assistance to all its needy distressed. It is the legislative intent that assistance shall be administered promptly and humanely, with due regard for the preservation of family life, and without discrimination on account of race, religion or political affiliation; and that assistance shall be so administered as to encourage self-respect, self-reliance, and the desire to be a good citizen, useful to society." The code also indicates that the welfare programs should be administered liberally, but in actual practice the manner in which the programs *are* administered is precisely opposite to the stated legislative intent.

While the federal government, too, advocates progressive and rehabilitative policies, it does not release funds to states without systematic requirements for eligibility that govern each category of assistance. Los Angeles County gives admirable attention to those sections of the federal handbook outlining eligibility requirements, but hardly notices the sections that call for actual services. The multitude of forms produced and insisted on by the federal and local bureaucracies cripples any social worker's efforts to obtain the funds and services for recipients that the law entitles them to.

Theoretically, welfare policies are supposed to help maintain and strengthen the family life of the recipients; in fact, the welfare department weakens family life by, for example, pressuring recipient mothers of youngsters to work, without making adequate provisions for proper child care or providing supplemental allowances for travel or clothing which would make the job more attractive: "Like the social worker might come in and say, 'Get a job,' and maybe I got kids from the ages of two months through twelve years old, and then on the other hand they will say, 'You need to be at home with your children.' So what do you do? Do you get a job or do you stay home with your children? So, okay, they tell me, 'This job is important,' and if I want my aid to continue, I have to go. Okay. But we don't have a day-care center here, so what am I supposed to do if I can't hire me some kind of a decent babysitter?"

Theoretically, every AFDC family is entitled to detailed help from the caseworkers; but because of understaffing and consequently heavy caseloads, the welfare workers rarely have enough time to sit down with the recipients and discuss with them all the advantages and disadvantages of a work situation. Thus, instead of being able to plan for the future, the recipients merely drift from day to day, from welfare check to welfare check.

Theoretically, welfare administrations should encourage recipients and their children to become self-supporting; in fact, the typical welfare bureau robs them of any incentive to do so by deducting, under most conditions, whatever is earned from their meager grants. In Los Angeles, it also permits the public housing authority to increase the monthly rent automatically when additional income is brought into the family: "Every time the Bureau of Public Assistance gives us a raise in our money—a small amount that they do—the housing authorities get it. So we still don't have anything, you know, and it's just like not getting it. Okay. Well, then they tell us we're getting a raise; all right, well, we figure that it can go to our food and so forth, but when we look around and get our rent statement, then they took the little nickel we get."

Recipients are urged to maintain physically decent homes, but the welfare department sometimes attempts to force the recipients to sell items of furniture and use the money to cut down on the grants: "If you come in with a nice record player or a living-room set, you get these things for a good reason—you're showing an interest in your own home. You know a woman can't help that. That's nature you know. But if your worker sees this and comes in, she wonders, 'Where did you get the money?' or 'How could you afford this?' Or if it's nice and so it looks expensive, she says, 'You could sell this and live off of this for certain months, for a certain length of time.' They'll stop your check or cut your check until you sell it. Now not all the caseworkers do it but some of them do it. Another thing about that, too, when I went down to apply for aid, they asked me did I have any kind of insurance policy, any money in the bank, some kind of property. I told them if I had all that I wouldn't be applying for aid, but if I did, in other words, you get explained that if I had any kind of insurance policy, I don't care what amount it was, I would have to sell it. And *live* off that money, *live* off it without any aid from them, *live* off that until it runs out!"

A welfare program should seek to help relieve family tensions, but the Los Angeles welfare department often tries to pressure wives and husbands to remain married even if the marriage is causing great distress in the family: "When the situation is so bad where a husband and wife cannot live together, I don't want a caseworker coming in and telling me, 'Well, try to make it, try this, try that.' When you been trying so many number of years, embarrassing the children and still going through the same thing and everything is getting worse and worse and worse. And especially somebody's going to end up hurt, dead, or in the hospital. If you say two words, he's down your throat; if he says two words, you're down his throat. So there's nothing left in a marriage. You're just there because of the kids, see, and that makes it bad, that makes it awful bad on the kids, because I do have that problem and I do see it right now. If I didn't, I wouldn't even apply for BPA, I would try to make it on the little money he makes right now. But I couldn't. I couldn't because it was affecting my oldest son very badly, he had to have therapy at school. I've been at school a number of times where maybe he have a mental block because he won't learn; it's something in the home. And it's still—even with the little money they're giving me now, it's not helping my problem because that stuff is too late now. When I needed it, they wouldn't give it to me. They wouldn't help me when I needed. But when they did give it to me, it was too late."

Finally, the welfare department and the recipients clash over whether or not sexual relationships outside of marriage should exist; the bureau attempts to force any unrelated man living in a household either to contribute to the family's support or leave, lest the family's grant be terminated: "If you have a boy friend or your ex-husband and they're going to come in, good enough in their hearts to give you enough to get junior a pair of shoes when you can't see getting them until the first or the sixteenth, and they got to go to school, they got to have those shoes or pants or what have you, I feel they need this extra money. And what we do in our private lives is our business. I don't feel that anybody from the Bureau of Public Assistance or anybody else should pry into a woman's private life, because that is private. You know, so I mean why suppress a woman of being able to release things, because they have to be done. Now our social workers, they got husbands, and if they don't have a husband, they got boy friends that they're going to do it, so how are they any better than we are? They're no better than we are; they have to have their release and we have to do the same thing. Unless they want us to just stay women and then go with other women, and then that's no good, then you're jeopardizing the children."

READING SELECTION 8: JACOBS, "THE WELFARE BUREAU"

COMPREHENSION AND ANALYSIS

Do not refer to the article to answer these questions. Choose one of the items that best answers each question, and mark the letter in the space provided.

1. _____ Before writing his essay, the author applied for welfare because (a) he needed money desperately (b) he wanted to experience what all recipients must go through (c) he was curious (d) he could not rely on getting interviews with welfare officials without contacts.

2. _____ Mark the two *major* criticisms against the welfare system that Jacobs emphasizes most. (a) the system is a monstrous bureaucratic tangle of red tape and excessive paper work (b) the system grossly violates the recipients' rights to privacy and control over his own affairs (c) the system fails to provide for a decent standard of living for recipients (d) the system's caseworkers are too overworked to give needed advice.

3. _____ To support his own conclusions, Jacobs cites evidence from (a) recipients' letters and direct statements (b) facts, figures and relevant statistics (c) comments from a few welfare department officials (d) all of the above (e) only a and b.

4. _____ According to Jacobs, which welfare program is the most controversial? (a) Aid to the Needy Disabled (b) General Home Relief (c) Aid to Families with Dependent Children (d) Aid to the Blind.

5. _____ The author states that the welfare system, contrary to its stated purposes, (a) keeps unemployed or unskilled people in a state of dependency (b) forces applicants to cheat to get enough aid to subsist (c) occasionally provides money below the federal minimum poverty level (d) assumes it should control every aspect of the recipient's life (e) all of the above (f) only a and d.

6. _____ Public assistance programs in America are derived from the English Poor Laws that were based on the assumption that (a) those who refused to work belonged in the poorhouse (b) only the disabled should be helped, for idleness was a vice (c) those who received help had to relinquish control over their lives (d) all of the above (e) b and c only.

7. _____ Which of the following faults with Aid to Dependent Chil-

dren did Jacobs *not* mention? The program (a) weakens family life by forcing mothers to work without adequate child care (b) weakens family life by causing tension between the working mother and the idle or disabled husband (c) fails to help recipients plan for the future (d) robs recipients of the incentive to work by deducting any wages they receive from their aid (e) advises married couples to remain together even under duress.

8. ———— What was the probable relationship between Los Angeles County's Welfare Department and the Watts' riot of 1965? (a) no direct relationship (b) only a slight relationship (c) a very strong relationship (d) any relationship is impossible to determine from the essay's evidence.

9. From the following list, choose the five popular misconceptions that Jacobs *directly* challenges.

A. ———— Welfare destroys people's initiative to work.

B. ———— Welfare is financed solely by local taxes.

C. ———— Welfare recipients are simply too lazy to work.

D. ———— Most people in California who apply for welfare are newcomers who have moved specifically to get immediate aid.

E. ———— Women on welfare tend to have many illegitimate children to get more aid.

F. ———— Most families, once on welfare, remain on welfare forever.

G. ———— Most welfare recipients spend their allotment on luxury items, such as color televisions, expensive cars, and liquor.

H. ———— The welfare system will eventually bankrupt the country.

I. ———— The average amount of welfare is more than sufficient to live comfortably.

10. Here are some suggestions for the welfare system. Based on the evidence in the essay, which would Jacobs probably approve (A) or disapprove (D)?

A. ———— a system that dispensed money, not as charity, but as a necessary requirement for a decent way of life

B. ———— a system that would provide the same guaranteed annual income for everyone, even those who refuse to work

C. ———— a system that dispensed money while the recipient trained for a useful job

D. ———— a system that appropriated money, not according to a standardized formula, but according to each family's needs

    E. _____ an increase in monthly welfare payments with no change in the system's operations or caseloads

    F. _____ abandoning the welfare system completely to force people to survive by their own wits

VOCABULARY

From the lettered choices, find the best definition for each vocabulary item, and mark the letter in the space provided.

1. _____ bears down *inexorably*
2. _____ organizational *modes*
3. _____ the *implicit* attitude
4. _____ their *subordinates*
5. _____ they seem to *deplore*
6. _____ the *sanctimonious* attitude
7. _____ *hordes* of people
8. _____ lead *marginal* lives
9. _____ an *abrasive* element
10. _____ *punitive* conditions
11. _____ a *meager* amount
12. _____ *illegitimacy* is a way
13. _____ laws were *coercive*
14. _____ the *indigent* poor
15. _____ idleness was a *vice*

A. minimal; on the fringe
B. those to be imitated
C. inflicting punishment, penalty
D. lacking means of survival or subsistence
E. relentlessly; mercilessly
F. state of giving birth out of marriage
G. unlawfulness; anarchy
H. manners; styles
I. packs; swarms
J. those who are subject; who belong to a lower order

K. causing friction; grating
L. forcible; compelling
M. implied; but not stated
N. lazy; slothful
O. displaying exaggerated gravity or solemnity
P. immoral habit; trait
Q. abhorrent; repelling
R. regret deeply; disapprove
S. scanty; inadequate
T. apparent; directly obvious

COMPREHENSION   No. right _____ × 5 = _____ %

VOCABULARY   No. right _____

No. of words 4450 ÷ time in seconds _____ × 60 = _____ WPM
WPM × Comprehension % = Reading Efficiency Rate _____

9

S. J. PERELMAN
Come on in, the Liability's Fine*

S. J. Perelman, one of the great American humorists, has contributed many humorous sketches for The New Yorker, *and during the Thirties, wrote for motion pictures. This sketch is a wonderful introduction to Perelman's humor and to his remarkable ability to handle the intricacies of the language.*

The sunlight was so benign one recent forenoon in the country, and the air laden with such promise of spring, that, on the verge of entering my web to spin a few merchandisable threads, I decided to take a turn about the place and see what catastrophes I could unearth to impair my efficiency. It looked quite unpromising for a while; none of the barn doors had blown off during the night, the ruts in the lane—thitherto as deep as the Union trenches before Vicksburg—had mysteriously filled up by themselves, and the cistern containing our auxiliary supply of rain water had stopped rotting and exuded a fresh, invigorating tang of resin. I was forlornly kicking a terrace wall, in the hope of loosening the stones and embroiling myself in a long, exasperating hassle with masons, when an azure-blue sedan rolled up, backed swiftly around, and splintered the lower branches of a magnolia just coming into flower. A thickset, forceful man of the type who models Shurons in opticians' windows jumped out and cursorily examined the damage. Then, whisking a briefcase from the trunk, he strode toward me with hand extended.

"Howdy," he said, all wind and geniality like a barber's cat. "Chicanery's my name—Walt Chicanery, I'm with the Hindsight Insurance Company, over in Doylestown. Is the owner here?" I explained that though my clothes belied it, I held the fief, and he chuckled tolerantly to assuage my embarrassment. "You sure fooled me," he said. "I thought you were the handyman."

* From *The Road to Miltown, or Under the Spreading Atrophy* (New York: Simon & Schuster, Inc., 1957), pp. 131–137.

"I am," I replied evenly. "I do all the odd jobs, like pruning these trees after people drive over them."

"That's where you're missing a bet, neighbor," he said, stabbing me in the breastbone with his forefinger. "Don't prune 'em—replace 'em. I've got a policy whereby you're fully protected against loss to shrubs, hedges, sedges, vines, pines, creepers, rushes, and ramblers."

"So have I," I disclosed. "I've got any kind of insurance you can name —hailstorm, shipwreck, volcano, libel, frostbite, all of them. I'm even insured against meteors or a rain of red frogs. And now, if you'll excuse me—"

"One moment there," he said patronizingly. "You're pretty cocky, aren't you? Think every possible contingency's provided for, eh? Well, think again. What happens if your bowling ball slips and you break the bones in your companion's foot?"

I knew I should have whistled up my syce and had the fellow beaten off the place with lathees, but the sun felt so good on my back that I let myself be drawn. "The only kind I've ever dropped was a matzo ball," I said, "and I doubt whether it affected Jed Harris's gait. No, sir," I went on, "I don't get involved in those trick mishaps. I'm probably less accident-prone than any man alive. I just sit indoors and do my work, and that's where I'm going now." Entering the outbuilding where I worry, I immersed myself in a sheaf of papers. Simultaneously, Chicanery's hand slid into my field of vision, holding a printed page.

"You owe this to your family, friend," his voice purred into my shoulder. "Just look it over before you send me away."

"What is it?" I asked peevishly.

"A list of typical accidents covered by our new Allstate Comprehensive Personal Liability policy," he said, buttering each word like Svengali. "Go ahead, read it. Go ahead, I dare you." Robbed of my will, I read.

The list was formidable, an encyclopedia of disaster. "A passer-by breaks arm in fall on your icy walk," it intoned. "Your dog bites the deliveryman. Your wife injures a passer-by with her umbrella. Mailman slips on your front step—suffers a concussion. Your child knocks down an elderly person with his sled. Handyman tumbles from your stepladder. Friend suffers a crippling fall on your freshly waxed floor. While hunting, you accidentally shoot another hunter. Your baby-sitter breaks ankle tripping over baby's toy. Neighbor's child falls into trash fire. Your child accidentally hits playmate in eye with ball. Your child runs into bystander with bicycle. You accidentally burn stranger with cigarette. A guest trips over your rug. Your child accidentally sails toy airplane into playmate's face. Your golf drive injures another player. Your back-yard swing breaks, injuring a neighbor's child. A fellow bus passenger trips over your suitcase or package. Baseball bat slips from your son's hands —hurtles into spectator's face. Your trash fire spreads to a neighbor's home. Your child accidentally breaks plate-glass window. Your cat claws visitor's expensive fur coat."

I looked up at Chicanery, who, while I was absorbed, had flipped open my checkbook and was examining the balance with amused contempt, and handed back the prospectus. "Listen, this is all very well for schlemiels," I said, "but I repeat—none of that stuff happens to yours truly. I've crisscrossed the ruddy globe, waded knee-deep in malarial swamps, slept cheek by jowl with hamadryads, shared my last catty of rice with head-hunters, and never even had a nosebleed. You're barking up the wrong tree, Tuan. Good day."

"Ta-ta," he said, without tensing a muscle. "Say, what's that whistling I hear down on your porch? A bird?" I admitted that I own a rather gifted myna acquired in Thailand, who speaks idiomatic Siamese, Chinese, and English, and who allows nobody but me to gentle him. "You don't say," he marveled. "What's he do when your guests reach into his cage?"

"Who—Tong Cha?" I asked carelessly. "Oh, he generally goes for their eyes. He thinks they're grapes."

"Be a shame to shell out fifty thousand damages for a grape," observed Chicanery with a yawn. "A party over here in Chalfont got hooked that way. His rooster bit off a little boy's nose. Time the courts finished with him, the poor devil was on relief."

"B-but Tong Cha wouldn't hurt anyone intentionally," I said, suddenly agitated. "I mean, basically he's sweet—he's just playful, full of beans—"

"Well, maybe he can explain that to the jury," said Chicanery. "Or maybe you'll be lucky enough to get a Siamese judge. Otherwise, you're going byebye with an iron ball soldered to your leg, as sure as you're born."

"Er—how much did you say that policy was?" I inquired, moistening my lips. "I might be able to swing it after all. I don't really need a bridge on these molars; I can chew on the other side."

"Sure you can," the agent agreed sympathetically. "Your cheeks are bound to cave in sooner or later, no matter what you do. Now, here's the deal." Within twenty minutes, and to the accompaniment of a spate of actuarial jargon I only half understood, I was formally indemnified against a host of actionable casualties that might befall me or my dependents, whether human or members of the brute creation.

As Chicanery finished ticking off the complex provisions, he caught himself abruptly. "Danged if I haven't forgot the drowning clause," he exclaimed. "That's what comes of somebody jabbering in your ear."

"There's no water on this place," I objected. "Just the little creek you drove through in the lane. You couldn't drown a chipmunk in that."

"Hunh, that's what Dr. Bundy over at Keller's Church thought," rejoined Chicanery. "His wife's brother came home one night drunk as a boiled owl, fell in the brook, and goodbye Charlie. Widow collected seventy-four grand and poor Bundy blew his brains out. I don't want you coming around with a beef if it happens to you."

"O.K., O.K.," I said impatiently. "Is the policy in effect from now on?"

"Yup, soon as your check clears," he said. "Personally, I always recommend paying cash so you get immediate protection." I at once yielded up what currency I had in my clothes, then repaired to the house and levied on the kitchen funds, and finally amassed the premium, a good share of it in pennies. Chicanery stowed it away in his poke and, teetering back in my mid-Victorian swivel chair, beamed paternally at me.

"Someday you'll bless me for this," he declared. "A stitch in time—" There was a fearful crack of wood and metal, the chair crumbled into matchwood, and Chicanery catapulted backward, describing the figure known among movie stunt men as the Hundred and Eight. In landing, he unfortunately dislodged a pile of atlases and gazetteers, which rained down on him like building blocks and almost hid him from view. I sprang up and flung aside the sailing directions for Macassar Strait and the copy of *Menaboni's Birds* resting on his head. His face had gone the color of an old Irish towel and he was breathing heavily through his mouth.

"Are you all right?" I demanded, seizing his shoulders and shaking him vigorously. Two years as a biology major, plus wide reading of illustrated hygiene magazines along Sixth Avenue, have taught me that in possible concussions the patient should be stimulated to keep the circulation brisk.

Chicanery opened his eyes and goggled about stupidly. "Where am I?" he murmured.

"Right here in the Pennsylvania Dutch country, about nine miles from Riegelsville," I assured him, endeavoring to keep my voice buoyant. "Is anything hurting you? Can you twist your neck?" With a grunt, he shook me off and clambered to his feet. A normal healthy flush was momentarily replacing his pallor. He looked fit as a fighting cock, and I said so.

"Leave that up to my doctor," he snapped, dusting off his pants. "It could be internal injuries, like as not. Whatever it is, we can settle it between us. You won't have to go to court."

I had some difficulty in enunciating clearly, but I made my point at last. "You just sold me a policy that covered this type of accident!" I bellowed. "I thought you were sincere! *I* was sincere! Now you tell me—"

"Look, Mister," said Chicanery, his eyeballs shrinking to two bits of flint. "No use trying to bluster your way out of it. If you wanted protection against falls sustained from furniture, you should have specified. That chair is a death-trap, and you could be jailed for using it. You'll hear from my lawyer." He sailed out, slamming the door with such force that a loose slate pitched off the roof and struck him between the shoulder blades. Through the window, I saw him sink to his knees in a position of deep meditation, like a Buddhist monk. Then he arose heavily and, making a notation on a pad, tottered to his car. Five seconds later, it disappeared over the brow of the hill, trailing a flowering magnolia from its bumper. I haven't heard a rumble out of him since, but one of these days my heirs and assigns will undoubtedly receive a bulky envelope with a Doylestown postmark. I must leave word behind to forward it on to Singapore.

READING SELECTION 9: PERELMAN, "COME ON IN;
THE LIABILITIES FINE

COMPREHENSION AND ANALYSIS

Do not refer to the article to answer these questions. Choose one of the
items that best answers each question, and mark the letter in the space
provided.

1. __A__ At the beginning of the selection, the narrator says he was
(a) hoping for a catastrophe to occur so he could find
something to do (b) repairing the barn doors (c) waiting
for the insurance man to come (d) fixing a stone terrace
wall.

2. __E__ The narrator failed to get rid of Chicanery after he arrived
because (a) he actually needed insurance (b) the warm
day put him in an exceptionally good mood (c) Chicanery
was very persuasive and didn't give him a chance to get rid
of him (d) all of the above (e) b and c only.

3. __C__ It is obvious from Perelman's description that Chicanery
was (a) a crook, only pretending to be an insurance salesman (b) a sincere believer in insurance for protection
against disaster (c) a shrewd, convincing, smooth-talking
con man (d) a failure as an insurance salesman.

4. __b__ Characters' names often suggest something about their personality and behavior. Judging from the selection, what can
you infer about the meaning of "chicanery"? It means (a)
rudeness, arrogance (b) underhanded deceit and trickery
(c) sincerity and honesty (d) evil, destruction.

5. __C__ What is the loophole in the policy Chicanery sells? (a) it
covers only accidents occurring indoors (b) it is not valid
until the purchaser's check clears (c) it deliberately ex-
cludes the kind of accident Chicanery has (d) it duplicates
the narrator's other policies.

6. __E__ In this sketch, Perelman pokes fun at (a) people who over-
insure themselves for every conceivable disaster (b) people
like himself who are gullible enough to fall for a line (c)
unscrupulous, smooth-talking door-to-door salesmen (d)
people who ask for disaster to have some excitement (e) all
of the above.

7. __D__ Chicanery insulted the narrator by (a) driving over his
magnolia bush and not apologizing (b) mistaking him for
the caretaker (c) looking in his checkbook (d) all of the
above (e) only a and b.

8. Based on the evidence in the article, mark T (true), F

(false), or X (not verifiable) for the inferences that follow.

A. __T__ The narrator was probably sloppily dressed.

B. __T__ The narrator already had several insurance policies.

C. __F__ The narrator agreed to buy a policy only to get rid of Chicanery.

D. __X__ The narrator probably has traveled extensively because of the foreign cities he mentions.

E. __T__ Chicanery probably deliberately planned his "accident."

F. __X__ From his description, the narrator thought Chicanery's accident was carefully rehearsed and polished.

G. __X__ The narrator kept, besides exotic birds, several dogs and cats.

H. __X__ Undoubtedly the narrator's wife was furious when she learned of the incident.

I. __X__ Chicanery eventually sued for damages.

J. __X__ The narrator undoubtedly learned that to ask for a disaster is foolish.

K. __X__ The next time a salesman comes to his house, the narrator will probably be less trusting.

9. __C__ Perelman's piece can best be described as (a) a moral tale to caution the reader against trusting door-to-door salesmen (b) an amusing criticism of all insurance salesmen (c) a witty, amusing account of a salesman who successfully cons a sucker (d) a story that proves the necessity of insurance to cover every disaster.

10. __C__ When the narrator says he must give his heirs instructions to forward Chicanery's envelope to Singapore, he implies that (a) he has learned his lesson and, given the chance, will trick Chicanery in the same way (b) he is planning a long trip around the world (c) if Chicanery ever tries to get the money, the narrator will send him on a wild goose chase (d) Chicanery probably will never have the nerve to sue for damages (e) a, c, and d only.

VOCABULARY

From the lettered choices, find the best definition for each vocabulary item, and mark the letter in the space provided.

1. __E__ to *impair* my efficiency
2. __P__ *auxiliary* supply
3. __K__ *cursorily* examined
4. __B__ all wind and *geniality*
5. __H__ to *assuage* my embarrassment

6. __R__ he said *patronizingly*
7. __D__ I *immersed* myself
8. __M__ the list was *formidable*
9. __C__ with amused *contempt*
10. __G__ this is for *schlemiels*
11. __O__ suddenly *agitated*
12. __I__ a *spate* of jargon
13. __B__ he beamed *paternally*
14. __J__ to keep my voice *buoyant*
15. __T__ replaced his *pallor*

A. in a fatherly way
B. cheerfulness; kindly warmth
C. disdain; scorn
D. engrossed; involved deeply
E. drowned
F. make worse; harm
G. stupid, easily duped people; dolts
H. make less severe; alleviate
I. overflow; outpouring
J. light; cheerful
K. hastily; superficially

L. carefully; thoroughly
M. causing fear or dread because of size; awesome
N. disbelief; incredulity
O. stirred up; disturbed
P. reserve; supplemental
Q. strongly; forcefully
R. condescendingly; lowering oneself to inferiors
S. calmed; soothed
T. paleness; lack of color

COMPREHENSION No. right _____ × 5 = _____ %

VOCABULARY   No. right _____

No. of words 1740 ÷ time in seconds _____ × 60 = _____ WPM
WPM × Comprehension % = Reading Efficiency Rate _____

10

THOMAS SZASZ
The Crime of Commitment*

Born in Hungary and educated in the United States, Thomas S. Szasz is a psychiatrist who contributes frequently to medical and psychiatric journals. In this article, he argues that our notions of mental illness are outmoded, that too frequently unacceptable or annoying behavior is defined as mental illness, and that involuntary commitment of mental patients is closer to imprisonment without trial than to therapeutic rehabilitation.

Physicians and laymen alike generally believe persons are involuntarily confined in mental hospitals because they are mentally ill, but don't know they are sick and need medical treatment. This view, to put it charitably, is nonsense. In my opinion, mental illness is a myth. People we label "mentally ill" are not sick, and involuntary mental hospitalization is not treatment. It is punishment.

Involuntary confinement for "mental illness" is a deprivation of liberty that violates basic human rights, as well as the moral principles of the Declaration of Independence and the U. S. Constitution. In short, I consider commitment a crime against humanity.

Any psychiatrist who accepts as his client a person who does not wish to be his client, who defines him as "mentally ill," who then incarcerates his client in an institution, who bars his client's escape from the institution and from the role of mental patient, and who proceeds to "treat" him against his will—such a psychiatrist, I maintain, creates "mental illness" and "mental patients." He does so in exactly the same way as the white man created slavery by capturing the black man, bringing him to America in shackles, and then selling and using the black man as if he were an animal.

To understand the injustice of commitment it is necessary to distinguish between *disease* as a *biological condition* and the *sick role* as a *social*

* From *Psychology Today,* March, 1969, pp. 55–57.

status. Though a simple one, this distinction is rarely made in articles on mental illness, and there is a good reason for this. For once this distinction is made, psychiatry ceases to be what it is officially proclaimed, namely a medical specialty, and becomes, instead, social engineering.

Strictly speaking, *illness* is a biological (physicochemical) abnormality of the body or its functioning. A person is sick if he has diabetes, a stroke, or cancer.

The *sick role,* on the other hand, refers to the social status of claiming illness or assuming the role of patient. Like husband, father or citizen, the *sick role* denotes a certain relationship to others in the society.

A person may be ill, but may prefer not to assume the sick role, as when we have a severe cold but go about our business. Conversely, a person may be healthy, but choose to assume the sick role, as when we feel perfectly well but offer illness as an excuse for avoiding an obligation to go to the office or a party. Soldiers often assume the sick role —called "malingering"—to avoid the dangers of combat.

Where does the distinction between illness and sick role leave the alleged mental patient? He is said to be "very sick" by his relatives and the psychiatrists retained by them, but the patient maintains he is perfectly well and rejects medical or psychiatric help. Society then uses the police power of the state to force such a person into the sick role: this is done by calling the person a "mental patient," by incarcerating him in a "mental hospital" and by "treating" him for his "mental illness" whether he likes it or not. The underlying issue, however, is whether or not an individual has the right to refuse to be cast into the role of mental patient.

To answer this question, it is necessary to consider the problem of what mental illness is. Mental illness is not a physicochemical abnormality of the body, that is, an organic illness. If it were, we would simply call it illness and have no need for the qualifying adjective "mental." Actually, what we call "functional" mental diseases are not diseases at all. Persons said to be suffering from such disorders are socially deviant or inept, or in conflict with individuals, groups or institutions.

Not only does mental illness differ fundamentally from physical illness, but mental hospitalization differs from medical hospitalization. Mental hospitalization is typically involuntary, whereas medical hospitalization is typically voluntary. In a free society, a person can't be committed and treated against his will for cancer or heart disease, but he can be committed for depression or schizophrenia.

Should future research establish that certain so-called functional mental illnesses are actual physical disorders, they would then be treated like other organic disorders and the question of involuntary hospitalization for them would become irrelevant.

If schizophrenia, for example, turns out to have a biochemical cause and cure, schizophrenia would no longer be one of the diseases for which a person would be involuntarily committed. Pellagra once sent many persons to mental hospitals with symptoms resembling schizophrenia until a vitamin deficiency was found to cause pellagra.

A person is said to be mentally ill if he behaves in certain "abnormal" ways. Since what is abnormal to one person is normal to another, mental illness is a kind of loose-fitting, quasi-medical synonym for bad or undesirable behavior. To a Christian Scientist, going to a doctor is abnormal. To a hypochondriac, *not* going is. To a Roman Catholic, using artificial birth control is abnormal. To a non-Catholic eager to avoid pregnancy, *not* using it is abnormal. The fact that mental illness designates a deviation from an ethical rule of conduct, and that such rules vary widely, explains why upper-middle-class psychiatrists can so easily find evidence of "mental illness" in lower-class individuals; and why so many prominent persons in the past 50 years or so have been diagnosed by their enemies as suffering from some type of insanity. Barry Goldwater was called a "paranoid schizophrenic"; Whittaker Chambers, a "psychopathic personality"; Woodrow Wilson, a "neurotic," frequently "very close to psychosis" (by no less a psychiatrist than Sigmund Freud!). Jesus himself, according to two psychiatrists quoted by Dr. Albert Schweitzer in his doctoral thesis, was a "born degenerate" with a "fixed delusional system"; manifesting a "paranoid clinical picture [so typical] it is hardly conceivable people can even question the accuracy of the diagnosis."

My argument that commitment is a crime against humanity is opposed on the grounds that commitment is necessary for the protection of the healthy members of society. To be sure, commitment does protect the community from certain threats. But the question should not be *whether* the community is protected, but precisely *from what,* and *how.*

Commitment shields nonhospitalized members of society from having to accommodate to the annoying or idiosyncratic demands of persons who have *not* violated any criminal statutes. The commitment procedure has already been used against General Edwin Walker and Ezra Pound. Conceivably it could be used against a Stokely Carmichael or an Eldridge Cleaver.

But what about those persons who are actually violent? Society could, if it were willing, protect itself from violence and threats of violence through our system of criminal laws, which provides for the imprisonment of violators in correctional institutions.

What about so-called emotionally disturbed persons who have not violated any statute but are believed to be violence-prone? Everything possible should be done to give them help, but is it just to hospitalize or treat them involuntarily for being "potentially dangerous?"

To be judged potentially violent, a patient must be interviewed by a psychiatrist, which in effect violates the patient's right under the Fifth Amendment to refuse to incriminate himself. Few "mental patients" receive legal advice prior to being committed, but if they refused to be seen or interviewed by a physician, commitment would be impossible.

Psychiatrists cannot predict whether a person will be violent. Many "mental patients" who lose their liberty never have been and never will be violent.

Being "potentially dangerous" is not a crime. Most of us equate emotional disturbance with being violence-prone. Studies show, however, that "mental" patients are no more violence-prone than "normals."

To further clarify the political dimensions and implications of commitment practices, let us note some of the fundamental parallels between master and slave on the one hand and the institutional psychiatrist and involuntarily hospitalized mental patient on the other. In each instance the former member of the pair defines the social role of the latter, and casts the latter in that role by force. The committed patient must accept the view that he is "sick," that his captors are "well," that the patient's own view of himself is false and his captors' view of him is true, and that to effect any change in his social situation, the patient must relinquish his "sick" views and adopt the "healthy" views of those who have power over him. By accepting himself as "sick" and the institutional environment and the various manipulations imposed by the staff as "treatment," the patient is compelled to authenticate the psychiatrist's role as that of benevolent physician curing mental illness. The patient who maintains the forbidden image of reality—that the psychiatrist is a jailer —is considered paranoid. Since most patients (like oppressed people generally) eventually accept the ideas imposed on them by their superiors, hospital psychiatrists are constantly immersed in an environment in which their identity as "doctor" is affirmed. The moral superiority of white men over black was similarly authenticated and affirmed.

Suppose a person wishes to study slavery. He might start by studying slaves—and he would then find that slaves are, in general, brutish, poor and uneducated. The student of slavery might then conclude that slavery is the slave's natural or appropriate social state. Such, indeed, have been the methods and conclusions of innumerable men through the ages. For example, Aristotle held that slaves were naturally inferior and hence justly subdued.

Another student, biased by contempt for slavery, might proceed differently. He would maintain there can be no slave without a master holding the slave in bondage. This student would accordingly consider slavery a type of human relationship, a social institution, supported by custom, law, religion and force. From this perspective, the study of masters is at least as relevant to the study of slavery as is the study of slaves. I hold that the study of institutional psychiatrists is as relevant to the study of involuntary hospitalization as is the study of mental patients.

Mental illness has been investigated for centuries, and continues to be investigated today, in much the same way slaves were studied in the antebellum South and before. Men took for granted the existence of slaves.

Scientists duly noted and classified the biological and social character-istics of the slaves. In the same way, we take for granted the existence of mental patients. Indeed, many Americans believe the number of such patients is steadily increasing. And it is generally believed that the psy-chiatrist's task is to observe and classify the biological, psychological and social characteristics of mental patients.

The defenders of slavery claimed the Negro was happier as a slave than as a free man because of the "peculiarities of his character." As his-torian S. M. Elkins has said, "The failure of any free workers to present themselves for enslavement can serve as one test of how much the analysis of the happy slave may have added to Americans' understand-ing of themselves." The failure of most persons with so-called mental illness to present themselves for hospitalization is a test of how much current analysis of mental health problems may have added to our un-derstanding of ourselves.

Today, of course, involuntary mental hospitalization is a universally accepted method of social control, much as slavery was in the past. Our unwillingness to look searchingly at this problem may be compared to the unwillingness of the South to look at slavery. "A democratic people," wrote Elkins, "no longer reasons with itself when it is all of the same mind." Today the Supreme Court of Iowa can say: "Such loss of liberty [as is entailed in commitment of the insane] is not such liberty as is within the meaning of the constitutional provision that 'no person shall be deprived of life, liberty or property without due process of law.'" I submit, however, that just as slavery is an evil, so is hospitalizing any-one without his consent, whether that person is depressed or paranoid, hysterical or schizophrenic.

Commitment practices flourished long before there were mental or psychiatric "treatments" for "mental diseases." Indeed madness, or mental illness, was not always a requirement for commitment. The Illinois com-mitment laws of 1851 specified that, "Married women . . . may be en-tered or detained in the hospital on the request of the husband of the woman . . . *without* the evidence of insanity required in other cases." Regulations for the Bicêtre and Salpêtrierè, the two Parisian "mental hospitals" that became world famous, made it possible in 1680 to lock up children (of artisans and poor people) who "refused to work or who used their parents badly." Girls "debauched or in evident danger of be-coming so," and prostitutes or "women who ran bawdy houses" were also considered fit subjects for incarceration.

Today, commitment laws usually specify that, for involuntary hospitali-zation, a person not only must be mentally ill, but must also be danger-ous to himself or to others. But even if a mental patient has expert legal advice, what facts can *he* offer to prove that he is not dangerous, when a psychiatrist claims he is? Clearly, it is impossible to *prove* that a person is not dangerous.

Involuntary mental hospitalization remains today what it has been ever since its inception in the 17th Century: an extra-legal, quasi-medical form of social control for persons who annoy or disturb others and whose nonconformity cannot be controlled through the criminal law. To be sure, the rhetoric has changed. Formerly, a housewife's commitment could be justified by her husband's disaffection and his unsupported complaints. Today, commitment must be justified by calling the housewife "mentally ill." The locus of confinement has changed. The Bedlams of old have been replaced by state mental hospitals and community mental-health centers. But the social reality remains the same: commitment is still punishment without trial, imprisonment without time limit, and stigmatization without hope of redress.

Reading Selection 10: Szasz, "The Crime of Commitment"

Comprehension and Analysis

Do not refer to the article to answer these questions. Choose one of the items that best answers each question, and mark the letter in the space provided.

1. __c__ The main idea of the article is that (a) mental illness is a biological and physical disorder (b) mental institutions are created to protect society, though they too often are ineffectual (c) committing a mentally ill person involuntarily is inhumane and a deliberate violation of his rights (d) mental institutions seldom cure patients, but only aggravate the illness.

2. __d__ Dr. Szasz justifies his opinion that commitment is unfair by stating that (a) psychiatrists may actually create mental illness in their patients (b) there is a difference between illness and the "sick role" (c) patients who insist they are well are forced to admit to illness because the state has the power to commit them (d) all of the above (e) a and c only.

3. __b__ According to the author, mental illness is defined as (a) a physicochemical disorder (b) the inability to adjust to society (c) a brain disorder causing tension or violence (d) a malfunctioning of the adrenals which produces schizophrenia.

4. __d__ What are the moral and ethical problems in committing a person who behaves abnormally? (a) abnormal and normal behavior are relative—what is abnormal for one group may be normal for another (b) a patient may be deprived of his right to life, liberty and the pursuit of happiness (c) commitment is a convenient way to dispose of politically undesirable or non-conformist people (d) all of the above (e) a and b only.

5. __c__ To prove that mental patients are powerless victims, Dr. Szasz relies extensively on the analogy of (a) imprisonment of criminals (b) discrimination against minority groups (c) the institution of slavery (d) concentration camps.

6. __d__ The author cites numerous examples of how earlier societies treated the mentally ill to prove that modern notions of mental illness are (a) more humane and scientific (b) less humane and scientific (c) basically unchanged in reality when compared to the seventeenth century (d) more scientific but less humane.

7. _____ For a person to be involuntarily confined, he must be both

mentally ill and dangerous to others. Dr. Szasz feels this is wrong because (a) a patient cannot prove he is *not* dangerous against his psychiatrist's claims (b) a patient may be committed because he is only potentially violent (c) the mentally ill are no more violent than normal people (d) a patient must incriminate himself during a psychiatric examination to be diagnosed (e) all of the above.

8. __e__ Dr. Szasz concludes by emphasizing that mental illness is (a) a convenient label, a quasi-medical form of social control (b) a shameful occurrence in a supposedly enlightened society (c) an unethical way to sentence people who cannot be punished by criminal law (d) all of the above (e) a and c only.

9. Based on the evidence in the article, mark T (true), F (false), or X (not verifiable) for the inferences that follow.

A. __X__ Recent studies suggest that schizophrenia may actually be a physical, rather than a mental, disorder.

B. __F__ Normal, stable people never pretend to be sick or assume the "sick role."

C. __F__ Mental patients, under present law, can refuse to be treated or committed.

D. __T__ Normal and abnormal behavior are nearly impossible to define precisely.

E. __F__ During psychiatric examinations, the doctor and patient are considered equals.

F. __X__ There is sufficient evidence to prove that state mental hospitals are only overcrowded prisons.

G. __T__ Dr. Szasz admits that some people do have to be committed for society's protection.

H. _____ Too often people are committed merely because their relatives find them annoying or because they behave oddly.

I. __X__ Research into mental illness has been ineffective because the student begins with preconceived, biased notions of what mental illness is.

J. __F__ Violent, anti-social behavior should be handled only through mental institutions, rather than through criminal laws.

K. __T__ We need a complete reevaluation of mental illness, its definition, and treatment.

10. __e__ The tone and purpose of the article can be described as (a) technical—to instruct other psychiatrists in the proper care of mental patients (b) informative—to eliminate popular misconceptions about mental illness (c) critical—to attack

current theories of mental illness and its treatment (d) the tone and purpose are not evident (e) b and c only.

VOCABULARY

From the lettered choices, find the best definition for each vocabulary item, and mark the letter in the space provided.

1. ___N___ *involuntarily* confined
2. ___J___ a *deprivation* of liberty
3. ___E___ *incarcerates* his client
4. ___G___ *abnormality* of the body
5. ___B___ socially deviant or *inept*
6. ___H___ depression or *schizophrenia*
7. ___R___ *quasi*-medical synonym
8. ___I___ to a *hypochondriac*
9. ___M___ the *idiosyncratic* demands
10. ___P___ to *incriminate* himself
11. ___T___ *relinquish* his views
12. ___A___ the *antebellum* South
13. ___D___ *debauched* girls
14. ___K___ her husband's *disaffection*
15. ___F___ without hope of *redress*

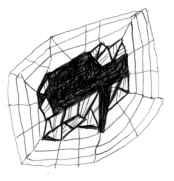

A. before the war
B. incompetent; out of place
C. annoying; provoking
D. morally corrupted; depraved
E. confines; imprisons
F. violation; illegal act
G. malformation; irregularity
H. group of severe psychic disorders involving deterioration of personality
I. person who persistently worries about health or imagined illnesses
J. denial; loss
K. estrangement; alienation of feelings; loyalty
L. asserts; states without proof
M. characterized by personal quirks or mannerisms
N. contrary to one's will or consent
O. treats; cures
P. imply guilt of; accuse
Q. correction; amends
R. not genuine; only resembling the real
S. exercising free will; choice
T. give up; surrender

COMPREHENSION   No. right _____ × 5 = _____ %

VOCABULARY   No. right _____

No. of words 2450 ÷ time in seconds _____ × 60 = _____ WPM
WPM × Comprehension % = Reading Efficiency Rate_____

TOM WOLFE

O Rotten Gotham—Sliding Down into the Behavioral Sink*

Tom Wolfe is a young journalist whose subjects on contemporary culture have ranged from Murray the K, a New York disc jockey whom he calls the "fifth Beatle," to a cult of California surfers. In this essay, he turns his attention to a more serious topic, the phenomenon of the "behavioral sink," the effects of overcrowding on all living organisms, particularly on the residents of New York City.

I just spent two days with Edward T. Hall, an anthropologist, watching thousands of my fellow New Yorkers short-circuiting themselves into hot little twitching death balls with jolts of their own adrenalin. Dr. Hall says it is overcrowding that does it. Overcrowding gets the adrenalin going, and the adrenalin gets them hyped up. And here they are, hyped up, turning bilious, nephritic, queer, autistic, sadistic, barren, batty, sloppy, hot-in-the-pants, chancred-on-the-flankers, leering, puling, numb—the usual in New York, in other words, and God knows what else. Dr. Hall has the theory that overcrowding has already thrown New York into a state of behavioral sink. Behavioral sink is a term from ethology, which is the study of how animals relate to their environment. Among animals, the sink winds up with a "population collapse" or "massive die-off." O rotten Gotham.

It got to be easy to look at New Yorkers as animals, especially looking down from some place like a balcony at Grand Central at the rush hour Friday afternoon. The floor was filled with the poor white humans, running around, dodging, blinking their eyes, making a sound like a pen full of starlings or rats or something.

"Listen to them skid," says Dr. Hall.

He was right. The poor old etiolate animals were out there skidding on their rubber soles. You could hear it once he pointed it out. They stop short to keep from hitting somebody or because they are disoriented and

* From *The Pump House Gang* (New York: Farrar, Straus & Giroux, Inc., 1968) pp. 295–309.

they suddenly stop and look around, and they skid on their rubber-sole shoes, and a screech goes up. They pour out onto the floor down the escalators from the Pan-Am Building, from 42nd Street, from Lexington Avenue, up out of subways, down into subways, railroad trains, up into helicopters—

"You can also hear the helicopters all the way down here," says Dr. Hall. The sound of the helicopters using the roof of the Pan-Am Building nearly fifty stories up beats right through. "If it weren't for this ceiling"— he is referring to the very high ceiling in Grand Central—"this place would be unbearable with this kind of crowding. And yet they'll probably never 'waste' space like this again."

They screech! And the adrenal glands in all those poor white animals enlarge, micrometer by micrometer, to the size of cantaloupes. Dr. Hall pulls a Minox camera out of a holster he has on his belt and starts shooting away at the human scurry. The Sink!

Dr. Hall has the Minox up to his eye—he is a slender man, calm, 52 years old, young-looking, an anthropologist who has worked with Navajos, Hopis, Spanish-Americans, Negroes, Trukese. He was the most important anthropologist in the government during the crucial years of the foreign aid program, the 1950's. He directed both the Point Four training program and the Human Relations Area Files. He wrote *The Silent Language* and *The Hidden Dimension,* two books that are picking up the kind of "underground" following his friend Marshall McLuhan started picking up about five years ago. He teaches at the Illinois Institute of Technology, lives with his wife, Mildred, in a high-ceilinged town house on one of the last great residential streets in downtown Chicago, Astor Street; has a grown son and daughter, loves good food, good wine, the relaxed, civilized life— but comes to New York with a Minox at his eye to record—perfect!—The Sink.

We really got down in there by walking down into the Lexington Avenue line subway stop under Grand Central. We inhaled those nice big fluffy fumes of human sweat, urine, effluvia, and sebaceous secretions. One old female human was already stroked out on the upper level, on a stretcher, with two policemen standing by. The other humans barely looked at her. They rushed into line. They bellied each other, haunch to paunch, down the stairs. Human heads shone through the gratings. The species North European tried to create bubbles of space around themselves, about a foot and a half in diameter—

"See, he's reacting against the line," says Dr. Hall.

—but the species Mediterranean presses on in. The hell with bubbles of space. The species North European resents that, this male human behind him presses forward toward the booth . . . *breathing* on him, he's disgusted, he pulls out of the line entirely, the species Mediterranean resents him for resenting it, and neither of them realizes what the hell they are getting irritable about exactly. And in all of them the old adrenals grow another micrometer.

Dr. Hall whips out the Minox. Too perfect! The bottom of The Sink.

It is the sheer overcrowding, such as occurs in the business sections of Manhattan five days a week and in Harlem, Bedford-Stuyvesant, southeast Bronx every day—sheer overcrowding is converting New Yorkers into animals in a sink pen. Dr. Hall's argument runs as follows: all animals, including birds, seem to have a built-in, inherited requirement to have a certain amount of territory, space, to lead their lives in. Even if they have all the food they need, and there are no predatory animals threatening them, they cannot tolerate crowding beyond a certain point. No more than two hundred wild Norway rats can survive on a quarter acre of ground, for example, even when they are given all the food they can eat. They just die off.

But why? To find out, ethologists have run experiments on all sorts of animals, from stickleback crabs to Sika deer. In one major experiment, an ethologist named John Calhoun put some domesticated white Norway rats in a pen with four sections to it, connected by ramps. Calhoun knew from previous experiments that the rats tend to split up into groups of ten to twelve and that the pen, therefore, would hold forty to forty-eight rats comfortably, assuming they formed four equal groups. He allowed them to reproduce until there were eighty rats, balanced between male and female, but did not let it get any more crowded. He kept them supplied with plenty of food, water, and nesting materials. In other words, all their more obvious needs were taken care of. A less obvious need—space—was not. To the human eye, the pen did not even look especially crowded. But to the rats, it was crowded beyond endurance.

The entire colony was soon plunged into a profound behavioral sink. "The sink," said Calhoun, "is the outcome of any behavioral process that collects animals together in unusually great numbers. The unhealthy connotations of the term are not accidental: a behavioral sink does act to aggravate all forms of pathology that can be found within a group."

For a start, long before the rat population reached eighty, a status hierarchy had developed in the pen. Two dominant male rats took over the two end sections, acquired harems of eight to ten females each, and forced the rest of the rats into the two middle pens. All the overcrowding took place in the middle pens. That was where the "sink" hit. The aristocrat rats at the ends grew bigger, sleeker, healthier, and more secure the whole time.

In The Sink, meanwhile, nest building, courting, sex behavior, reproduction, social organization, health—all of it went to pieces. Normally, Norway rats have a mating ritual in which the male chases the female, the female ducks down into a burrow and sticks her head up to watch the male. He performs a little dance outside the burrow, then she comes out, and he mounts her, usually for a few seconds. When The Sink set in, however, no more than three males—the dominant males in the middle sections—kept up the old customs. The rest tried everything from satyrism to homosexuality or else gave up on sex altogether. Some of the subordinate males spent all their time chasing females. Three or four might chase one female at the same time, and instead of stopping at the burrow entrance for the ritual, they would charge right in. Once mounted, they would hold on for minutes instead of the usual seconds.

Homosexuality rose sharply. So did bisexuality. Some males would mount anything—males, females, babies, senescent rats, anything. Still other males dropped sexual activity altogether, wouldn't fight and, in fact, would hardly move except when the other rats slept. Occasionally a female from the aristocrat rats' harems would come over the ramps and into the middle sections to sample life in The Sink. When she had had enough, she would run back up the ramp. Sink males would give chase up to the top of the ramp, which is to say, to the very edge of the aristocratic preserve. But one glance from one of the king rats would stop them cold and they would return to The Sink.

The slumming females from the harems had their adventures and then returned to a placid, healthy life. Females in The Sink, however, were ravaged, physically and psychologically. Pregnant rats had trouble continuing pregnancy. The rate of miscarriages increased significantly, and females started dying from tumors and other disorders of the mammary glands, sex organs, uterus, ovaries, and Fallopian tubes. Typically, their kidneys, livers, and adrenals were also enlarged or diseased or showed other signs associated with stress.

Child-rearing became totally disorganized. The females lost the interest or the stamina to build nests and did not keep them up if they did build them. In the general filth and confusion, they would not put themselves out to save offspring they were momentarily separated from. Frantic, even sadistic competition among the males was going on all around them and rendering their lives chaotic. The males began unprovoked and senseless assaults upon one another, often in the form of tail-biting. Ordinarily, rats will suppress this kind of behavior when it crops up. In The Sink, male rats gave up all policing and just looked out for themselves. The "pecking order" among males in The Sink was never stable. Normally, male rats set up a three-class structure. Under the pressure of overcrowding, however, they broke up into all sorts of unstable subclasses, cliques, packs—and constantly pushed, probed, explored, tested one another's power. Anyone was fair game, except for the aristocrats in the end pens.

Calhoun kept the population down to eighty, so that the next stage, "population collapse" or "massive die-off," did not occur. But the autopsies showed that the pattern—as in the diseases among the female rats—was already there.

The classic study of die-off was John J. Christian's study of Sika deer on

James Island in the Chesapeake Bay, west of Cambridge, Maryland. Four or five of the deer had been released on the island, which was 280 acres and uninhabited, in 1916. By 1955 they had bred freely into a herd of 280 to 300. The population density was only about one deer per acre at this point, but Christian knew that this was already too high for the Sikas' inborn space requirements, and something would give before long. For two years the number of deer remained 280 to 300. But suddenly, in 1958, over half the deer died; 161 carcasses were recovered. In 1959 more deer died and the population steadied at about 80.

In two years, two-thirds of the herd had died. Why? It was not starvation. In fact, all the deer collected were in excellent condition, with well-developed muscles, shining coats, and fat deposits between the muscles. In practically all the deer, however, the adrenal glands had enlarged by 50 per cent. Christian concluded that the die-off was due to "shock following severe metabolic disturbance, probably as a result of prolonged adrenocortical hyperactivity. . . . There was no evidence of infection, starvation, or other obvious cause to explain the mass mortality." In other words, the constant stress of overpopulation, plus the normal stress of the cold of the winter, had kept the adrenalin flowing so constantly in the deer that their systems were depleted of blood sugar and they died of shock.

Well, the white humans are still skidding and darting across the floor of Grand Central. Dr. Hall listens a moment longer to the skidding and the darting noises, and then says, "You know, I've been on commuter trains here after everyone has been through one of these rushes, and I'll tell you, there is enough acid flowing in the stomachs in every car to dissolve the rails underneath."

Just a little invisible acid bath for the linings to round off the day. The ulcers the acids cause, of course, are the one disease people have already been taught to associate with the stress of city life. But overcrowding, as Dr. Hall sees it, raises a lot more hell with the body than just ulcers. In everyday life in New York—just the usual, getting to work, working in massively congested areas like 42nd Street between Fifth Avenue and Lexington, especially now that the Pan-Am Building is set in there, working in cubicles such as those in the editorial offices at Time-Life, Inc., which Dr. Hall cites as typical of New York's poor handling of space, working in cubicles with low ceilings and, often, no access to a window, while construction crews all over Manhattan drive everybody up the Masonite wall with air-pressure generators with noises up to the boil-a-brain decibel levels, then rushing to get home, piling into subways and trains, fighting for time and for space, the usual day in New York—the whole now-normal thing keeps shooting jolts of adrenalin into the body, breaking down the body's defenses and winding up with the work-a-daddy human animal stroked out at the breakfast table with his head apoplexed like a cauliflower out of his $6.95 semi-spread Pima-cotton shirt, and nosed over into a plate of No-Kloresto egg substitute, signing off with the black thrombosis, cancer, kidney, liver, or stomach failure, and the adrenals ooze to a halt, the size of eggplants in July.

One of the people whose work Dr. Hall is interested in on this score is René Dubos at the Rockefeller Institute. Dubos's work indicates that specific organisms, such as the tuberculosis bacillus or a pneumonia virus, can seldom be considered "the cause" of a disease. The germ or virus, apparently, has to work in combination with other things that have already broken the body down in some way—such as the old adrenal hyperactivity. Dr. Hall would like to see some autopsy studies made to record the size of adrenal glands in New York, especially of people crowded into slums and people who go through the full rush-hour-work-rush-hour cycle every day. He is afraid that until there is some clinical, statistical data on how overcrowding actually ravages the human body, no one will be willing to do anything about it. Even in so obvious a thing as air pollution, the pattern is familiar. Until people can actually see the smoke or smell the sulphur or feel the sting in their eyes, politicians will not get excited about it, even though it is well known that many of the lethal substances polluting the air are invisible and odorless. For one thing, most politicians are like the aristocrat rats. They are insulated from The Sink by practically sultanic buffers—limousines, chauffeurs, secretaries, aides-de-camp, doormen, shuttered houses, high-floor apartments. They almost never ride subways, fight rush hours, much less live in the slums or work in the Pan-Am Building.

We took a cab from Grand Central to go up to Harlem, and by 48th Street we were already socked into one of those great, total traffic jams on First Avenue on Friday afternoon. Dr. Hall motions for me to survey the scene, and there they all are, humans, male and female, behind the glass of their automobile windows, soundlessly going through the torture of their own adrenalin jolts. This male over here contracts his jaw muscles so hard that they bunch up into a great cheese Danish pattern. He twists his lips, he bleeds from the eyeballs, he shouts . . . soundlessly behind glass . . . the fat corrugates on the back of his neck, his whole body shakes as he pounds the heel of his hand into the steering wheel. The female human in the car ahead of him whips her head around, she bares her teeth, she screams . . . soundlessly behind glass . . . she throws her hands up in the air, Whaddya expect me—Yah, yuh stupid—and they all sit there, trapped in their own congestion, bleeding hate all over each other, shorting out the ganglia and—goddam it—

Dr. Hall sits back and watches it all. This is it! The Sink! And where is everybody's wandering boy?

Dr. Hall says, "We need a study in which drivers who go through these rush hours every day would wear GSR bands."

GSR?

"Galvanic skin response. It measures the electric potential of the skin, which is a function of sweating. If a person gets highly nervous, his palms begin to sweat. It is an index of tension. There are some other fairly simple devices that would record respiration and pulse. I think everybody who goes through this kind of experience all the time should take his own pulse —not literally—but just be aware of what's happening to him. You can usually tell when stress is beginning to get you physically."

In testing people crowded into New York's slums, Dr. Hall would like to take it one step further—gather information on the plasma hydrocortisone level in the blood or the corticosteroids in the urine. Both have been demonstrated to be reliable indicators of stress, and testing procedures are simple.

The slums—we finally made it up to East Harlem. We drove into 101st Street, and there was a new, avant-garde little church building, the Church of the Epiphany, which Dr. Hall liked—and, next to it, a pile of rubble where a row of buildings had been torn down, and from the back windows of the tenements beyond several people were busy "airmailing," throwing garbage out the window, into the rubble, beer cans, red shreds, the No-Money-Down Eames roller stand for a TV set, all flying through the air onto the scaggy sump. We drove around some more in Harlem, and a sequence was repeated, trash, buildings falling down, buildings torn down, rubble, scaggy sumps or, suddenly, a cluster of high-rise apartment projects, with fences around the grass.

"You know what this city looks like?" Dr. Hall said. "It looks bombed out. I used to live at Broadway and 124th Street back in 1946 when I was studying at Columbia. I can't tell you how much Harlem has changed in twenty years. It looks bombed out. It's broken down. People who live in New York get used to it and don't realize how filthy the city has become. The whole thing is typical of a behaviorial sink. So is something like the Kitty Genovese case—a girl raped and murdered in the courtyard of an apartment complex and forty or fifty people look on from their apartments and nobody even calls the police. That kind of apathy and anomie is typical of the general psychological deterioration of The Sink."

He looked at the high-rise housing projects and found them mainly testimony to how little planners know about humans' basic animal requirements for space.

"Even on the simplest terms," he said, "it is pointless to build one of these blocks much over five stories high. Suppose a family lives on the fifteenth floor. The mother will be completely cut off from her children if they are playing down below, because the elevators are constantly broken in these projects, and it often takes half an hour, literally half an hour, to get the elevator if it is running. That's very common. A mother in that situation is just as much a victim of overcrowding as if she were back in the tenement block. Some Negro leaders have a bitter joke about how the white man is solving the slum problem by stacking Negroes up vertically, and there is a lot to that."

For one thing, says Dr. Hall, planners have no idea of the different space requirements of people from different cultures, such as Negroes and Puerto Ricans. They are all treated as if they were minute, compact middle-class whites. As with the Sika deer, who are overcrowded at one per acre, over-crowding is a relative thing for the human animal, as well. Each species has its own feeling for space. The feeling may be "subjective," but it is quite real.

Dr. Hall's theories on space and territory are based on the same information, gathered by biologists, ethologists, and anthropologists, chiefly, as Robert Ardrey's. Ardrey has written two well-publicized books, *African Genesis* and *The Territorial Imperative*. *Life* magazine ran big excerpts from *The Territorial Imperative*, all about how the drive to acquire territory and property and add to it and achieve status is built into all animals, including man, over thousands of centuries of genetic history, etc., and is a more powerful drive than sex. *Life*'s big display prompted Marshall McLuhan to crack, "They see this as a great historic justification for free enterprise and Republicanism. If the birds do it and the stickleback crabs do it, then it's right for man." To people like Hall and McLuhan, and Ardrey, for that matter, the right or wrong of it is irrelevant. The only thing they find inexcusable is the kind of thinking, by influential people, that isn't even aware of all this. Such as the thinking of most city planners.

"The planners always show you a bird's-eye of what they are doing," he said. "You've seen those scale models. Everyone stands around the table and looks down and says that's great. It never occurs to anyone that they are taking a bird's eye view. In the end, these projects do turn out fine, when viewed from an airplane."

As an anthropologist, Dr. Hall has to shake his head every time he hears planners talking about fully integrated housing projects for the year 1980 or 1990, as if by then all cultural groups will have the same feeling for space and will live placidly side by side, happy as the happy burghers who plan all the good clean bird's-eye views. According to his findings, the very fact that every cultural group does have its own peculiar, unspoken feeling for space is what is responsible for much of the uneasiness one group feels around the other.

It is like the North European and the Mediterranean in the subway line. The North European, without ever realizing it, tries to keep a bubble of space around himself, and the moment a stranger invades that sphere, he feels threatened. Mediterranean peoples tend to come from cultures where everyone is much more involved physically, publicly, with one another on a day-to-day basis and feels no uneasiness about mixing it up in public, but may have very different ideas about space inside the home. Even Negroes brought up in America have a different vocabulary of space and gesture from the North European Americans who, historically, have been their models, according to Dr. Hall. The failure of Negroes and whites to communicate well often boils down to things like this: some white will be interviewing a Negro for a job; the Negro's culture has taught him to show somebody you are interested by looking right at him and listening intently to what he has to say. But the species North European requires something more. He expects his listener to nod from time to time, as if to say, "Yes, keep going." If he doesn't get this nodding, he feels anxious, for fear the listener doesn't agree with him or has switched off. The Negro may learn that the white expects this sort of thing, but he isn't used to the precise kind of nodding that is customary, and so he may start overresponding, nodding like mad, and at this point the North European is liable to think he has some kind of stupid Uncle Tom on his hands, and the guy still doesn't get the job.

The whole handling of space in New York is so chaotic, says Dr. Hall, that even middle-class housing now seems to be based on the bird's-eye models for slum projects. He took a look at the big Park West Village development, set up originally to provide housing in Manhattan for families in the middle-income range, and found its handling of space very much like a slum project with slightly larger balconies. He felt the time has come to start subsidizing the middle class in New York on its own terms—namely, the kind of truly "human" spaces that still remain in brownstones.

"I think New York City should seriously consider a program of encouraging the middle-class development of an area like Chelsea, which is already starting to come up. People are beginning to renovate houses there on their own, and I think if the city would subsidize that sort of thing with tax reliefs and so forth, you would be amazed at what would result. What New York needs is a string of minor successes in the housing field, just to show everyone that it can be done, and I think the middle class can still do that for you. The alternative is to keep on doing what you're doing now, trying to lift a very large lower class up by main force almost and finding it a very slow and discouraging process."

"But before deciding how to redesign space in New York," he said, "people must first simply realize how severe the problem already is. And the handwriting is already on the wall."

"A study published in 1962," he said, "surveyed a representative sample of people living in New York slums and found only 18 per cent of them free from emotional symptoms. Thirty-eight per cent were in need of psychiatric help, and 23 per cent were seriously disturbed or incapacitated. Now, this study was published in 1962, which means the work probably went on from 1955 to 1960. There is no telling how bad it is now. In a behavioral sink, crises can develop rapidly."

Dr. Hall would like to see a large-scale study similar to that undertaken by two sociopsychologists, Chombart de Lauwe and his wife, in a French working-class town. They found a direct relationship between crowding and general breakdown. In families where people were crowded into the apartment so that there was less than 86 to 108 square feet per person, social and physical disorders doubled. That would mean that for four people the smallest floor space they could tolerate would be an apartment, say, 12 by 30 feet.

What would one find in Harlem? "It is fairly obvious," Dr. Hall wrote in *The Hidden Dimension*, "that the American Negroes and people of Spanish culture who are flocking to our cities are being very seriously stressed. Not only are they in a setting that does not fit them, but they have passed the limits of their own tolerance of stress. The United States is faced with the fact that two of its creative and sensitive peoples are in the process of being destroyed and like Samson could bring down the structure that houses us all."

Dr. Hall goes out to the airport, to go back to Chicago, and I am coming back in a cab, along the East River Drive. It is four in the afternoon, but already the damned drive is clogging up. There is a 1959 Oldsmobile just to the right of me. There are about eight people in there, a lot of pop-eyed silhouettes against a leopard-skin dashboard, leopard-skin seats— and the driver is classic. He has a mustache, sideburns down to his jaw socket, and a tattoo on his forearm like a Rossetti painting of Jane Burden Morris with her hair long. All right; it is even touching, like a postcard photo of the main drag in San Pedro, California. But suddenly Sideburns guns it and cuts in front of my cab so that my driver has to hit the brakes, and then hardly 100 feet ahead Sideburns hits a wall of traffic himself and has to hit his brakes, and then it happens. A stuffed white Angora animal, a dog, no, it's a Pekingese cat, is mounted in his rear window—as soon as he hits the brakes its *eyes* light up, Nighttown pink. To keep from ramming him, my driver has to hit the brakes again, too, and so here I am, out in an insane, jammed-up expressway at four in the afternoon, shuddering to a stop while a stuffed Pekingese grows bigger and bigger and brighter in the eyeballs directly in front of me. Jolt! Nighttown pink! Hey—that's me the adrenalin is hitting, *I* am this white human sitting in a projectile heading amid a mass of clotted humans toward a white Angora stuffed goddam leopard-dash Pekingese freaking cat—kill that damned Angora— Jolt!—got me—another micrometer on the old adrenals—

READING SELECTION 11: WOLFE, "O ROTTEN GOTHAM—
SLIDING DOWN INTO THE BEHAVIORAL SINK"

COMPREHENSION AND ANALYSIS

Do not refer to the article to answer these questions. Choose one of the items that best answers each question, and mark the letter in the space provided.

1. _____ The author defines ethology as the study of (a) the effects of overpopulation on animals (b) the relationship of animals to their environment (c) the psychology of man's environment (d) man's relationship to his environment.

2. _____ A Behavioral Sink refers to (a) overcrowding beyond a species' endurance level (b) an increase in the size of the adrenal glands (c) undue tension and stress from congestion or the frenzied pace of city life (d) a massive population collapse or die-off.

3. _____ Which groups did Wolfe *not* list as subjects for completed population experiments? (a) white Norway rats (b) Sika deer (c) residents of Harlem (d) stickleback crabs (e) French working class families.

4. _____ From this list, mark the *three* reasons that explain why animals die in an overcrowded environment: (a) their hereditary requirements for living space are violated (b) the stronger, dominant animals kill off the weak ones who are the least equipped to survive (c) the adrenalin output decreases which causes eventual death from inertia and apathy (d) overcrowding causes a lack of food and water and allows predatory animals to kill their victims (e) stress causes the adrenal glands to increase, which in turn produces metabolic disturbances, hyperactivity, loss of blood sugar, and death from shock (f) stress produces severe changes in the group's behavior which in turn produces enough physical damage to cause death.

5. _____ Aside from the problem of overpopulation in New York, residents experience their own kind of Behavioral Sink because of (a) traffic congestion (b) intolerable noise levels (c) poorly designed office space (d) the frantic competition for time and space (e) all of the above (f) only a and d.

6. _____ One can infer from the experiments with animals, as well as from the problem of human crowding, that over-population causes (a) mainly adverse physical or organic disorders (b) mainly adverse social or behavioral disorders (c) mainly

adverse psychological disorders (d) all three—adverse physical, social, and psychological disorders.

7. ——— According to Wolfe, Dr. Hall and other scientists would like
to study humans to determine (a) whether stress in combination with viruses or bacteria makes disease more likely
(b) the effects of urban life on the adrenal glands (c) the
skin responses, respiration, and pulse of rush-hour drivers
(d) the levels of plasma hydrocortisone in the blood and
corticosteroids in the urine of ghetto residents (e) all of the
above.

8. ——— Dr. Hall cited a study published in 1962 which showed that
the most tragic result of overcrowded New York slums was
(a) lack of privacy (b) the high incidence of emotional and
psychiatric disorders (c) a kind of mass anomie from poverty and unemployment (d) a disrespect for property and
an ignorance of health standards (e) none of the above.

9.   Based on the evidence in the essay, mark T (true), F (false),
or X (not verifiable) for the inferences that follow.

A. ——— The only scientists concerned with studying the
population problem are anthropologists.

B. ——— Attempts to study ghetto residents have failed
because the people resent the invasion of privacy.

C. ——— City planners have mistakenly assumed that poor
people can change their living habits quickly.

D. ——— It is probably true that Negroes and Puerto
Ricans have an inborn requirement for more space than
whites have.

E. ——— Most politicians do nothing about the problem
of overcrowding because they know that voters are indifferent.

10.   Based on the evidence in the essay, mark J (justified) or NJ
(not justified) for the conclusions that follow.

A. ——— Overpopulation affects the poor more than the
rich.

B. ——— A group's living requirements cannot be forcibly changed without causing adverse effects.

C. ——— Housing projects have failed because of insufficient recreation areas and lack of educational programs on
maintaining proper living standards.

D. ——— Many of the city's racial problems can very
likely be traced to unpleasant and overcrowded conditions
in the ghetto.

E. ——— Eventually, all city dwellers may experience a
total population collapse if the present trends are not reversed.

VOCABULARY

From the lettered choices, find the best definition for each vocabulary item, and mark the letter in the space provided.

1. _____ no *predatory* animals
2. _____ to *aggravate* all forms
3. _____ a status *hierarchy*
4. _____ a *placid,* healthy life
5. _____ *sadistic* competition
6. _____ senseless *assaults*
7. _____ the mass *mortality*
8. _____ the adrenals *ooze* to a halt
9. _____ *ravages* the body
10. _____ the *lethal* substances
11. _____ they are *insulated* from
12. _____ a new, *avant-garde* church
13. _____ apathy and *anomie*
14. _____ *subsidizing* the middle class
15. _____ to *renovate* houses

A. any group systematically arranged in graded order
B. healthy; salutary
C. death; loss of life
D. repair; renew
E. make worse; intensify
F. isolated; detached
G. calm; unruffled
H. advanced; daring in technique or style
I. annoy; provoke
J. lays waste; destroys

K. state of profound alienation
L. characterizing those who live by preying off others
M. ethics; moral virtues
N. cripples; distorts
O. violent attacks
P. tendency to enjoy inflicting pain or cruelty
Q. abasement; depravity
R. leak, seep slowly
S. supporting with a grant
T. deadly; fatal

COMPREHENSION   No. right _____ × 5 = _____ %

VOCABULARY   No. right _____

No. of words 4400 ÷ time in seconds _____ × 60 = _____ WPM
WPM × Comprehension % = Reading Efficiency Rate _____

12

MIKE THELWELL

Fish Are Jumping an' the Cotton Is High: Notes from the Mississippi Delta*

Mike Thelwell was born in Jamaica and now teaches creative writing at the University of Massachusetts. He has been active in the civil rights movement as a worker for the Student Non-violent (now National) Co-ordinating Committee and as director of the Washington office of the Mississippi Freedom Democratic Party. In this essay, he describes with sensitivity and compassion the Mississippi Delta and the almost desperate plight of its rural black inhabitants.

There is an immense mural in the Hinds County Courthouse in Jackson, Mississippi. On the wall behind the judge's bench is this mansion. White, gracefully colonnaded in a vaguely classical style, it overlooks vast fields, white with cotton which rows of darkies are busily (and no doubt, happily) picking. In the foreground to the left stands a family. The man is tall, well-proportioned with a kind of benevolent nobility shining from his handsome Anglo-Saxon face. He is immaculate in white linen and a planter's stetson as he gallantly supports his wife, who is the spirit of demure grace and elegance in her lace-trimmed gown. To the right, somewhat in the background to be sure, stands a buxom, grinning hand-kerchief-headed Aunt Jemima, everyone's good-humored black Mammy. In this mural, progress is represented by a work-gang of Negroes, building under the direction of a white overseer what appears to be an addition to the great house. Although this painting is not wired for sound—a concession, one imagines, to the dignity of the court—it requires little imagination to hear the soothing, homey sound of a spiritual wafting on the gentle wind from the cotton fields. The general tone is certainly one of orderly industry, stability, and a general contentment. "Take a good look at them," a Negro lawyer said to me, "because they are the last happy darkies you are likely to see here."

* From the *Massachusetts Review*, Volume VII, No. 2, 1966.

Actually, this mural is so inept in technique and execution, that at first flush one is inclined to mistake it for parody. But Mississippians, especially the politicians, have never demonstrated the sense of security or humor that would permit them consciously to parody themselves, although they seem incapable of escaping this in their public utterances. That this mural, consciously or not, is a burlesque of a parody of a stereotype which has never had historical or social reality goes without saying, but the mere fact that the mural exists and is intended to be taken seriously, or at least with a straight face, is equally important. Because, despite the fact that the Deep South is an area of as vast geographic, economic, and even sociological differentiation as any region in the nation, it is this plantation image of the South that persists in the sentimental subconscious of the American popular imagination. It is this image, or some derivative of it, that people tend to see when the Deep South is mentioned.

In point of fact the area in which huge cotton plantations of *Gone with the Wind* popular fame existed, and to an extent still do, is limited to a relatively small, specific geographic area. This is a narrow band of very level, fertile black earth which runs erratically south, then west from the bottom of Virginia through parts of the Carolinas, central Alabama, picks up in southwest Georgia, and runs through northwestern Mississippi and into Arkansas. This very generally describes the region known as the "Black belt," where the institutional replacements of the huge antebellum plantations exist, and where the descendants of the slaves still greatly outnumber the descendants of their masters, and where the relationship between these two groups shows only a superficial formal change. In Mississippi, this area is called the Delta, a term which, in its precise geographic meaning, refers only to the wedge of land between the Mississippi and Yazoo rivers, but which extends in popular usage to most of the northwestern quarter of the state. The area of the Delta coincides almost exactly with the Second Congressional District of Mississippi, the home of Senator Eastland, the Citizens' Council, and of the densest population of Negroes in the state. It is here, were it to exist anywhere, that one would find the image of the mural translated into reality.

What can be said about this place that will express the impact of a land so surrealistic and monotonous in its flatness that it appears unnatural, even menacing? Faulkner comes close to expressing the physical impact of the region: ". . . Crossing the last hill, at the foot of which the rich unbroken alluvial flatness began as the sea began, at the base of its cliffs, dissolving away in the unhurried rain as the sea itself would dissolve away."

This description suggests the dominant quality: a flatness like an ocean of land, but within that vast flatness, a sense of confinement, a negation of distance and space that the sea does not have. And there are the rivers

—in the east the headwaters of the river called Big Black, and sluggish tributaries, the Skuna, Yalabusha, and Yacona which flow into the Tallahatchie, which in turn meets the Sunflower to become the Yazoo which was called by the Indians the river of the dead. The Yazoo flows south and west until it meets the Mississippi at the city of Vicksburg. These rivers are, in Faulkner's words, ". . . thick, black, slow, unsunned streams almost without current, which once each year ceased to flow at all, then reversed, spreading, drowning the rich land and subsiding again leaving it even richer."

I once entered the Delta from the west, from Arkansas, over a long, narrow old bridge that seemed to go for miles over the wide and uncertain Mississippi. It was midsummer and a heat that seemed independent of the sun rose from the land. The slightest indentation in the road's surface became a shimmering sheet of water that disappeared as you approached it. The numbing repetition of cotton fields blurring in the distance wore on one's nerves and perceptions. This has been called the richest agricultural soil in the world. So it may have been, but it also is tough and demanding—no longer boundlessly fecund, it now yields its fruits only after exacting disproportionate prices in human sweat and effort. An old man told me, "For every man it enriches it kills fifty," and some folks joke that "The Delta will wear out a mule in five years, a white man in ten, and a nigger in fifteen."

For long stretches of highway where the fields are unbroken by any structure or sign of habitation, one might be in another century, except that a few things serve to place you in time. Even if tractors are not visible they are suggested by the certainty that there could not be, no, not in all the Southland, enough Negroes and mules to have planted all this. And there are the planes. On smooth strips next to the cotton these toy-like little craft, fragile and buoyant as children's kites, are tethered to the ground. The gentlest wind causes them to rear and buck against their moorings like colts. At times they are seen at absurdly low heights, skimming the top of the crops they are "dusting" against the boll weevil. They are used increasingly on the large plantations. One pilot, unnecessarily reckless, you think, crosses the highway *underneath* the telegraph wires and directly over your car. You remember, in that moment, the outdoor rally in Indianola that was bombed from one of these planes one night.

The billboards along the highway are also indices, not only of time but of place. They exhort you to support your Citizens' Council, to save America by impeaching Earl Warren, and challenge you to deny that "In Your Heart, You Know He Is Right." "Kills 'em Fast, Keeps 'em Dying," is the message of another, and it is only when you are nearly abreast of the sign that the small print reveals that an insecticide is being advertised, and nothing larger than a boll weevil is the proposed victim.

But the combination of plane and grisly advertisement reminds you of a report from Panola County, in the heart of the Delta. The SNCC worker who wrote the report is distressed by the fact that many small Negro children in that area are plagued by running, chancre-like sores on their faces or limbs. These lingering and persistent ulcers are attributed by the community to a side-effect of the "pizen" sprayed on the cotton. Children of all ages pick cotton in the Delta, and apparently this insecticide enters any exposed break in the skin and eats away at the flesh like an acid. "What can we do," the report asks, "isn't there some law? . . ." Perhaps, you think, it may be this particular brand of pesticide that "keeps 'em dying."

This is "The Heart of Dixie"—as numerous signs proclaim—the very center of the myth and the image, but what is its reality? For you right now its only reality is heat, and an almost unbearable cumulative discomfort, sweat burning your eyes, oven blasts of dusty air when you open the window, the metal edge of the window that keeps scorching your arm, and all around a punitive white glare that is painful to look into.

For the SNCC workers who are your companions the reality seems to be a certain tense caution. They work the Delta and know the road, but in curious terms. Their knowledge is of the condition of the jails, idiosyncrasies of the lawmen, and the make, model, and color of the cars they drive. They choose a route, not necessarily the most direct, but one that avoids certain towns and the jurisdictions of certain local officers. They watch the backroad intently for the car that may be the sheriff, the Highway Patrol, or one of the new radio-equipped prowl cars of the Klan. A car or pick-up truck filled with youngish white men, stripped of license tags, is always ominous, especially if they keep passing and inspecting your car. Often, because it is legal to carry openly displayed weapons here, the cars will be fitted with racks on which rifles and shotguns are conspicuous. This should not suggest that violence is an inevitable consequence of using the highways. But the tension is always present, for when a car follows you a few miles, passes you a number of times, then streaks off down the highway, you have no way of knowing their intentions. "Man, watch for a '63 Chevvy, light gray, no plate on front an' a long aerial. See anything that look like it, shout."

The tension in the car draws to a fine edge. All know the car, and the reputation of the patrolman who polices the next fifty or so miles of highway. Two of the young men in the car have been "busted"—arrested by him—and as one says, "Once is enough. That man would rather whup yore head than eat shrimp . . . an' he's a seafood lover."

This trooper is regarded with a mixture of fear and contempt by the Negroes in the county. He is reputed to stop every Negro he encounters, driving or on foot, to check their licenses and to find out where they are going and why. He is particularly fond of "interrogating" adolescent girls. As your companions talk about him a sort of grim, parodic humor attaches to him. His first statement, they say, is invariably, "All right, Nigger, pull to the side, take off your hat, spit out your gum, an' lemme see your license." It makes no difference if you are hatless and have never chewed gum. And because, for SNCC workers anyway, the response is either silent compliance or a denial that their name is Nigger, his next utterance is usually, "Dammit, Nigger, don't you know to say Sir?" But this day he does not appear.

On another occasion I saw him making an arrest. Like most things in the Delta, he verges on being a caricature, drawn with too heavy a hand. He is not tall, but blocky and heavy. His hair is thinning, his face is round, full-cheeked, cherubic save for small pale-blue eyes behind absolutely innocuous gold-rimmed glasses. In the heat his complexion could not be called merely florid, it was red, deeply and truly red. His khaki-colored military-style uniform was too tight and stained with damp circles at the armpits and the seat of his pants. His ponderous, hard-looking belly sags over the belt which slopes down almost to the junction of his thighs. Most striking are his hands: blunt, stubby, very wide—with the skin of the fingers stretched tight, like so many plump, freckled, and hairy link sausages. Two images stay with me: one of a boneless, formless, shapeless face; another of the chunky figure, standing spraddle-legged and tugging at the cloth of his trousers where it bunched in tight wrinkles between his thighs. I often wonder about this man. From all accounts he is a sadist, and one with entirely too much opportunity to indulge his impulses, but there is also present a pathetic, somehow pitiable banality about him. Besides, he represents the most easily solved of the problems in the Delta.

Driving along the highways in the Delta you occasionally pass people walking—a single man, two, or sometimes what appears to be an entire family. Usually the man is in front in overalls, or blue denim pants and jacket and with a wide-brimmed straw hat against the sun. The children follow behind in single file, with the woman usually at the end. They often carry tools, but more often cardboard boxes and newspaper-wrapped bundles tied with string. These little caravans become visible while you are some distance down the highway. If they have shoes then they walk on the hot but smooth asphalt; if they are barefoot they take to the weeds. When they hear your car approaching they step off the highway and face the road, motionless, waiting with a quality of dogged, expressionless patience to resume their plodding journey. Sometimes, but rarely, a child will wave a vague and tentative motion of the arm somewhere between greeting and dismissal, and that is the only sign. No smiles. Often you find such a group miles from any house, village, side road, or anything that might be called a town. One wonders where they sprang from, where they hope to go, and why. They are almost always— I cannot remember seeing any white families walking—Negroes.

Indianola is the capital of Sunflower County, a county distinguished because it contains the 4,800-acre plantation of U.S. Senator James O. Eastland, the state prison farm at Parchman, and is the home of Mrs.

Fannie Lou Hamer, the ex-plantation worker who has become the symbol of the resistance.

Although this is your first time there, you recognize when you have come home. When the pavement runs out—the streetlights become fewer or nonexistent and the rows of weather-textured, gray-grained clapboard shacks begin—you experience feelings of relief, almost love. This chaotic, dilapidated shantytown represents community, safety in numbers, friendship, and some degree of security after the exposed vulnerability of the highway.

Even if you wanted to, you could not escape the children of all sizes and shades who abandon their games in the dusty streets or weed-filled lots for the excitement of a new arrival. Noisy with impatient curiosity and quick vitality they surround you, shooting questions. "Is yo' a freedom fighter? Yo' come for the meeting? Is yo' gon' start up the school? Have any money?" Or proudly, "We does leafletting, yo' want us to give out any?" Big-eyed and solemn they await the answers, ignoring their elders' warnings, shouted from the porches, "Yo' all don't be botherin' that man now, heah?" They must have some bit of information so that they can go scampering importantly up the porches to inform the old people. The community grapevine.

And on the porches, the people are almost always old, at least no longer young. Frequently they are the grandparents of the children because the true parents, the generation in between, are at work, or have left the state in search of work. This gap between generations lies like a blight on every Negro community, and especially in the Delta. You see it in any kind of meeting, in the churches—any gathering of Negroes in Mississippi consists predominantly of teenagers and older people.

So the old people on the porch rock and fan and listen politely, perhaps too politely, expressing a cautious, noncommittal agreement that is somehow too glib and practiced. And their eyes flick over your shoulder to see who may be watching. It may be the Man. The quiescent, easy agreement is another aspect of the mask, and one has no right to judge the only practical response that they have fashioned, the only defense they had. For if they survived yessing the white man to death, why not you? "Thou seest this man's fall, but thou knowest not his wrasslin'."

The motion and energy, the openness and thirst to know of the children in the road forms a tragic counterpoint to the neutral caution of the porches. So short a journey and symbolically so final. The problem comes clear: to create within the community those new forms, new relationships, new alternatives that will preserve this new generation from the paralysis of fear and hopelessness.

In all the shantytowns that cluster on the edge of every Delta city and town the population steadily increases as increasing numbers of Negroes are driven off the plantations and off the land. Everywhere you get the impression of hopelessness and waiting. Large numbers of human beings in a kind of limbo, physically present and *waiting*. And what they wait for is the cotton. At planting time, chopping time, and picking time, busses and trucks come into the shantytowns before the sun is well up. The people—men, women, and children—file on in the numbers needed and are taken to the plantations where they work a twelve-hour day for $2.50 or 30 cents an hour. Each year fewer and fewer people are needed for less and less work. If the fall is unusually wet, then it is a little better. The dust becomes a black and adhesive mud miring down the ponderous cotton-picking machines. Then, for a few hectic weeks almost the entire community can find work getting the crop in before it rots. Still, denied education and the skills that would give them mobility, these waiting people are superfluous, the obsolete victims of a vicious system that depended on large numbers of human beings being kept available in case they were needed. One plantation owner in the county is quoted as saying, "Niggers went out like the mule."

One way to understand this primitive and haunting place and the gratuitous human misery that it breeds is to figure out who is in charge. Two forces rule the Delta: racism and cotton. Though the whitefolks put up a great show of control and dominance they are at the mercy of both. It is Cotton—not even Anglo-Saxon, but an immigrant from Egypt—that determines how the society is organized. And as a ruler, he is as ruthless, capricious, and sickly as the final issue of some inbred and decadent European House. Delicate, it must be protected from more vigorous hybrid weeds and from a small beetle from Mexico. Drought will burn it out, water will rot it. Extravagant and demanding, it has—in alliance with human cupidity—all but exhausted a land of once incredible fertility which must now be pampered and fertilized excessively before it will produce. This process is so expensive that the final, grudging yield must be bought by the U.S. government which alone can afford it. The federal government has a surplus at present of some 14,000,000 bales. This spring the federal cotton allotment has been reduced by one-third in the Delta. Even fewer Negroes will have work of any kind. The millionaire planter Eastland and other landlords, however, will still profit handsomely from their federal subsidy. While awaiting a federal check that runs into hundreds of thousands of dollars, the Senator will, if he maintains his average, make three speeches deploring the immorality of government handouts and creeping socialism, by which he must mean the distribution of food surpluses to starving families in his county.

At suppertime the "freedom house" is full of bustle, the local kids pass in and out, a couple of carloads of SNCC workers from other parts of the state have stopped by on their way through. The shouted laughter and greetings are loud, the exchange of news marked by a wry humor. A young man from the southwest corner around Natchez tell stories about a local judge, nicknamed by the lawyers "Necessity," because in Horace's observation "necessity knows no law." But this judge is a favorite, because his records invariably contain so much error that although he never fails to convict, the higher court hardly ever fails to reverse him. Frequently, they say, his mind wanders, and he interrupts the proceedings of his own court with, "Your Honor, I object."

Another worker just down from Sharkey County, which is very rural and contains no city of any size, complains loudly about conditions. "Even the mosquitoes threatening to leave the county. They organized and sent Johnson a telegram saying that if the Red Cross didn't come down and distribute blood, they weren't staying." He wouldn't be surprised, he adds, to find when he returned that they had gotten relief.

The meeting is called for eight, but will not really get started much before nine, as the women must feed their whitefolks their suppers before going home to feed their own families. But folks start gathering from seven. They use the time to "testify": to talk about whatever troubles their mind—mostly the absence of food, money, work, and the oppressiveness of the police. They talk about loss of credit, eviction, and voting, three things which form an inseparable unity in the Delta. Some young men are there from Washington County. They say the people over there got together and told the owners that they wouldn't work any more for thirty cents. After the evictions they started a tent city, have a "strike fund" collected in the community, and are planting a "freedom garden" for winter food. Everyone cheers. What they want is cooperation. "If they sen' busses from Washington County don't go. Be workin' gainst us if you do."

"Thass right. Nevah. Freedom."

In the clapping, shouting, stomping excitement there is brief release from tension and fear. But over it all hovers an unease, the desperation of the unanswered question, "Whut *is* we gon' do?" Winter is coming. "*Whut is we gon' do?*"

A lady wants to know. She is from "out in the rural" she says and two nights ago was awakened by what sounded like people crying. A man, his wife, and seven children were coming down the road carrying bundles. The children were crying and tears were in the man's eyes. They had no shoes. He said that that evening the owner had given him twenty dollars and told him to find someplace else. He had worked that plantation all his life, had less than three years of school, and had never been outside the county. "Ah tell yo' that man was *shock*, he wuz *confused*. I want to know, what is we gon' do?"

A portly, middle-aged lady answers her. This lady is known for a tough nerviness, insouciant streak of daring best characterized by the Yiddish word *chutzpah*, or by the sheriff in the term "smart nigger." She also has a heart condition of some fame and strategic value. (As she gets up, you recall the time she was in jail and convinced the jailer, after two minor attacks and a constant and indignant harangue, that she was quite likely to die, and that he was certain to be held responsible, if she were not allowed to have her "heart prescription." And she got it, too. You remember her, dramatically clutching her ailing heart, breathing laboriously, and accepting with a quick wink the druggist's bottle of sour mash bourbon.) There were two little boys walking down the road, she says. They were throwing stones at everything they met. They came upon a chicken which the larger boy sent off with a well-placed stone. He does the same for a pig, a cow, and a mule. Then, they come to a hornets' nest. When the bigger boy makes no effort to hit that target the other asks, "Ain't yo' gonna pop that nes'?" "Nope, sho' ain't." "Why ain't yo' gonna hit thet nes'?" the smaller asks. "Well, Ah ain't gonna hit thet nes',"— she pauses, looks at the audience, winks, shakes her head—"I ain't gonna hit thet nes' *because dey's organized.*"

They like that story, even if it is only a partial answer, saying *what,* but not *how.* So they nod agreement and murmur that "we' uns gotta be *together,* an' we gotta keep on, keeping on, no matter how mean times git." There is in these Delta communities a great spirit of closeness and cooperation. When a family is evicted, the children may be absorbed into the community, two here, one there. Or an entire family that finds itself suddenly homeless (landlords aren't required by any law to give notice) may be taken in by another family whose home is already too small. Without these traditions the folks could not have endured.

In the meetings, everything—uncertainty, fear, even desperation—finds expression, and there is comfort and sustenance in "talkin' bout hit." A preacher picks the theme up with a story of his own. "Wunst times wuz very bad fer the rabbits."

"Fo' the *whut?*" comes a chorus. The old man smiles, "Fer the *rabbits.* Yes sir, Ah tells yo' they wuz bein' hard *pressed.* Them ol' houn's wuz runnin' them *ragged.* Got so bad it seem like they couldn't git down to the fiel's to nibble a little grass. It looked like they wasn't gonna be able to make it."

"*Yeah, yeah, tellit,*" the people shake their heads in sympathy.

"They wuz *hard pressed* fo' a fack. So fin'lly, not knowin' what else to do, they calls a meetin'. Yessir, they call a *mass meetin'.*"

"*Ahuh, Freedom.*"

"So they talked an' talked, discussed it back an' fo'th, how the houn's wasn't givin' them space even to live."

"*Thass right, tell it.*"

"But they couldn't meet with no solution. It jes' didn't seem like hit was nothin' they could do." The speaker shakes his head. "No, it didn't seem like they could make it. So fin'ly thisyer ol' rabbit, he wuz ol' anyways an' fixin' to die anyhow, he sugges' that since they wuzn't making it *nohow,* they should all jes' join together an' run down to the *river an' drown theyself.*"

Everyone in the church is listening very closely. There is the beginning of a low murmur of rejection.

"But since nobody said any better, they put hit in the form of a motion, an' someone secon' hit an' they take a vote. It passed [pause] *unanimous*. So on the nex' moonlight night, they all git together jes' as the motion call fer, link they arms, and start fer the river, fo' to drown theyself. Hit wuz *a-a-l* the rabbits in the county, an' thet wuz a long line, jes' hoppin' along in the moonlight to go drown theyse'f. It wuz somethin' to see, chillun, it sho' wuz. An, yo' know, they hadn't gon far befo' they come upon the houn's, out looking fo' rabbits to chase. Them ol' houn's be so surprise at seein' all them rabbits commin' towards them steady, *they thought they time had come*. They be so surprised they turn roun' an' run so fas' they was outen the county, befo' sun come up. Rabbits had no mo' trouble."

"Talk 'bout Freedom."

There is little of subtlety or delicacy here; it is a region of extremes and nothing occurs in small measure. All is blatant, even the passing of time. Night in the Delta is sudden and intense, an almost tangible curtain of blue-purple darkness that comes abruptly, softening and muting the starkness of the day. The moon and stars seem close, shining with a bright yellow haziness like ripe fruit squashed against a blackboard. The wind is warm, very physical and furry as it moves with suggestive intimacy over your face and body. Like the sea, the Delta is at its most haunting and mysterious in the dark. The air is heavy with the ripe smell of honeysuckle and night-blooming jasmine, at once cloying and aphrodisiac. A woman's voice deep-timbered, husky, and *negro* is singing an old plaintive song of constant sorrow with new words. The song becomes part of the rich-textured night, like the tracings of the fireflies. In the restless and erotic night you believe. For the first time you can believe the blues, tales of furtive and shameful passions, madness, incest, rape, and violence. Half-intoxicated by the night, by its sensuous, textured restlessness, it is possible to believe all the secret, shameful history that everyone seems to know and none will admit except in whispers. It is easy to believe that the land is finally and irrevocably cursed. That faceless voice singing to the darkness an old song with new words, *"They say that freedom . . . is a constant sorrow."*

Just off the road stands the shack. There is a quality of wildness to the scrubby bush around it, and because it is set on short wood piles it appears to have been suddenly set down on the very top of the carpet of weeds around it. The grayed wood siding has long since warped, so that a fine line shows between each plank, giving the shack the appearance of a cage. Crossing the porch you step carefully, avoiding the rotted holes. The woman inside turns dull eyes toward where you stand in the doorway. She is sharing out a pot of greens onto tin plates. The cabin is windowless and dim but is crisscrossed by rays of light beaming through the cracks in the siding and from gaps in the roof where the shingles have rotted and blown away. This light creates patterns of light and shadow on everything in the room. As the woman watches you, at least inclines her head in your direction, her children sidle around her so that she is between them and the door. You see that there are only five—at first it seemed as though the cabin was full. None of them is dressed fully, and the two smallest are completely nude. As the mother gives you the directions back to the highway, she ladles out the greens and each child seizes a plate but stands looking at you. They are all eyes, and these eyes in thin tight faces blaze at you. The full, distended bellies of the children contrast with the emaciated limbs, big prominent joints, narrow chests in which each rib stands out, the black skin shiny, almost luminous. You cannot leave, so you stand gently talking with the mother, who answers your questions with an unnatural candor. She seems beyond pride. As you talk, she sits on a box and gives her breast to the smallest child even though he seems to be about five. This doesn't surprise you unduly for you have learned that in the Delta Negro mothers frequently do not wean their children until the next one arrives. What will substitute when there is not enough food?

You find out that she is twenty-four, was married at fifteen, had seven children but two died, the father is in Louisiana chopping pulpwood, the nearest work he could find. He sends money when he works. She lives in this abandoned cabin because it was the only rent-free house she could find after they were put off the plantation. As you leave, you see them framed in the doorway, the mother in unlaced man's shoes, one brown, the other black, holding her smallest child with the unnaturally big head and eyes.

You wonder how they are to survive the winter in a cabin with walls that cannot even keep the dust out. But this is Tallahatchie County, where 33 per cent of all Negro babies die in the first year of life, where Negroes live, grow old, and die without ever being properly examined by a doctor, and children die of cold and hunger in the winter. One reason given for the high infant mortality rate—you meet women who admit to having birthed ten children of which three or four survived—is that in this completely agricultural county, families survive the winter, when there is no work for the men, on the ten or twelve dollars the mother makes working as a cook or maid. When her time of labor approaches she dares not stop working.

But all of this was some time ago. All I know of the Delta now is what I hear. I am told that snow blanketed it in January and I am glad I was not there to see it. I am told that in December 250 families were given notice to be off the plantations by January 1st. This means that some 2,200 human beings are without home or livelihood, and none of the programs of the federal government—social security, unemployment compensation, or job retraining—affects them. By spring, they say, some 12,000 people will be homeless. I am glad I was not there to see the ghostly silent caravans trudging through the snow at the side of the highway. A lady in Sunflower County told me on the phone that families were at the tent city asking to be taken in.

Throughout the Delta the plantations are automating, driven by the dual pressure of cutting costs and the potential effect of the 1965 voting rights bill in a region with a Negro majority. The state of Mississippi wants its Negro population thinned out. They make no secret of it. Governor Johnson has said in praise of his predecessor that under Ross Barnett's regime "116,000 Negroes fled the state." And the state has still not been able to find any way to use the 1.6 million dollars appropriated by the Office of Economic Opportunity to be used to finance the distribution of surplus food in the Delta. Before this grant, it had been Mississippi's position that they simply could not afford the cost of *distributing* the free food. I am just cowardly enough to be glad I am not there to see.

READING SELECTION 12: THELWELL, "FISH ARE JUMPIN' AN' THE COTTON IS HIGH"

COMPREHENSION AND ANALYSIS

Do not refer to the article to answer these questions. Choose one of the items that best answers each question, and mark the letter in the space provided.

1. _____ At the beginning of the essay, what is significant about the mural at Jackson, Mississippi, that Thelwell describes in detail? (a) it establishes his purpose—to dispel the myth of what the mural portrays (b) it illustrates that most Americans subconsciously imagine the South with naiveté and sentimentality (c) it reveals in part the way white Southerners consider Negroes (d) it contrasts sharply and effectively with the reality—the poverty and misery—later described (e) all of the above.

2. _____ To record his observations of the Delta, Thelwell relies on (a) his own experiences while traveling with SNCC workers (b) his childhood memories of growing up in the Delta (c) his experiences working with the Mississippi Legal Aid Society (d) reports and articles he has read (e) his experiences as an adult living in the Delta.

3. _____ The author describes the land of the Delta region as (a) fruitful and abundant; easy to farm (b) once fertile but now depleted; tough and demanding to farm (c) poor, barren; impossible to farm (d) impressively beautiful and rich.

4. _____ According to the essay, civil rights workers must take precautions in traveling certain highways because of occasional harassment from (a) white sheriffs (b) Ku Klux Klan members (c) white citizens who dislike outside intruders (d) all of the above.

5. _____ From Thelwell's description of the white sheriff who stops every Negro for interrogation, it is apparent that he regards the sheriff as (a) pathetic, trite; a slightly ridiculous caricature (b) contemptuous, unmerciful, and sadistic (c) responsible and efficient (d) concerned and helpful (e) an anachronism.

6. _____ Thelwell states that the two forces which rule the Delta are (a) cotton and racism (b) poverty and injustice (c) cotton and poverty (d) racism and illiteracy (e) the law and cotton.

7. _____ The essay tries to convey the impression that most Negroes in the Delta view life with (a) naive courage and determina-

tion (b) hopelessness and desperation; with a sense of eternally "waiting" (c) idealistic hope and optimism (d) stubbornness and remarkable endurance.

8. _____ The primary economic problem which confronts Negroes in the Delta is (a) a lack of decent, inexpensive housing (b) their inability to get skilled jobs close to home (c) the seasonal nature of work in cotton fields and increasingly automated farms (d) an inadequate welfare system.

9. Based on the evidence in the essay, mark T (true), F (false), or X (not verifiable) for the inferences that follow.

A. _____ The reality of the Delta is much harsher than its mythic characteristics.

B. _____ There are more whites than blacks in the Delta.

C. _____ Civil rights workers who come to the Delta are distrusted by young, as well as old, blacks.

D. _____ Most Negroes who travel on Mississippi's highways and roads ignore the sheriffs' or state troopers' orders.

E. _____ Because there are so few doctors or hospitals, blacks seldom receive proper medical care.

F. _____ Black residents in the Delta would probably have enough food to survive on if the surplus supplies were distributed evenly.

10. Based on the evidence in the essay, mark J (justified) or NJ (not justified) for the conclusions that follow.

A. _____ Despite the civil rights laws passed during recent years, the living standards and political rights of Delta Negroes have probably changed little since the Civil War.

B. _____ Blacks in the Delta lack the most basic requirements to survive: money; useful year-round employment; decent housing, food, and medical care.

C. _____ Cotton rules Mississippi, for blacks and whites alike.

D. _____ The state of Mississippi deliberately and openly wants blacks to leave the state.

E. _____ Federally financed job retraining programs are useless in Mississippi because there is so little industry where new skills could be employed.

F. _____ Although the author was sickened by what he saw in the Delta, he is optimistic about better living conditions for blacks in the future.

VOCABULARY

From the lettered choices, find the best definition for each vocabulary item, and mark the letter in the space provided.

1. _____ *demure* grace and elegance
2. _____ his face is *cherubic*
3. _____ behind *innocuous* glasses
4. _____ a *banality* about him
5. _____ with *dogged* patience
6. _____ a *noncommittal* agreement
7. _____ agreement is too *glib*
8. _____ these people are *superfluous*
9. _____ the *gratuitous* human misery
10. _____ he is *capricious*
11. _____ with human *cupidity*
12. _____ a constant *harangue*
13. _____ all is *blatant*
14. _____ an old *plaintive* song
15. _____ tales of *furtive* passion

A. lacking cause, justification
B. mournful; expressing a sub-
   dued sadness
C. not holding to any opinion
D. silly; childish
E. merciless; unrelenting
F. harmless; inoffensive;
   undistinctive
G. pretentious
H. callous; hardened
I. greed; avarice
J. pleas; entreaties
K. triteness; hackneyed from
   overuse

L. loud speech; tirade
M. angelic; round and chubby
N. stubborn; obstinate
O. offensively obvious; tastelessly
   conspicuous
P. sedate; reserved; prim
Q. done in secret; sly
R. fickle; whimsical
S. unnecessary; irrelevant; un-
   wanted surplus
T. overly smooth, easy; done
   without thought or sincerity

COMPREHENSION No. right _____ × 5 = _____ %

VOCABULARY No. right _____

No. of words 5200 ÷ time in seconds _____ × 60 = _____ WPM
WPM × Comprehension % = Reading Efficiency Rate _____

PART III

SHORT STORIES

1

FRANK CONROY
Car Games[*]

Frank Conroy, (1936–   ), a young American writer, is best known for his autobiographical novel, Stop-Time, *a story of his own painful and confused youth in Florida and New York. This story, "Car Games," begins with seemingly unimportant details of a successful businessman's reminiscence—until one day . . .*

The first time he'd ever driven a car entirely by himself was on his twelfth birthday. His uncle, owner of a Model A, had up until then allowed him to take the wheel for only a moment or two, retaining adult control of accelerator, brake, and gears, but on July 24, 1946, in a burst of largesse induced partly by the bourbon Uncle Charlie had already drunk and partly in anticipation of the bourbon they were on their way to the liquor store to pick up, the old man had got in on the right side and pushed the boy into the driver's seat.

"You mean I can drive?" Jack asked. The scope of the sudden, entirely unexpected present overwhelmed him.

"You know the gears," Uncle Charlie said. "Let the clutch out gradual and give it gas gradual."

"Wow."

Jack first looked at everything—pedals, shift, wheel, and instruments—to make sure it was all still there. Had the car shyly withdrawn its various protuberances, turtlelike, he would not have been surprised. He rattled the shift, pushed the pedals, and began the moves he'd studied for years. The car jumped forward, lurched, and stalled.

"What did I do wrong?"

"I don't know. Let's go."

He started the engine, and the Model A took several large jumps forward. Jack was frozen at the wheel, while Uncle Charlie dipped back and forth like a rodeo rider. Scared, Jack shouted at the windshield.

* From *The New Yorker,* January 17, 1970, pp. 27–29.

"What's wrong? What should I do?"

"Keep going. You'll get the feel of it."

In fear, when he meant to push the clutch, he pushed the accelerator and the car moved smoothly up the hill toward the paved road into town.

"Good," said Uncle Charlie. "Try not to stall when you stop at the corner."

Jack was rapturously involved with the controls, adjusting the wheel, playing with the gearshift, experimenting with the gas. At the corner he simply turned to the left and accelerated.

"You should've stopped there," Uncle Charlie said, burping quietly as they shot down the hill.

"Wow," Jack said. "This is terrific."

He remembers all this as he sits waiting for his wife to bring coffee into the living room. At the age of thirty-five he finds himself daydreaming constantly, remembering his past with such clarity it's like going to the movies. The previous afternoon, while on the phone half listening to an important client, he'd gone back to the age of six, reliving a mysterious formal lunch in a country house where he'd asked for more strawberries, please. The client had undoubtedly thought he was making silent decisions. Neither does his wife know the extent of his daydreaming, putting his abstraction down to worry about the market, or perhaps, in her most fearful moments, to simple withdrawal after a hard marriage of twelve years.

She pours herself a brandy. "You want one?" She'd started drinking when the youngest child had started school.

"I'm going to sell the car."

"You are?" She becomes alert—the special, slightly masked alertness she assumes when she discovers something has been going on inside his head without her knowing it. "To get a new one?"

"No. Just sell it. Cheaper to take cabs." He lets his obviously inadequate answer hang in the air, asking her to believe that after living as if there were no tomorrow for his entire life he has suddenly got sensible. The truth is he doesn't know why he no longer wants the car—any more than he knows why he no longer wants to sleep with his wife. The car (a delicate, expensive, and painfully beautiful Aston Martin) is no fun anymore. His passion (the pleasantly dreamy sensation as his hand goes under saucy chrome to release the catch of a hood, the lump in his throat, the ridiculous lump in his throat when he walked away from the Ford convertible for the last time) is gone, as if he had once possessed a separate automobile-loving heart that has atrophied and disappeared. His lack of feeling for the Aston pains him. He wants to sell the car and become old.

"It's hard to imagine you without a car," she says. "You've always had one."

He drifts away, remembering sophomore year and the old Mercury he'd bought from Elvin Marsdale in French House. A big, top-heavy brute of a car, it had broken down constantly, forcing him to spend as much time in junkyards looking for parts as on the road. When, finally, his tuned ear told him the engine itself was dying—inexorable death, from the inside, rings totally worn, valves gasping, drive shaft groaning—he'd sold it to an ignorant graduate student at a slight profit.

For a while he had no car, and then an extraordinary piece of luck occurred—he won a Ford convertible in a lottery, a new model fully equipped with accessories, white-walls, and a St. Christopher medal. He suspected fraud, a telephone prank on the part of his classmates, but when he showed up at the rectory of an enormous church in downtown New Haven the car was indeed there, parked in an inner courtyard, and when he handed over the lottery ticket a fat priest gave him a set of keys, the registration, and a slap on the back. In the courtyard, he walked around the car several times. The chrome gleamed with almost unbearable intensity. He could see a distorted image of himself in the waxed black body, his face slipping like oil over the curved surfaces. He was afraid to touch the car. When he got in, he was afraid to start the engine. He stared at his eyes in the mirror (familiar blue—he was apparently there) for several moments before adjusting the glass. Then he pushed the seat back a couple of notches, turned the ignition, and rolled slowly out of the courtyard onto the street.

The car became his in time, of course, but it was never *entirely* his. There was an aura of the supernatural clinging to it until the end, until trade-in. In dreams the fat priest asked for it back.

He treated the car badly. The first month or two, he'd fussed over it, trying to keep it new, but as little scratches appeared here and there, as small electrical parts began to fail, as the smell of newness evaporated, he lost interest. He could not bring himself to clean the interior, and the floor gradually filled with newspapers, sweat socks, beer cans, and Howard Johnson boxes. He began racing. A continuous night-to-night contest with Herb Maglio, owner of an old but well-tuned Plymouth. At first they simply raced from Starkey and Sheen's, the college bar, to the campus line—a distance of one mile, each man balancing his desire to win against his fear and the abuse of his gearbox, each man coming up with a slightly different formula every night. Eventually the race extended into the campus itself, along a difficult route they had tacitly agreed on—through the first parking lot, down the long curve to French House, a slalom through the trees bordering College Lane, up past the tennis courts and out over the grass to the cinder track around the football field.

Jack stares at his wife without seeing her and remembers the cinder track. Cold autumn air at 3 A.M. The lights of the cars were shut down for secrecy, and starlight, moonlight, points of window light from distant dorms needled the air. He stood beer-drunk with beer-drunk Herb at the edge of the grass and waited for his eyes to adjust to the dark. The smell of hot oil. A faint tang from swollen, burnt brake linings. In the open car he gunned the engine, pumping gas like an organist pumping his bellows. Leaning back, half standing in the seat, he threw a beer can into the night sky. When it hit the ground the engines roared and cinders flew. Wind swirled around his head. In the darkness the cinder track was absolutely black. An unearthly, perfect black. Follow the black.

He stands up abruptly, walks to the center of the room, and looks around.

His wife watches him, and after a moment asks, "What's wrong?"

He feels himself to be in some extraordinary state. The room around him is particularly vivid, each object clear and hard in space, the colors glowing, all of it entirely familiar, and yet he is no longer part of it, or, more precisely, at once part of it and not part of it. Simultaneously a sense of great power fills him. Profound changes occur in the dark parts of his brain, as if the lobes, like sliding blocks in a wooden puzzle, are gliding momentously into new positions and new alignments. He walks out of the room and out of the house.

At the entrance to the East River Drive, a dark-blue Chrysler passes on the wrong side, cutting him off, and, rocking slightly, disappears up the ramp.

"Stupid bastard," he says as he negotiates the turn. "Goddam bubble-head." He allows himself to rave at other drivers, insulting them as he never insults real people. He plays a game, spewing out a stream of oaths as he drives, ridiculing everyone on the road. He feels justified, since he knows he is a better driver than any of them.

He accelerates off the ramp onto the highway and catches a glimpse of the blue Chrysler crossing lanes on a curve up ahead. The Aston pulls him as he presses the gas pedal half an inch closer to the floor. Sweeping through the slower traffic, he changes lanes smoothly and carefully. The speedometer needle rests at seventy and the engine purls.

One night, after a light snowfall, he and Maglio had taken their cars down to the new, unfinished parking lot behind the college Field House. At the brink of a gentle hill they stared down at a perfectly flat, unbroken surface the size of two football fields, a smooth, unmarked coating of snow over the virgin asphalt.

"Beautiful!" he shouted across to the other car.

"You go first," Herb yelled back. "Break the seal."

Jack reached up and opened the roof clamps. With his other hand he pulled the switch, and the power top folded into itself and disappeared behind the back seat. He turned up the collar of his jacket and started down the hill, timing his acceleration carefully so that the rear wheels maintained traction. He entered the lot on a straight line. Nearing the center, he turned the wheel to the left and pressed the gas gently. The rear wheels broke loose, slipping to the right, and he steered into the skid. As the car stabilized, drifting perfectly over the snow at an angle of fifteen degrees, he repeated the same movements in reverse, swinging the car slowly through zero and over to fifteen degrees in the other direction. Approaching the edge of the lot, he pressed the gas to the floor, spun the steering wheel hard, and turned the car completely around in a four-wheel skid. For several moments he went backward, in a straight line, until the rear wheels collected enough traction to stop the car. His eye ran back along the elegant curves of his tracks in the snow to Herb's Plymouth, which was just starting down the incline. Jack slid out from under the wheel, raised himself up, and sat on the back of the seat, staring through the snow-flecked air, listening to the faint rodeo yells of his skylarking friend.

After a mile, he catches up with the Chrysler. The woman behind the wheel has black hair falling to her shoulders and her pale face is distorted. Alone in the car, she talks and gesticulates as if in the midst of a conversation. She drives abstractedly, the big car drifting back and forth across the wide road. Jack pulls the Aston into the lane beside her, and she glances over quickly. She accelerates suddenly, but he is prepared and keeps up with her. At eighty miles an hour, they pass a string of cars, Jack on the outside, the woman on the inside. As the speed increases he feels a calmness come over his soul.

They'd played tag in the snow, spinning the cars around, slipping this way and that, Herb trying to touch bumpers, Jack trying to get away, their eyes blurred from the wind and the tears of their laughter. What times they'd had! What easy times, gliding, gently gliding over the snow like a pair of skaters.

As the road temporarily narrows to two lanes where some construction is going on, the woman in the Chrysler refuses to move over. He begins to pass, but she moves closer to him and he is forced to touch the brakes. Side by side, they enter the narrow part of the road. Before he can pull in behind her, he has struck two rubber pylons, sending them high into the air, across the divider into the oncoming traffic. He is vaguely aware of workmen in the closed lane dropping their tools and starting for the barrier, but he is already past them. The light is beginning to fail as, on the other side of the city, the sun sets.

He pulls up beside her again, at ninety miles an hour. She is no longer talking to herself, but sits rigidly, staring straight ahead. She drifts into his lane but he does not give ground. The automobiles touch, side to side, with a soft sound like a tin can crushed underfoot. Her mouth opens in a silent O of surprise. He pulls away for a moment, and then bumps her side again, somewhat harder than before. Pointlessly, mysteriously, she begins to blow the Chrysler's horn. When she decides to steer into him, she starts the move so clumsily, so obviously, he is ready, and with a hard punch of his brakes he slows abruptly and she drifts into his lane, directly in front of him.

Ahead there is only a single clear lane. They enter at ninety miles an hour, the Aston two feet behind the Chrysler. Jack glances at the tachometer, shifts down into third, and closes the distance between the two cars. The slight jar as the bumpers touch is almost imperceptible. He feels a remote, faraway pain from his clamped teeth. He presses the gas to the floor and listens to the Aston's big engine open up.

He pushes the Chrysler up to ninety-five, and then to a hundred before the first curve. She plows through a low iron railing and bounces high into the air. He follows her through the hole and for a split second they travel along the pedestrian walkway. Suddenly, as if a tire had blown, the Chrysler swerves, crashes through the high railing, and sails out into the open air over the river.

That is the last image he sees—the big blue Chrysler suspended magically in the air above the black water, the woman inside comically prim, motionless as a mannequin. In another moment he would laugh, but the Aston strikes a concrete abutment and his head goes through the windshield.

Conroy, "Car Games"

QUESTIONS FOR COMPREHENSION AND DISCUSSION

1. What role have cars played in Jack's life?
2. From the author's brief description of Jack and his wife, what do you know about their married life?
3. Why does Jack daydream? What do his flashbacks to his youth suggest?
4. Explain this passage: "He feels himself to be in some extraordinary state. The room around him is particularly vivid, each object clear and hard in space, the colors glowing, all of it entirely familiar, and yet he is no longer part of it, or, more precisely, at once part of it and not part of it."
5. Why does Jack ridicule other drivers as he plays his "game"? Why is the "game" metaphor both ironic and tragic?
6. As Jack drives to his death, what is he thinking about?
7. What is the meaning (and the effect) of the ending?

VOCABULARY

From the lettered choices, find the best definition for each vocabulary item, and mark the letter in the space provided.

1. _____ its various *protuberances*
2. _____ was *rapturously* involved
3. _____ remembering with *clarity*
4. _____ putting his *abstraction* down
5. _____ an *aura* of the supernatural
6. _____ the smell of newness *evaporated*
7. _____ they had *tacitly* agreed
8. _____ light *needled* the air
9. _____ he *negotiates* a turn
10. _____ to *rave* at others
11. _____ *spewing* out a stream
12. _____ the *virgin* asphalt
13. _____ she talks and *gesticulates*
14. _____ the jar is *imperceptible*
15. _____ the woman comically *prim*

A. silently; implied
B. ecstatically; carried away by emotion
C. discharging; vomiting
D. daydreaming; reverie
E. talk wildly, as in a delirium
F. maneuvers; clears successfully
G. things that bulge, stick out
H. pure; sexually naive
I. turned to, converted to vapor
J. arranges by discussion and settlement
K. clearness; lucidity
L. affectedly proper; stiff
M. annoyed; badgered
N. distinctive air, atmosphere
O. an impractical or general idea
P. very slight; barely noticeable

Q. pierced; cut through

R. makes gestures in an excited manner

S. untouched; unused

T. disappeared; vanished

VOCABULARY   No. right _____

JAMES THURBER

*The Greatest Man in the World**

James Thurber (1894–1961), the American humorist and artist, is best known for his portrayals of humorous, charming characters. In this story, "The Greatest Man in the World," Thurber satirizes the power of the press to transform a sneering, boorish young man, Jack Smurch, into a perfect American "good-guy" hero, until Smurch's violations of propriety become nearly a national disaster.

Looking back on it now, from the vantage point of 1950, one can only marvel that it hadn't happened long before it did. The United States of America had been, ever since Kitty Hawk, blindly constructing the elaborate petard by which, sooner or later, it must be hoist. It was inevitable that some day there would come roaring out of the skies a national hero of insufficient intelligence, background, and character successfully to endure the mounting orgies of glory prepared for aviators who stayed up a long time or flew a great distance. Both Lindbergh and Byrd, fortunately for national decorum and international amity, had been gentlemen; so had our other famous aviators. They wore their laurels gracefully, withstood the awful weather of publicity, married excellent women, usually of fine family, and quietly retired to private life and the enjoyment of their varying fortunes. No untoward incidents, on a worldwide scale, marred the perfection of their conduct on the perilous heights of fame. The exception to the rule was, however, bound to occur and it did, in July, 1937, when Jack ("Pal") Smurch, erstwhile mechanic's helper in a small garage in Westfield, Iowa, flew a second-hand, single-motored Bresthaven Dragon-Fly III monoplane all the way around the world, without stopping.

Never before in the history of aviation had such a flight as Smurch's ever been dreamed of. No one had even taken seriously the weird floating

* From *The Middle-Aged Man on the Flying Trapeze* (New York: Harper & Row, Publishers, 1945), pp. 154–160.

auxiliary gas tanks, invention of the mad New Hampshire professor of astronomy, Dr. Charles Lewis Gresham, upon which Smurch placed full reliance. When the garage worker, a slightly built, surly, unprepossessing young man of twenty-two, appeared at Roosevelt Field in early July, 1937, slowly chewing a great quid of scrap tobacco, and announced, "Nobody ain't seen no flyin' yet," the newspapers touched briefly and satirically upon his projected twenty-five-thousand-mile flight. Aëronautical and automotive experts dismissed the idea curtly, implying that it was a hoax, a publicity stunt. The rusty, battered, second-hand plane wouldn't go. The Gresham auxiliary tanks wouldn't work. It was simply a cheap joke.

Smurch, however, after calling on a girl in Brooklyn who worked in the flap-folding department of a large paper-box factory, a girl whom he later described as his "sweet patootie," climbed nonchalantly into his ridiculous plane at dawn of the memorable seventh of July, 1937, spit a curve of tobacco juice into the still air, and took off, carrying with him only a gallon of bootleg gin and six pounds of salami.

When the garage boy thundered out over the ocean the papers were forced to record, in all seriousness, that a mad, unknown young man—his name was variously misspelled—had actually set out upon a preposterous attempt to span the world in a rickety, one-engined contraption, trusting to the long-distance refuelling device of a crazy schoolmaster. When, nine days later, without having stopped once, the tiny plane appeared above San Francisco Bay, headed for New York, spluttering and choking, to be sure, but still magnificently and miraculously aloft, the headlines, which long since had crowded everything else off the front page—even the shooting of the Governor of Illinois by the Vileti gang—swelled to unprecedented size, and the news stories began to run to twenty-five and thirty columns. It was noticeable, however, that the accounts of the epoch-making flight touched rather lightly upon the aviator himself. This was not because facts about the hero as a man were too meagre, but because they were too complete.

Reporters, who had been rushed out to Iowa when Smurch's plane was first sighted over the little French coast town of Serly-le-Mer, to dig up the story of the great man's life, had promptly discovered that the story of his life could not be printed. His mother, a sullen short-order cook in a shack restaurant on the edge of a tourists' camping ground near Westfield, met all inquiries as to her son with an angry "Ah, the hell with him; I hope he drowns." His father appeared to be in jail somewhere for stealing spotlights and laprobes from tourists' automobiles; his young brother, a weak-minded lad, had but recently escaped from the Preston, Iowa, Reformatory and was already wanted in several Western towns for the theft of money-order blanks from post offices. These alarming discoveries were still piling up at the very time that Pal Smurch, the greatest hero of the twentieth century, blear-eyed, dead for sleep, half-starved, was piloting his crazy junk-heap high above the region in which the lamentable story of his private life was being unearthed, headed for New York and a greater glory than any man of his time had ever known.

The necessity for printing some account in the papers of the young man's career and personality had led to a remarkable predicament. It was of course impossible to reveal the facts, for a tremendous popular feeling in favor of the young hero had sprung up, like a grass fire, when he was halfway across Europe on his flight around the globe. He was, therefore, described as a modest chap, taciturn, blond, popular with his friends, popular with girls. The only available snapshot of Smurch, taken at the wheel of a phony automobile in a cheap photo studio at an amusement park, was touched up so that the little vulgarian looked quite handsome. His twisted leer was smoothed into a pleasant smile. The truth was, in this way, kept from the youth's ecstatic compatriots; they did not dream that the Smurch family was despised and feared by its neighbors in the obscure Iowa town, nor that the hero himself, because of numerous unsavory exploits, had come to be regarded in Westfield as a nuisance and a menace. He had, the reporters discovered, once knifed the principal of his high school—not mortally, to be sure, but he had knifed him; and on another occasion, surprised in the act of stealing an altar-cloth from a church, he had bashed the sacristan over the head with a pot of Easter lilies; for each of these offences he had served a sentence in the reformatory.

Inwardly, the authorities, both in New York and in Washington, prayed that an understanding Providence might, however awful such a thing seemed, bring disaster to the rusty, battered plane and its illustrious pilot, whose unheard-of flight had aroused the civilized world to hosannas of hysterical praise. The authorities were convinced that the character of the renowned aviator was such that the limelight of adulation was bound to reveal him to all the world as a congenital hooligan mentally and morally unequipped to cope with his own prodigious fame. "I trust," said the Secretary of State, at one of many secret Cabinet meetings called to consider the national dilemma, "I trust that his mother's prayer will be answered," by which he referred to Mrs. Emma Smurch's wish that her son might be drowned. It was, however, too late for that—Smurch had leaped the Atlantic and then the Pacific as if they were millponds. At three minutes after two o'clock on the afternoon of July 17, 1937, the garage boy brought his idiotic plane into Roosevelt Field for a perfect three-point landing.

It had, of course, been out of the question to arrange a modest little reception for the greatest flier in the history of the world. He was received at Roosevelt Field with such elaborate and pretentious ceremonies as rocked the world. Fortunately, however, the worn and spent hero promptly swooned, had to be removed bodily from his plane, and was spirited from the field without having opened his mouth once. Thus he did not jeopardize the dignity of this first reception, a reception illumined by the presence of the Secretaries of War and the Navy, Mayor Michael J. Moriarity of New York, the Premier of Canada, Governors Fanniman, Groves, McFeely, and Critchfield, and a brilliant array of European diplomats. Smurch did not, in fact, come to in time to take part in the gigantic hullabaloo arranged at City Hall for the next day. He was rushed to a secluded nursing home and confined to bed. It was nine days before he was able to get up, or to be more exact, before he was permitted to get up. Meanwhile the greatest minds in the country, in solemn assembly, had arranged a secret conference of city, state, and government officials, which Smurch was to attend for the purpose of being instructed in the ethics and behavior of heroism.

On the day that the little mechanic was finally allowed to get up and dress and, for the first time in two weeks, took a great chew of tobacco, he was permitted to receive the newspapermen—this by way of testing him out. Smurch did not wait for questions. "Youse guys," he said—and the *Times* man winced—"youse guys can tell the cock-eyed world dat I put it over on Lindbergh, see? Yeh—an' made an ass o' them two frogs." The "two frogs" was a reference to a pair of gallant French fliers who, in attempting a flight only halfway round the world, had, two weeks before, unhappily been lost at sea. The *Times* man was bold enough, at this point, to sketch out for Smurch the accepted formula for interviews in cases of this kind; he explained that there should be no arrogant statements belittling the achievements of other heroes, particularly heroes of foreign nations. "Ah, the hell with that," said Smurch. "I did it, see? I did it, an' I'm talkin' about it." And he did talk about it.

None of this extraordinary interview was, of course, printed. On the contrary, the newspapers, already under the disciplined direction of a secret directorate created for the occasion and composed of statesmen and editors, gave out to a panting and restless world that "Jacky," as he had been arbitrarily nicknamed, would consent to say only that he was very happy and that anyone could have done what he did. "My achievement has been, I fear, slightly exaggerated," the *Times* man's article had him protest, with a modest smile. These newspaper stories were kept from the hero, a restriction which did not serve to abate the rising malevolence of his temper. The situation was, indeed, extremely grave, for Pal Smurch was, as he kept insisting, "rarin' to go." He could not much longer be kept from a nation clamorous to lionize him. It was the most desperate crisis the United States of America had faced since the sinking of the *Lusitania*.

On the afternoon of the twenty-seventh of July, Smurch was spirited away to a conference-room in which were gathered mayors, governors, government officials, behaviorist psychologists, and editors. He gave them each a limp, moist paw and a brief unlovely grin. "Hah ya?" he said. When Smurch was seated, the Mayor of New York arose and, with obvious pessimism, attempted to explain what he must say and how he must act when presented to the world, ending his talk with a high tribute to the hero's courage and integrity. The Mayor was followed by Governor Fanniman of New York, who, after a touching declaration of faith, introduced Cameron Spottiswood, Second Secretary of the American Embassy in Paris, the gentleman selected to coach Smurch in the amenities of public ceremonies. Sitting in a chair, with a soiled yellow tie in his hand and his shirt open at the throat, unshaved, smoking a rolled cigarette, Jack Smurch listened with a leer on his lips. "I get ya, I get ya," he cut in, nastily. "Ya want me to ack like a softy, huh? Ya want me to ack like that —— —— baby-faced Lindbergh, huh? Well, nuts to that, see?" Everyone took in his breath sharply; it was a sigh and a hiss. "Mr. Lindbergh," began a United States Senator, purple with rage, "and Mr. Byrd—" Smurch, who was paring his nails with a jackknife, cut in again. "Byrd!" he exclaimed. "Aw fa God's sake, dat big—" Somebody shut off his blasphemies with a sharp word. A newcomer had entered the room. Everyone stood up, except Smurch, who, still busy with his nails, did not even glance up. "Mr. Smurch," said someone sternly, "the President of the United States!" It had been thought that the presence of the Chief Executive might have a chastening effect upon the young hero, and the former had been, thanks to the remarkable coöperation of the press, secretly brought to the obscure conference-room.

A great, painful silence fell. Smurch looked up, waved a hand at the President. "How ya comin'?" he asked, and began rolling a fresh cigarette. The silence deepened. Someone coughed in a strained way. "Geez, it's hot, ain't it?" said Smurch. He loosened two more shirt buttons, revealing a hairy chest and the tattooed word "Sadie" enclosed in a stencilled heart. The great and important men in the room, faced by the most serious crisis in recent American history, exchanged worried frowns. Nobody seemed to know how to proceed. "Come awn, come awn," said Smurch. "Let's get the hell out of here! When do I start cuttin' in on de parties, huh? And what's they goin' to be *in* it?" He rubbed a thumb and forefinger together meaningly. "Money!" exclaimed a state senator, shocked, pale. "Yeh, money," said Pal, flipping his cigarette out of a window. "An' big money." He began rolling a fresh cigarette. "Big money," he repeated, frowning over the rice paper. He tilted back in his chair, and leered at each gentleman, separately, the leer of an animal that knows its power, the leer of a leopard loose in a bird-and-dog shop. "Aw fa God's sake, let's get some place where it's cooler," he said. "I been cooped up plenty for three weeks!"

Smurch stood up and walked over to an open window, where he stood staring down into the street, nine floors below. The faint shouting of newsboys floated up to him. He made out his name. "Hot dog!" he cried, grinning, ecstatic. He leaned out over the sill. "You tell 'em, babies!" he shouted down. "Hot diggity dog!" In the tense little knot of men standing behind him, a quick, mad impulse flared up. An unspoken word of appeal, of command, seemed to ring through the room. Yet it was deadly silent. Charles K. L. Brand, secretary to the Mayor of New York City, happened to be standing nearest Smurch; he looked inquiringly at the President of the United States. The President, pale, grim, nodded shortly. Brand, a tall, powerfully built man, once a tackle at Rutgers, stepped forward, seized the greatest man in the world by his left shoulder and the seat of his pants, and pushed him out the window.

"My God, he's fallen out the window!" cried a quick-witted editor.

"Get me out of here!" cried the President. Several men sprang to his side and he was hurriedly escorted out of a door toward a side-entrance of the building. The editor of the Associated Press took charge, being used to such things. Crisply he ordered certain men to leave, others to stay; quickly he outlined a story which all the papers were to agree on, sent two men to the street to handle that end of the tragedy, commanded a Senator to sob and two Congressmen to go to pieces nervously. In a word, he skillfully set the stage for the gigantic task that was to follow, the task of breaking to a grief-stricken world the sad story of the untimely, accidental death of its most illustrious and spectacular figure.

The funeral was, as you know, the most elaborate, the finest, the solemnest, and the saddest ever held in the United States of America. The monument in Arlington Cemetery, with its clean white shaft of marble and the simple device of a tiny plane carved on its base, is a place for pilgrims, in deep reverence, to visit. The nations of the world paid lofty tributes to little Jacky Smurch, America's greatest hero. At a given hour there were two minutes of silence throughout the nation. Even the inhabitants of the small, bewildered town of Westfield, Iowa, observed this touching ceremony; agents of the Department of Justice saw to that. One of them was especially assigned to stand grimly in the doorway of a little shack restaurant on the edge of the tourists' camping ground just outside the town. There, under his stern scrutiny, Mrs. Emma Smurch bowed her head above two hamburger steaks sizzling on her grill—bowed her head and turned away, so that the Secret Service man could not see the twisted, strangely familiar, leer on her lips.

Name _____   Date _____

Thurber, "The Greatest Man in the World"

1. Why is Smurch not a "proper" hero for the American public? By implication, what does Thurber reveal about what Americans expect in their heroes?
2. What does Thurber suggest about the role of the press in handling spectacular events? How does the press finally describe Smurch's feat?
3. Why do the country's leaders decide that Smurch's feat is a national disaster? How do they solve the situation?
4. What customs and practices in American society does Thurber poke fun at in his story?

VOCABULARY

From the lettered choices, find the best definition for each vocabulary item, and mark the letter in the space provided.

1. __d__ for national *decorum*
2. __m__ international *amity*
3. ____ no *untoward* incidents
4. ____ *perilous* heights of fame
5. ____ *unprepossessing* young man
6. __b__ climbed *nonchalantly*
7. __k__ the *lamentable* story
8. __f__ his twisted *leer*
9. __o__ the *obscure* Iowa town
10. ____ limelight of *adulation*
11. ____ his *prodigious* fame
12. __L__ the *Times* man *winced*
13. __E__ the *malevolence* of his temper
14. __I__ to *lionize* him
15. ____ a *chastening* effect

A. extravagant, hypocritical praise
B. coolly; casually
C. sullenly; morosely
D. seemliness; propriety
E. evil; malice
F. a sly look expressing lewd desire or malicious intent
G. good nature; generosity
H. hazardous; dizzying
I. treat as a celebrity
J. regrettable; distressing
K. mournful; plaintive
L. flinched; shrank back from
M. peaceful relations; good will
N. publicity; fame
O. without distinction, fame; unknown

P. vast; extraordinary in size
Q. unseemly; uncouth
R. giving an unfavorable
impression

S. moderating; refining
T. brutalize; victimize

VOCABULARY   No. right ———

JEAN PAUL SARTRE

The Wall*

*Jean Paul Sartre (1905–   ), one of Europe's great existential philoso-
phers, has written many plays, novels, critical essays and philosophical
works. In this famous story set in Spain during the Revolution, Pablo
Ibbieta is faced with the horror of execution, and as the story progresses,
he recognizes the futility and the meaningless nature of human existence.*

They pushed us into a large white room and my eyes began to blink
because the light hurt them. Then I saw a table and four fellows seated
at the table, civilians, looking at some papers. The other prisoners were
herded together at one end and we were obliged to cross the entire room
to join them. There were several I knew, and others who must have
been foreigners. The two in front of me were blond with round heads.
They looked alike. I imagine they were French. The smaller one kept
pulling at his trousers, out of nervousness.

This lasted about three hours. I was dog-tired and my head was empty.
But the room was well-heated, which struck me as rather agreeable; we
had not stopped shivering for twenty-four hours. The guards led the
prisoners in one after another in front of the table. Then the four fellows
asked them their names and what they did. Most of the time that was all
—or perhaps from time to time they would ask such questions as: "Did
you help sabotage the munitions?" or, "Where were you on the morning
of the ninth and what were you doing?" They didn't even listen to the
replies, or at least they didn't seem to. They just remained silent for a
moment and looked straight ahead, then they began to write. They asked
Tom if it was true he had served in the International Brigade. Tom
couldn't say he hadn't because of the papers they had found in his jacket.

* Trans. Marie Jolas, from *Bedside Book of Famous French Stories*, ed. Belle
Becker and Robert N. Linscott (New York: Random House, Inc., 1945), pp. 397–
414.

They didn't ask Juan anything, but after he told them his name, they wrote for a long while.

"It's my brother José who's the anarchist," Juan said. "You know perfectly well he's not here now. I don't belong to any party. I never did take part in politics." They didn't answer.

Then Juan said, "I didn't do anything. And I'm not going to pay for what the others did."

His lips were trembling. A guard told him to stop talking and led him away. It was my turn.

"Your name is Pablo Ibbieta?"

I said yes.

The fellow looked at his papers and said, "Where is Ramon Gris?"

"I don't know."

"You hid him in your house from the sixth to the nineteenth."

"I did not."

They continued to write for a moment and the guards led me away. In the hall, Tom and Juan were waiting between two guards. We started walking. Tom asked one of the guards, "What's the idea?" "How do you mean?" the guard asked. "Was that just the preliminary questioning, or was that the trial?" "That was the trial," the guard said. "So now what? What are they going to do with us?" The guard answered drily, "The verdict will be told you in your cell."

In reality, our cell was one of the cellars of the hospital. It was terribly cold there because it was very drafty. We had been shivering all night long and it had hardly been any better during the day. I had spent the preceding five days in a cellar in the archbishop's palace, a sort of dungeon that must have dated back to the Middle Ages. There were lots of prisoners and not much room, so they housed them just anywhere. But I was not homesick for my dungeon. I hadn't been cold there, but I had been alone, and that gets to be irritating. In the cellar I had company. Juan didn't say a word; he was afraid, and besides, he was too young to have anything to say. But Tom was a good talker and knew Spanish well.

In the cellar there were a bench and four straw mattresses. When they led us back we sat down and waited in silence. After a while Tom said, "Our goose is cooked."

"I think so too," I said. "But I don't believe they'll do anything to the kid."

Tom said, "They haven't got anything on him. He's the brother of a fellow who's fighting, and that's all."

I looked at Juan. He didn't seem to have heard.

Tom continued, "You know what they do in Saragossa? They lay the guys across the road and then they drive over them with trucks. It was a Moroccan deserter who told us that. They say it's just to save ammunition."

I said, "Well, it doesn't save gasoline."

I was irritated with Tom; he shouldn't have said that.

He went on, "There are officers walking up and down the roads with their hands in their pockets, smoking, and they see that it's done right. Do you think they'd put 'em out of their misery? Like hell they do. They just let 'em holler. Sometimes as long as an hour. The Moroccan said the first time he almost puked."

"I don't believe they do that here," I said, "unless they really are short of ammunition."

The daylight came in through four air vents and a round opening that had been cut in the ceiling, to the left, and which opened directly onto the sky. It was through this hole, which was ordinarily closed by means of a trapdoor, that they unloaded coal into the cellar. Directly under the hole, there was a big pile of coal dust; it had been intended for heating the hospital, but at the beginning of the war they had evacuated the patients and the coal had stayed there unused; it even got rained on from time to time, when they forgot to close the trapdoor.

Tom started to shiver. "God damn it," he said, "I'm shivering. There, it is starting again."

He rose and began to do gymnastic exercises. At each movement, his shirt opened and showed his white, hairy chest. He lay down on his back, lifted his legs in the air and began to do the scissors movement. I watched his big buttocks tremble. Tom was tough, but he had too much fat on him. I kept thinking that soon bullets and bayonet points would sink into that mass of tender flesh as though it were a pat of butter.

I wasn't exactly cold, but I couldn't feel my shoulders or my arms. From time to time, I had the impression that something was missing and I began to look around for my jacket. Then I would suddenly remember they hadn't given me a jacket. It was rather awkward. They had taken our clothes to give them to their own soldiers and had left us only our shirts and these cotton trousers the hospital patients wore in mid-summer. After a moment, Tom got up and sat down beside me, breathless.

"Did you get warmed up?"

"Damn it, no. But I'm all out of breath."

Around eight o'clock in the evening, a Major came in with two falangists.

"What are the names of those three over there?" he asked the guard.

"Steinbock, Ibbieta and Mirbal," said the guard.

The Major put on his glasses and examined his list.

"Steinbock—Steinbock . . . Here it is. You are condemned to death. You'll be shot tomorrow morning."

He looked at his list again.

"The other two, also," he said.

"That's not possible," said Juan. "Not me."

The Major looked at him with surprise. "What's your name?"

"Juan Mirbal."

"Well, your name is here," said the Major, "and you're condemned to death."

"I didn't do anything," said Juan.

The Major shrugged his shoulders and turned toward Tom and me.

"You are both Basque?"

"No, nobody's Basque."

He appeared exasperated.

"I was told there were three Basques. I'm not going to waste my time running after them. I suppose you don't want a priest?"

We didn't even answer.

Then he said, "A Belgian doctor will be around in a little while. He has permission to stay with you all night."

He gave a military salute and left.

"What did I tell you?" Tom said. "We're in for something swell."

"Yes," I said. "It's a damned shame for the kid."

I said that to be fair, but I really didn't like the kid. His face was too refined and it was disfigured by fear and suffering, which had twisted all his features. Three days ago, he was just a kid with a kind of affected manner some people like. But now he looked like an aging fairy, and I thought to myself he would never be young again, even if they let him go. It wouldn't have been a bad thing to show him a little pity, but pity makes me sick, and besides, I couldn't stand him. He hadn't said anything more, but he had turned gray. His face and hands were gray. He sat down again and stared, round-eyed, at the ground. Tom was good-hearted and tried to take him by the arm, but the kid drew himself away violently and made an ugly face. "Leave him alone," I said quietly. "Can't you see he's going to start to bawl?" Tom obeyed regretfully. He would have liked to console the kid; that would have kept him occupied and he wouldn't have been tempted to think about himself. But it got on my nerves. I had never thought about death, for the reason that the question had never come up. But now it had come up, and there was nothing else to do but think about it.

Tom started talking. "Say, did you ever bump anybody off?" he asked me. I didn't answer. He started to explain to me that he had bumped off six fellows since August. He hadn't yet realized what we were in for, and I saw clearly he didn't *want* to realize it. I myself hadn't quite taken it in. I wondered if it hurt very much. I thought about the bullets; I imagined their fiery hail going through my body. All that was beside the real question; but I was calm, we had all night in which to realize it. After a while Tom stopped talking and I looked at him out of the corner of my eye. I saw that he, too, had turned gray and that he looked pretty miserable. I said to myself, "It's starting." It was almost dark, a dull light filtered through the air vents across the coal pile and made a big spot under the sky. Through the hole in the ceiling I could already see a star. The night was going to be clear and cold.

The door opened and two guards entered. They were followed by a blond man in a tan uniform. He greeted us.

"I'm the doctor," he said. "I've been authorized to give you any assistance you may require in these painful circumstances."

He had an agreeable, cultivated voice.

I said to him, "What are you going to do here?"

"Whatever you want me to do. I shall do everything in my power to lighten these few hours."

"Why did you come to us? There are lots of others: the hospital's full of them."

"I was sent here," he answered vaguely. "You'd probably like to smoke, wouldn't you?" he added suddenly. "I've got some cigarettes and even some cigars."

He passed around some English cigarettes and some *puros*, but we refused them. I looked him straight in the eye and he appeared uncomfortable.

"You didn't come here out of compassion," I said to him. "In fact, I know who you are. I saw you with some fascists in the barracks yard the day I was arrested."

I was about to continue, when all at once something happened to me which surprised me: the presence of this doctor had suddenly ceased to interest me. Usually, when I've got hold of a man I don't let go. But somehow the desire to speak had left me. I shrugged my shoulders and turned away. A little later, I looked up and saw he was watching me with an air of curiosity. The guards had sat down on one of the mattresses. Pedro, the tall thin one, was twiddling his thumbs, while the other one shook his head occasionally to keep from falling asleep.

"Do you want some light?" Pedro suddenly asked the doctor. The other fellow nodded, "Yes." I think he was not over-intelligent, but doubtless he was not malicious. As I looked at his big, cold, blue eyes, it seemed to me the worst thing about him was his lack of imagination. Pedro went out and came back with an oil lamp which he set on the corner of the bench. It gave a poor light, but it was better than nothing; the night before we had been left in the dark. For a long while I stared at the circle of light the lamp threw on the ceiling. I was fascinated. Then, suddenly, I came to, the light circle paled, and I felt as if I were being crushed under an enormous weight. It wasn't the thought of death, and it wasn't fear; it was something anonymous. My cheeks were burning hot and my head ached.

I roused myself and looked at my two companions. Tom had his head in his hands and only the fat, white nape of his neck was visible. Juan was by far the worst off; his mouth was wide open and his nostrils were trembling. The doctor came over to him and touched him on the shoulder, as though to comfort him; but his eyes remained cold. Then I saw the Belgian slide his hand furtively down Juan's arm to his wrist. Indifferent, Juan let himself be handled. Then, as though absentmindedly, the Belgian laid three fingers over his wrist; at the same time, he drew away somewhat and managed to turn his back to me. But I leaned over backward and saw him take out his watch and look at it a moment before relinquishing the boy's wrist. After a moment, he let the inert hand fall and went and leaned against the wall. Then, as if he had suddenly remembered something very important that had to be noted down immediately, he took a notebook from his pocket and wrote a few lines in it. "The son-of-a-bitch," I thought angrily. "He better not come and feel my pulse; I'll give him a punch in his dirty jaw."

He didn't come near me, but I felt he was looking at me. I raised my head and looked back at him. In an impersonal voice, he said, "Don't you think it's frightfully cold here?"

He looked purple with cold.

"I'm not cold," I answered him.

He kept looking at me with a hard expression. Suddenly I understood, and I lifted my hands to my face. I was covered with sweat. Here, in this cellar, in mid-winter, right in a draft, I was sweating. I ran my fingers through my hair, which was stiff with sweat; at the same time, I realized my shirt was damp and sticking to my skin. I had been streaming with perspiration for an hour, at least, and had felt nothing. But this fact hadn't escaped that Belgian swine. He had seen the drops rolling down my face and had said to himself that it showed an almost pathological terror; and he himself had felt normal and proud of it because he was cold. I wanted to get up and go punch his face in, but I had hardly started to make a move before my shame and anger had disappeared. I dropped back onto the bench with indifference.

I was content to rub my neck with my handkerchief because now I felt the sweat dripping from my hair onto the nape of my neck and that was disagreeable. I soon gave up rubbing myself, however, for it didn't do any good; my handkerchief was already wringing wet and I was still sweating. My buttocks, too, were sweating, and my damp trousers stuck to the bench.

Suddenly, Juan said, "You're a doctor, aren't you?"

"Yes," said the Belgian.

"Do people suffer—very long?"

"Oh! When . . . ? No, no," said the Belgian, in a paternal voice, "it's quickly over."

His manner was as reassuring as if he had been answering a paying patient.

"But I . . . Somebody told me—they often have to fire two volleys."

"Sometimes," said the Belgian, raising his head, "it just happens that the first volley doesn't hit any of the vital organs."

"So then they have to reload their guns and aim all over again?" Juan thought for a moment, then added hoarsely, "But that takes time!"

He was terribly afraid of suffering. He couldn't think about anything else, but that went with his age. As for me, I hardly thought about it any more and it certainly was not fear of suffering that made me perspire.

I rose and walked toward the pile of coal dust. Tom gave a start and
looked at me with a look of hate. I irritated him because my shoes
squeaked. I wondered if my face was as putty-colored as his. Then I
noticed that he, too, was sweating. The sky was magnificent; no light at
all came into our dark corner and I had only to lift my head to see the
Big Bear. But it didn't look the way it had looked before. Two days ago,
from my cell in the archbishop's palace, I could see a big patch of sky and
each time of day brought back a different memory. In the morning, when
the sky was a deep blue, and light, I thought of beaches along the Atlantic;
at noon, I could see the sun, and I remembered a bar in Seville where I
used to drink manzanilla and eat anchovies and olives; in the afternoon,
I was in the shade, and I thought of the deep shadow which covers half of
the arena while the other half gleams in the sunlight: it really gave me a
pang to see the whole earth reflected in the sky like that. Now, however,
no matter how much I looked up in the air, the sky no longer recalled anything. I liked it better that way. I came back and sat down next to Tom.
There was a long silence.

Then Tom began to talk in a low voice. He had to keep talking, otherwise he lost his way in his own thoughts. I believe he was talking to me,
but he didn't look at me. No doubt he was afraid to look at me, because
I was gray and sweating. We were both alike and worse than mirrors for
each other. He looked at the Belgian, the only one who was alive.

"Say, do you understand? I don't."

Then I, too, began to talk in a low voice. I was watching the Belgian.

"Understand what? What's the matter?"

"Something's going to happen to us that I don't understand."

There was a strange odor about Tom. It seemed to me that I was more
sensitive to odors than ordinarily. With a sneer, I said, "You'll understand,
later."

"That's not so sure," he said stubbornly. "I'm willing to be courageous,
but at least I ought to know . . . Listen, they're going to take us out into
the courtyard. All right. The fellows will be standing in line in front of us.
How many of them will there be?"

"Oh, I don't know. Five, or eight. Not more."

"That's enough. Let's say there'll be eight of them. Somebody will
shout 'Shoulder arms!' and I'll see all eight rifles aimed at me. I'm sure I'm
going to feel like going through the wall. I'll push against the wall as hard
as I can with my back, and the wall won't give in. The way it is in a nightmare. . . . I can imagine all that. Ah, if you only knew how well I can
imagine it!"

"Skip it!" I said. "I can imagine it too."

"It must hurt like the devil. You know they aim at your eyes and mouth
so as to disfigure you," he added maliciously. "I can feel the wounds already. For the last hour I've been having pains in my head and neck. Not

real pains—it's worse still. They're the pains I'll feel tomorrow morning. And after that, then what?"

I understood perfectly well what he meant, but I didn't want to seem to understand. As for the pains, I, too, felt them all through my body, like a lot of little gashes. I couldn't get used to them, but I was like him, I didn't think they were very important.

"After that," I said roughly, "you'll be eating daisies."

He started talking to himself, not taking his eyes off the Belgian, who didn't seem to be listening to him. I knew what he had come for, and that what we were thinking didn't interest him. He had come to look at our bodies, our bodies which were dying alive.

"It's like in a nightmare," said Tom. "You want to think of something, you keep having the impression you've got it, that you're going to understand, and then it slips away from you, it eludes you and it's gone again. I say to myself, afterwards, there won't be anything. But I don't really understand what that means. There are moments when I almost do—and then it's gone again. I start to think of the pains, the bullets, the noise of the shooting. I am a materialist, I swear it; and I'm not going crazy, either. But there's something wrong. I see my own corpse. That's not hard, but it's *I* who see it, with *my* eyes. I'll have to get to the point where I think— where I think I won't see anything more. I won't hear anything more, and the world will go on for the others. We're not made to think that way, Pablo. Believe me, I've already stayed awake all night waiting for something. But this is not the same thing. This will grab us from behind, Pablo, and we won't be ready for it."

"Shut up," I said. "Do you want me to call a father confessor?"

He didn't answer. I had already noticed that he had a tendency to prophesy and call me "Pablo" in a kind of pale voice. I didn't like that very much, but it seems all the Irish are like that. I had a vague impression that he smelled of urine. Actually, I didn't like Tom very much, and I didn't see why, just because we were going to die together, I should like him any better. There are certain fellows with whom it would be different —with Ramon Gris, for instance. But between Tom and Juan, I felt alone. In fact, I liked it better that way. With Ramon I might have grown soft. But I felt terribly hard at that moment, and I wanted to stay hard.

Tom kept on muttering, in a kind of absent-minded way. He was certainly talking to keep from thinking. Naturally, I agreed with him, and I could have said everything he was saying. It's not *natural* to die. And since I was going to die, nothing seemed natural any more: neither the coal pile, nor the bench, nor Pedro's dirty old face. Only it was disagreeable for me to think the same things Tom thought. And I knew perfectly well that all night long, within five minutes of each other, we would keep on thinking things at the same time, sweating or shivering at the same time. I looked at him sideways and, for the first time, he seemed strange to me. He had death written on his face. My pride was wounded. For twenty-four hours

I had lived side by side with Tom, I had listened to him, I had talked to him, and I knew we had nothing in common. And now we were as alike as twin brothers, simply because we were going to die together. Tom took my hand without looking at me.

"Pablo, I wonder . . . I wonder if it's true that we just cease to exist."

I drew my hand away.

"Look between your feet, you dirty dog."

There was a puddle between his feet and water was dripping from his trousers.

"What's the matter?" he said, frightened.

"You're wetting your pants," I said to him.

"It's not true," he said furiously. "I can't be . . . I don't feel anything."

The Belgian had come closer to him. With an air of false concern, he asked, "Aren't you feeling well?"

Tom didn't answer. The Belgian looked at the puddle without comment.

"I don't know what that is," Tom said savagely, "but I'm not afraid. I swear to you, I'm not afraid."

The Belgian made no answer. Tom rose and went to the corner. He came back, buttoning his fly, and sat down, without a word. The Belgian was taking notes.

We were watching the doctor. Juan was watching him too. All three of us were watching him because he was alive. He had the gestures of a living person, the interests of a living person; he was shivering in this cellar the way living people shiver; he had an obedient, well-fed body. We, on the other hand, didn't feel our bodies any more—not the same way, in any case. I felt like touching my trousers, but I didn't dare to. I looked at the Belgian, well-planted on his two legs, master of his muscles —and able to plan for tomorrow. We were like three shadows deprived of blood; we were watching him and sucking his life like vampires.

Finally he came over to Juan. Was he going to lay his hand on the nape of Juan's neck for some professional reason, or had he obeyed a charitable impulse? If he had acted out of charity, it was the one and only time during the whole night. He fondled Juan's head and the nape of his neck. The kid let him do it, without taking his eyes off him. Then, suddenly, he took hold of the doctor's hand and looked at it in a funny way. He held the Belgian's hand between his own two hands and there was nothing pleasing about them, those two gray paws squeezing that fat red hand. I sensed what was going to happen and Tom must have sensed it, too. But all the Belgian saw was emotion, and he smiled paternally. After a moment, the kid lifted the big red paw to his mouth and started to bite it. The Belgian drew back quickly and stumbled toward the wall. For a second, he looked at us with horror. He must have suddenly understood that we were not men like himself. I began to laugh, and one of the guards started up. The other had fallen asleep with his eyes wide open, showing only the whites.

I felt tired and over-excited at the same time. I didn't want to think any

more about what was going to happen at dawn—about death. It didn't
make sense, and I never got beyond just words, or emptiness. But whenever I tried to think about something else I saw the barrels of rifles aimed
at me. I must have lived through my execution twenty times in succession;
one time I thought it was the real thing; I must have dozed off for a moment. They were dragging me toward the wall and I was resisting; I was
imploring their pardon. I woke with a start and looked at the Belgian. I
was afraid I had cried out in my sleep. But he was smoothing his mustache;
he hadn't noticed anything. If I had wanted to, I believe I could have slept
for a while. I had been awake for the last forty-eight hours, and I was worn
out. But I didn't want to lose two hours of life. They would have had to
come and wake me at dawn. I would have followed them, drunk with
sleep, and I would have gone off without so much as "Gosh!" I didn't want
it that way. I didn't want to die like an animal. I wanted to understand.
Besides, I was afraid of having nightmares. I got up and began to walk
up and down and, so as to think about something else, I began to think
about my past life. Memories crowded in on me, helter-skelter. Some
were good and some were bad—at least that was how I had thought of
them *before*. There were faces and happenings. I saw the face of a little
novilero who had gotten himself horned during the *Feria*, in Valencia. I
saw the face of one of my uncles, of Ramon Gris. I remembered all kinds
of things that had happened: how I had been on strike for three months
in 1926, and had almost died of hunger. I recalled a night I had spent on
a beach in Granada; I hadn't eaten for three days, I was nearly wild, I
didn't want to give up the sponge. I had to smile. With what eagerness I
had run after happiness, and women, and liberty! And to what end? I had
wanted to liberate Spain, I admired Py Margall, I had belonged to the
anarchist movement, I had spoken at public meetings. I took everything as
seriously as if I had been immortal.

At that time I had the impression that I had my whole life before me,
and I thought to myself, "It's all a god-damned lie." Now it wasn't worth
anything because it was finished. I wondered how I had ever been able to
go out and have a good time with girls. I wouldn't have lifted my little
finger if I had ever imagined that I would die like this. I saw my life
before me, finished, closed, like a bag, and yet what was inside was not
finished. For a moment I tried to appraise it. I would have liked to say to
myself, "It's been a good life." But it couldn't be appraised, it was only an
outline. I had spent my time writing checks on eternity, and had understood nothing. Now, I didn't miss anything. There were a lot of things I
might have missed: the taste of manzanilla, for instance, or the swims I
used to take in summer in a little creek near Cadiz. But death had taken
the charm out of everything.

Suddenly the Belgian had a wonderful idea.

"My friends," he said to us, "if you want me to—and providing the military authorities give their consent—I could undertake to deliver a word or some token from you to your loved ones. . . ."

Tom growled, "I haven't got anybody."

I didn't answer. Tom waited for a moment, then he looked at me with curiosity. "Aren't you going to send any message to Concha?"

"No."

I hated that sort of sentimental conspiracy. Of course, it was my fault, since I had mentioned Concha the night before, and I should have kept my mouth shut. I had been with her for a year. Even as late as last night, I would have cut my arm off with a hatchet just to see her again for five minutes. That was why I had mentioned her. I couldn't help it. Now I didn't care any more about seeing her. I hadn't anything more to say to her. I didn't even want to hold her in my arms. I loathed my body because it had turned gray and was sweating—and I wasn't even sure that I didn't loathe hers too. Concha would cry when she heard about my death; for months she would have no more interest in life. But still it was I who was going to die. I thought of her beautiful, loving eyes. When she looked at me something went from her to me. But I thought to myself that it was all over; if she looked at me *now* her gaze would not leave her eyes, it would not reach out to me. I was alone.

Tom too, was alone, but not the same way. He was seated astride his chair and had begun to look at the bench with a sort of smile, with surprise, even. He reached out his hand and touched the wood cautiously, as though he were afraid of breaking something, then he drew his hand back hurriedly, and shivered. I wouldn't have amused myself touching that bench, if I had been Tom, that was just some more Irish play-acting. But somehow it seemed to me too that the different objects had something funny about them. They seemed to have grown paler, less massive than before. I had only to look at the bench, the lamp or the pile of coal dust to feel I was going to die. Naturally, I couldn't think clearly about my death, but I saw it everywhere, even on the different objects, the way they had withdrawn and kept their distance, tactfully, like people talking at the bedside of a dying person. It was *his own death* Tom had just touched on the bench.

In the state I was in, if they had come and told me I could go home quietly, that my life would be saved, it would have left me cold. A few hours, or a few years of waiting are all the same, when you've lost the illusion of being eternal. Nothing mattered to me any more. In a way, I was calm. But it was a horrible kind of calm—because of my body. My body—I saw with its eyes and I heard with its ears, but it was no longer I. It sweat and trembled independently, and I didn't recognize it any longer. I was obliged to touch it and look at it to know what was happening to it, just as if it had been someone else's body. At times I still felt it, I felt a slipping, a sort of headlong plunging, as in a falling airplane, or else I

heard my heart beating. But this didn't give me confidence. In fact, everything that came from my body had something damned dubious about it.
Most of the time it was silent, it stayed put and I didn't feel anything other
than a sort of heaviness, a loathsome presence against me. I had the impression of being bound to an enormous vermin.

The Belgian took out his watch and looked at it.

"It's half-past three," he said.

The son-of-a-bitch! He must have done it on purpose. Tom jumped up.
We hadn't yet realized the time was passing. The night surrounded us like
a formless, dark mass; I didn't even remember it had started.

Juan started to shout. Wringing his hands, he implored, "I don't want to
die! I don't want to die!"

He ran the whole length of the cellar with his arms in the air, then he
dropped down onto one of the mattresses, sobbing. Tom looked at him
with dismal eyes and didn't even try to console him any more. The fact
was, it was no use; the kid made more noise than we did, but he was less
affected, really. He was like a sick person who defends himself against his
malady with a high fever. When there's not even any fever left, it's much
more serious.

He was crying. I could tell he felt sorry for himself; he was thinking
about death. For one second, one single second, I too felt like crying, crying out of pity for myself. But just the contrary happened. I took one look
at the kid, saw his thin, sobbing shoulders, and I felt I was inhuman. I
couldn't feel pity either for these others or for myself. I said to myself, "I
want to die decently."

Tom had gotten up and was standing just under the round opening looking out for the first signs of daylight. I was determined, I wanted to die
decently, and I only thought about that. But underneath, ever since the
doctor had told us the time, I felt time slipping, flowing by, one drop at a
time.

It was still dark when I heard Tom's voice.

"Do you hear them?"

"Yes."

People were walking in the courtyard.

"What the hell are they doing? After all, they can't shoot in the dark."

After a moment, we didn't hear anything more. I said to Tom, "There's
the daylight."

Pedro got up yawning, and came and blew out the lamp. He turned to
the man beside him. "It's hellish cold."

The cellar had grown gray. We could hear shots at a distance.

"It's about to start," I said to Tom. "That must be in the back courtyard."

Tom asked the doctor to give him a cigarette. I didn't want any; I
didn't want either cigarettes or alcohol. From that moment on, the shooting didn't stop.

"Can you take it in?" Tom said.

He started to add something, then he stopped and began to watch the door. The door opened and a lieutenant came in with four soldiers. Tom dropped his cigarette.

"Steinbock?"

Tom didn't answer. Pedro pointed him out.

"Juan Mirbal?"

"He's the one on the mattress."

"Stand up," said the Lieutenant.

Juan didn't move. Two soldiers took hold of him by the armpits and stood him up on his feet. But as soon as they let go of him he fell down.

The soldiers hesitated a moment.

"He's not the first one to get sick," said the Lieutenant. "You'll have to carry him, the two of you. We'll arrange things when we get there." He turned to Tom. "All right, come along."

Tom left between two soldiers. Two other soldiers followed, carrying the kid by his arms and legs. He was not unconscious; his eyes were wide open and tears were rolling down his cheeks. When I started to go out, the Lieutenant stopped me.

"Are you Ibbieta?"

"Yes."

"You wait here. They'll come and get you later on."

They left. The Belgian and the two jailers left too, and I was alone. I didn't understand what had happened to me, but I would have liked it better if they had ended it all right away. I heard the volleys at almost regular intervals; at each one, I shuddered. I felt like howling and tearing my hair. But instead, I gritted my teeth and pushed my hands deep into my pockets, because I wanted to stay decent.

An hour later, they came to fetch me and took me up to the first floor in a little room which smelt of cigar smoke and was so hot it seemed to me suffocating. Here there were two officers sitting in comfortable chairs, smoking, with papers spread out on their knees.

"Your name is Ibbieta?"

"Yes."

"Where is Ramon Gris?"

"I don't know."

The man who questioned me was small and stocky. He had hard eyes behind his glasses.

"Come nearer," he said to me.

I went nearer. He rose and took me by the arms, looking at me in a way calculated to make me go through the floor. At the same time he pinched my arms with all his might. He didn't mean to hurt me; it was quite a game; he wanted to dominate me. He also seemed to think it was necessary to blow his fetid breath right into my face. We stood like that for a mo-

ment, only I felt more like laughing than anything else. It takes a lot more
than that to intimidate a man who's about to die: it didn't work. He
pushed me away violently and sat down again.

"It's your life or his," he said. "You'll be allowed to go free if you tell
us where he is."

After all, these two bedizened fellows with their riding crops and boots
were just men who were going to die one day. A little later than I, perhaps, but not a great deal. And there they were, looking for names among
their papers, running after other men in order to put them in prison or
do away with them entirely. They had their opinions on the future of
Spain and on other subjects. Their petty activities seemed to me to be offensive and ludicrous. I could no longer put myself in their place. I had the
impression they were crazy.

The little fat fellow kept looking at me, tapping his boots with his riding
crop. All his gestures were calculated to make him appear like a spirited,
ferocious animal.

"Well? Do you understand?"

"I don't know where Gris is," I said. "I thought he was in Madrid."

The other officer lifted his pale hand indolently. This indolence was also
calculated. I saw through all their little tricks, and I was dumbfounded
that men should still exist who took pleasure in that kind of thing.

"You have fifteen minutes to think it over," he said slowly. "Take him
to the linen-room, and bring him back here in fifteen minutes. If he continues to refuse, he'll be executed at once."

They knew what they were doing. I had spent the night waiting. After
that, they had made me wait another hour in the cellar, while they shot
Tom and Juan, and now they locked me in the linen-room. They must
have arranged the whole thing the night before. They figured that sooner
or later people's nerves wear out and they hoped to get me that way.

They made a big mistake. In the linen-room I sat down on a ladder
because I felt very weak, and I began to think things over. Not their
proposition, however. Naturally I knew where Gris was. He was hiding
in his cousins' house, about two miles outside the city. I knew, too, that I
would not reveal his hiding place, unless they tortured me (but they didn't
seem to be considering that). All that was definitely settled and didn't interest me in the least. Only I would have liked to understand the reasons
for my own conduct. I would rather die than betray Gris. Why? I no
longer liked Ramon Gris. My friendship for him had died shortly before
dawn along with my love for Concha, along with my own desire to live.
Of course I still admired him—he was hard. But it was not for that reason
that I was willing to die in his place; his life was no more valuable than
mine. No life was of any value. A man was going to be stood up against a
wall and fired at till he dropped dead. It didn't make any difference
whether it was I or Gris or somebody else. I knew perfectly well he was
more useful to the Spanish cause than I was, but I didn't give a God damn

about Spain or anarchy, either; nothing had any importance now. And yet, there I was. I could save my skin by betraying Gris and I refused to do it. It seemed more ludicrous to me than anything else; it was stubbornness.

I thought to myself, "Am I hard-headed!" And I was seized with a strange sort of cheerfulness.

They came to fetch me and took me back to the two officers. A rat darted out under our feet and that amused me. I turned to one of the falangists and said to him, "Did you see that rat?"

He made no reply. He was gloomy, and took himself very seriously. As for me, I felt like laughing, but I restrained myself because I was afraid that if I started, I wouldn't be able to stop. The falangist wore mustaches. I kept after him, "You ought to cut off those mustaches, you fool."

I was amused by the fact that he let hair grow all over his face while he was still alive. He gave me a kind of half-hearted kick, and I shut up.

"Well," said the fat officer, "have you thought things over?"

I looked at them with curiosity, like insects of a very rare species.

"I know where he is," I said. "He's hiding in the cemetery. Either in one of the vaults, or in the gravediggers' shack."

I said that just to make fools of them. I wanted to see them get up and fasten their belts and bustle about giving orders.

They jumped to their feet.

"Fine. Moles, go ask Lieutenant Lopez for fifteen men. And as for you," the little fat fellow said to me, "if you've told the truth, I don't go back on my word. But you'll pay for this, if you're pulling our leg."

They left noisily and I waited in peace, still guarded by the falangists. From time to time I smiled at the thought of the face they were going to make. I felt dull and malicious. I could see them lifting up the grave-stones, or opening the doors of the vaults one by one. I saw the whole situation as though I were another person: the prisoner determined to play the hero, the solemn falangists with their mustaches and the men in uniform running around among the graves. It was irresistibly funny.

After half an hour, the little fat fellow came back alone. I thought he had come to give the order to execute me. The others must have stayed in the cemetery.

The officer looked at me. He didn't look at all foolish.

"Take him out in the big courtyard with the others," he said. "When military operations are over, a regular tribunal will decide his case."

I thought I must have misunderstood.

"So they're not—they're not going to shoot me?" I asked.

"Not now, in any case. Afterwards, that doesn't concern me."

I still didn't understand.

"But why?" I said to him.

He shrugged his shoulders without replying, and the soldiers led me away. In the big courtyard there were a hundred or so prisoners, women, children and a few old men. I started to walk around the grass plot in the middle. I felt absolutely idiotic. At noon we were fed in the dining hall. Two or three fellows spoke to me. I must have known them, but I didn't answer. I didn't even know where I was.

Toward evening, about ten new prisoners were pushed into the court-yard. I recognized Garcia, the baker.

He said to me, "Lucky dog! I didn't expect to find you alive."

"They condemned me to death," I said, "and then they changed their minds. I don't know why."

"I was arrested at two o'clock," Garcia said.

"What for?"

Garcia took no part in politics.

"I don't know," he said. "They arrest everybody who doesn't think the way they do."

He lowered his voice.

"They got Gris."

I began to tremble.

"When?"

"This morning. He acted like a damned fool. He left his cousins' house Tuesday because of a disagreement. There were any number of fellows who would have hidden him, but he didn't want to be indebted to anybody any more. He said, 'I would have hidden at Ibbieta's, but since they've got him, I'll go hide in the cemetery.'"

"In the cemetery?"

"Yes. It was the god-damnedest thing. Naturally they passed by there this morning; that had to happen. They found him in the gravediggers' shack. They opened fire at him and they finished him off."

"In the cemetery!"

Everything went around in circles, and when I came to I was sitting on the ground. I laughed so hard the tears came to my eyes.

Sartre, "The Wall"

Questions for Comprehension and Discussion

1. What part have Pablo and Tom played in the Spanish War?
2. In what different ways do Tom, Pablo, and Juan react to the prospect of execution?
3. At the beginning, Pablo says twice that dying and the fear of suffering are not the "real questions," are not important. What is important to him?
4. Does Pablo experience any sort of change in the story? Describe.
5. What is the significance of Pablo's remark, "I want to die decently"?
6. Explain this passage: "I would rather die than betray Gris. Why? I no longer liked Ramon Gris. My friendship for him had died shortly before dawn along with my love for Concha, along with my own desire to live. Of course I still admired him—he was hard. But it was not for that reason that I was willing to die in his place; his life was no more valuable than mine. No life was of any value." Can the last sentence be interpreted to mean "life has no value"? Why or why not?
7. What does Pablo feel when he learns that Gris has been found? Why does he say: "I laughed so hard the tears came to my eyes"?
8. In what ways does Sartre use the title, "The Wall"?

Vocabulary

From the lettered choices, find the best definition for each vocabulary item, and mark the letter in the space provided.

1. __M__ to *sabotage* the munitions
2. __S__ *disfigured* by fear
3. __H__ to *console* the kid
4. __B__ an *air* of curiosity
5. __Q__ he was not *malicious*
6. __C__ slide his hand *furtively*
7. __F__ before *relinquishing* his wrist
8. __I__ let the *inert* hand fall
9. __K__ an almost *pathological* terror
10. __J__ the *anarchist* movement
11. __L__ I *loathed* my body
12. __N__ something *dubious* about it
13. __R__ bound to an enormous *vermin*
14. __E__ lifted his hand *indolently*
15. __N__ it seemed more *ludicrous*

A. alienate; estrange
B. characteristic manner
C. slyly; stealthily
D. good-natured; benevolent

E. idly; lazily
F. letting go; dropping
G. boldly; aggressively
H. comfort in grief or sorrow

421 Words

I. doubtful; uncertain
J. terrorist; one who is against an
   authoritarian regime
K. caused by a physical, rather
   than a mental, disorder
L. detested; abhorred
M. destroy, damage to stop the
   enemy

N. frivolous; silly
O. gripping; grasping
P. ridiculous; absurd
Q. spiteful; evil in motives
R. repulsive, parasitic organism
S. deformed; marred
T. unmoving; sluggish

VOCABULARY   No. right ———

MACHADO DE ASSIS
*The Secret Heart**

Machado de Assis (1839–1908) has only been recently translated into English from the Portuguese. A shy, epileptic mulatto, de Assis wrote about nineteenth-century Rio de Janeiro society, but his fiction is much more universal in theme and structure. "The Secret Heart," written in 1885, reveals his understanding of the recesses of the human heart.

Garcia, who was standing, studied his finger nails, and snapped them from time to time. Fortunato, in the rocking chair, looked at the ceiling. Maria Luiza, by the window, was putting the final touches to a piece of needlework. Five minutes had now passed without their saying a word. They had spoken of the day, which had been fine, of Catumby, where Fortunato and his wife lived, and of a private hospital that will be explained later.

They had also spoken of something else, something so grim and unpleasant that it took away all desire to talk of the day, the surroundings, and the hospital. Their conversation in respect to it had been constrained. Even now, Maria Luiza's hands still trembled, while Garcia's face had a severe look—something not usual with him. As a matter of fact, what happened was of such a nature that to make the situation clear it will be necessary to go back to its very beginning.

Garcia had obtained his M.D. the year before, 1861. In the year 1860, while he was still in medical school, he had seen Fortunato for the first time, at the entrance to the Santa Casa hospital. He was going in as the other was coming out. He had been struck by Fortunato's appearance, but even so would have forgotten him, if it had not been for a second encounter only a few days later. He lived on the Rua Dom Manuel. One of his rare diversions was to go to the Theater São Januário, which was close by, between that street and the bay. He was in the habit of going

* Trans. Helen Caldwell, from *The Psychiatrist and Other Stories* (Berkeley: University of California Press, 1966), pp. 66–75.

once or twice a month, and never found more than forty persons in the
audience. Only the most intrepid were bold enough to extend their travels
to that out-of-the-way corner of the city. One night as he was sitting in
the orchestra, Fortunato came in and sat down beside him.

The play was a heavy melodrama, stabbed through and through with
daggers, bristling with curses and remorse, but Fortunato heard it with
singular interest. In the painful scenes his attention redoubled, his eyes
kept going avidly from one character to another—so much so that the
medical student began to suspect that the play stirred personal memories
in the man. At the end of the drama, a farce came on, but Fortunato did
not wait to see it, and left the theater. Garcia followed him. Fortunato
went down the Beco do Cotovelo, along the Rua de São José to the Largo
da Carioca. He walked slowly, with lowered head, stopping now and
then to whack with his cane some dog that was lying asleep. The dog
would howl and *he* would keep on going. In the Largo da Carioca he
climbed into a Tilbury and went off in the direction of the Praça da
Constituição. Garcia went home without learning more than this.

Several weeks passed. One night, about nine o'clock, as he sat at home
in his garret apartment, he heard the sound of voices on the stairway.
He went down at once to the second floor, where an employee of the
Army Arsenal lived: several men were helping him upstairs, and he was
covered with blood. His colored serving man came running to the door,
the man groaned, there was a jumble of voices, the light was dim. When
the wounded man had been set down on his bed, Garcia said they must
send for a doctor.

"One's already on the way," someone replied.

Garcia glanced toward the speaker; it was the man he had seen at the
hospital and in the theater. He supposed he was a relative or friend of
the wounded man, but he dismissed the idea when he heard him ask
if the fellow had a family or any close relative. The colored man said he
had not; then the stranger took full charge. He asked the others to leave,
paid the porters, and gave the necessary orders for seeing to the wounded
man. Learning that Garcia was a neighbor and a medical student, he
asked him to remain and assist the doctor. Then he told what had happened.

"It was a gang of *capoeiras.** I was coming from the Moura Barracks,
where I had gone to visit a cousin, when I heard a lot of yelling and then
a scuffle. It seems they wounded another fellow who was going by and
he turned down one of those side streets, but all I saw was this gentleman,
who was crossing the street, at the moment one of the ruffians brushed
against him and stuck a dagger in him. He didn't fall immediately; he
told me where he lived, and, since it was but a few steps away, I thought
it best to bring him home."

* Members of gangs who menaced the streets of Rio de Janeiro during the
greater part of the nineteenth century. They were finally wiped out by Ferraz, the
first police chief of the Republic, in 1890.

"Did you know him before?" asked Garcia.

"No, I'd never laid eyes on him. Who is he?"

"He's a good man, an employee of the Army Arsenal. His name is Gouvêa."

"No, I don't know him."

The doctor and the police inspector soon arrived. The man's wound was dressed, and the information taken down. The stranger said his name was Fortunato Gomes da Silveira, that he was a bachelor, living on his income, a resident of Catumby. The wound was considered serious. While it was being dressed with the help of the medical student, Fortunato acted as servant, holding the basin, the candle, the cloths, without fuss, and looking coldly at the wounded man, who groaned a good deal. Afterwards he had a private conversation with the doctor, walked with him as far as the landing, and again assured the inspector that he was ready to assist the police with their investigation. After these two had left, he and the medical student remained in the bedroom. Garcia was dumbfounded. He glanced toward him, saw him calmly sit down, stretch out his legs, put his hands in his trousers pockets, and fix his eyes on the sick man. His eyes were a clear gray, the color of lead, they moved slowly and had a hard, cold, indifferent expression. His face was thin and pale, with a narrow band of sparse red beard clipped close and extending from beneath his chin to either temple. He was perhaps forty years old. From time to time he turned to the student and asked some question about the wounded man, but immediately returned his gaze to him while the young man answered. The feeling the student got was at once one of repulsion and of curiosity; he could not deny that he was witnessing an act of rare dedication, and, if he was disinterested, as he seemed, there was nothing else to do but accept the human heart as a well of mysteries.

It was almost one o'clock when Fortunato left. He returned on the succeeding days, but the cure progressed rapidly, and before it was completed he disappeared without telling the wounded man where he lived. It was the student who gave him the information as to name, street, and number.

"I'm going to thank him for the kindness he did me, as soon as I can go out," said the convalescent.

Six days afterward, he hurried to Catumby. Fortunato received him with a constrained air, listened impatiently to his words of thanks, replied in a bored manner, and ended by swinging the cord of his dressing gown against his knee. Gouvêa, sitting silent before him, smoothed his hat with his fingers, lifted his eyes from time to time without finding anything to say. At the end of ten minutes he asked permission to leave, and left.

"Watch out for capoeiras!" said his host with a laugh.

The poor devil left there mortified, humiliated, scarcely able to swallow his dislike, making an effort to forget it, to explain it away or excuse it, so that only the memory of the kind deed would remain in his heart, but the effort was vain. Resentment, a new and exclusive lodger moved in and kicked out the kind deed so that the poor thing had no recourse but to climb up into the brain and take refuge there as a mere idea. So it was that the benefactor himself forced upon this man the sentiment of ingratitude.

All this astonished Garcia. The young man possessed in germ the ability to decipher men, to unravel human character. He had a love of analysis, and felt a special pleasure, which he called exquisite, in penetrating layer after layer of spiritual strata until he touched the secret heart of an organism. Pricked on by curiosity, he thought of going to see the man of Catumby, but it occurred to him that he had not received a definite invitation to call on him. He needed an excuse, at least, and he could think of none.

Many months later, after he had obtained his degree and was living on the Rua de Matacavallos, near the Rua do Conde, he happened to meet Fortunato on an omnibus, and he ran into him a number of other times: these meetings brought acquaintance. One day Fortunato invited him to come visit him in near-by Catumby.

"Did you know I was married?"

"No."

"I got married four months ago—it seems like four days. Come have dinner with us Sunday."

"Sunday?"

"Don't go making up excuses. I won't take excuses. Come, Sunday."

Garcia went on Sunday. Fortunato gave him a good dinner, good cigars, and good conversation, in company with his wife, who was interesting. He had not changed in appearance. His eyes were the same steely disks, hard and cold; his other features were no more attractive than before. His courtesy, however, if it did not redeem his nature, at least offered considerable compensation. It was Maria Luiza who possessed charm both of person and of manners. She was slender and graceful, with gentle, submissive eyes. She was twenty-one, and looked nineteen. The second time Garcia went there he noticed a certain dissonance in their natures, that little or no spiritual affinity existed between them, and in the wife's manner toward her husband there was something that went beyond respect and bordered on subjection and fear. One day when the three were together, Garcia asked Maria Luiza if she knew the circumstances under which he had met her husband.

"No," she answered.

"You are going to hear of a handsome deed."

"It's not worth the telling," interrupted Fortunato.

"She shall decide whether it's worth telling or no," insisted the doctor.

He told the story of the Rua Dom Manuel. The girl listened in amazement. Little by little she stretched out her hand and clasped her husband's wrist; she was smiling and grateful, as if she had just discovered his heart. Fortunato shrugged his shoulders but he did not hear the tale with indifference. At the end of it, he himself told of the visit the wounded man had paid him, with all the details of his appearance, gestures, his hesitant words, tongue-tied silences—in short a clown. And he kept laughing as he told it. It was not the laughter of a two-faced man, which is evasive and sly. *His* laugh was frank and genial.

"A strange fellow!" thought Garcia.

Maria Luiza was upset by her husband's mockery, but Garcia restored her to her former contentment by again mentioning his dedication and rare qualities as a nurse—"such a good nurse," he concluded, "that if I ever start a private hospital, I'll ask him to be my partner."

"You mean it?"

"Mean what?"

"That we are going to start a hospital?"

"No, I was joking."

"We *could* do it. And for you, just beginning your practice, it might not be a bad idea. It so happens I have a house that is going to fall vacant; it will be the very thing."

Garcia refused to consider the proposal on that day, and on the next; but the idea had become fixed in the other's head, and he would not be put off. As a matter of fact, it would be a good beginning for a doctor, and might turn out to be a good business for both of them. Garcia definitely accepted a few days later. It was a disappointment to Maria Luiza. The high-strung, delicate girl suffered at the very thought of her husband living in contact with human illnesses, but she did not dare oppose him, and bowed her head. The plans were quickly drawn up and carried into effect. The truth is, Fortunato gave no thought to anything else, either then or later. After the hospital opened, it was he who served as administrator and head nurse: he inspected everything, supervised everything—purchases, broths, drugs, and accounts.

Garcia could see that the dedication to the wounded man on the Rua Dom Manuel was not a matter of chance but suited with his nature. He saw him perform menial and obnoxious tasks: he did not shrink from anything, did not find any disease distressing or repulsive, and was ready for anything at any time of day or night. Everyone admired and applauded. Fortunato studied, and closely followed the operations. He, and he alone, handled the caustics. "I have great faith in caustics," he would say.

The sharing of a common interest tightened the bonds of friendship. Garcia became a familiar of the house. He dined there almost every day, and there he observed Maria Luiza and saw her life of spiritual loneliness. And somehow this loneliness of hers increased her loveliness. Garcia began to feel troubled when she came into the room, when she spoke, when she worked quietly by the window, or played sweet, sad music on the piano. Gently, imperceptibly, love entered his heart. When he found it there, he tried to thrust it out, that there might be no other bond but friendship between him and Fortunato. But he did not succeed. He succeeded only in locking it in. Maria Luiza understood—both his love and his silence—but she never let on.

In the beginning of October, something happened that opened the doctor's eyes still more to the young woman's plight. Fortunato had taken up the study of anatomy and physiology, and busied himself in his spare time with ripping open and poisoning cats and dogs. Since the animals' cries disturbed the patients, he moved his laboratory home, and his wife, with her nervous temperament, had to endure them. One day, when she could stand no more, she went to the doctor and asked him to get her husband—as if it was his own idea—to give up these experiments.

"But you yourself . . ."

Maria Luiza answered with a smile. "He probably considers me childish. What I would like is for you, as a doctor, to tell him that this is bad for me. And, believe me, it is."

Garcia promptly got Fortunato to put an end to these experiments. If he performed them somewhere else, no one knew of it, but it may be that he did. Maria Luiza thanked the physician not only for herself but also for the animals, which she could not see suffer. She coughed, as she spoke. Garcia asked her if she was ill. She answered, "No."

"Let me feel your pulse."

"There's nothing wrong with me."

She did not let him feel her pulse, and went out of the room. Garcia was worried. He thought, on the contrary, there might be something wrong with her, that it was necessary to observe her and warn her husband in time.

Two days later—it was the very day on which we first glimpsed them —Garcia came to dinner. In the hall he was told that Fortunato was in his study, and he started toward that room. As he arrived at the study door, Maria Luiza came out in a state of great distress.

"What's the matter?" he asked.

"The rat! the rat!" she cried in a choked voice and went on.

Garcia remembered hearing Fortunato complain the day before of a rat that had carried off an important paper, but he never expected to see what he did see. He saw Fortunato seated at the table, which was in the middle of the study, and on which was placed a plate with spirits of alcohol in it. The liquid was on fire. Between the thumb and index finger of his left hand Fortunato held a hook from the point of which the rat hung by its tail. In his right hand he had a pair of scissors. At the moment Garcia entered the room, he was cutting off one of the rat's paws. Then he lowered the poor thing into the flame, rapidly in order not to

kill it, and made ready to do the same to the third paw, for he had already cut off the first. Garcia stopped short in horror.

"Kill it at once!" he said.

"In a minute."

And with a strange smile, reflection of a soul replete with satisfaction,
a smile that told of an inward savoring of the most exquisite sensation,
Fortunato cut off the rat's third paw, and for the third time made the
same movement into the flame. The wretched animal squealed and
twisted its bloodied, singed body, and would not die. Garcia turned away
his eyes, then looked again, and put out his hand as if to prevent the
torture from continuing, but he did not complete the gesture, because the
devil of a man compelled fear, with that radiant serenity of countenance.

It only remained to cut off the fourth paw. He cut it off very slowly,
keeping his eyes on the scissors. The paw dropped and he remained looking at the rat, now half cadaver. He lowered it into the flame for the
fourth time, still more rapidly, to save if he could some tatters of life.

Garcia, who stood on the other side of the table, mastered his re-
pugnance and looked intently at Fortunato's face. Neither rage nor hate;
only a vast pleasure, quiet and deep, such pleasure as another man might
derive from hearing a beautiful sonata or from seeing a sublime statue—
something resembling pure, aesthetic feeling. It appeared to Garcia, and
it was actually the case, that Fortunato had entirely forgotten him. He
could not have been putting it on, no, it was impossible. The flame was
dying, it may have been that the rat still had a bit of life left, a shadow
of a shadow: Fortunato took advantage of it to cut off the animal's little
muzzle, and, for the last time, to bring its flesh to the flame. Finally he
let the dead thing drop on the plate, and pushed from him all that mess
of scorched flesh and blood.

As he stood up he came face to face with the physician and started.
Then he displayed rage against the animal that had carried off his paper,
but the anger was plainly counterfeit.

"Punishment without anger," thought the doctor, "the need for a sensation of pleasure that only another creature's pain can give—that is the
secret heart of this man."

Fortunato expatiated upon the importance of the document . . . only
loss of time, it was true, but time was precious to him right now. Garcia
listened without a word, without belief. He recalled other actions of
Fortunato's, serious and trifling things: he found the same explanation for
all of them, a ringing of changes on the same set of sensations, a unique
kind of dilettantism—a miniature Caligula.

When Maria Luiza returned to the study a few minutes later, her
husband went up to her, laughingly took her hands, and said gently,
"Coward!" And, turning toward the doctor, "Would you believe it? She
almost fainted."

Maria Luiza timidly protested: she was nervous, and a woman. Then she went and sat by the window, with her colored wools and needles, and her fingers still trembling, just as we saw her at the beginning of this story. It will be recalled that after speaking of other matters, the three fell silent: the husband sat looking at the ceiling, the physician snapping his finger nails.

Not long after, they went in to dinner; but dinner was not cheerful. Maria Luiza's thoughts kept straying and she coughed frequently. The doctor asked himself if she might not be exposed to some vicious excess in the company of such a man. It was barely possible, but his love transformed the possibility into a certainty: he trembled for her and determined to keep a close watch over both of them.

Her cough grew worse, and it was not long before the disease put off its mask. It was tuberculosis, insatiate old hag that sucks the life and leaves a pulp of bones. Fortunato received the news as a blow. He really loved his wife, in his way, was used to her, it was hard to lose her. He spared nothing—doctors, medicines, change of air, all the remedies, all the palliatives. But it was in vain. The illness was mortal.

In the final days, in the presence of her last terrible torments, the husband's peculiar bent dominated whatever other feeling he may have had. He never left her for an instant, fastened a cold, dull eye on that slow, painful dissolution of life, drank in, one by one, the suffering moments of this beautiful woman, now thin and transparent, consumed by fever and sapped by death. His relentless egoism, ravening after sensations, refused to renounce a single minute of her agony, or repay her with a single tear, in public or in private. Only when she died—then he was stunned. When he came to his senses he saw that he was again alone.

In the night, a female relative of Maria Luiza's, who had been with her when she died, went to get some rest. Fortunato and Garcia stayed on in the parlor, watching with the corpse, both thoughtful. But the husband, too, was exhausted. The doctor told him to rest for a while.

"Go lie down and sleep for an hour or two. I'll do the same afterward."

Fortunato went into an adjoining sitting room, stretched out on the sofa, and fell asleep at once. Twenty minutes later he awoke, tried to go back to sleep, dozed a few minutes, then got up and returned to the parlor. He walked on tiptoe so as not to awaken the relative, who was asleep close by. As he reached the door, he stopped in astonishment.

Garcia had gone up to the corpse, had raised the face-covering and gazed for some seconds at the dead woman's features. Then, as if death spiritualized everything, he leaned down and kissed her forehead. It was at this moment that Fortunato reached the door. He stopped in astonishment. Impossible that it was the kiss of friendship, it must have been the epilogue to a long book of adultery. He was not jealous, be it noted. Nature had so mixed the elements in him as not to give him either jealousy or envy, but she had given him vanity, which is no less subject to resentment. He stared in astonishment, biting his lips.

Meanwhile, Garcia again leaned down to kiss the dead woman; but this time he could not bear his grief. The kiss gave way to sobs, and his eyes could no longer hold their tears, which poured forth in a flood, tears of love that had been stilled—of love and of hopeless despair. Fortunato, from the doorway, where he had remained, quietly savored this outburst of spiritual pain, which was long, very long, delightfully long.

De Assis, "The Secret Heart"

QUESTIONS FOR COMPREHENSION AND DISCUSSION

1. Why does Fortunato treat Gouvêa, the wounded man, so curtly when he comes to pay his thanks?
2. Fortunato's eyes are described several times in detail. How does this description help reveal his character?
3. What does Garcia think about Fortunato's dedication to human illness?
4. What are Fortunato's motives? What is finally revealed about his "secret heart"?
5. What is Garcia's relationship with Maria Luiza? Why is Fortunato not jealous of Garcia's affection for her?
6. At the end of the story, Fortunato's evil nature is revealed. What incidents prior to the rat experiment suggest his strange predilection?

VOCABULARY

From the lettered choices, find the best definition for each vocabulary item, and mark the letter in the space provided.

1. __P__ their conversation had been *constrained*
2. __C__ one of his rare *diversions*
3. __H__ only the most *intrepid*
4. __L__ a heavy *melodrama*
5. __E__ bristling with *remorse*
6. __S__ he left *mortified*
7. __N__ he had no *recourse*
8. __R__ a *dissonance* in their natures
9. __A__ no spiritual *affinity*
10. __G__ a soul *replete* with satisfaction
11. __T__ the anger was *counterfeit*
12. __M__ Fortunato *expatiated* upon
13. __B__ a unique kind of *dilletantism*
14. __K__ *insatiate* old hag
15. __Q__ painful *dissolution* of life

A. natural; spiritual attraction
B. amateur interest for sake of amusement
C. distractions; amusements
D. specialties; areas of vast knowledge
E. hopeless anguish; distressing self-reproach
F. empty; meaningless
G. full; abundantly supplied

H. bold; fearless
I. frustration; anxiety
J. ephemeral; transitory
K. incapable of being satisfied; greedy
L. romantic drama displaying violent or extravagant emotions
M. spoke at length; elaborated
N. access to help or protection

O. tragedy
P. confined; forced; unnatural
Q. disintegration; death
R. harsh disagreement;
   incongruity

S. humiliated; shamed
T. pretended; feigned; fake

VOCABULARY No. right _____

5

FLANNERY O'CONNOR
Good Country People*

Although Flannery O'Connor (1925–1964) did not like to be regarded as only a Southern writer, she nevertheless has won a large reading public from her remarkable fiction about the people of the South. Until her death from a long illness, she lived in Millidgeville, Georgia, where she raised hundreds of pea fowl. "Good Country People" is from a collection of short novels and fiction, Three by Flannery O'Connor *(Signet). The story relates with pathos and humor two of her most unforgettable characters.*

Besides the neutral expression that she wore when she was alone, Mrs. Freeman had two others, forward and reverse, that she used for all her human dealings. Her forward expression was steady and driving like the advance of a heavy truck. Her eyes never swerved to left or right but turned as the story turned as if they followed a yellow line down the center of it. She seldom used the other expression because it was not often necessary for her to retract a statement, but when she did, her face came to a complete stop, there was an almost imperceptible movement of her black eyes, during which they seemed to be receding, and then the observer would see that Mrs. Freeman, though she might stand there as real as several grain sacks thrown on top of each other, was no longer there in spirit. As for getting anything across to her when this was the case, Mrs. Hopewell had given it up. She might talk her head off. Mrs. Freeman could never be brought to admit herself wrong on any point. She would stand there and if she could be brought to say anything, it was something like, "Well, I wouldn't of said it was and I wouldn't of said it wasn't," or letting her gaze range over the top kitchen shelf where there was an assortment of dusty bottles, she might remark, "I see you ain't ate many of them figs you put up last summer."

* From *A Good Man Is Hard to Find* (New York: Harcourt Brace Jovanovich, Inc., 1959), pp. 169–196.

They carried on their most important business in the kitchen at breakfast. Every morning Mrs. Hopewell got up at seven o'clock and lit her
gas heater and Joy's. Joy was her daughter, a large blonde girl who had
an artificial leg. Mrs. Hopewell thought of her as a child though she was
thirty-two years old and highly educated. Joy would get up while her
mother was eating and lumber into the bathroom and slam the door, and
before long, Mrs. Freeman would arrive at the back door. Joy would hear
her mother call, "Come on in," and then they would talk for a while in
low voices that were indistinguishable in the bathroom. By the time Joy
came in, they had usually finished the weather report and were on one or
the other of Mrs. Freeman's daughters, Glynese or Carramae. Joy called
them Glycerin and Caramel. Glynese, a redhead, was eighteen and had
many admirers; Carramae, a blonde, was only fifteen but already married
and pregnant. She could not keep anything on her stomach. Every morning Mrs. Freeman told Mrs. Hopewell how many times she had vomited
since the last report.

Mrs. Hopewell liked to tell people that Glynese and Carramae were
two of the finest girls she knew and that Mrs. Freeman was a *lady* and
that she was never ashamed to take her anywhere or introduce her to
anybody they might meet. Then she would tell how she had happened to
hire the Freemans in the first place and how they were a godsend to her
and how she had had them four years. The reason for her keeping them
so long was that they were not trash. They were good country people.
She had telephoned the man whose name they had given as a reference
and he had told her that Mr. Freeman was a good farmer but that his
wife was the nosiest woman ever to walk the earth. "She's got to be into
everything," the man said. "If she don't get there before the dust settles,
you can bet she's dead, that's all. She'll want to know all your business.
I can stand him real good," he had said, "but me nor my wife neither
could have stood that woman one more minute on this place." That had
put Mrs. Hopewell off for a few days.

She had hired them in the end because there were no other applicants
but she had made up her mind beforehand exactly how she would handle
the woman. Since she was the type who had to be into everything, then,
Mrs. Hopewell had decided, she would not only let her be into everything, she would *see to it* that she was into everything—she would give
her the responsibility of everything, she would put her in charge. Mrs.
Hopewell had no bad qualities of her own but she was able to use other
people's in such a constructive way that she never felt the lack. She had
hired the Freemans and she had kept them four years.

Nothing is perfect. This was one of Mrs. Hopewell's favorite sayings.
Another was: that is life! And still another, the most important, was: well,
other people have their opinions too. She would make these statements,
usually at the table, in a tone of gentle insistence as if no one held them
but her, and the large hulking Joy, whose constant outrage had obliterated

every expression from her face, would stare just a little to the side of her, her eyes icy blue, with the look of someone who has achieved blindness by an act of will and means to keep it.

When Mrs Hopewell said to Mrs. Freeman that life was like that, Mrs. Freeman would say, "I always said so myself." Nothing had been arrived at by anyone that had not first been arrived at by her. She was quicker than Mr. Freeman. When Mrs. Hopewell said to her after they had been on the place a while, "You know, you're the wheel behind the wheel," and winked, Mrs. Freeman had said, "I know it. I've always been quick. It's some that are quicker than others."

"Everybody is different," Mrs. Hopewell said.

"Yes, most people is," Mrs. Freeman said.

"It takes all kinds to make the world."

"I always said it did myself."

The girl was used to this kind of dialogue for breakfast and more of it for dinner; sometimes they had it for supper too. When they had no guest they ate in the kitchen because that was easier. Mrs. Freeman always managed to arrive at some point during the meal and to watch them finish it. She would stand in the doorway if it were summer but in the winter she would stand with one elbow on top of the refrigerator and look down on them, or she would stand by the gas heater, lifting the back of her skirt slightly. Occasionally she would stand against the wall and roll her head from side to side. At no time was she in any hurry to leave. All this was very trying on Mrs. Hopewell but she was a woman of great patience. She realized that nothing is perfect and that in the Freemans she had good country people and that if, in this day and age, you get good country people, you had better hang onto them.

She had had plenty of experience with trash. Before the Freemans she had averaged one tenant family a year. The wives of these farmers were not the kind you would want to be around you for very long. Mrs. Hopewell, who had divorced her husband long ago, needed someone to walk over the fields with her; and when Joy had to be impressed for these services, her remarks were usually so ugly and her face so glum that Mrs. Hopewell would say, "If you can't come pleasantly, I don't want you at all," to which the girl, standing square and rigid-shouldered with her neck thrust slightly forward, would reply, "If you want me, here I am— LIKE I AM."

Mrs. Hopewell excused this attitude because of the leg (which had been shot off in a hunting accident when Joy was ten). It was hard for Mrs. Hopewell to realize that her child was thirty-two now and that for more than twenty years she had had only one leg. She thought of her still as a child because it tore her heart to think instead of the poor stout girl in her thirties who had never danced a step or had any *normal* good times. Her name was really Joy but as soon as she was twenty-one and away from home, she had had it legally changed. Mrs. Hopewell was certain that she had thought and thought until she had hit upon the ugliest name in any language. Then she had gone and had the beautiful name, Joy, changed without telling her mother until after she had done it. Her legal name was Hulga.

When Mrs. Hopewell thought the name, Hulga, she thought of the broad blank hull of a battleship. She would not use it. She continued to call her Joy to which the girl responded but in a purely mechanical way.

Hulga had learned to tolerate Mrs. Freeman who saved her from taking walks with her mother. Even Glynese and Carramae were useful when they occupied attention that might otherwise have been directed at her. At first she had thought she could not stand Mrs. Freeman for she had found that it was not possible to be rude to her. Mrs. Freeman would take on strange resentments and for days together she would be sullen but the source of her displeasure was always obscure; a direct attack, a positive leer, blatant ugliness to her face—these never touched her. And without warning one day, she began calling her Hulga.

She did not call her that in front of Mrs. Hopewell who would have been incensed but when she and the girl happened to be out of the house together, she would say something and add the name Hulga to the end of it, and the big spectacled Joy-Hulga would scowl and redden as if her privacy had been intruded upon. She considered the name her personal affair. She had arrived at it first purely on the basis of its ugly sound and then the full genius of its fitness had struck her. She had a vision of the name working like the ugly sweating Vulcan who stayed in the furnace and to whom, presumably, the goddess had to come when called. She saw it as the name of her highest creative act. One of her major triumphs was that her mother had not been able to turn her dust into Joy, but the greater one was that she had been able to turn it herself into Hulga. However, Mrs. Freeman's relish for using the name only irritated her. It was as if Mrs. Freeman's beady steel-pointed eyes had penetrated far enough behind her face to reach some secret fact. Something about her seemed to fascinate Mrs. Freeman and then one day Hulga realized that it was the artificial leg. Mrs. Freeman had a special fondness for the details of secret infections, hidden deformities, assaults upon children. Of diseases, she preferred the lingering or incurable. Hulga had heard Mrs. Hopewell give her the details of the hunting accident, how the leg had been literally blasted off, how she had never lost consciousness. Mrs. Freeman could listen to it any time as if it had happened an hour ago.

When Hulga stumped into the kitchen in the morning (she could walk without making the awful noise but she made it—Mrs. Hopewell was certain—because it was ugly-sounding), she glanced at them and did not speak. Mrs. Hopewell would be in her red kimono with her hair tied around her head in rags. She would be sitting at the table, finishing her breakfast and Mrs. Freeman would be hanging by her elbow outward from the refrigerator, looking down at the table. Hulga always put her eggs on the stove to boil and then stood over them with her arms folded, and Mrs. Hopewell would look at her—a kind of indirect gaze divided between her and Mrs. Freeman—and would think that if she would only keep herself up a little, she wouldn't be so bad looking. There was nothing wrong with her face that a pleasant expression wouldn't help. Mrs. Hopewell said that people who looked on the bright side of things would be beautiful even if they were not.

Whenever she looked at Joy this way, she could not help but feel that it would have been better if the child had not taken the Ph.D. It had certainly not brought her out any and now that she had it, there was no more excuse for her to go to school again. Mrs. Hopewell thought it was nice for girls to go to school to have a good time but Joy had "gone through." Anyhow, she would not have been strong enough to go again. The doctors had told Mrs. Hopewell that with the best of care, Joy might see forty-five. She had a weak heart. Joy had made it plain that if it had not been for this condition, she would be far from these red hills and good country people. She would be in a university lecturing to people who knew what she was talking about. And Mrs. Hopewell could very well picture her there, looking like a scarecrow and lecturing to more of the same. Here she went about all day in a six-year-old skirt and a yellow sweat shirt with a faded cowboy on a horse embossed on it. She thought this was funny; Mrs. Hopewell though it was idiotic and showed simply that she was still a child. She was brilliant but she didn't have a grain of sense. It seemed to Mrs. Hopewell that every year she grew less like other people and more like herself—bloated, rude, and squint-eyed. And she said such strange things! To her own mother she had said—without warning, without excuse, standing up in the middle of a meal with her face purple and her mouth half full—"Woman! do you ever look inside? Do you ever look inside and see what you are *not?* God!" she had cried sinking down again and staring at her plate, "Male-branche was right: we are not our own light. We are not our own light!" Mrs. Hopewell had no idea to this day what brought that on. She had only made the remark, hoping Joy would take it in, that a smile never hurt anyone.

The girl had taken the Ph.D. in philosophy and this left Mrs. Hopewell at a complete loss. You could say, "My daughter is a nurse," or "My daughter is a school teacher," or even, "My daughter is a chemical engineer." You could not say, "My daughter is a philosopher." That was something that had ended with the Greeks and Romans. All day Joy sat on her neck in a deep chair, reading. Sometimes she went for walks but she didn't like dogs or cats or birds or flowers or nature or nice young men. She looked at nice young men as if she could smell their stupidity.

One day Mrs. Hopewell had picked up one of the books the girl had just put down and opening it at random, she read, "Science, on the other hand, has to assert its soberness and seriousness afresh and declare that it is concerned solely with what-is. Nothing—how can it be for science anything but a horror and a phantasm? If science is right, then one thing stands firm: science wishes to know nothing of nothing. Such is after all the strictly scientific approach to Nothing. We know it by wishing to know nothing of Nothing." These words had been underlined with a blue pencil and they worked on Mrs. Hopewell like some evil incantation in gibberish. She shut the book quickly and went out of the room as if she were having a chill.

This morning when the girl came in, Mrs. Freeman was on Carramae. "She thrown up four times after supper," she said, "and was up twict in the night after three o'clock. Yesterday she didn't do nothing but ramble in the bureau drawer. All she did. Stand up there and see what she could run up on."

"She's got to eat," Mrs. Hopewell muttered, sipping her coffee, while she watched Joy's back at the stove. She was wondering what the child had said to the Bible salesman. She could not imagine what kind of a conversation she could possibly have had with him.

He was a tall gaunt hatless youth who had called yesterday to sell them a Bible. He had appeared at the door, carrying a large black suitcase that weighted him so heavily on one side that he had to brace himself against the door facing. He seemed on the point of collapse but he said in a cheerful voice, "Good morning, Mrs. Cedars!" and set the suitcase down on the mat. He was not a bad-looking young man though he had on a bright blue suit and yellow socks that were not pulled up far enough. He had prominent face bones and a streak of sticky-looking brown hair falling across his forehead.

"I'm Mrs. Hopewell," she said.

"Oh!" he said, pretending to look puzzled but with his eyes sparkling, "I saw it said 'The Cedars,' on the mailbox so I thought you was Mrs. Cedars!" and he burst out in a pleasant laugh. He picked up the satchel and under cover of a pant, he fell forward into her hall. It was rather as if the suitcase had moved first, jerking him after it. "Mrs. Hopewell!" he said and grabbed her hand. "I hope you are well!" and he laughed again and then all at once his face sobered completely. He paused and gave her a straight earnest look and said, "Lady, I've come to speak of serious things."

"Well, come in," she muttered, none too pleased because her dinner was almost ready. He came into the parlor and sat down on the edge of a straight chair and put the suitcase between his feet and glanced around the room as if he were sizing her up by it. Her silver gleamed on the two sideboards; she decided he had never been in a room as elegant as this.

"Mrs. Hopewell," he began, using her name in a way that sounded almost intimate, "I know you believe in Chrustian service."

"Well yes," she murmured.

"I know," he said and paused, looking very wise with his head cocked one one side, "that you're a good woman. Friends have told me."

Mrs. Hopewell never liked to be taken for a fool. "What are you selling?" she asked.

"Bibles," the young man said and his eye raced around the room before he added, "I see you have no family Bible in your parlor, I see that is the one lack you got!"

Mrs. Hopewell could not say, "My daughter is an atheist and won't let me keep the Bible in the parlor." She said, stiffening slightly, "I keep my Bible by my bedside." This was not the truth. It was in the attic somewhere.

"Lady," he said, "the word of God ought to be in the parlor."

"Well, I think that's a matter of taste," she began. "I think . . ."

"Lady," he said, "for a Chrustian, the word of God ought to be in every room in the house besides in his heart. I know you're a Chrustian because I can see it in every line of your face."

She stood up and said, "Well, young man, I don't want to buy a Bible and I smell my dinner burning."

He didn't get up. He began to twist his hands and looking down at them, he said softly, "Well lady, I'll tell you the truth—not many people want to buy one nowadays and besides, I know I'm real simple. I don't know how to say a thing but to say it. I'm just a country boy." He glanced up into her unfriendly face. "People like you don't like to fool with country people like me!"

"Why!" she cried, "good country people are the salt of the earth! Besides, we all have different ways of doing, it takes all kinds to make the world go 'round. That's life!"

"You said a mouthful," he said.

"Why, I think there aren't enough good country people in the world!" she said, stirred. "I think that's what's wrong with it!"

His face had brightened. "I didn't inraduce myself," he said. "I'm Manley Pointer from out in the country around Willohobie, not even from a place, just from near a place."

"You wait a minute," she said. "I have to see about my dinner." She went out to the kitchen and found Joy standing near the door where she had been listening.

"Get rid of the salt of the earth," she said, "and let's eat."

Mrs. Hopewell gave her a pained look and turned the heat down under the vegetables. "I can't be rude to anybody," she murmured and went back into the parlor.

He had opened the suitcase and was sitting with a Bible on each knee.

"You might as well put those up," she told him. "I don't want one."

"I appreciate your honesty," he said. "You don't see any more real honest people unless you go way out in the country."

"I know," she said, "real genuine folks!" Through the crack in the door she heard a groan.

"I guess a lot of boys come telling you they're working their way through college," he said, "but I'm not going to tell you that. Somehow," he said, "I don't want to go to college. I want to devote my life to Chrustian service. See," he said, lowering his voice, "I got this heart condition. I may not live long. When you know it's something wrong with you and you may not live long, well then, lady . . ." He paused, with his mouth open, and stared at her.

He and Joy had the same condition! She knew that her eyes were filling with tears but she collected herself quickly and murmured, "Won't you stay for dinner? We'd love to have you!" and was sorry the instant she heard herself say it.

"Yes mam," he said in an abashed voice, "I would sher love to do that!"

Joy had given him one look on being introduced to him and then throughout the meal had not glanced at him again. He had addressed several remarks to her, which she had pretended not to hear. Mrs. Hopewell could not understand deliberate rudeness, although she lived with it, and she felt she had always to overflow with hospitality to make up for Joy's lack of courtesy. She urged him to talk about himself and he did. He said he was the seventh child of twelve and that his father had been crushed under a tree when he himself was eight year old. He had been crushed very badly, in fact, almost cut in two and was practically not recognizable. His mother had got along the best she could by hard working and she had always seen that her children went to Sunday School and that they read the Bible every evening. He was now nineteen year old and he had been selling Bibles for four months. In that time he had sold seventy-seven Bibles and had the promise of two more sales. He wanted to become a missionary because he thought that was the way you could do most for people. "He who losest his life shall find it," he said simply and he was so sincere, so genuine and earnest that Mrs. Hopewell would not for the world have smiled. He prevented his peas from sliding onto the table by blocking them with a piece of bread which he later cleaned his plate with. She could see Joy observing sidewise how he handled his knife and fork and she saw too that every few minutes, the boy would dart a keen appraising glance at the girl as if he were trying to attract her attention.

After dinner Joy cleared the dishes off the table and disappeared and Mrs. Hopewell was left to talk with him. He told her again about his childhood and his father's accident and about various things that had happened to him. Every five minutes or so she would stifle a yawn. He sat for two hours until finally she told him she must go because she had an appointment in town. He packed his Bibles and thanked her and prepared to leave, but in the doorway he stopped and wrung her hand and said that not on any of his trips had he met a lady as nice as her and he asked if he could come again. She had said she would always be happy to see him.

Joy had been standing in the road, apparently looking at something in the distance, when he came down the steps toward her, bent to the side with his heavy valise. He stopped where she was standing and confronted her directly. Mrs. Hopewell could not hear what he said but she trembled to think what Joy would say to him. She could see that after a minute Joy said something and that then the boy began to speak again, making an excited gesture with his free hand. After a minute Joy said something else at which the boy began to speak once more. Then to her amazement, Mrs. Hopewell saw the two of them walk off together, toward the gate. Joy had walked all the way to the gate with him and Mrs. Hopewell could not imagine what they had said to each other, and she had not yet dared to ask.

Mrs. Freeman was insisting upon her attention. She had moved from the refrigerator to the heater so that Mrs. Hopewell had to turn and face her in order to seem to be listening. "Glynese gone out with Harvey Hill again last night," she said. "She had this sty."

"Hill," Mrs. Hopewell said absently, "is that the one who works in the garage?"

"Nome, he's the one that goes to chiropracter school," Mrs. Freeman said. "She had this sty. Been had it two days. So she says when he brought her in the other night he says, 'Lemme get rid of that sty for you,' and she says, 'How?' and he says, 'You just lay yourself down acrost the seat of that car and I'll show you.' So she done it and he popped her neck. Kept on a-popping it several times until she made him quit. This morning," Mrs. Freeman said, "she ain't got no sty. She ain't got no traces of a sty."

"I never heard of that before," Mrs. Hopewell said.

"He ast her to marry him before the Ordinary," Mrs. Freeman went on, "and she told him she wasn't going to be married in no *office*."

"Well, Glynese is a fine girl," Mrs. Hopewell said. "Glynese and Carramae are both fine girls."

"Carramae said when her and Lyman was married Lyman said it sure felt sacred to him. She said he said he wouldn't take five hundred dollars for being married by a preacher."

"How much would he take?" the girl asked from the stove.

"He said he wouldn't take five hundred dollars," Mrs. Freeman repeated.

"Well we all have work to do," Mrs. Hopewell said.

"Lyman said it just felt more sacred to him," Mrs. Freeman said. "The doctor wants Carramae to eat prunes. Says instead of medicine. Says them cramps is coming from pressure. You know where I think it is?"

"She'll be better in a few weeks," Mrs. Hopewell said.

"In the tube," Mrs. Freeman said. "Else she wouldn't be as sick as she is."

Hulga had cracked her two eggs into a saucer and was bringing them to the table along with a cup of coffee that she had filled too full. She sat down carefully and began to eat, meaning to keep Mrs. Freeman there by questions if for any reason she showed an inclination to leave. She could perceive her mother's eye on her. The first round-about question would be about the Bible salesman and she did not wish to bring it on. "How did he pop her neck?" she asked.

Mrs. Freeman went into a description of how he had popped her neck. She said he owned a '55 Mercury but that Glynese said she would rather marry a man with only a '36 Plymouth who would be married by a preacher. The girl asked what if he had a '32 Plymouth and Mrs. Freeman said what Glynese had said was a '36 Plymouth.

Mrs. Hopewell said there were not many girls with Glynese's common sense. She said what she admired in those girls was their common sense. She said that reminded her that they had had a nice visitor yesterday, a young man selling Bibles. "Lord," she said, "he bored me to death but he was so sincere and genuine I couldn't be rude to him. He was just good country people, you know," she said, "—just the salt of the earth."

"I seen him walk up," Mrs. Freeman said, "and then later—I seen him walk off," and Hulga could feel the slight shift in her voice, the slight insinuation, that he had not walked off alone, had he? Her face remained expressionless but the color rose into her neck and she seemed to swallow it down with the next spoonful of egg. Mrs. Freeman was looking at her as if they had a secret together.

"Well, it takes all kinds of people to make the world go 'round," Mrs. Hopewell said. "It's very good we aren't all alike."

"Some people are more alike than others," Mrs. Freeman said.

Hulga got up and stumped, with about twice the noise that was necessary, into her room and locked the door. She was to meet the Bible salesman at ten o'clock at the gate. She had thought about it half the night. She had started thinking of it as a great joke and then she had begun to see profound implications in it. She had lain in bed imagining dialogues for them that were insane on the surface but that reached below to depths that no Bible salesman would be aware of. Their conversation yesterday had been of this kind.

He had stopped in front of her and had simply stood there. His face was bony and sweaty and bright, with a little pointed nose in the center of it, and his look was different from what it had been at the dinner table. He was gazing at her with open curiosity, with fascination, like a child watching a new fantastic animal at the zoo, and he was breathing as if he had run a great distance to reach her. His gaze seemed somehow familiar but she could not think where she had been regarded with it before. For almost a minute he didn't say anything. Then on what seemed an insuck of breath, he whispered, "You ever ate a chicken that was two days old?"

The girl looked at him stonily. He might have just put this question up for consideration at the meeting of a philosophical association. "Yes," she presently replied as if she had considered it from all angles.

"It must have been mighty small!" he said triumphantly and shook all over with little nervous giggles, getting very red in the face, and subsiding finally into his gaze of complete admiration, while the girl's expression remained exactly the same.

"How old are you?" he asked softly.

She waited some time before she answered. Then in a flat voice she said, "Seventeen."

His smiles came in succession like waves breaking on the surface of a little lake. "I see you got a wooden leg," he said. "I think you're real brave. I think you're real sweet."

The girl stood blank and solid and silent.

"Walk to the gate with me," he said. "You're a brave sweet little thing and I liked you the minute I seen you walk in the door."

Hulga began to move forward.

"What's your name?" he asked, smiling down on the top of her head.

"Hulga," she said.

"Hulga," he murmured, "Hulga. Hulga. I never heard of anybody name Hulga before. You're shy, aren't you, Hulga?" he asked.

She nodded, watching his large red hand on the handle of the giant valise.

"I like girls that wear glasses," he said. "I think a lot. I'm not like these people that a serious thought don't ever enter their heads. It's because I may die."

"I may die too," she said suddenly and looked up at him. His eyes were very small and brown, glittering feverishly.

"Listen," he said, "don't you think some people was meant to meet on account of what all they got in common and all? Like they both think serious thoughts and all?" He shifted the valise to his other hand so that the hand nearest her was free. He caught hold of her elbow and shook it a little. "I don't work on Saturday," he said. "I like to walk in the woods and see what Mother Nature is wearing. O'er the hills and far away. Picnics and things. Couldn't we go on a pic-nic tomorrow? Say yes, Hulga," he said and gave her a dying look as if he felt his insides about to drop out of him. He had even seemed to sway slightly toward her.

During the night she had imagined that she seduced him. She imagined that the two of them walked on the place until they came to the storage barn beyond the two back fields and there, she imagined, that things came to such a pass that she very easily seduced him and that then, of course, she had to reckon with his remorse. True genius can get an idea across even to an inferior mind. She imagined that she took his remorse in hand and changed it into a deeper understanding of life. She took all his shame away and turned it into something useful.

She set off for the gate at exactly ten o'clock, escaping without drawing Mrs. Hopewell's attention. She didn't take anything to eat, forgetting that food is usually taken on a picnic. She wore a pair of slacks and a dirty white shirt, and as an afterthought, she had put some Vapex on the collar of it since she did not own any perfume. When she reached the gate no one was there.

She looked up and down the empty highway and had the furious feeling that she had been tricked, that he had only meant to make her walk to the gate after the idea of him. Then suddenly he stood up, very tall, from behind a bush on the opposite embankment. Smiling, he lifted his hat which was new and wide-brimmed. He had not worn it yesterday and she wondered if he had bought it for the occasion. It was toast-colored with a red and white band around it and was slightly too large for him. He stepped from behind the bush still carrying the black valise. He had on the same suit and the same yellow socks sucked down in his shoes from walking. He crossed the highway and said, "I knew you'd come!"

The girl wondered acidly how he had known this. She pointed to the valise and asked, "Why did you bring your Bibles?"

He took her elbow, smiling down on her as if he could not stop. "You can never tell when you'll need the word of God, Hulga," he said. She had a moment in which she doubted that this was actually happening and then they began to climb the embankment. They went down into the pasture toward the woods. The boy walked lightly by her side, bouncing on his toes. The valise did not seem to be heavy today; he even swung it. They crossed half the pasture without saying anything and then, putting his hand easily on the small of her back, he asked softly, "Where does your wooden leg join on?"

She turned an ugly red and glared at him and for an instant the boy looked abashed. "I didn't mean you no harm," he said. "I only meant you're so brave and all. I guess God takes care of you."

"No," she said, looking forward and walking fast, "I don't even believe in God."

At this he stopped and whistled. "No!" he exclaimed as if he were too astonished to say anything else.

She walked on and in a second he was bouncing at her side, fanning with his hat. "That's very unusual for a girl," he remarked, watching her out of the corner of his eye. When they reached the edge of the wood, he put his hand on her back again and drew her against him without a word and kissed her heavily.

The kiss, which had more pressure than feeling behind it, produced that extra surge of adrenalin in the girl that enables one to carry a packed trunk out of a burning house, but in her, the power went at once to the brain. Even before he released her, her mind, clear and detached and ironic anyway, was regarding him from a great distance, with amusement but with pity. She had never been kissed before and she was pleased to discover that it was an unexceptional experience and all a matter of the mind's control. Some people might enjoy drain water if they were told it was vodka. When the boy, looking expectant but uncertain, pushed her gently away, she turned and walked on, saying nothing as if such business, for her, were common enough.

He came along panting at her side, trying to help her when he saw a root that she might trip over. He caught and held back the long swaying blades of thorn vine until she had passed beyond them. She led the way and he came breathing heavily behind her. Then they came out on a sunlit hillside, sloping softly into another one a little smaller. Beyond, they could see the rusted top of the old barn where the extra hay was stored.

The hill was sprinkled with small pink weeds. "Then you ain't saved?" he asked suddenly, stopping.

The girl smiled. It was the first time she had smiled at him at all. "In my economy," she said, "I'm saved and you are damned but I told you I didn't believe in God."

Nothing seemed to destroy the boy's look of admiration. He gazed at her now as if the fantastic animal at the zoo had put its paw through the bars and given him a loving poke. She thought he looked as if he wanted to kiss her again and she walked on before he had the chance.

"Ain't there somewheres we can sit down sometime?" he murmured, his voice softening toward the end of the sentence.

"In that barn," she said.

They made for it rapidly as if it might slide away like a train. It was a large two-story barn, cool and dark inside. The boy pointed up the ladder that led into the loft and said, "It's too bad we can't go up there."

"Why can't we?" she asked.

"Yer leg," he said reverently.

The girl gave him a contemptuous look and putting both hands on the ladder, she climbed it while he stood below, apparently awestruck. She pulled herself expertly through the opening and then looked down at him and said, "Well, come on if you're coming," and he began to climb the ladder, awkwardly bringing the suitcase with him.

"We won't need the Bible," she observed.

"You never can tell," he said, panting. After he had got into the loft, he was a few seconds catching his breath. She had sat down in a pile of straw. A wide sheath of sunlight, filled with dust particles, slanted over her. She lay back against a bale, her face turned away, looking out the front opening of the barn where hay was thrown from a wagon into the loft. The two pink-speckled hillsides lay back against a dark ridge of woods. The sky was cloudless and cold blue. The boy dropped down by her side and put one arm under her and the other over her and began methodically kissing her face, making little noises like a fish. He did not remove his hat but it was pushed far enough back not to interfere. When her glasses got in his way, he took them off of her and slipped them into his pocket.

The girl at first did not return any of the kisses but presently she began to and after she had put several on his cheek, she reached his lips and remained there, kissing him again and again as if she were trying to draw all the breath out of him. His breath was clear and sweet like a child's and the kisses were sticky like a child's. He mumbled about loving her and about knowing when he first seen her that he loved her, but the mumbling was like the sleepy fretting of a child being put to sleep by his mother. Her mind, throughout this, never stopped or lost itself for a second to her feelings. "You ain't said you loved me none," he whispered finally, pulling back from her. "You got to say that."

She looked away from him off into the hollow sky and then down at a black ridge and then down farther into what appeared to be two green swelling lakes. She didn't realize he had taken her glasses but this landscape could not seem exceptional to her for she seldom paid any close attention to her surroundings.

"You got to say it," he repeated. "You got to say you love me."

She was always careful how she committed herself. "In a sense," she began, "if you use the word loosely, you might say that. But it's not a word I use. I don't have illusions. I'm one of those people who see *through* to nothing."

The boy was frowning. "You got to say it. I said it and you got to say it," he said.

The girl looked at him almost tenderly. "You poor baby," she murmured. "It's just as well you don't understand," and she pulled him by the neck, face-down, against her. "We are all damned," she said, "but some of us have taken off our blindfolds and see that there's nothing to see. It's a kind of salvation."

The boy's astonished eyes looked blankly through the ends of her hair. "Okay," he almost whined, "but do you love me or don'tcher?"

"Yes," she said and added, "in a sense. But I must tell you something. There mustn't be anything dishonest between us." She lifted his head and looked him in the eye. "I am thirty years old," she said. "I have a number of degrees."

The boy's look was irritated but dogged. "I don't care," he said. "I don't care a thing about what all you done. I just want to know if you love me or don'tcher?" and he caught her to him and wildly planted her face with kisses until she said, "Yes, yes."

"Okay then," he said, letting her go. "Prove it."

She smiled, looking dreamily out on the shifty landscape. She had seduced him without even making up her mind to try. "How?" she asked, feeling that he should be delayed a little.

He leaned over and put his lips to her ear. "Show me where your wooden leg joins on," he whispered.

The girl uttered a sharp little cry and her face instantly drained of color. The obscenity of the suggestion was not what shocked her. As a child she had sometimes been subject to feelings of shame but education had removed the last traces of that as a good surgeon scrapes for cancer; she would no more have felt it over what he was asking than she would have believed in his Bible. But she was as sensitive about the artificial leg as a peacock about his tail. No one ever touched it but her. She took care of it as someone else would his soul, in private and almost with her own eyes turned away. "No," she said.

"I known it," he muttered, sitting up. "You're just playing me for a sucker."

"Oh no no!" she cried. "It joins on at the knee. Only at the knee. Why do you want to see it?"

The boy gave her a long penetrating look. "Because," he said, "it's what makes you different. You ain't like anybody else."

She sat staring at him. There was nothing about her face or her round freezing-blue eyes to indicate that this had moved her; but she felt as if her heart had stopped and left her mind to pump her blood. She decided that for the first time in her life she was face to face with real innocence. This boy, with an instinct that came from beyond wisdom, had touched the truth about her. When after a minute, she said in a hoarse high voice, "All right," it was like surrendering to him completely. It was like losing her own life and finding it again, miraculously, in his.

Very gently he began to roll the slack leg up. The artificial limb, in a white sock and brown flat shoe, was bound in a heavy material like canvas and ended in an ugly jointure where it was attached to the stump. The boy's face and his voice were entirely reverent as he uncovered it and said, "Now show me how to take it off and on."

She took it off for him and put it back on again and then he took it off himself, handling it as tenderly as if it were a real one. "See!" he said with a delighted child's face. "Now I can do it myself!"

"Put it back on," she said. She was thinking that she would run away with him and that every night he would take the leg off and every morning put it back on again. "Put it back on," she said.

"Not yet," he murmured, setting it on its foot out of her reach. "Leave it off for a while. You got me instead."

She gave a little cry of alarm but he pushed her down and began to kiss her again. Without the leg she felt entirely dependent on him. Her brain seemed to have stopped thinking altogether and to be about some other function that it was not very good at. Different expressions raced back and forth over her face. Every now and then the boy, his eyes like two steel spikes, would glance behind him where the leg stood. Finally she pushed him off and said, "Put it back on me now."

"Wait," he said. He leaned the other way and pulled the valise toward him and opened it. It had a pale blue spotted lining and there were only two Bibles in it. He took one of these out and opened the cover of it. It was hollow and contained a pocket flask of whiskey, a pack of cards, and a small blue box with printing on it. He laid these out in front of her one at a time in an evenly-spaced row, like one presenting offerings at the shrine of a goddess. He put the blue box in her hand. THIS PRODUCT TO BE USED ONLY FOR THE PREVENTION OF DISEASE, she read, and dropped it. The boy was unscrewing the top of the flask. He stopped and pointed, with a smile, to the deck of cards. It was not an ordinary deck but one with an obscene picture on the back of each card. "Take a swig," he said, offering her the bottle first. He held it in front of her, but like one mesmerized, she did not move.

Her voice when she spoke had an almost pleading sound. "Aren't you," she murmured, "aren't you just good country people?"

The boy cocked his head. He looked as if he were just beginning to understand that she might be trying to insult him. "Yeah," he said, curling his lip slightly, "but it ain't held me back none. I'm as good as you any day in the week."

"Give me my leg," she said.

He pushed it farther away with his foot. "Come on now, let's begin to have us a good time," he said coaxingly. "We ain't got to know one another good yet."

"Give me my leg!" she screamed and tried to lunge for it but he pushed her down easily.

"What's the matter with you all of a sudden?" he asked, frowning as he screwed the top on the flask and put it quickly back inside the Bible. "You just a while ago said you didn't believe in nothing. I thought you was some girl!"

Her face was almost purple. "You're a Christian!" she hissed. "You're a fine Christian! You're just like them all—say one thing and do another. You're a perfect Christian, you're . . ."

The boy's mouth was set angrily. "I hope you don't think," he said in a lofty indignant tone, "that I believe in that crap! I may sell Bibles but I know which end is up and I wasn't born yesterday and I know where I'm going!"

"Give me my leg!" she screeched. He jumped up so quickly that she barely saw him sweep the cards and the blue box back into the Bible and throw the Bible into the valise. She saw him grab the leg and then she saw it for an instant slanted forlornly across the inside of the suitcase with a Bible at either side of its opposite ends. He slammed the lid shut and snatched up the valise and swung it down the hole and then stepped through himself.

When all of him had passed but his head, he turned and regarded her with a look that no longer had any admiration in it. "I've gotten a lot of interesting things," he said. "One time I got a woman's glass eye this way. And you needn't to think you'll catch me because Pointer ain't really my name. I use a different name at every house I call at and don't stay nowhere long. And I'll tell you another thing, Hulga," he said, using the name as if he didn't think much of it, "you ain't so smart. I been believing in nothing ever since I was born!" and then the toast-colored hat disappeared down the hole and the girl was left, sitting on the straw in the dusty sunlight. When she turned her churning face toward the opening, she saw his blue figure struggling successfully over the green speckled lake.

Mrs. Hopewell and Mrs. Freeman, who were in the back pasture, digging up onions, saw him emerge a little later from the woods and head across the meadow toward the highway. "Why, that looks like that nice dull young man that tried to sell me a Bible yesterday," Mrs. Hopewell said, squinting. "He must have been selling them to the Negroes back in there. He was so simple," she said, "but I guess the world would be better off if we were all that simple."

Mrs. Freeman's gaze drove forward and just touched him before he disappeared under the hill. Then she returned her attention to the evil-smelling onion shoot she was lifting from the ground. "Some can't be that simple," she said. "I know I never could."

O'CONNOR, "GOOD COUNTRY PEOPLE"

QUESTIONS FOR COMPREHENSION AND DISCUSSION

1. From Mrs. Hopewell's many references to "good country people," what do you learn about her attitudes and her perception of real life?
2. What purpose in the story does Mrs. Freeman serve?
3. Hulga is obviously educated, but can you accept her claims to believe in nothing? Why or why not?
4. Apart from their literal meaning, how does Miss O'Connor use Hulga's wooden leg and her degree in philosophy as symbols?
5. The story might be interpreted as showing the discrepancy between appearance and reality. How does this help explain Hulga's relationship with the Bible salesman? Mrs. Hopewell's tolerance of Mrs. Freeman's constant chatter about her daughters? Her politeness toward the Bible salesman?
6. Why is the Bible salesman so successful in deceiving Mrs. Hopewell and finally Hulga?
7. At the end of the story, how was Hulga changed?

VOCABULARY

From the lettered choices, find the best definition for each vocabulary item, and mark the letter in the space provided.

1. _____ an *imperceptible* movement
2. _____ the large *hulking* Joy
3. _____ *obliterated* every expression
4. _____ her face so *glum*
5. _____ she would be *sullen*
6. _____ the source was always *obscure*
7. _____ *blatant* ugliness
8. _____ like some evil *incantation*
9. _____ a tall *gaunt* youth
10. _____ in an *abashed* voice
11. _____ *stifle* a yawn
12. _____ the slight *insinuation*
13. _____ he stood, *awestruck*
14. _____ like one *mesmerized*
15. _____ in a *lofty*, indignant tone

A. obstinately ill-humored; morose
B. arrogant; haughty
C. disconcerted; astonished
D. destroyed completely; wiped out
E. emaciated; hollow-eyed; lean
F. embarrassed
G. ugly
H. slight; barely noticeable
I. corrupted; warped
J. entranced; hypnotized

K. obvious; obtrusive
L. magic words; prayer to
   produce magic results
M. sly hint; innuendo
N. moody and silent
O. filled with reverential fear

P. pathetic
Q. not clear; hidden
R. self-satisfied
S. suppress; keep back
T. big and clumsy

VOCABULARY   No. right ——

6

JOHN UPDIKE

*Eros Rampant**

*Born in Shillington, Pennsylvania, and educated at Harvard, John Updike
(1932–   ) is one of this country's most important and well-respected
young writers. "Eros Rampant" is an excellent example of Updike's ability
to use evocative language. In this story, the writer depicts modern marriage, with the peculiar twists, frustrations, and deceptive appearances
which govern the Maples' lives.*

The Maples' house is full of love. Bean, the six-year-old baby, loves
Hecuba, the dog. John, who is eight, an angel-faced mystic serenely unable
to ride a bicycle or read a clock, is in love with his Creepy Crawlers, his
monster cards, his dinosaurs, and his carved rhinoceros from Kenya. He
spends hours in his room after school drifting among these things, rear-
ranging, gloating, humming. He experiences pain only when his older
brother, Richard Jr., sardonically attempts to enter his room and pierces his
placenta of contemplation. Richard is in love with life, with all outdoors,
with Carl Yastrzemski, Babe Parelli, the Boston Bruins, the Beatles, and
with that shifty apparition who, comb in hand, peeps back shiny-eyed at
him out of the mirror in the mornings, wearing a moustache of toothpaste.
He receives strange challenging notes from girls—*Dickie Maple you stop
looking at me*—which he brings home from school carelessly crumpled
along with his spelling papers and hectographed notices about eye, tooth,
and lung inspection. His feelings about young Mrs. Brice, who confronts
his section of the fifth grade with the enameled poise and diction of an airline hostess, are so guarded as to be suspicious. He almost certainly loves,
has always deeply loved, his older sister, Judith. Verging on thirteen, she
has become difficult to contain, even within an incestuous passion. Large
and bumptious, she eclipses his view of the television screen, loudly frugs
while he would listen to the Beatles, teases, thrashes, is bombarded and
jogged by powerful rays from outer space. She hangs for hours by the

* From *Harper's*, June, 1968, pp. 59–64.

corner where Mr. Lunt, her history teacher, lives; she pastes effigies of the
Monkees on her walls, French-kisses her mother good-night, experiences
the panic of sleeplessness, engages in long languorous tussles on the sofa
with the dog. Hecuba, a spayed golden retriever, races from room to room,
tormented as if by fleas by the itch for adoration, ears flattened, tail thumping, until at last she runs up against the cats, who do not love her, and she
drops exhausted, in grateful defeat, on the kitchen linoleum, and sleeps.
The cats, Esther and Esau, lick each other's fur and share a bowl. They
had been two of a litter. Esther, the mother of more than thirty kittens
mostly resembling her brother, but with a persistent black minority vindi-
cating the howled appeal of a neighboring tom, has been "fixed"; Esau,
sentimentally allowed to continue unfixed, now must venture from the
house in quest of the bliss that had once been purely domestic. He returns
scratched and battered. Esther licks his wounds while he leans dazed beside the refrigerator; even his purr is ragged. Nagging for their supper,
they sit like bookends, their backs discreetly touching, an expert old married couple on the dole. One feels, unexpectedly, that Esau still loves
Esther, while she merely accepts and understands him. She seems scornful of his merely dutiful attentions. Is she puzzled by her abrupt surgical
lack of what drastically attracts him? But it is his big square tomcat's head
that seems puzzled, rather than her triangular feminine feline one. The
children feel a difference; both Bean and John cuddle Esau more, now
that Esther is sterile. Perhaps, obscurely, they feel that she has deprived
them of a miracle, of the semiannual miracle of her kittens, of drowned
miniature piglets wriggling alive from a black orifice vaster than a cave.
Richard Jr., as if to demonstrate his superior purchase on manhood and its
righteous compassion, makes a point of petting the two cats equally, stroke
for stroke. Judith claims she hates them both; it is her chore to feed them
supper, and she hates the smell of horsemeat. She loves, at least in the
abstract, horses.

Mr. Maple loves Mrs. Maple. He goes through troublesome periods,
often on Saturday afternoons, of being unable to take his eyes from her,
of being captive to the absurd persuasion that the curve of her solid
haunch conceals, enwraps, a precarious treasure mistakenly confided to his
care. He cannot touch her enough. The sight of her body contorted by one
of her yoga exercises, in her elastic black leotard riddled with runs, twists
his heart so that he cannot breathe. Her gesture as she tips the dregs of
white wine into a potted geranium seems infinite, like one of Vermeer's
moments frozen in an eternal light from the left. At night he tries to press
her into himself, to secure her drowsy body against his breast like a clasp,
as if without it he will come undone. He cannot sleep in this position, yet
maintains it long after her breathing has become steady and oblivious: can
love be defined, simply, as the refusal to sleep? Also he loves Penelope
Vogel, a quaint little secretary at his office who is recovering from a dis-
astrous affair with an Antiguan; and he is in love with the memories of six

or so other women, beginning with a seven-year-old playmate who used to steal his hunter's cap; and is half in love with death. He as well seems to love, perhaps alone in the nation, President Johnson, who is unaware of his existence. Along the same lines, Richard adores the moon; he studies avidly all the photographs beamed back from its uncongenial surface.

And Joan? Whom does she love? Her psychiatrist, certainly. Her father, inevitably. Her yoga instructor, probably. She has a part-time job in a museum and returns home flushed and quick-tongued, as if from sex. She must love the children, for they flock to her like sparrows to suet. They fight bitterly for a piece of her lap and turn their backs upon their father, as if he, the source and shelter of their life, were a grotesque intruder, a chimney sweep in a snow palace. None of his impersonations with the children—scoutmaster, playmate, confidant, financial bastion, factual wizard, watchman of the night—win them over; Bean still cries for Mommy when hurt, John approaches her for the money to finance yet more monster cards, Dickie demands that hers be the last good-night, and even Judith, who should be his, kisses him timidly, and saves her open-mouthed passion for her mother. Joan swims through their love like a fish through water, ignorant of any other element. Love slows her footsteps, pours upon her from the radio, hangs about her, in the kitchen, in the form of tacked-up children's drawings of houses, families, cars, cats, dogs, and flowers. Her husband cannot touch her; she is solid but hidden, like the World Bank, presiding yet immaterial, like the federal judiciary. Some cold uncoordinated thing pushes at his hand as it hangs impotent; it is Hecuba's nose. Obese spayed golden-eyed bitch, like him she abhors exclusion and strains to add her warmth to the tumble, in love with them all, in love with the smell of food, in love with the smell of love.

Penelope Vogel takes care to speak without sentimentality; five years younger than Richard, she has endured a decade of amorous ordeals and, still single at twenty-nine, preserves herself by speaking dryly, in the flip phrases of a still younger generation.

"We had a good thing," she says of her Antiguan, "that became a bad scene."

She handles, verbally, her old affairs like dried flowers; sitting across the restaurant table from her, Richard is made jittery by her delicacy, as if he and a grandmother are together examining an array of brittle, enigmatic mementos. "A very undesirable scene," Penelope adds. "The big time was too much for him. He got in with the drugs crowd. I couldn't see it."

"He wanted to marry you?" Richard asks timidly; this much is office gossip.

She shrugs, admitting, "There was that pitch."

"You must miss him."

"There is that. He was the most beautiful man I ever saw. His shoulders. In Dickinson's Bay, he'd have me put my hand on his shoulder in the water and that way he'd pull me along for miles, swimming. He was a snorkel instructor."

"His name?" Jittery, fearful of jarring these reminiscences, which are also negotiations, he spills the last of his Gibson, and jerkily signals to order another.

"Hubert," Penelope says. She is patiently mopping with her napkin. "Like a girl friend told me, Never take on a male beauty, you'll have to fight for the mirror." Her face is small and very white, and her nose very long, her pink nostrils inflamed by a perpetual cold. Only a Negro, Richard thinks, could find her beautiful; the thought gives her, in the restless shadowy restaurant light, beauty. The waiter, colored, comes and changes their tablecloth. Penelope continues so softly Richard must strain to hear, "When Hubert was eighteen he had a woman divorce her husband and leave her children for him. She was one of the old planter families. He wouldn't marry her. He told me, If she'd do that to him, next thing she'd leave me. He was very moralistic, until he came up here. But imagine an eighteen-year-old boy having an effect like that on a mature married woman in her thirties."

"I better keep him away from my wife," Richard jokes.

"Yeah." She does not smile. "They *work* at it, you know. Those boys are *pros.*"

Penelope has often been to the West Indies. In St. Croix, it delicately emerges, there was Andrew, with his goatee and his septic-tank business and his political ambitions; in Guadeloupe, there was Ramon, a customs inspector; in Trinidad, Castlereigh, who played the alto pans in a steel band and also did the limbo. He could go down to nine inches. But Hubert was the worst, or best. He was the only one who had followed her north. "I was supposed to come live with him in this hotel in Dorchester but I was scared to go near the place, full of cop-out types and the smell of pot in the elevator. I got two offers from guys just standing there pushing the Up button. It was not a healthy scene." The waiter brings them rolls; in his shadow her profile seems wan and he yearns to pluck her, pale flower, from the tangle she has conjured. "It got so bad," she says, "I tried going back to an old boy friend, an awfully nice guy with a mother and a nervous stomach. He's a computer systems analyst, very dedicated, but I don't know, he just never impressed me. All he can talk about is his gastritis and how she keeps telling him to move out and get a wife, but he doesn't know if she means it. His mother."

"He is . . . white?"

Penelope glances up; there is a glint off her halted butter knife. Her voice slows, goes drier. "No, as a matter of fact. He's what they call an Afro-American. You mind?"

"No, no, I was just wondering—his nervous stomach. He doesn't sound like the others."

"He's not. Like I say, he doesn't impress me. Don't you find, once you have something that works, it's hard to back up?" More seems meant than is stated; her level gaze, as she munches her thickly buttered bun, feels like one tangent in a complicated geometrical problem: find the point at which she had switched from white to black lovers.

The subject is changed for him; his heart jars, and he leans forward hastily to say, "See that woman who just came in? Leather suit, gypsy earrings, sitting down now? Her name is Eleanor Dennis. She lives down our street from us. She's divorced."

"Who's the man?"

"I have no idea. Eleanor's moved out of our circles. He looks like a real thug." Along the far wall, Eleanor adjusts the great loop of her earring; her sideways glance, in the shuffle of shadows, flicks past his table. He doubts that she saw him.

Penelope says, "From the look on your face, that was more than a circle she was in with you."

He pretends to be disarmed by her guess, but in truth considers it providential that one of his own old loves should appear, to countervail the dark torrent of hers. For the rest of the meal they talk about *him*, him and Eleanor and Marlene Bossman and Joan and the little girl who used to steal his hunter's cap. In the lobby of Penelope's apartment house, the elevator summoned, he offers to go up with her.

She says carefully, "I don't think you want to."

"But I *do*." The building is Back Bay modern; the lobby is garishly lit and furnished with plastic plants that need never be watered, Naugahyde chairs that were never sat upon, and pointless tessellated plaques. The light is an absolute presence, as even and clean as the light inside a freezer, as ubiquitous as ether or as the libido that, Freud says, permeates all of us from infancy on.

"No," Penelope repeats. "I've developed a good ear for sincerity in these things. I think you're too wrapped up back home."

"The dog likes me," he confesses, and kisses her good-night there, encased in brightness. Dry voice to the contrary, her lips are shockingly soft, wide, warm, and sorrowing.

"So," Joan says to him. "You slept with that little office mouse." It is Saturday; the formless erotic suspense of the afternoon is over. The Maples are in their room dressing for a party, by the ashen light of dusk, and the watery blue of a distant streetlamp.

"I never have," he says, thereby admitting, however, that he knows who she means.

"Well you took her to dinner."

"Who says?"

"Mack Dennis. Eleanor saw the two of you in a restaurant.

"When do they converse? I thought they were divorced."

"They talk all the time. He's still in love with her. Everybody knows that."

"Okay. When do he and *you* converse?"

Oddly, she has not prepared an answer. "Oh—" His heart falls through her silence. "Maybe I saw him in the hardware store this afternoon."

"And maybe you didn't. Why would he blurt this out anyway? You and he must be on cozy terms."

He says this to trigger her denial; but she mutely considers and, sauntering toward her closet, admits, "We understand each other."

How unlike her, to bluff this way. "When was I supposedly seen?"

"You mean it happens often? Last Wednesday, around eight-thirty. You *must* have slept with her."

"I couldn't have. I was home by ten, you may remember. You had just gotten back yourself from the museum."

"What went wrong, darley? Did you offend her with your horrible pro-Vietnam stand?"

In the dim light he hardly knows this woman, her broken gestures, her hasty voice. Her silver slip glows and crackles as she wriggles into a black knit cocktail dress; with a kind of determined agitation she paces around the bed, to the bureau and back. As she moves, her body seems to be gathering bulk from the shadows, bulk and a dynamic elasticity. He tries to placate her with a token offering of truth. "No, it turns out Penelope only goes with Negroes. I'm too pale for her."

"You admit you tried?"

He nods.

"Well," Joan says, and takes a half-step toward him, so that he flinches in anticipation of being hit, "do you want to know who *I* was sleeping with Wednesday?"

He nods again, but the two nods feel different, as if, transposed by a terrific unfelt speed, a continent had lapsed between them.

She names a man he knows only slightly, an assistant director in the museum, who wears a collar pin and has his gray hair cut long and tucked back in the foppish English style. "It was *fun*," Joan says, kicking at a shoe. "He thinks I'm *beau*tiful. He cares for me in a way you just *don't*." She kicks away the other shoe. "You look pale to me too, buster."

Stunned, he needs to laugh. "But we all think you're beautiful."

"Well you don't make me *feel* it."

"*I* feel it," he says.

"You make me feel like an ugly drudge." As they grope to understand their new positions, they realize that she, like a chess player who has impulsively swept forward her queen, has nowhere to go but on the defensive. In a desperate attempt to keep the initiative, she says, "Divorce me. Beat me."

He is calm, factual, admirable. "How often have you been with him?"

"I don't know. Since April, off and on." Her hands appear to embarrass her; she places them at her sides, against her cheeks, together on the bedpost, off. "I've been trying to get out of it, I've felt horribly guilty, but he's never been at all pushy, so I could never really arrange a fight. He gets this hurt look."

"Do you want to keep him?"

"With you knowing? Don't be grotesque."

"But he cares for you in a way I just don't."

"Any lover does that."

"God help us. You're an expert."

"Hardly."

"What *about* you and Mack?"

She is frightened. "Years ago. Not for very long."

"And Freddy Vetter?"

"No, we agreed not. He knew about me and Mack."

Love, a cloudy heavy ink, inundates him from within, suffuses his palms with tingling pressure as he steps close to her, her murky face held tense against the expectation of a blow. "You whore," he breathes, enraptured. "My sweet bride." He kisses her hands; they are corrupt and cold. "Who else?" he begs, as if each name is a burden of treasure she lays upon his bowed serf's shoulders. "Tell me all your men."

"I've told you. It's a pretty austere list. You know *why* I told you? So you wouldn't feel guilty about this Vogel person."

"But nothing happened. When you do it, it happens."

"Sweetie, I'm a woman," she explains, and they do seem, in this darkening room above the muted hubbub of television, to have reverted to the bases of their marriage, to the elemental constituents. Woman. Man. House.

"What does your psychiatrist say about all this?"

"Not much." The triumphant swell of her confession has passed; her drier manner prepares for days, weeks of his questions. She retrieves the shoes she kicked away. "That's one of the reasons I went to him, I kept having these affairs—"

"*Kept* having? You're killing me."

"Please don't interrupt. It was somehow very innocent. I'd go into his office, and lie down, and say, 'I've just been with Mack, or Otto—'"

"Otto. What's that joke? Otto is 'toot' spelled inside out."

" '—and it was wonderful, or awful, or so-so,' and then we'd talk about my childhood masturbation. It's not his business to scold me, it's his job to get me to stop scolding myself."

"The poor bastard, all the time I've been jealous of him, and he's been suffering with this for years; he had to listen every *day*. You'd go in there and plunk yourself still warm down on his couch—"

"It wasn't every day at all. Weeks would go by. I'm not Otto's only woman."

The artificial tumult of television below merges with a real commotion, a screaming and bumping that mounts the stairs and threatens the aquarium where the Maples are swimming, dark fish in ink, their outlines barely visible, known to each other only as eddies of warmth, as mysterious animate chasms in the surface of space. Fearing that for years he will not again be so close to Joan, or she be so open, he hurriedly asks, "And what about the yoga instructor?"

"Don't be silly," Joan says, clasping her pearls at the nape of her neck. "He's an elderly vegetarian."

The door crashes open; their bedroom explodes in shards of electric light. Richard Jr. is frantic, sobbing.

"Mommy, Judy keeps teasing me and getting in front of the television!"

"I did not. I did not." Judith speaks very distinctly, "Mother and Father, he is a retarded liar."

"She can't help she's growing," Richard tells his son, picturing poor Judith trying to fit herself among the intent childish silhouettes in the little television room, pitying her for her bulk, much as he pities Johnson for his Presidency. Bean bursts into the bedroom, frightened by violence, and Hecuba leaps upon the bed with rolling golden eyes, and Judith gives Dickie an impudent and unrepentant sideways glance, and he, gagging on a surfeit of emotion, bolts from the room. Soon there arises from the other end of the upstairs an anguished squawk as Dickie invades John's room and punctures his communion with his dinosaurs. Downstairs, a woman, neglected and alone, locked in a box, sings about *amore*. Bean hugs Joan's legs so she cannot move.

Judith asks with parental sharpness, "What were you two talking about?"

"Nothing," Richard says. "We were getting dressed."

"Why were all the lights out?"

"We were saving electricity," her father tells her.

"Why is Mommy crying?" He looks, disbelieving, and discovers that indeed, her cheeks coated with silver, she is.

At the party, amid clouds of friends and smoke, Richard resists being parted from his wife's side. She has dried her tears, and faintly swaggers, as when, on the beach, she dares wear a bikini. But her nakedness is only in his eyes. Her head beside his shoulder, her grave soft voice, the plump unrepentant cleft between her breasts, all seem newly treasurable and intrinsic to his own identity. As a cuckold, he has grown taller, attenuated, more elegant and humane in his opinions, airier and more mobile. When the usual argument about Vietnam commences, he hears himself sounding like a dove. He concedes that Johnson is unlovable. He allows that Asia is infinitely complex, devious, ungrateful, feminine: but must we abandon her therefore? When Mack Dennis, grown burly in bachelorhood, comes and asks Joan to dance, Richard feels unmanned and sits on the sofa with such an air of weariness that Marlene Brossman sits down beside him and, for the first time in years, flirts. He tries to tell her with his voice, beneath the meaningless words he is speaking, that he loved her, and could love her again, but that at the moment he is terribly distracted and must be excused. He goes and asks Joan if it isn't time to go. She resists; "It's too rude." She is safe here among proprieties and foresees that his exploitation of the territory she has surrendered will be thorough. Love is pitiless. They drive home at midnight under a slim moon nothing like its photographs—shadow-caped canyons, gimlet mountain ranges, gritty circular depressions around the metal feet of the mechanical intruder sent from the blue ball in the sky.

They do not rest until he has elicited from her a world of details: dates, sites, motel interiors, precisely mixed emotions. They make love, self-critically. He exacts the new wantonness she owes him, and in compensation tries to be, like a battered old roué, skillful. He satisfies himself that in some elemental way he has never been displaced; that for months she has been struggling in her lover's grasp, in the gauze net of love, her wings pinioned by tact. She assures him that she seized on the first opportunity for confession; she confides to him that Otto spray-sets his hair and uses perfume. She, weeping, vows that nowhere, never, has she encountered his, Richard's, passion, his pleasant bodily proportions and backwards-reeling grace, his invigorating sadism, his male richness. Then why . . . ? She is asleep. Her breathing has become oblivious. He clasps her limp body to his, wasting forgiveness upon her ghostly form. A receding truck pulls the night's silence taut. She has left him a hair short of satiety; her confession feels still a fraction unplumbed. The lunar face of the electric clock says three. He turns, flips his pillow, restlessly adjusts his arms, turns again, and seems to go downstairs for a glass of milk.

To his surprise, the kitchen is brightly lit, and Joan is on the linoleum floor, in her leotard. He stands amazed while she serenely twists her legs into the lotus position. He asks her again about the yoga instructor.

"Well, I didn't think it counted if it was part of the exercise. The whole point, darley, is to make mind and body one. This is Pranayama—breath control." Stately, she pinches shut one nostril and slowly inhales, then pinches shut the other and exhales. Her hands return, palm up, to her knees. And she smiles. "This one is fun. It's called the Twist." She assumes a new position, her muscles elastic under the black cloth tormented into runs. "Oh, I forgot to tell you, I've slept with Harry Saxon."

"Joan, no. How often?"

"When we felt like it. We used to go out behind the Little League field. That heavenly smell of clover."

"But sweetie, why?"

Smiling, she inwardly counts the seconds of this position. "You know why. He asked. It's hard, when men ask. You mustn't insult their male natures. There's a harmony in everything."

"And Freddy Vetter? You lied about Freddy, didn't you?"

"Now *this* pose is wonderful for the throat muscles. It's called the Lion. You mustn't laugh." She kneels, her buttocks on her heels, and tilts back her head, and from gaping jaws thrusts out her tongue as if to touch the ceiling. Yet she continues speaking. "The whole theory is, we hold our heads too high, and blood can't get to the brain."

His chest hurts; he forces from it the cry, "Tell me everybody!"

She rolls toward him and stands upright on her shoulders, her face flushed with the effort of equilibrium and the downflow of blood. Her legs slowly scissor open and shut. "Some men you don't know," she goes on. "They come to the door to sell you septic tanks." Her voice is coming from her belly. Worse, there is a humming. Terrified, he awakes, and sits up. His chest is soaked.

He locates the humming as a noise from the transformer on the telephone pole near their windows. All night, while its residents sleep, the town communes with itself electrically. Richard's terror persists, generating mass as the reality of his dream sensations is confirmed. Joan's body seems small, scarcely bigger than Judith's, and narrower with age, yet infinitely deep, an abyss of secrecy, perfidy, and acceptingness; acrophobia launches sweat from his palms. He leaves the bed as if scrambling backward from the lip of a vortex. He again goes downstairs; his wife's revelations have steepened the treads and left the walls slippery.

The kitchen is dark; he turns on the light. The floor is bare. The familiar objects of the kitchen seem discovered in a preservative state of staleness, wearing a look of tension, as if they are about to burst with the strain of being so faithfully themselves. Esther and Esau pad in from the living room, where they have been sleeping on the sofa, and beg to be fed, sitting like bookends, expectant and expert. The clock says four. Watchman of the night. But in searching for signs of criminal entry, for traces of his dream, Richard finds nothing but—clues mocking in their very abundance—the tacked-up drawings done by children's fingers ardently bunched around a crayon, of houses, cars, cats, and flowers.

UPDIKE, "EROS RAMPANT"

QUESTIONS FOR COMPREHENSION AND DISCUSSION

1. What is ironic about the story's opening line: "The Maples' house is full of love"?

2. What is "erotic" love? In what ways does Updike use the title, "Eros Rampant"?

3. Does Mr. Maple change in any way during the story? Why is he so curious about his wife's affairs?

4. Is Mr. Maple dreaming the entire incident or are his wife's confessions real? How can you support your answer?

5. From the entire story, what do you know about their marriage? What holds it together? What kind of society do the Maples move in?

6. What is the effect of the last line? "But in searching for signs of criminal entry, for traces of his dream, Richard finds nothing but—clues mocking in their very abundance—the tacked-up drawings done by children's fingers ardently bunched around a crayon, of houses, cars, cats, and flowers." Why are these clues "mocking"? Do these images suggest something more than the drawings of innocent children?

VOCABULARY

From the lettered choices, find the best definition for each vocabulary item, and mark the letter in the space provided.

1. _____ *sardonically* attempts
2. _____ an *incestuous* passion
3. _____ long *languorous* tussles
4. _____ she seems *scornful*
5. _____ a *precarious* treasure
6. _____ it hangs *impotent*
7. _____ an array of *enigmatic* mementoes
8. _____ as *ubiquitous* as ether
9. _____ she *mutely* considers
10. _____ he tries to *placate* her
11. _____ a pretty *austere* list
12. _____ a *surfeit* of emotion
13. _____ the new *wantonness*
14. _____ short of *satiety*
15. _____ an abyss of *perfidy*

A. sexual attraction between relatives; forbidden

B. baffling; puzzling

C. subject to continual risk; uncertain

D. complicated; impressively long

E. childish; innocent

F. excess; rush

G. cynically; mockingly

H. surreptitiously; sneakily

I. existing everywhere at once
J. appease; pacify one's distress
K. lazily and sentimentally
   dreamy, tender
L. act of violating faith; trust
M. very simple; in this case, ironi-
   cally—suggesting moral strict-
   ness

N. fickleness; whimsicality
O. contemptuous; disdainful
P. silently
Q. overpowering; deadening
R. state of being full; satisfied
S. powerless to act; helpless
T. lustful, extravagant, dissolute
   behavior

VOCABULARY   No. right _____

PROGRESS CHARTS

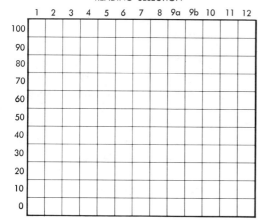

CHART 1
Comprehension

For each reading selection, compute your comprehension score, from 0 to 100, and record it in the appropriate square to make a bar graph. Draw lines connecting each bar.

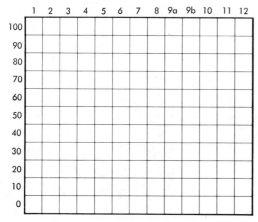

CHART 2
Vocabulary

For each reading selection, compute your vocabulary score, from 0 to 100, and record it in the appropriate square to make a bar graph. Draw lines connecting each bar.

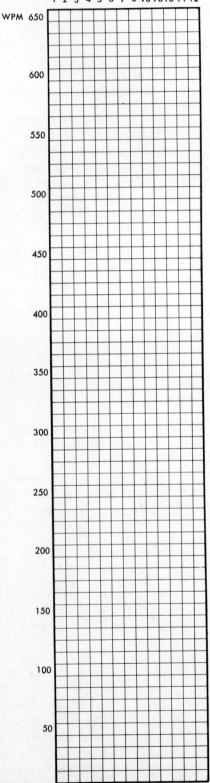

Chart 3
Reading Rate

For each reading selection, compute your reading rate (WPM), using either the speed conversion tables or the formula provided. Record your score in the appropriate square. If your score is not divisible by 10, fill in only the appropriate portion of the square. (■) Draw lines connecting each bar.

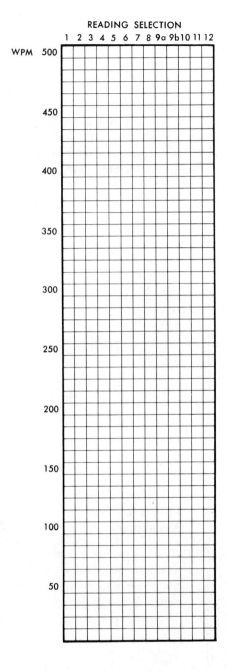

READING SELECTION

1 2 3 4 5 6 7 8 9a 9b 10 11 12

WPM 500
450
400
350
300
250
200
150
100
50

CHART 4
Reading Efficiency Rate

For each reading selection, compute your reading efficiency rate according to the formula provided and record your score in the appropriate square to make a bar graph. Draw lines connecting each bar.

Part II

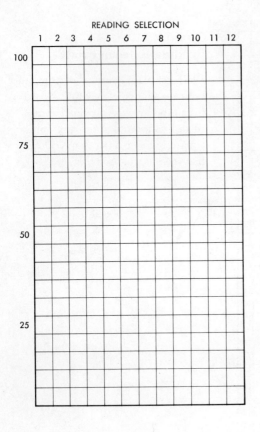

Chart 5
Comprehension

For each reading selection, compute your comprehension score and record it in the appropriate square to make a bar graph. Draw lines connecting each bar.

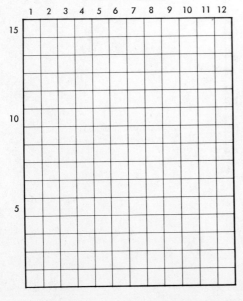

Chart 6
Vocabulary

For each reading selection, compute your vocabulary score and record it in the appropriate square to form a bar graph. Draw lines connecting each bar.

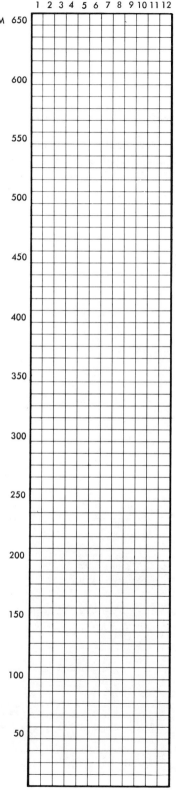

READING SELECTION

WPM

Chart 7
Reading Rate

For each reading selection, compute your reading rate (WPM), using either the speed conversion tables or the formula provided. Record your score in the appropriate square. If your score is not divisible by 10, fill in only the appropriate portion of the square. (▩). Draw lines connecting each bar.

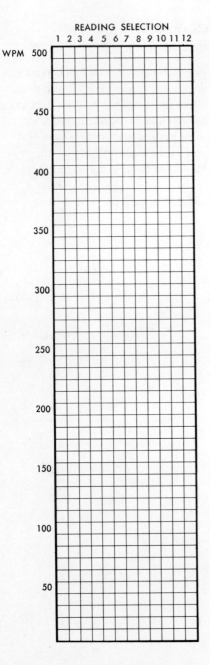

READING SELECTION
1 2 3 4 5 6 7 8 9 10 11 12

WPM 500

450

400

350

300

250

200

150

100

50

Chart 8
Reading Efficiency Rate

For each reading selection, compute your reading efficiency rate according to the formula provided and record your score in the appropriate square to make a bar graph. Draw lines connecting each bar.

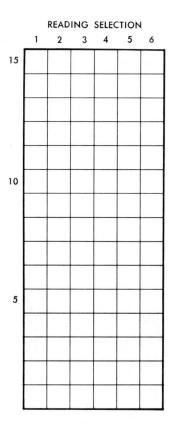

READING SELECTION

CHART 9
Vocabulary

For each reading selection, compute your vocabulary score and record it in the appropriate square to form a bar graph. Draw lines connecting each bar.

SPEED CONVERSION TABLES

	1	2	3	4	5	6	7	8	9	10	11	12	13	14	15	16	17	18	19	20	21	22	23	24	25	26	27	28	29	30
1-550	550	275	183	138	110	92	79	69	61	55	50	46	42																	
2-780	780	390	260	195	156	130	111	98	87	78	71	65	60																	
3-850	850	425	283	213	170	142	121	106	94	85	77	71	65	61																
4-1060	1060	530	353	265	212	177	151	133	118	106	96	88	82	76	71	66	62													
5-1200		600	400	300	240	200	171	150	133	120	109	100	92	86	80	75	71	67	63	60										
6-750	750	375	250	188	150	125	107	94	83	75	68	63	58																	
7-1250		625	417	313	250	208	179	156	139	125	114	104	96	89	83	78	74	69	66	63	60									
8-600	600	300	200	150	120	100	86	75	67	60																				
9A-450	450	225	150	113	90	75	64	56																						
9B-850	850	425	283	213	170	142	121	106	94	85	77	71	65	61																
10-875	875	438	292	219	175	146	125	109	97	88	80	73	67	63	58															
11-1325		663	442	331	265	221	189	166	147	133	120	110	102	95	88	83	78	74	70	66	63	60								
12-1075	1075	538	358	269	215	179	154	134	119	108	98	90	83	77	72	67	63	60												

SPEED CONVERSION TABLE—PART I

	1	2	3	4	5	6	7	8	9	10	11	12	13	14	15	16	17	18	19	20	21	22	23	24	25	26	27	28	29	30
1-1850			617	463	370	308	264	231	206	185	168	154	142	132	123	116	109	103	97	93	88	84	80	77	74	71	69	66	64	62
2-3100					620	517	443	388	344	310	282	258	238	221	207	194	182	172	163	155	148	141	135	129	124	119	115	111	107	103
3-3400					680	567	486	425	378	340	309	283	262	243	227	213	200	189	179	170	162	155	148	142	136	131	126	121	117	113
4-2300			767	575	460	383	329	288	256	230	209	192	177	164	153	144	135	128	121	115	110	105	100	96	93	88	85	82	79	77
5-2050			683	513	410	342	293	256	228	205	186	171	158	146	137	128	121	114	108	104	98	93	89	85	82	79	76	73	71	68
6-4200							600	525	467	420	382	350	323	300	280	263	247	233	221	210	200	191	183	175	168	162	156	150	145	140
7-4450							636	556	494	445	405	371	342	318	297	278	262	247	234	223	212	202	193	185	178	171	165	159	153	148
8-5125								641	569	513	466	427	394	366	342	320	301	285	270	256	244	233	223	214	205	197	190	183	177	171
9-2430				608	486	405	347	304	270	243	221	203	187	174	162	152	143	135	128	122	116	110	106	101	97	93	90	87	84	81
10-2450				613	490	408	350	306	272	245	224	204	188	175	163	153	144	136	129	123	117	111	107	102	98	94	91	88	84	82
11-4400							629	550	489	440	400	367	338	314	293	275	259	244	231	220	210	200	191	183	176	169	164	157	152	147
12-5200								650	578	520	473	433	400	371	347	325	306	289	274	260	248	236	226	217	208	200	193	186	179	173

SPEED CONVERSION TABLE—PART II